Programming for Mixed Reality with Windows 10, Unity, Vuforia, and UrhoSharp

Dawid Borycki

PROGRAMMING FOR MIXED REALITY WITH WINDOWS 10, UNITY, VUFORIA, AND URHOSHARP

Published with the authorization of Microsoft Corporation by:
Pearson Education, Inc.

Copyright © 2019 by Pearson Education, Inc.

ISBN-13: 9781509306879
ISBN-10: 1509306870

Library of Congress Control Number: 2018952317

TRADEMARKS

Microsoft and the trademarks listed at http://www.microsoft.com on the "Trademarks" webpage are trademarks of the Microsoft group of companies. All other marks are property of their respective owners.

WARNING AND DISCLAIMER

Every effort has been made to make this book as complete and as accurate as possible, but no warranty or fitness is implied. The information provided is on an "as is" basis. The author, the publisher, and Microsoft Corporation shall have neither liability nor responsibility to any person or entity with respect to any loss or damages arising from the information contained in this book or from the use of the programs accompanying it.

SPECIAL SALES

For information about buying this title in bulk quantities, or for special sales opportunities (which may include electronic versions; custom cover designs; and content particular to your business, training goals, marketing focus, or branding interests), please contact our corporate sales department at corpsales@pearsoned.com or (800) 382-3419.

For government sales inquiries, please contact governmentsales@pearsoned.com.

For questions about sales outside the U.S., please contact intlcs@pearson.com.

Editor-in-Chief: Brett Bartow

Executive Editor: Laura Norman

Development Editor: Kate Shoup/ Polymath Publishing

Managing Editor: Sandra Schroeder

Senior Project Editor: Tracey Croom

Production Editor: Danielle Foster

Copy Editor: Kate Shoup/ Polymath Publishing

Indexer: Valerie Haynes Perry

Proofreader: Dan Foster

Technical Editor: John Ray

Cover Designer: Twist Creative, Seattle

Compositor: Danielle Foster

Graphics: Vived Graphics

Without hard work, nothing grows but weeds.
—GORDON B. HINCKLEY

Contents at a Glance

Contents

About the Author

 **DAWID BORYCKI** is a software engineer and biomedical researcher experienced in Microsoft technologies. He has completed a broad range of challenging projects involving the development of software for device prototypes (mostly medical equipment), embedded device interfacing, and desktop and mobile programming.

Introduction

If you've ever watched any of the *Iron Man* movies starring Robert Downey Jr., you're probably familiar with Jarvis. Jarvis, short for "Just a Rather Very Intelligent System," is a highly advanced computerized AI system. Recently, Jarvis inspired Mark Zuckerberg to build his own AI-powered home-automation system (https://youtu.be/ZGLPxEv_EWo).

Incredibly, you can build your own wearable Jarvis-like system by combining the thrilling power of novel holographic devices like HoloLens with Microsoft Cognitive Services and Microsoft Mixed Reality. Such systems can quickly process visual content and describe it via spoken words or text displayed on screen. With just a few voice commands or air gestures, you can ask your Mixed Reality "Jarvis" system to look up what you see on the web and tell you more about it. You could use this system with AI to, say, develop a device to support visually impaired persons (https://youtu.be/R2mC-NUAmMk).

In this book you will learn how to develop AI-powered Mixed Reality apps using various strategies and technologies, including Universal Windows Platform (UWP), Microsoft Cognitive Services, Unity, Vuforia, and Xamarin UrhoSharp. First, you will learn how to set up the development environment, install the necessary tools, and use the HoloLens emulator and Mixed Reality simulators. Then you will start writing UWP two-dimensional apps that run across every Windows 10 device (including HoloLens and immersive headsets) and adjust their views and functionalities to specific devices. Subsequently, you will learn how to transfer images from the world-facing camera of the headset to the machine learning modules of the computer vision service to obtain image descriptions that are spoken by the device or displayed in text form. Afterward, you will use sensor readings from the mobile device to control content displayed on the Windows Mixed Reality headset.

After learning about 2D app development, you will move on to building 3D apps. You'll learn how to do this from the ground up. First, you'll explore the fundamental concepts of 3D graphics. You will then learn how to use Unity Editor to build 3D Mixed Reality apps, including setting up scenes, adding built-in and custom 3D objects, and formatting these objects with materials to create holograms. Afterward, you will learn how to make your holograms behave like real objects with various physics simulations and to interact with these holograms through air gestures and voice commands. Next, you will learn how to attach augmented reality to real objects with Vuforia. Finally, you will build a Mixed Reality app with UrhoSharp—a library for writing cross-platform 3D apps. This will enable you to transfer your skills to other platforms, such as iOS or Android.

Audience and Expected Skills

This book is devoted to developers, students, engineers, enthusiasts, designers, scientists, and researchers who would like to use their existing programming skills to develop software for Windows Mixed Reality (HoloLens and immersive headsets) with Unity, Vuforia, and UrhoSharp. I assume the reader knows fundamental aspects of C# programming and is experienced in Windows programming. I do not, however, assume any previous knowledge of Unity, Vuforia, or UrhoSharp.

Tools and Required Hardware

To implement all examples presented in this book, you will need a system that runs Windows 10 (Creators Update or later) and uses Visual Studio 2017 Community as the development environment.

Organization of This Book

The book is divided into three parts:

- **Part I: Fundamentals**   Chapters 1 through 3 introduce Mixed Reality in Windows 10, define all related terms, show you how to prepare your development environment, and explain possible approaches to developing apps for Windows Mixed Reality.

- **Part II: Developing 2D UWP Apps**   Chapters 4 through 7 cover 2D app development with a special focus on Universal Windows Platform (UWP) programming interfaces. Programmers familiar with UWP can easily port their existing apps to new holographic or Mixed Reality platforms and thereby extend the spectrum of their users.

- **Part III: Developing 3D Apps**   Chapters 8 through 15 teach you how to create 3D Windows Mixed Reality apps with Unity, Vuforia, and UrhoSharp. These chapters assume no prior knowledge of those tools. The aim of this part is to guide you through all the steps and leave you with all the skills necessary to create exciting AI-powered 3D apps for Windows Mixed Reality.

Conventions

The following conventions are used in this book:

- **Boldface** type is used to indicate text that you type.

- *Italic* type is used to indicate new terms and file names.

- Code elements appear in a `monospaced` font.

About the Companion Content

This book includes companion code to enrich your learning experience. The companion code for this book can be downloaded from the following page:

https://github.com/dawidborycki/MixedReality-Samples.

As shown in Figure I-1, the code is partitioned into subfolders, which correspond to particular chapters. To improve book readability, in many places I refer to the companion code rather than showing the full listings, so it is good to have the solution open while reading this book.

You can also find the companion files at *https://aka.ms/ProgMixedReality/downloads.*

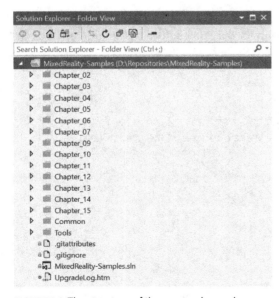

FIGURE I-1 The structure of the companion code.

Acknowledgments

The publication of this book would not have been possible without Loretta Yates and Laura Norman, who accepted my book proposal and provided initial feedback. I am grateful to John Ray for thoroughly checking every project presented in this book and providing useful, positive comments on the content. Many thanks, too, to Kate Shoup for copyediting the book. Finally, I appreciate ongoing support from my family: my wife, Agnieszka; my daughter, Zuzanna; and my son, Ksawery. I would achieve nothing without them.

Errata and Book Support

We have made every effort to ensure the accuracy of this book and its companion content. Any errors that have been reported since this book was published are listed on our Microsoft Press site at:

> *https://aka.ms/ProgMixedReality/errata*

If you find an error that is not already listed, you can report it to us through the same page.

If you need additional support, email Microsoft Press Book Support at *mspinput@microsoft.com*.

Please note that product support for Microsoft software is not offered through the addresses above.

Stay in Touch

Let's keep the conversation going! We're on Twitter: @MicrosoftPress.

Fundamentals

CHAPTER 1

Introduction to Windows Mixed Reality

Windows Mixed Reality is a platform that delivers a completely new way of mixing digitally generated three-dimensional content with the real world or environment. To understand what this means, let's first discuss how people use traditional computing systems for work or fun. Typically, we work with two-dimensional screens, in which we use perspective drawing to depict three-dimensional objects. Although this approach is suitable for designing and implementing various elements, we cannot directly interact with digitally created objects. So, our ability to present or interact with what we create is limited. Windows Mixed Reality aims to suppress this barrier by providing a revolutionary way of computing. To that end, Windows Mixed Reality delivers software and hardware components that enable us to mix virtual and real worlds to accomplish much more than we ever could in traditional computing.

This chapter covers the concepts related to Windows Mixed Reality. It starts by defining virtual, augmented, and mixed realities. Then, it discusses Windows Mixed Reality headsets and the concept of holograms as it relates to Windows Mixed Reality. Afterward, the chapter discusses several Windows Mixed Reality–enabled utilities available in Windows 10 (with the Fall Creators update or above)—for example, Microsoft Paint 3D, which lets you create and interact with 3D objects through Windows Mixed Reality.

Virtual, Augmented, and Mixed Reality

Windows Mixed Reality (WMR) involves a broad range of software and hardware technologies, including virtual and augmented reality. There are also several devices supported by WMR. At the moment, only Microsoft HoloLens provides a true mixed reality experience. Other WMR headsets provide a virtual reality experience. To understand the key differences between these headsets, let's define virtual, augmented, and mixed reality.

Virtual Reality

Virtual reality (VR) refers to a realistic and immersive 3D simulation of an environment. This simulation is generated with the help of interactive software and hardware and is controlled by the user's voice, gestures, gaze, or body movements.

Predecessors of the current VR systems were called stereoscopes and were introduced during the 19th century by Sir Charles Wheatstone, David Brewster, and Oliver Wendell Holmes, who developed them independently (http://bit.ly/stereoscopes). During the early 20th century their ideas were extended by Sawyer Service Inc. to develop View-Master (http://bit.ly/viewmaster_sawyer). Nintendo made important advances in VR with its introduction of the VR-enabled Virtual Boy game console in 1995 (http://bit.ly/virtual-boy). The Virtual Boy came equipped with a controller and a viewer, which, like stereoscopes and the View-Master, generated a stereo pair of images. These images, called stereopair, created the illusion of depth in a 3D scene. In 1989, a company called VPL Research went even further. It developed a VR headset as part of a full-body outfit that contained sensors to measure body movement. This immersed the user even more in the VR simulation. Although these old VR devices did not succeed commercially, they are precursors of modern VR headsets.

> ## Stereoscopy
>
> Stereoscopy works by providing two two-dimensional images of the same environment. These images differ slightly from each other and are displayed independently for the left and right eye. The brain combines these two images to build a sense of depth in a 2D plane to create the virtual 3D scene.
>
> Perhaps the easiest way to grasp this effect is to raise your thumb a few inches in front of your face and then quickly alternate blinking with your left and right eye. Notice how the location of your thumb appears to be different depending on which eye you use to view it, and how its correct location is restored when you have both eyes open. That's how stereoscopy works.

Currently, we are seeing a rapid revival of VR. In recent years, Facebook acquired a company called Oculus to further develop its VR headset technology; HTC released the Vive headset; Sony created PlayStation VR; and Google released the Cardboard, based on the View-Master, to enable users to cheaply convert nearly any smartphone into a VR headset. October 2017 brought the release of numerous new headsets dedicated for use with Windows Mixed Reality. (These are described in detail in the next section.)

Augmented Reality

Augmented reality (AR) is another technology that has recently taken off. In general, AR uses digital elements such as sound and images generated by a computer system to augment the human perception system.

The most exciting aspect of AR is its ability to overlay three-dimensional synthetic elements on real objects. AR can be further used to create an interaction between virtual and real objects. For example, with additional environment-understanding cameras, you can "touch" the synthetic objects and manipulate them with your hands or air gestures.

AR became well-known after the remarkable success of the AR-enabled game, Pokémon GO, which was itself preceded by Niantic's Ingress. These games inspired manufacturers of mobile devices to create several programming kits to speed up AR development. Although modern mobile phones are equipped with powerful processors and various inertial sensors, they do not exhibit the full potential of AR, as they are very rarely equipped with sensors to understand the environment, which precisely sense the phone's distance to various real objects in the scene. Moreover, displays on current mobile devices cannot generate stereoscopic 3D objects without the use of additional hardware (like Cardboard, for example). Instead, mobile devices overlay digital elements on real objects captured by the camera. Then, both the synthetic and the real objects are displayed on the same screen. In other words, mobile devices offer a relatively quick way to blend real with synthetic objects, but the AR experience is limited.

The Microsoft HoloLens takes a completely different approach. It uses a head-mounted AR module that creates stereoscopic 3D images of synthetic objects, which are displayed directly on the real scene. Because HoloLens does not use an opaque display, real and synthetic objects "live" in the same environment. Moreover, HoloLens is equipped with numerous cameras and sensors to probe your near environment. This enables HoloLens to understand the scene in which you are embedded, allowing real objects to occlude and interact with virtual ones. HoloLens can also recognize the user's hand gestures and voice input, and can generate stereoscopic sound to provide the best possible AR experience.

Virtuality Continuum

VR and AR are tightly coupled to the concept of the *virtuality continuum*, which was introduced in a paper by Paul Milgram and Fumio Kishino (http://bit.ly/mixed_reality). You can think of the virtuality continuum as a spectrum of real and virtual environments. The real environment (RE) is composed only of real objects. The virtual environment (VE) comprises only digitally created elements.

As shown in Figure 1-1, VR is closer to the VE extreme, though not all the way there. This is because VR relies primarily on digital elements but does not yet allow for a completely virtual environment and requires the use of real elements (like hand and body movements) to control the simulation. In contrast, AR is closer to the RE extreme because AR blends digitally created objects with reality. With AR, synthetic objects are displayed in the real environment, and the user can both interact with synthetic objects and occlude real ones.

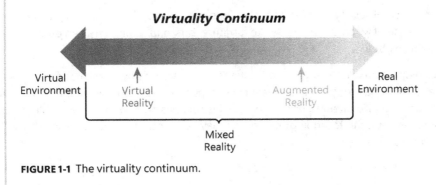

FIGURE 1-1 The virtuality continuum.

Mixed Reality

In Figure 1-1, VR and AR are shown as points on the virtuality continuum. These points represent only specific combinations (or blended ratios) of virtual and real environments. The set of all other combinations of blending virtual and real environments is denoted as mixed reality (MR). As shown in Figure 1-1, mixed reality is more general than VR and AR separately. MR includes both AR and VR as well as many more points on the virtuality continuum.

The blending of virtual and physical worlds enabled by MR advances human–device interaction to a whole new level, introducing a broad range of possibilities. With MR, developers are now equipped with all necessary tools to combine real environments, human input, and digital content to provide experiences restricted only by their imagination.

When desktops were the most popular computing systems, people mostly used a mouse and keyboard to control them. For most people, this became a convenient way to communicate with the device. However, touchscreens on mobile devices have significantly simplified human–device interaction. Every day, experiences show that even small children can easily unlock a smartphone to watch their favorite videos on YouTube. This is because touchscreens provide a more natural way to interact with a device. A similar significant step forward is now being made by MR.

MR provides an entirely new and exciting way to create apps that blend seamlessly and naturally with the real world. Users can now control apps using air gestures and head movements. More importantly, digital content can interact with the physical world because MR devices can be equipped with sensors that understand the user's near environment. In other words, both the device and the app can now perceive your near environment. Accordingly, developers can now create apps by placing virtual content in the user's surroundings. In practice, this means various communicator apps can provide virtual content (avatars) representing other people. As a result, users can talk to people located thousands of miles away as if they were in the same room!

Other currently explored MR applications include (but are not limited to) the following:

- **Tutorial or teaching**   With these types of apps, students can see complex structures in 3D (such as images of the human body) and easily highlight or zoom selected parts to understand how they work. A good example is shown here: http://bit.ly/case_western.

- **Visualizations**   These types of apps enable users to visualize objects on real physical surfaces in full size—useful when buying items like furniture, cars, and so on. Here's an example: http://bit.ly/HoloLens_Volvo.

- **Remote help**   With these types of applications, users can employ an MR headset to transfer information about a problem in their near environment to a remote consultant. This consultant can then add digital content to provide precise instructions on how to fix the problem. Several companies now use this technology on an everyday basis, including thyssenkrupp (http://bit.ly/HoloLens_thyssenkrupp).

Windows Mixed Reality Hardware

To provide MR experiences, Windows Mixed Reality requires hardware components. One of these components is a head-mounted display (HMD). The other is either a clicker (for HoloLens; see Figure 1-2) or a motion controller (for Mixed Reality headsets; see Figure 1-3), which the user holds in his or her hands.

FIGURE 1-2 HoloLens clicker. (Courtesy of https://developer.microsoft.com.)

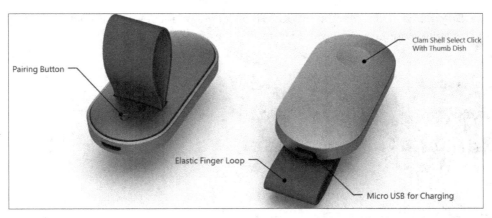

FIGURE 1-3 Windows Mixed Reality motion controllers. (Courtesy of https://developer.microsoft.com.)

There are two distinct groups of Windows Mixed Reality HMDs:

- **Holographic headsets** Holographic headsets use *see-through* displays, which embed synthetic 3D objects in the real environment. Accordingly, holographic headsets are on the AR side of the virtuality continuum.

- **Immersive headsets** Immersive headsets have *opaque displays*, which block the physical environment. As such, they are on the VR side of the virtuality continuum.

Both holographic and immersive devices fall under the class of MR devices. The following sections describe HMDs in a more detail.

Holograms

Microsoft defines a hologram as an *"object made of light and sound that can appear in the world around you."* This definition can give pause to people familiar with holography, however. In holography, the term hologram is reserved to describe a recording (stored in the appropriate medium) that encodes complex information (amplitude and phase) about the optical field in the form of an interference fringe pattern. This pattern can be then illuminated by a laser light to display a fully 3D image of the object without the help of any special headset or intermediate optics. Here, conforming to the Microsoft definition, I will use the term hologram to describe synthetic objects created by a holographic device, keeping in mind that this does not precisely adhere to the traditional meaning of the term.

Microsoft HoloLens

Microsoft HoloLens (see Figure 1-4) is the leading untethered, head-mounted device for providing Mixed Reality experiences.

Note *Untethered* means that the HoloLens is an independent device. It is a wearable, fully independent computing system. It does not require a separate PC.

FIGURE 1-4 Microsoft HoloLens. (Courtesy of https://developer.microsoft.com.)

The HoloLens features see-through holographic lenses. These lenses enable the user to view his or her surroundings. They also double as a screen to enable the user to view stereo pairs of digital 3D objects, which are generated by two RGB LED projectors. (See Figure 1-5.) Although these projectors are much smaller than the digital projector you might use at work or at home, the principles behind their operation are similar.

> **Note** The HoloLens screens, which are translucent, use waveguides. These waveguides reflect the light projected onto the screen by the RGB LED projectors while also transmitting light reflected from real objects contained in the surrounding scene. The screens then blend these images to provide an MR experience. (Of course, the technical implementation of the HoloLens optics is much more complex, as it relies on specific properties of light propagation. This book describes their operation only in general terms.)

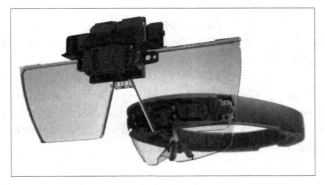

FIGURE 1-5 The see-through display of the Microsoft HoloLens. (Courtesy of https://developer.microsoft.com.)

The HoloLens provides an automatically adjustable element to optimize the creation of the stereo images based on the user's interpupillary distance (IPD). As for their clarity, these stereo images contain more than 2 million points and more than 2,500 points per radian. Some critique of HoloLens is related to its limited field of view (FOV). This, however, is more of a technical challenge than a conceptual one—meaning the FOV will likely be significantly increased in the near future.

The HoloLens is equipped with a custom processor to control the optical system. This processor, called the Microsoft Holographic Processing Unit (HPU), is a multiprocessor unit that processes information from various HoloLens sensors. (See Figure 1-6.) These include the following:

- **Four cameras**   These help the HoloLens ascertain the near environment.

- **Depth or time-of-flight camera**   This is used to determine the distance of various real objects in the environment from the HoloLens.

- **Inertial measurement unit (IMU)**   This tracks head movements.

- **Ambient light sensor**   This measures the intensity of ambient light for adjusting the brightness of holograms.

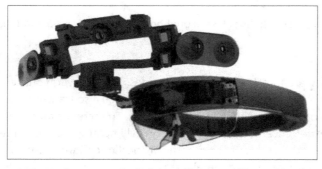

FIGURE 1-6 Sensors on the HoloLens. (Courtesy of https://developer.microsoft.com.)

> **Note** The next generation of the HPU will also contain an integrated coprocessor to handle computations for implementing deep neural networks to support artificial intelligence. (For more information, see http://bit.ly/HPU_2.)

In addition to the HPU, HoloLens also has a 32-bit Intel central processing unit (CPU), which—along with 2 GB of RAM and 64 GB of flash memory—serves the hardware basis for the Windows 10 operating system. HoloLens also has built-in speakers, which generate spatial sound. All this hardware is powered by a battery, which lasts for about 2 to 3 hours of active use.

Immersive Headsets

Unlike the HoloLens, currently available immersive headsets are tethered, so they require a PC running Windows 10 with the Fall Creators update or above. Detailed requirements for PC hardware are given here: http://bit.ly/wmr_pc.

Like the HoloLens, however, immersive headsets use stereoscopy to create 3D objects. Therefore, one of the most important specifications is the display technology. Table 1-1 lists currently available immersive devices along with their key specifications. As shown, apart from the Samsung HMD Odyssey, they're all quite similar. Each one uses two liquid crystal displays (LCDs), each with a resolution of 1,440 x 1,440 and a field of view of 105°. In contrast, the Samsung HMD Odyssey uses an AMOLED display with the same horizontal resolution as the two LCDs in the other devices (2,880) and a higher vertical resolution (1600). Additionally, the Samsung headset provides a slightly larger field of view (110°). Figures 1-7 to 1-11 depict each of these headsets.

TABLE 1-1 A Summary of Immersive Mixed Reality Headsets

Device name	Display technology	Field of view
Acer Windows Mixed Reality headset	Two LCD displays at 1440 x 1440 points each	105°
Dell Visor Windows Mixed Reality headset	Two LCD displays at 1440 x 1440 points each	105°
HP Windows Mixed Reality headset	Two LCD displays at 1440 x 1440 points each	105°
Lenovo Explorer Windows Mixed Reality headset	Two LCD displays at 1440 x 1440 points each	105°
Samsung HMD Odyssey Windows Mixed Reality headset	AMOLED 2880 x 1600	110°

Note All immersive headsets come with the controllers shown in Figure 1-3. These controllers are not yet compatible with HoloLens, however. Each immersive headset also uses an HDMI cable for display purposes and USB for connectivity.

FIGURE 1-7 The Acer Windows Mixed Reality Headset. (Courtesy of https://www.microsoft.com/.)

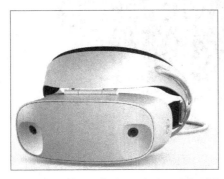 

FIGURE 1-8 The Dell Visor Windows Mixed Reality headset. (Courtesy of https://www.microsoft.com/.)

FIGURE 1-9 The HP Windows Mixed Reality headset. (Courtesy of https://www.microsoft.com/.)

FIGURE 1-10 The Lenovo Windows Mixed Reality headset. (Courtesy of https://www.microsoft.com/.)

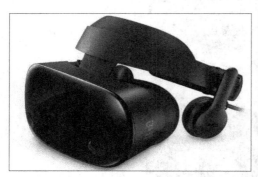

FIGURE 1-11 The Samsung HMD Odyssey Windows Mixed Reality headset. (Courtesy of https://www.microsoft.com/.)

Placing Windows Mixed Reality Hardware on the Virtuality Continuum

Now that you've explored the available hardware for Windows Mixed Reality, you can place it on the virtuality continuum. (Refer to Figure 1-1.) Given the current capabilities of the HoloLens, you can place this device at the RE position on the continuum and moving across the spectrum to the midpoint. This covers a broad range of the virtuality continuum and defines a blending of real and virtual environments. (See Figure 1-12.) As for immersive headsets, their range on the continuum spans from the VE position to roughly the one-third point. Mobile devices cover only a small range of the virtuality continuum on both ends, as they offer a limited VR and AR experience.

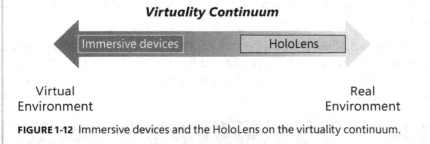

FIGURE 1-12 Immersive devices and the HoloLens on the virtuality continuum.

Mixed Reality in Windows 10

Windows 10 has several built-in apps that support Mixed Reality. One of the most exciting of these is Paint 3D. (See Figure 1-13.) Paint 3D complements the 2D functionality of Microsoft Paint, one of the best-known Windows apps.

FIGURE 1-13 Paint 3D in Windows 10.

With Paint 3D, you can quickly create 3D scenes using primitive 3D models like cubes, spheres, hemispheres, cones, and pyramids. You can also draw your own primitives using Doodle—a free drawing tool that turns your sketches into 3D objects. Finally, you can import 3D models of various scenes, people, or animals from the Remix 3D online repository. To import a 3D model into Paint 3D, follow these steps:

1. Click the **Remix 3D** tab in Paint 3D.

2. A collection of 3D models opens. Scroll this collection or type a description in the search box to find a model you like. (In Figure 1-14, I searched for a 3D model of a firefighter.)

3. Click the model you want to use. Then place it on the Paint 3D canvas by clicking the selected model.

4. To preview the scene containing the model, click the **View in Mixed Reality** icon above the Paint 3D canvas. (It's the one that features a rotated 3D cube in front of a screen.) This opens the Mixed Reality Viewer app, which overlays your scene on the real environment (captured by your device's camera).

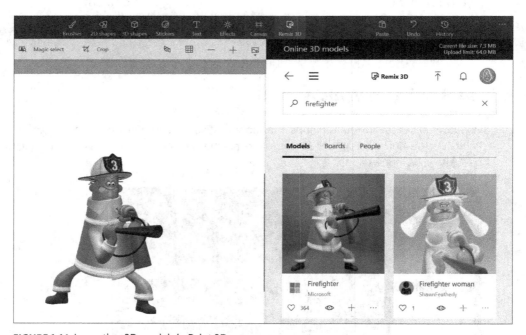

FIGURE 1-14 Importing 3D models in Paint 3D.

In addition to the Paint 3D (and Mixed Reality Viewer) app, several other Microsoft products are equipped with Mixed Reality features. These include the following:

- **Microsoft Word**   Microsoft Word also enables you to import 3D models from Remix 3D.

- **3D Builder**   With 3D Builder, you can create 3D scenes and then print them in 3D. You can also use 3D Builder to import any image and turn it into a 3D model. Figure 1-15 shows this capability in action. It contains a hexagon and a sphere, which I drew using primitives I accessed from the 3D Builder toolbar. Then, I added a photograph of the Samsung HMD Odyssey Windows Mixed Reality headset. (Refer to Figure 1-11.) With just a few mouse clicks, I created a 3D scene!

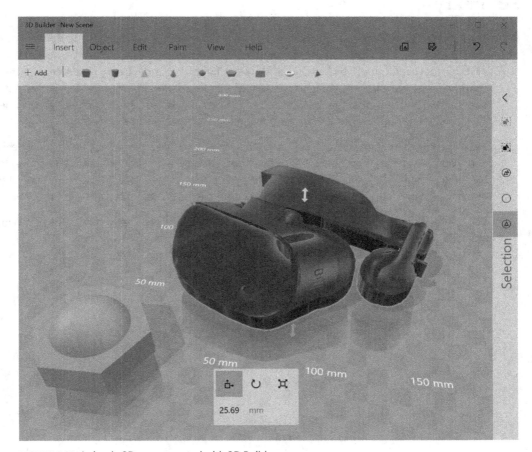

FIGURE 1-15 A simple 3D scene created with 3D Builder.

Note You can use a 3D modeling app (such as Paint 3D, 3D Builder, or a more advanced tool) to quickly create models or scenes. Then, you can use 3D Builder to export them to a file. Finally, you can import the model or scene contained in that file into the app you are developing to quickly create a virtual environment. Part III of this book explores these capabilities in a more detail.

Summary

The aim of this chapter was to further engage you in Windows Mixed Reality app development. It started by defining important terms relating to Windows Mixed Reality. Then it reviewed the concept of the virtual continuum, which describes the blending of real and mixed environments. After that, the chapter discussed where VR, AR, and MR exist within the continuum. You then learned about currently available hardware, including the HoloLens and immersive devices. Finally, you got an overview of Windows 10 apps that can support 3D modeling for Windows Mixed Reality apps.

At present, the Microsoft HoloLens is the leading Mixed Reality headset, being the only device capable of providing a true MR experience. Immersive headsets are oriented more toward VR and less toward blending with physical world than the HoloLens, as they are not equipped with see-through stereoscopy displays. However, all apps for Mixed Reality headsets can be implemented in a very similar way.

Chapter 2 discusses the development tools and models you can use to create apps for Windows Mixed Reality.

Development Tools

Now that you're familiar with the concepts behind mixed reality and the various Microsoft Mixed Reality hardware components, let's review the development tools. Because Windows Mixed Reality headsets run Windows 10—either directly (as with the HoloLens) or indirectly through an associated PC (as with immersive headsets)—they are also a part of the Universal Windows Platform (UWP). UWP delivers a common API. Therefore, the easiest and most straightforward way to start developing apps for Windows Mixed Reality is through the UWP API.

UWP apps, however, are usually 2D—meaning that although you can view the 2D digital content they generate using a HoloLens or immersive device, the apps cannot achieve the full potential of Windows Mixed Reality. To achieve this full potential, you must instead develop 3D apps. This requires the use of Microsoft DirectX, SharpDX, Unity (supported by the Mixed Reality Toolkit and Vuforia), or UrhoSharp. This chapter summarizes and reviews all these tools.

Universal Windows Platform

The Universal Windows Platform (UWP) was introduced along with Windows 10. As noted, it provides a common API that you can use to develop apps with a consistent set of programming tools. You can also use UWP to distribute apps via the Microsoft Store.

UWP apps can target various device families, including Mixed Reality, Xbox, mobile, Internet of Things (IoT), desktop, and Surface Hub. (See Figure 2-1.) UWP provides a common core API that applies for each device family as well as access to tools to support device family–specific hardware functionality. To access these tools, you simply obtain an SDK extension dedicated to a specific device family. Then, to use the extension, you simply select it in the Reference Manager. An app that uses a device-specific API can still run across all other Windows 10 device families. However, an attempt to access the device-specific API on a device that does not support it will result in an exception of type `System.TypeLoadException`.

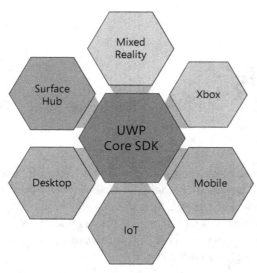

FIGURE 2-1 A sketch of the UWP API.

Adaptive Coding and Target Device Families

Both Windows 10 and UWP are still evolving, with new features frequently added to both. As a result, there may be times when an API you want to use might not be available for a particular device. To avoid this problem, you can use adaptive coding. Alternatively, you can make your UWP app non-universal by indicating the device families and minimum Windows 10 versions supported by your app.

In an adaptive coding, you use the methods of the Windows.Foundation.Metadata. ApiInformation class to infer whether a type (IsTypePresent), a method (IsMethodPresent), an event (IsEventPresent), a property (IsPropertyPresent), an enumeration value (IsEnumNamedValuePresent), or an API contract (IsApiContractPresent) is available for the device on which an app is running. For instance, the following statement checks whether the Windows.ApplicationModel.Preview.Holographic.HolographicApplicationPreview class can be used:

```
var isTypePresent = Windows.Foundation.Metadata.ApiInformation.IsTypePresent(
    "Windows.ApplicationModel.Preview.Holographic.HolographicApplicationPreview");
```

Adaptive coding is a little like the conditional preprocessor directives (#if, #else, #elif, and #endif), which you use to compile the same code for various platforms. With these, you typically enable or disable specific code snippets depending on the compilation constants representing the particular platform. For instance, you could write something like the following:

```
public sealed partial class MainPage : Page
{
    public MainPage()
    {
        InitializeComponent();
```

```
#if WMR

        if (Windows.ApplicationModel.Preview.Holographic.HolographicApplicationPreview.
            IsCurrentViewPresentedOnHolographicDisplay())
        {
            // Do something with holographic preview
        }

#endif
    }
}
```

In this case, the code between the `#if` and `#endif` clauses will be compiled only when the WMR symbol is defined. You can define symbols using the `#define` directive (for example, `#define WMR`), provided it is the first clause in the file, or by entering them in the Conditional Compilation Symbols box in the project properties. (See Figure 2-2.)

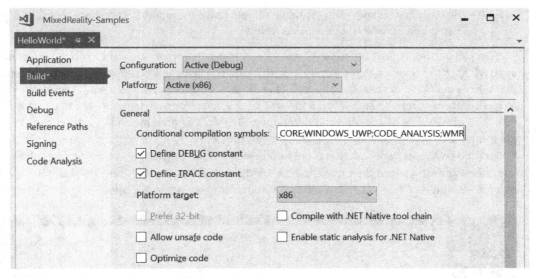

FIGURE 2-2 Setting conditional compilation symbols.

Although preprocessor directives are widely used for developing multi-platform apps, they require you to recompile the code for each platform independently by manually changing conditional compilation symbols. In contrast, adaptive coding allows you to check API availability during runtime. As a result, you compile the source code only once for all platforms and then poll for the particular API, when the app is being executed.

To set target device families for your app, you edit the app package manifest (Package.appxmanifest). This XML file, contained in every UWP project, describes your app to the operating system. To edit this file, follow these steps:

1. Open the package-manifest file in the text or XML Editor. To do this quickly in Visual Studio, right-click the **Package.appxmanifest** file in Solution Explorer and choose **View Code** from the menu that appears.

2. In the **<Dependencies>** node, declare which device families your app should support. For example, to make your UWP app compatible only with the HoloLens, you would modify the node as follows:

```
<Dependencies>
    <TargetDeviceFamily Name="Windows.Holographic" MinVersion="10.0.0.0"
                        MaxVersionTested="10.0.0.0"/>
</Dependencies>
```

Each target device family appears within a `TargetDeviceFamily` tag. This tag has three attributes:

- **Name**   This attribute references the name of the device family that your app is targeting. (For a complete list of device family names, see http://bit.ly/target_device_family.)

- **MinVersion**   This attribute references the minimum version number of the device family with which your app is compatible.

- **MaxVersionTested**   This attribute references the maximum version number of the device family against which your app was tested.

Being able to implement universal 2D apps is very important when you want to apply new or existing UWP apps to Windows Mixed Reality. In such cases, you just need to use adaptive coding to ensure that the needed API is accessible. Later, you can tailor the views of your apps to HoloLens or Windows Mixed Reality headsets. You'll learn how in Part II of this book. For now, I simply want to demonstrate how the same UWP app looks on various Windows 10 devices without making a single change to the source code (again, assuming the code contains the necessary APIs). Figure 2-3 shows a simple HelloWorld UWP app (which you'll explore further in subsequent chapters) in the Windows Mobile emulator. Figure 2-4 shows the same app on a Windows desktop. Finally, Figure 2-5 shows the app in a HoloLens emulator. As you can see, the app automatically adjusts to the device.

FIGURE 2-3 The HelloWorld UWP app executed in the Windows Mobile emulator.

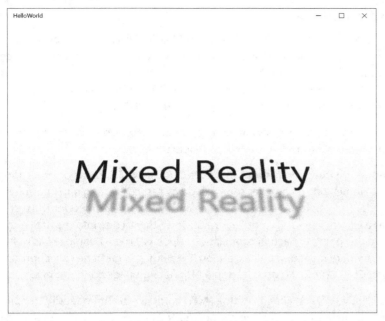

FIGURE 2-4 The HelloWorld UWP app executed in a Windows desktop environment.

FIGURE 2-5 The HelloWorld UWP app executed in the HoloLens emulator.

.NET Core and .NET Native

You can use a variety of programming languages to develop UWP apps. This book, however, focuses on C#. UWP apps built with C# use the Microsoft .NET Core Framework, which is a general-purpose and modular implementation of the Microsoft .NET Framework. In C# UWP apps, you access the Microsoft .NET Core Framework through the `Microsoft.NETCore.UniversalWindowsPlatform` NuGet package. This package is referenced by default whenever you create a UWP project.

The .NET Core Framework contains two tools to manage program execution—one for debug build configurations and one for release build configurations. (See Figure 2-6.)

- **Core Common Language Runtime (CoreCLR)**   Core CLR is a .NET Core-tailored version of the CLR for the .NET Framework. It compiles source code by first converting it to intermediate language (IL) code. Then, before a particular piece of this code is executed for the first time, Core CLR uses a just-in-time (JIT) compiler to transform the IL code into the native code for a given device. At this point, the actual compilation happens. (The JIT compiler, as well as additional tools for memory management, exception handling, and garbage collection, are provided by the CoreCLR.) CoreCLR is used by default for debug build configurations.

- **.NET Native**   .NET Native uses an ahead-of-time (AOT) compiler to automatically compile your app's code into the native code for a specific device. The native code is then executed by the Minimal CLR runtime (MRT.dll), which is similar to the C runtime (CRT.dll) used to execute C/C++ apps. Because .NET Native uses similar tools as C/C++ compilers, it offers clear performance benefits. .NET Native is used by default in release build configurations.

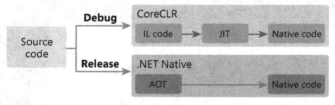

FIGURE 2-6 A sketch of UWP app compilation. Notice that the compilation mode differs depending on whether the compilation configuration is set to a debug build or a release build.

Microsoft DirectX

Microsoft DirectX is a set of APIs for creating high-performance 2D and 3D games or multimedia apps. The C++ UWP toolkit for Visual Studio 2017 includes several project templates for developing universal apps with DirectX. Like C# templates, these project templates enable you to create an app that can be deployed across various Windows 10 devices.

One template extends the capabilities of the default C++ DirectX project templates and is tailored specifically for Windows Mixed Reality: the Holographic DirectX 11 App (Visual C++) template. The default app created by this template features a holographic spinning cube positioned 2 meters along the gaze direction (that is, the direction the user is looking). This default app consists of the following elements. (See the companion code in the Chapter_02/HolographicAppDirectXMain folder.)

- **An entry point**   This is the `main` method. It creates an instance of the `AppViewSource` class (discussed in an upcoming bullet).

- **Holographic content processor**   The class name of this processor depends on the project name. (Here, I will call it `HolographicAppDirectXMain`.)

- **Shaders**   These elements transform vertices. (See Chapter 8 for more information.)

- **AppViewSource**   This class runs the UWP app using a static Run method from the `CoreApplication` class. It has one method, `CreateView`, which creates the `AppView` class. (See the next bullet.)

- **AppView**   This manages the app window and handles the app lifecycle. It is similar to the App class from the UWP project template. The `AppView` class has several methods. Two are of particular importance for creating and rendering holographic content:

  - **`Initialize`**   This method creates an instance of the holographic content processor.

  - **Run**   This method continuously updates and renders holographic content with the help of methods from the `HolographicAppDirectXMain` class (discussed in the next bullet).

- **HolographicAppDirectX**   This class manages and updates holographic content. `HolographicAppDirectX` uses two objects:

  - **SpinningCubeRenderer**   This is a sample implementation of the rendering pipeline (defined in Chapter 8). Here, it renders the spinning cube.

  - **SpatialInputHandler**   This is the gesture handler.

Figure 2-7 shows this app running in the HoloLens emulator.

FIGURE 2-7 A HoloLens app created with the Holographic DirectX 11 App (Visual C++) template.

Note The holographic template allows access to various Windows Mixed Reality features and enables you to fully control the rendering pipeline. This comes at the cost of increased app complexity. For instance, a quick glance at the source code of the SpinningCubeRenderer class reveals that it handles a lot of low-level stuff to create the spinning cube, which is then programmatically added to the scene.

SharpDX

SharpDX is a .NET wrapper for the DirectX API. DirectX holographic templates include a C# project template that uses SharpDX to implement the same holographic app as the C++ DirectX template discussed in this section. The SharpDX template has the same structure as the DirectX template. The only difference is that everything is implemented with C# instead of C++. (See the companion code in the *Chapter_02/HolographicAppSharpDX* folder.)

Unity

Unity is a cross-platform tool created by Unity Technologies for developing 2D and 3D apps. Although Unity is called a game engine, I consider it a cross-platform app engine because it supports various VR, AR, and MR platforms—including Windows Mixed Reality—which are not necessarily used for games.

In Unity, you need not create scene objects programmatically, as in DirectX. Instead you drag and drop objects in the Unity Editor (a stand-alone app included with Unity) to create the scene. You can implement any additional logic—for example, to handle object interactions or user input—with C# scripts. Figure 2-8 shows a scene created in Unity Editor for a Windows Mixed Reality app.

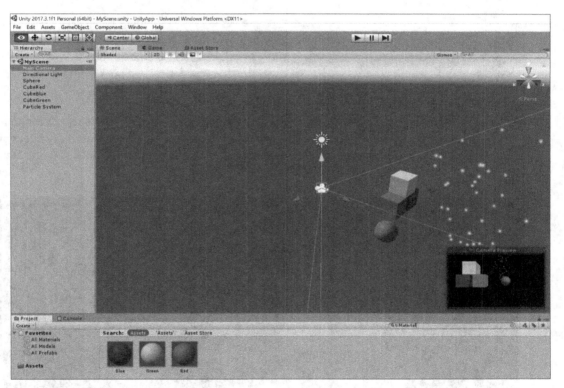

FIGURE 2-8 Unity Editor with a simple scene.

After you design an app in Unity Editor, you build, or export, it from the Unity Editor as a UWP app. (See Figure 2-9.) This produces a Visual Studio solution, which you can deploy to a HoloLens, a Windows Mixed Reality headset, or any other Windows 10 device. (Unity also offers build tools for other platforms, including iOS, tvOS, Android, Tizen, Xbox One, Mac, Linux, Samsung TV, PS Vita, PS4, and WebGL.)

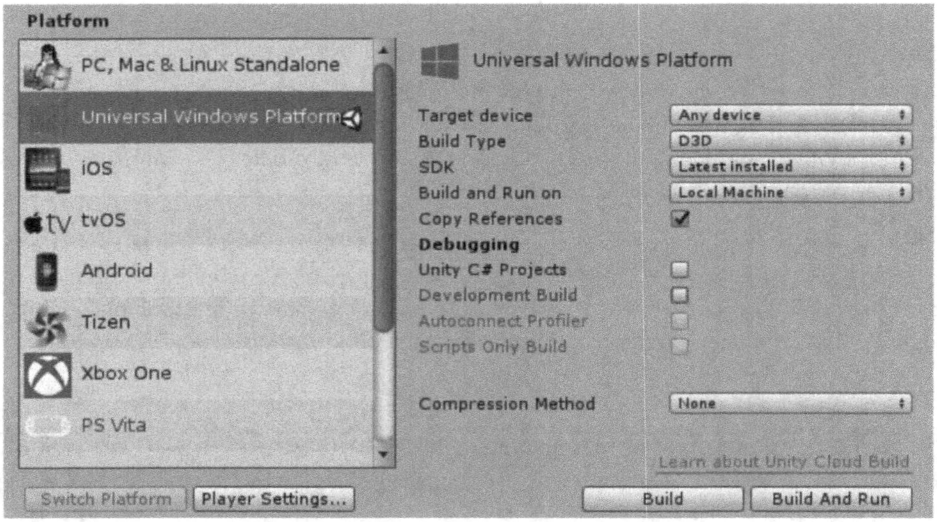

FIGURE 2-9 Build settings in the Unity Editor.

Figure 2-10 shows an example of a UWP Windows Mixed Reality app created in Unity Editor. To build this app, I built a scene using three cubes, one sphere, and a particle system composed of white moving balls. I then exported the scene as a UWP app and deployed it in the HoloLens emulator. (You'll learn more about this process beginning with Chapter 9.)

FIGURE 2-10 An example of a Windows Mixed Reality app developed with Unity Editor. (Compare this with the camera preview in the bottom-right corner of Figure 2-8.)

> **Note** This app, exported from the Unity Editor as a Visual Studio solution, uses the same DirectX interface as a holographic template. Specifically, the entry point is the static `Main` method of the `App` class. The `Main` method is responsible for initializing and running the Windows Mixed Reality app. During this initialization, the `App` class sets the `WinRTBridge`, being part of Unity, to process all Unity app callbacks.

Unity development for Windows Mixed Reality can be accelerated with two packages: Mixed Reality Toolkit and Vuforia. These are discussed next.

The Mixed Reality Toolkit

The Mixed Reality Toolkit is a collection of APIs, written in C++, that you can use to speed up development for Windows Mixed Reality. You access this toolkit in Unity through the Mixed Reality Toolkit–Unity extension (MRTKu). The MRTKu provides multiple features, which can be used for the following:

- Handling input from gaze, gesture, voice, and motion controllers

- Spatial sound and spatial understanding

- Spatial mapping for integrating real and virtual worlds

- Rendering the floor and boundaries in Mixed Reality headsets

- Implementing collaboration across various devices

The MRTKu provides handy tools for applying common configurations to your projects. For instance, you can adjust your app for use with a HoloLens, see-through headsets, or immersive headsets by selecting the appropriate checkbox in the Project Settings window. (See Figure 2-11.) In addition, the MRTKu simplifies the build process. For example, you can use the Build Window (see Figure 2-12) to build and run your app in the headset or emulator directly from Unity Editor. This greatly accelerates development.

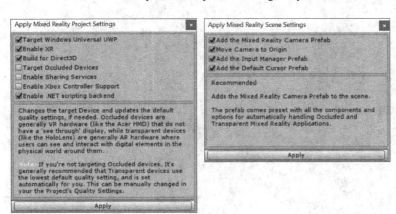

FIGURE 2-11 The Project Settings (left) and Scene Settings windows in the MRTKu. You use these to quickly configure your Mixed Reality app.

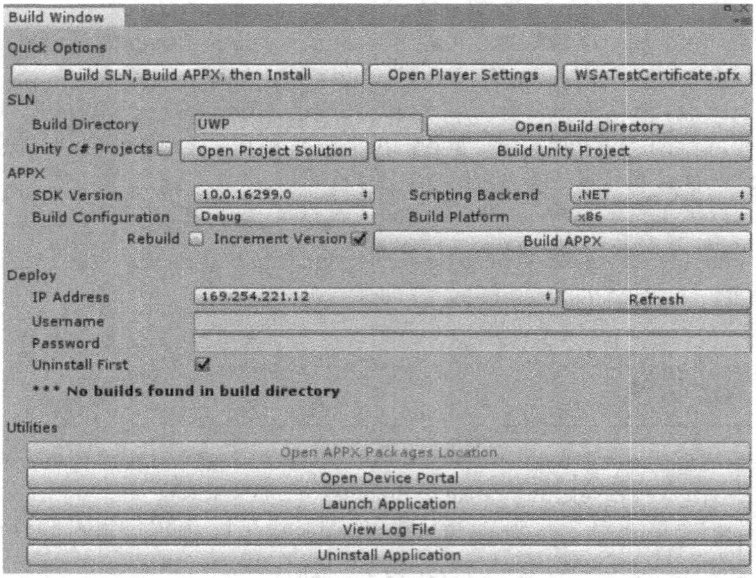

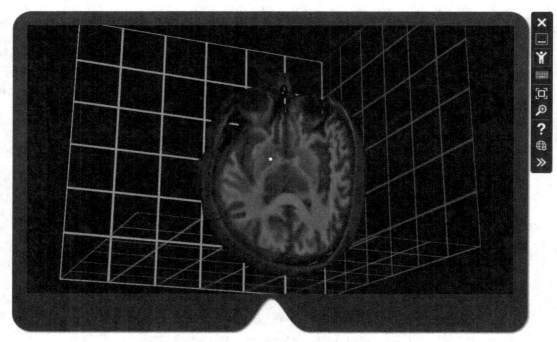

FIGURE 2-12 A Build Window in the MRTKu.

MRTKu also provides several samples you can use to create your own apps. For example, the medical sample shown in Figure 2-13 renders volumetric data from the human head acquired with magnetic resonance imaging (MRI). With this app, you can use air gestures to quickly visualize brain sections.

FIGURE 2-13 A medical app, rendering MRI images of the human head.

Vuforia

The Vuforia AR SDK supports mobile devices and headsets, including HoloLens. It implements object, text, and image recognition. Recognized elements can be then robustly tracked, even when they get out of view. In this way, Vuforia helps you provide AR experiences by blending real and virtual worlds. For example, you can specify objects or images that, when detected, trigger your app to generate specific 3D content. For instance, suppose you want to place a virtual flowerpot on the real table in your room. You could configure Vuforia to recognize that table and trigger the placement of the virtual flowerpot on it. Extended tracking capabilities in Vuforia can even help you keep the virtual flowerpot in the field of view—even when the table becomes invisible. You'll learn how to use Vuforia in Chapter 14.

UrhoSharp

UrhoSharp, developed by Xamarin, constitutes a .NET binding to Urho3D. This enables developers to create cross-platform C# apps for iOS, tvOS, MacOS, Android, and Windows 10—including Windows Mixed Reality. UrhoSharp wraps the Urho3D API much like SharpDX wraps the DirectX API. With UrhoSharp, you can create 3D scenes programmatically or by using the Urho Editor. UrhoSharp comes with several C# samples (http://bit.ly/urho-samples) that demonstrate the creation of holographic content. Figure 2-14 shows a mutant sample app running in the HoloLens emulator. You'll learn how to create apps with UrhoSharp in Chapter 15. You'll learn where the mutant model actually comes from in Chapter 11.

FIGURE 2-14 The mutant UrhoSharp sample app running in the HoloLens emulator.

Summary

This chapter reviewed the main tools for developing Windows Mixed Reality apps. It started with a broad description of the UWP API, which is commonly used to create apps for various Windows 10 devices. The chapter then briefly described the DirectX and SharpDX project templates for creating holographic content. These tools provide comprehensive access to APIs for creating Windows Mixed Reality apps at the cost of increased complexity.

DirectX and SharpDX projects require users to programmatically create objects and control their rendering. As noted in this chapter, this barrier can be overcome with Unity, which enables users to create scenes visually. Several Unity assets and packages, including MRTKu and Vuforia, can speed up development for Windows Mixed Reality.

Finally, this chapter introduced UrhoSharp, the .NET porting of Urho3D, which serves as an alternative to Unity. Future chapters will explore several of these tools—including how to use them to create Mixed Reality experiences—in more detail.

CHAPTER 3

Configuring the Development Environment, Emulators, and Hardware

This chapter shows you how to set up the development environment to make sure you have all the tools you will need to implement the applications discussed in this book. I explain which components or workloads of Visual Studio 2017 you will need and how to obtain Unity, Vuforia, and UrhoSharp. Then I show you how to develop a HelloWorld app and guide you through the process of installing the HoloLens emulator and Mixed Reality simulator. Finally, I tell you how to execute the HelloWorld app in these emulators.

Setting Up the Development Environment

As explained in Chapter 2, I will use the following tools throughout this book:

- Windows 10 SDK

- Visual Studio 2017

- Unity 2017

- Vuforia

- UrhoSharp

- HoloLens emulator

- Mixed Reality simulator

> **Tip** If you have some of these components already installed, just skip ahead to the sections that cover the components you do not yet have.

Windows 10

To develop Mixed Reality apps, you will need a PC with Windows 10 with the Creators Update (or later) installed (Windows 10 Version 1703 or above). To check your operating system (OS) version, simply open the **Windows Start** menu and type **winver**. This opens an About Windows dialog box, which contains information about your OS version and edition (see Figure 3-1). To obtain all the screenshots in this chapter, I used the Windows 10 Creators Update. If you are using Windows 10 Fall Creators Update, some of the screens (especially those of the Mixed Reality simulator) will look slightly different. However, all steps are the same.

> **Note** The HoloLens emulator cannot be used in Windows 10 Home Edition because it does not support the Hyper-V.

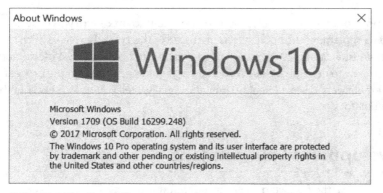

FIGURE 3-1 The About Windows dialog box showing the Windows version.

After verifying that you have the correct OS (or downloading it if you do not), you need to enable Developer mode. Follow these steps:

1. Launch the Settings app.

2. Click the **Update & Security** group.

3. Click the **For Developers** tab.

4. Click the **Developer Mode** option button (see Figure 3-2).

5. Another two switches become available: **Enable Device Portal** and **Device Discovery**. Leave these at their default (off) values.

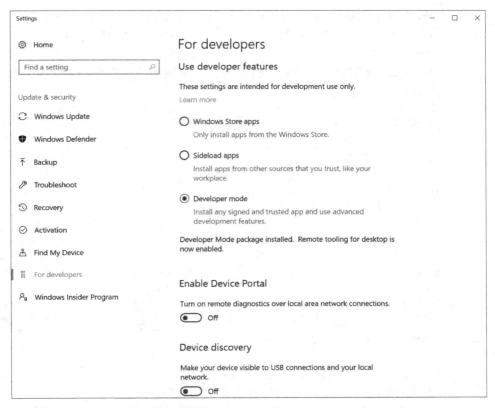

FIGURE 3-2 Enabling Developer mode.

Visual Studio 2017

Visual Studio 2017 is available in three different versions:

- Community
- Professional
- Enterprise

The Community version is available free of charge and contains all the features we need. So, let's download and install it:

1. Type **visualstudio.com/vs** in your web browser's address bar.

2. Move your cursor over the **Download Visual Studio** button. A drop-down list with version options appears.

3. Choose **Community**.

4. Download and run the installer.

5. Click the **Continue** button as needed to accept the privacy statements. The main Visual Studio installer will be launched, and you'll see the window shown in Figure 3-3.

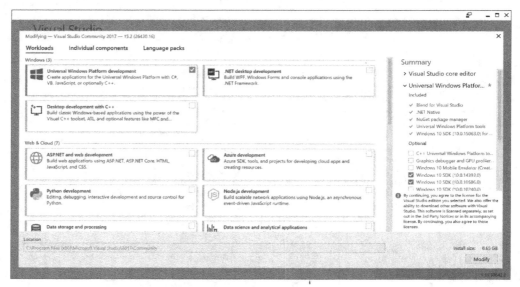

FIGURE 3-3 The Visual Studio 2017 installer.

All Visual Studio components are partitioned into workloads. These correspond to a specific development group. For instance, the first workload listed in the upper-left corner of the installer window shown in Figure 3-3, Universal Windows Platform Development, contains tools you need to implement Universal Windows Platform (UWP) apps. Select the following workloads in the installer window (you may need to scroll down to see them all):

- **Universal Windows Platform Development**

- **Game Development with Unity**

6. All examples presented in this book are compatible with Unity Editor 2017.2 and above. If your version precedes this one, deselect **Unity Editor** on the Summary pane. As Figure 3-3 shows, this pane displays the list of individual components included in selected workloads. (I will tell you how to install the proper Unity Editor in the next section.)

7. Then make sure the **Windows 10 SDK (10.0.14393.0)** and **Windows 10 SDK (10.0.10586)** checkboxes are selected in the Summary panel on the right (refer to Figure 3-3).

8. Finally, click the **Modify** button. An installer will download and install all selected components (see Figure 3-4). Note that it may take a while. In my case, the installation size was about 6 GB.

FIGURE 3-4 Progress of a Visual Studio 2017 installation.

Unity Editor

To develop 3D apps for Mixed Reality headsets, you will need Unity 2017.2 or above. You can download it here: bit.ly/unity-personal. (In this chapter the personal version is used. Differences between Unity versions are described in detail in Chapter 9.) When I was writing this chapter, the stable Unity version was 2017.3.

To download and install Unity Editor, follow these steps:

1. Use the preceding hyperlink to download an app called Unity Download Assistant.

2. Run the app and accept the license agreement.

3. In the Choose Components screen, select the following options before clicking the **Next** button (see Figure 3-5):

   - **Unity 2017.2** (or higher)

   - **Standard Assets**

   - **Windows Store .NET Scripting Backend**

   - **Vuforia Augmented Reality Support**

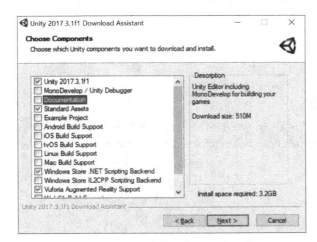

FIGURE 3-5 Selecting Unity components to install.

4. Specify where the files will be downloaded and choose an installation directory (see Figure 3-6). Configure them according to your preference. Then click **Next** to run the installation.

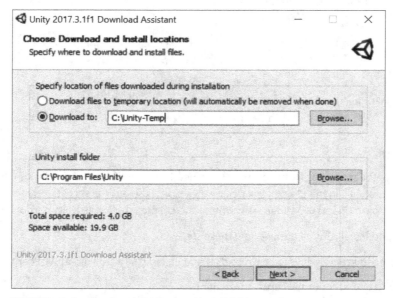

FIGURE 3-6 Configuring download and install folders.

5. When you run the Unity Editor for the first time, it will ask you to enter your Unity ID. If you do not have one, create it at bit.ly/unity-id.

Vuforia

To get the Vuforia SDK, use the following link: bit.ly/vuforia-sdk. This page contains SDK downloads. By default, there are four entries for the following platforms:

- Android

- iOS

- UWP

- Unity

Starting with Unity 2017.2, the Vuforia Engine is integrated with the Unity Editor. The above link also includes a legacy Vuforia version, which can be used for project migrations.

UrhoSharp

UrhoSharp is distributed as a NuGet package. To install such a package, you first need to create a project. Follow these steps:

1. Open Visual Studio.

2. Open the **File** menu and choose **New Project** to open the New Project dialog box.

3. Type **Blank App C#** in the **Filter** field in the upper-right corner of the dialog box.

4. Choose the **Blank App (Universal Windows) Visual C#** project template.

5. Type **HelloWorld** in the **Name** field and click **OK** (see Figure 3-7).

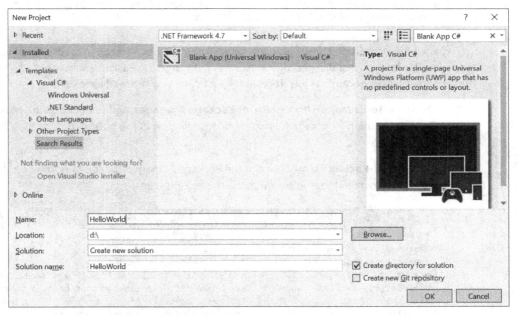

FIGURE 3-7 Creating a blank UWP Visual C# app.

6. Before Visual Studio creates the project, it will display a dialog box asking you to set the minimum and target versions of Windows 10 that will be supported by your app (see Figure 3-8). Leave these settings as they are. (We will get back to this topic in the next chapter.)

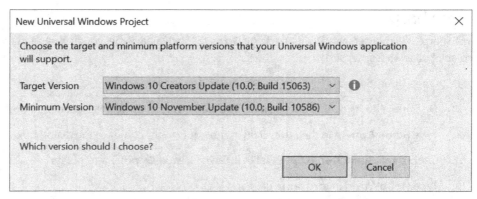

FIGURE 3-8 Configuring the Target Version and Minimum Version settings to specify which versions of Windows 10 will be supported by the app.

To install the UrhoSharp NuGet package (or any other NuGet package), you use the NuGet Package Manager. This lets you install a package in two ways: through the Package Manager Console or through the Package Manager graphical interface. In the first case, you proceed as follows:

1. Open the **Tools** menu, choose **NuGet Package Manager**, and select **Package Manager Console** to open a Package Manager Console window in the bottom part of the Visual Studio editor.

2. Type **Install-Package UrhoSharp** in the Package Manager Console window. The UrhoSharp package is installed for the current project (see Figure 3-9).

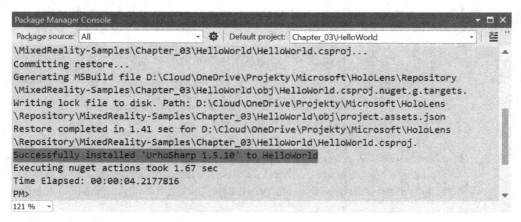

FIGURE 3-9 Installing the UrhoSharp NuGet package using the console.

If you prefer to use the graphical interface of the NuGet Package Manager (see Figure 3-10) to install a package, follow these steps:

1. Open the **Tools** menu, choose **NuGet Package Manager**, and select **Manage NuGet Packages for Solution** to open the NuGet Package Manager graphical interface.

2. Click the **Browse** tab.

3. In the search box, type **UrhoSharp**. A list of packages whose names contain the text you typed appears.

4. Click **UrhoSharp**.

5. Click the **Install** button on the right, confirm the changes to the project, and wait until the package and all its dependencies are installed. When the installation is complete, the NuGet package will appear on the Installed tab.

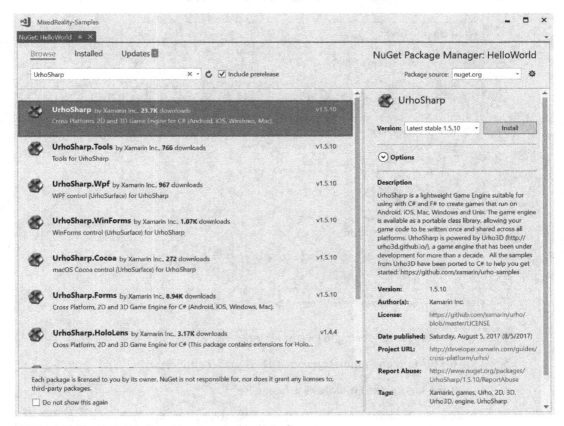

FIGURE 3-10 The NuGet Package Manager graphical interface.

Note that the graphical interface of the NuGet Package Manager lets you specify the version of the NuGet package. You can do the same in the console by supplementing the `Install-Package` command with the `Version` parameter like this:

```
Install-Package UrhoSharp -Version 1.5.2
```

You can also get a list of the latest package versions using the `Find-Package` command:

```
Find-Package UrhoSharp -AllVersions
```

HoloLens Emulator

The HoloLens emulator works as a virtual machine. Therefore, to install and use the emulator, you must ensure that the Hyper-V function of your PC is turned on. To do so, follow these steps:

1. Open the Windows **Start** menu and type **Turn Windows Features**.

2. Click the **Turn Windows Features On or Off** entry on the search list to open the Windows Features dialog box, shown in Figure 3-11.

3. Ensure that the **Hyper-V** checkbox is selected and click **OK**.

FIGURE 3-11 The Windows Features dialog box.

To install the HoloLens emulator, follow these steps:

1. Type **bit.ly/hololens-emulator** in your web browser's address bar.

2. Download and run the **EmulatorSetup.exe** file.

3. After you download and run the file, the installer will ask you to specify a location for the emulator (Figure 3-12). Choose the first option, **Install the Microsoft HoloLens Emulator to This Computer**, and click the **Next** button.

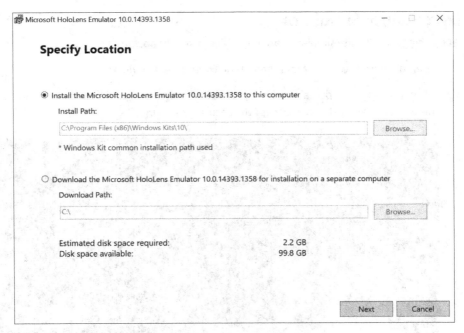

FIGURE 3-12 HoloLens Emulator setup.

4. In the next screen, choose **Yes** to allow the Windows kits to collect anonymous data or **No** to disable this feature. Choose according to your preference.

5. Accept the license agreement.

6. From the list of available features, choose **Microsoft HoloLens Emulator** (see Figure 3-13). (The other feature, Microsoft HoloLens App Templates, also installs DirectX project templates for Visual Studio, which we do not use in this book.)

7. Click **Install** to start the installation.

8. After the installation is complete, restart your PC.

FIGURE 3-13 Selecting features to install.

Mixed Reality Simulator

To set up the Mixed Reality simulator, open the Mixed Reality portal.

1. Open the **Windows Start** menu and type **Mixed Reality Portal**.

2. When you open the portal for the first time, a welcome screen appears (see Figure 3-14). Click the **Get Started** button and accept the security warning.

FIGURE 3-14 The Windows Mixed Reality portal.

3. The screen shown in Figure 3-15 appears. It summarizes the hardware capabilities of your PC to run Windows Mixed Reality. (As shown in Figure 3-15, my laptop can run Windows Mixed Reality, but the graphics card cannot guarantee optimal performance.) Even if your PC does not meet minimal hardware requirements, you can still set it up for simulation. So, go ahead and click the **Set Up Simulation (for Developers)** link. (See the bottom-left corner of Figure 3-15.)

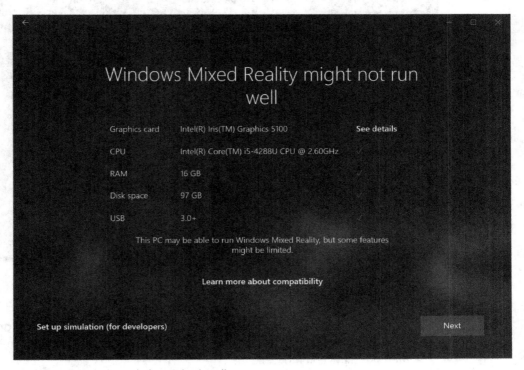

FIGURE 3-15 Setting up Windows Mixed Reality.

4. A pop-up window appears asking you to confirm this decision. Click **Set Up** and wait for the Mixed Reality portal to download all the necessary components.

5. Click the **For Developers** icon (it features a wrench and a screwdriver and is located in the bottom-left corner of Mixed Reality Portal) to expand the For Developers pane.

6. Switch the **Simulation** setting to **On**, as shown in Figure 3-16. (If you are using the Windows 10 Fall Creators Update, then this switch will be labeled **Headset**.)

FIGURE 3-16 The Mixed Reality simulator.

Note The Start menu for the Mixed Reality simulator looks like the one for the HoloLens emulator. You also control the Mixed Reality simulator using similar methods (keys and mouse).

HelloWorld Project

Before going further, let's write some code, which we will then execute using the headset emulator. The project we will develop will use a 3D projection and shadowing effect from the Visual layer (see Figure 3-17). A projection and a linear gradient brush are used to create a simple depth effect, while shadowing presents sample usage of the Visual layer.

FIGURE 3-17 A HelloWorld app using 3D effects and shadow from the Visual layer.

To implement the app, shown in Figure 3-17, we'll edit the HelloWorld project we created earlier in this chapter in the "UrhoSharp" section. Specifically, we'll open the MainPage.xaml file and modify the declarations between the Page tags as outlined in Listing 3-1.

LISTING 3-1 Declarations of the MainPage.xaml file

```
<Page.Resources>
    <Style TargetType="TextBlock">
        <Setter Property="HorizontalAlignment"
                Value="Center" />
        <Setter Property="VerticalAlignment"
                Value="Center" />
        <Setter Property="FontSize"
                Value="80" />
        <Setter Property="TextWrapping"
```

```
                         Value="WrapWholeWords" />
        </Style>

        <Style TargetType="Grid">
            <Setter Property="Background">
                <Setter.Value>
                    <LinearGradientBrush StartPoint="0,0"
                                         EndPoint="0,1">
                        <GradientStop Color="Transparent"
                                      Offset="0.3" />
                        <GradientStop Color="LightGoldenrodYellow"
                                      Offset="0.6" />
                    </LinearGradientBrush>
                </Setter.Value>
            </Setter>
        </Style>
    </Page.Resources>

    <Grid x:Name="MainGrid">
        <Grid.Projection>
            <PlaneProjection RotationX="-35" />
        </Grid.Projection>

        <TextBlock x:Name="TextBlockMixedReality"
                   Text="Mixed Reality" />
    </Grid>
```

Listing 3-1 creates the 3D plane projection using the PlaneProjection class. This class represents the perspective transform to create the 3D effect. You configure this transform using several public properties of the PlaneProjection class instance. You can configure the angle of rotation (RotationX, RotationY, RotationZ) and its center around three different axes (CenterOfRotationX, CenterOfRotationY, CenterOfRotationZ). You can also set the distance that the object (Grid) is translated along the specific axis of the plane of the object (LocalOffsetX, LocalOffsetY, LocalOffsetZ) and the screen (GlobalOffsetX, GlobalOffsetY, GlobalOffsetZ). Here, we only use the RotationX property to rotate the plane projection by −35 degrees around the x-axis.

Listing 3-1 creates a label with the text "Mixed Reality" using the TextBlock class and defining two anonymous XAML styles. The first style sets the vertical and horizontal alignment of the label so it is centered in the application view. It also has a larger font size and is configured for word wrapping so that the "Mixed Reality" string will be split into two lines if it is too wide to fit in the app window. The second style is used to set the background of the view to a linear gradient. Listing 3-1 uses the LinearGradientBrush class and configures its StartPoint and EndPoint properties so that the linear gradient starts at the top and ends at the bottom of the screen. In general, for the StartPoint and EndPoint properties, you use a pair of values of type Windows.Foundation.Point ranging from 0 to 1. These values specify the coordinates of the point where the gradient should begin or end. I encourage you to modify StartPoint and EndPoint in Listing 3-1 to see how they affect a final gradient.

After configuring a gradient, the listing creates two gradient stops (instances of the GradientStop class). These are the points at which the gradient changes color. The first stop is transparent. The second stop is set to LightGoldenrodYellow. The relative positions of both stops within the gradient are set to 0.3 (30%) and 0.6 (60%), respectively. To that end the listing uses the Offset property of the GradientStop class.

Once the UI is declared, you implement the code-behind by modifying MainPage.xaml.cs as shown in Listing 3-2. This listing adds a statement to the MainPage constructor. This statement wires an event handler with the LayoutUpdated event of the label.

LISTING 3-2 Drop shadow is updated whenever the layout of the text block changes

```
public MainPage()
{
    InitializeComponent();

    TextBlockMixedReality.LayoutUpdated += TextBlockMixedReality_LayoutUpdated;
}
```

When the LayoutUpdated event is raised, the drop shadow for the label is created using the Visual layer. Listing 3-3 illustrates how to achieve this. First it contains an instance of the Composition class, which manages the session between the app and low-level system composition process. Then it invokes the CreateSpriteVisual method to instantiate the SpriteVisual object. It represents a two-dimensional rectangular visual element, which can be rendered in the application view. Next, it sets the size of this component to be equal to that of the label and creates the drop shadow (using the CreateDropShadowForTextBlock method, shown in Listing 3-4). Finally, it displays an instance of the SpriteVisual object using the SetElementChildVisual method of the ElementCompositionPreview class. The latter is used to access the Visual layer associated with the XAML elements.

LISTING 3-3 Creating the sprite visual

```
private void TextBlockMixedReality_LayoutUpdated(
    object sender, object e)
{
    // Get compositor and create sprite visual
    var compositor = ElementCompositionPreview.
        GetElementVisual(MainGrid).Compositor;
    var visual = compositor.CreateSpriteVisual();

    // Adjust visual size to text block size
    visual.Size = TextBlockMixedReality.DesiredSize.ToVector2();

    // Create drop shadow
    visual.Shadow = CreateDropShadowForTextBlock(
        compositor, TextBlockMixedReality);

    // Add visual to the composition preview
    ElementCompositionPreview.SetElementChildVisual(
        MainGrid, visual);
}
```

To create the drop shadow, we implement a method from Listing 3-4. It validates the input arguments (compositor and textBlock) and creates the DropShadow effect using the CreateDropShadow method of the Compositor class instance. This method returns an instance of the DropShadow class, representing a shadow. Subsequently, we configure the shadow using the following three properties of this instance:

- **Color** This property configures the color of the shadow. Setting a color does not require any additional comments. We simply use the DarkOrange static property of the Colors class.

- **Offset** This property specifies the location of the shadow. (More on that after Listing 3-4.)

- **Mask** This property determines the shadow' shape. In this case, Mask is set to the label shape, which we obtain using the GetAlphaMask property of the TextBlock class instance.

LISTING 3-4 Creating the drop shadow

```
private DropShadow CreateDropShadowForTextBlock(
    Compositor compositor, TextBlock textBlock)
{
    // Check arguments
    Check.IsNull(compositor, "Compositor");
    Check.IsNull(textBlock, "TextBlock");

    var shadow = compositor.CreateDropShadow();

    // Configure shadow
    shadow.Color = Colors.DarkOrange;
    shadow.Offset = GetShadowOffset(textBlock);
    shadow.Mask = TextBlockMixedReality.GetAlphaMask();

    return shadow;
}
```

To determine the location of the shadow, we write another helper method, GetShadowOffset, shown in Listing 3-5. It determines the location of the label in the view. It constructs an instance of the System.Numerics.Vector3 class so that its X and Y components correspond to the top-left corner of the label. It also sets the Z component value to the fixed number.

LISTING 3-5 Calculating the shadow location so it will be always located below the label

```
private Vector3 GetShadowOffset(TextBlock textBlock)
{
    // Z offset
    const float zOffset = -100.0f;

    // Calculate TextBlock origin
    var transform = textBlock.TransformToVisual(
        Window.Current.Content);
    var origin = transform.TransformPoint(new Point());

    // Return the resulting offset
    return new Vector3((float)origin.X,
        (float)origin.Y, zOffset);
}
```

Listing 3-4 also uses the Check static class. I implemented this class in a separate project, MixedReality.Common, which I made with the Shared Library (Universal Windows) project template. I added this project to the current solution (to do this, you right-click the solution name, choose **Add**, and select **New Project**) and used it to implement a functionality, which will be shared between all other UWP apps we will create in this book. Here, in MixedReality.Common, I renamed the default file from Class1.cs to Check.cs and then modified it as shown in Listing 3-6. Then I referenced MixedReality.Common in the HelloWorld app using the Reference Manager. (To do this, you right-click the **References** node of the HelloWorld project and choose **Add Reference**.) Finally, in the Reference Manager, I selected the **MixedReality.Common** option on the **Projects/Solution** tab.

LISTING 3-6 A definition of the Check class

```
public static class Check
{
    public static void IsNull(object obj, string paramName)
    {
        if (obj == null)
        {
            throw new ArgumentNullException(paramName);
        }
    }
}
```

You can now execute the HelloWorld app in Visual Studio. To do so, do one of the following:

- Open the **Debug** menu and choose **Start Debugging**.

- Open the **Debug** menu and choose **Start Without Debugging**.

- Use the appropriate shortcut keys (which are displayed next to the preceding options).

The app will be built, deployed, and run in your PC (refer to Figure 3-17). Note that you can resize the app window and the drop shadow below the label will be always in the correct position. This is because whenever the layout of the label is changed, an appropriate method from Listing 3-3 is invoked to render the shadow again.

Let's execute this sample app in the HoloLens emulator and in the simulator of the Mixed Reality headset.

Deploying Apps to the HoloLens Emulator

You can use the HoloLens emulator to execute the HelloWorld app. Because the HelloWorld app is universal, it can be deployed to the HoloLens emulator without any changes. You only need to specify the target machine. To do so, open the **Target** drop-down list as shown in Figure 3-18, and choose **HoloLens Emulator**.

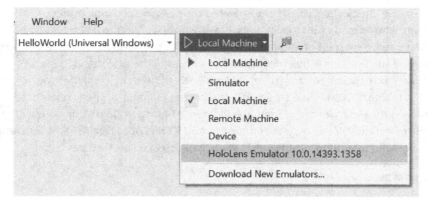

FIGURE 3-18 Selecting the target machine on which the HelloWorld app will be executed.

When the HoloLens emulator is set as the target, you can run the HelloWorld app there. First, though, Visual Studio will set up the emulator. (It may take a while when running for the first time.) After the emulator is ready, the app will be deployed and executed in the emulator.

You will see the HelloWorld app window with a green pointer with the label "Tap to Place." Move the app window by pressing and holding the left mouse button as you drag the pointer. When you reach the desired location, press the right mouse button. This emulates the tap gesture of the HoloLens. The app window will be placed and should look like the one shown in Figure 3-19.

FIGURE 3-19 The HelloWorld app in the HoloLens emulator (compare with Figure 3-17).

Using the Emulator

To control the HoloLens emulator, you use the following keyboard keys:

- **W, A, S, D** Use these keys to emulate walking forward, backward, left, and right, respectively.

- **Left, right, up, and down arrows** Use these keys to look left, right, up, or down, respectively. To look around you can also use the mouse while pressing and holding the left mouse button.

HoloLens accepts several hand or gaze gestures. The best way to learn these gestures is through the Learn Gestures app. To run this app, go to the emulator and press the Windows key or the F2 key to open a Start menu. Right-click (to emulate an air tap or select gesture) the Learn Gestures entry (in the bottom-left corner of the menu), place the Learn Gestures app, and follow the instructions to learn about HoloLens gestures.

HoloLens Device Portal

Although the HoloLens is controlled by Windows 10, it does not have the tools you typically use to configure and control the desktop platform—for example, Control Panel or Task Manager. Instead, similar tools are available through the web-based HoloLens Device Portal. These tools give you control over more advanced features of the HoloLens device. For instance, you can capture mixed reality, see active processes (like in Task Manager), or run the file explorer (see the System group). When using the emulator, you can access this portal by clicking the globe icon located on the Tools pane of the HoloLens emulator. This opens the Device Portal in your default web browser (see Figure 3-20).

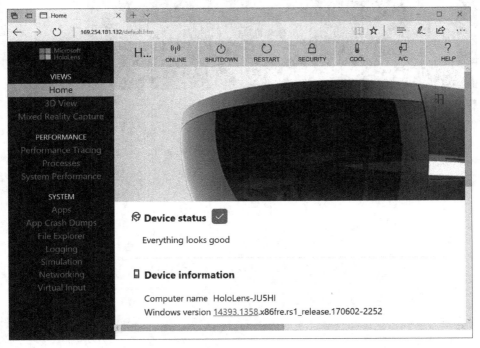

FIGURE 3-20 The HoloLens Device Portal.

Running Apps in the Mixed Reality Simulator

To run the HelloWorld app in the Mixed Reality simulator, follow these steps:

1. Change the target device to **Local Machine** (refer to Figure 3-18).

2. Open the Mixed Reality portal.

3. Open the **Start** menu and tap the plus (+) icon. You'll see a list of installed apps. Scroll down this list to find the **HelloWorld** app (see Figure 3-21) and tap it.

FIGURE 3-21 A list of all installed apps.

4. The app window opens with a Select to Place icon displayed. Pin the window exactly as you did in the HoloLens emulator. The HelloWorld app becomes active (see Figure 3-22).

FIGURE 3-22 The HelloWorld app running in the Mixed Reality simulator. Compare this result with Figure 3-17 and Figure 3-19.

Summary

In this chapter you prepared the development environment you will use in this book. Then you learned how to implement the UWP app, displaying a label with a drop shadow created with the Visual layer. Lastly, you learned how to deploy the app in the HoloLens emulator and Mixed Reality simulator. You will employ these tools in the next part of the book to develop more advanced 2D apps.

Developing 2D UWP Apps

CHAPTER 4

UWP Basics

I n this chapter, you will discover the exact structure of the UWP app. You will learn the execution flow, from the entry point up to displaying the view. You will also see how views are implemented, explore common programming approaches for improving code maintainability and testability, study data binding, and examine the Model–View–ViewModel (MVVM) software architectural pattern. Finally, you'll see how UWP apps can run across various Windows 10 devices and how to use intrinsic UWP programming interfaces to adjust the app's view and logic for various platforms. These concepts will be used throughout this part of the book.

XAML and UI

The HelloWorld app we developed in Chapter 3 has three main elements:

- The auto-generated `Program` class with the `Main` method, representing the entry point of every C# app

- The `App` class, which handles all the logic related to the app lifecycle and app services

- `MainPage`, which implements a default view

To better understand the app execution model, let's briefly analyze the UWP app lifecycle. Figure 4-1 presents a simple flowchart of this lifecycle and associated events. Initially, the app is not running. It leaves this idle state after being launched by the user (in which case the `OnLaunched` event of the App class is raised) or activated by the operating system (in which case the `OnActivated` event is raised). After the app is launched or activated, it enters the running in background state, in which the UI is still invisible. From here on, the app can periodically switch between the running in background, running in foreground (in which case the UI is visible), and suspended states.

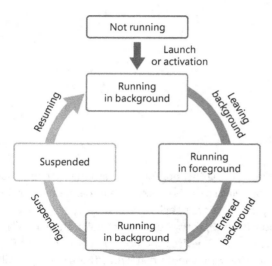

FIGURE 4-1 The UWP app lifecycle.

As shown in Figure 4-1, Windows 10 can suspend the app to save resources. When the transition between each lifecycle state occurs, one of the following corresponding events is raised:

- **LeavingBackground** This is fired when the app transitions from the running in background state to the running in foreground state.

- **EnteredBackground** This is raised when the app transitions from the running foreground state to the running in background state.

- **Suspending** This is fired when the app is suspended—that is, transitioned from the running in background state to the suspended state.

- **Resuming** This occurs when the app transitions from the suspended state to the running in background state.

Before Windows 10, version 1607 (Anniversary Edition), the app lifecycle did not include the running in background and running in foreground states. Therefore, the app could periodically transition between running and suspended states.

Let's now see where the lifecycle fits in. Listing 4-1 shows the automatically generated `Program` class. This class is created whenever you compile your UWP app. You can find the resulting code in the App.g.i.cs file under the obj folder. As Listing 4-1 shows, the `Program.Main` method has only one statement, which is responsible for initializing the App class. From this point, the control flow is directed to that class.

LISTING 4-1 The automatically generated `Program` class

```
public static class Program
{
    [global::System.CodeDom.Compiler.GeneratedCodeAttribute(
        "Microsoft.Windows.UI.Xaml.Build.Tasks"," 14.0.0.0")]
    [global::System.Diagnostics.DebuggerNonUserCodeAttribute()]
```

```
    static void Main(string[] args)
    {
        global::Windows.UI.Xaml.Application.Start((p) => new App());
    }
}
```

Listing 4-2 shows a constructor of the App class. This constructor invokes the InitializeComponent method. This method is also automatically generated in the App.g.i.cs file. The constructor then registers the OnSuspending method to handle the App.Suspending event. You use this event to save the app state. If the code responsible for saving an app state is asynchronous, an event handler can complete before you save data. Hence, to delay its execution, you use an instance of SuspendingDeferral. Listing 4-2 shows how to get such an instance with the GetDeferral method of the SuspendingEventArgs. SuspendingOperation class instance. When the asynchronous code has finished, you invoke the Complete method of the SuspendingDeferral class instance to inform the system that it can safely suspend your app. Starting with the Anniversary Edition of Windows 10, it is recommended that you use the EnteredBackground event to save the app state. You can wire to this event as shown in Listing 4-3.

LISTING 4-2 A fragment of the App class

```
public App()
{
    InitializeComponent();
    Suspending += OnSuspending;
}

private void OnSuspending(object sender, SuspendingEventArgs e)
{
    var deferral = e.SuspendingOperation.GetDeferral();
    deferral.Complete();
}
```

LISTING 4-3 Wiring to the EnteredBackground event

```
public App()
{
    InitializeComponent();
    Suspending += OnSuspending;

    EnteredBackground += App_EnteredBackground;
}

private void App_EnteredBackground(object sender, EnteredBackgroundEventArgs e)
{
    // Starting from Windows 10 Anniversary Edition, it is recommended
    // to use this event to store app state
}
```

As shown in Figure 4-1, the App class uses several other events during the app lifecycle. One is the OnLaunched event, invoked when the user executes the app. A default implementation of this method appears in Listing 4-4. Briefly, this method creates a Frame object, which displays application views and handles navigation between them. Subsequently, depending on the previous activation (the PreviousExecutionState property of the event arguments), OnLaunched checks whether the app state and/or last view should be restored. Typically, when you run the app for the first time and it is not activated from the background, the OnLaunched event will reach the following statement:

```
rootFrame.Navigate(typeof(MainPage), e.Arguments);
```

This creates and displays a view, declared in the MainPage class. From this point, the control flow is redirected to that view.

LISTING 4-4 A default implementation of the OnLaunched event handler

```
protected override void OnLaunched(LaunchActivatedEventArgs e)
{
    Frame rootFrame = Window.Current.Content as Frame;

    if (rootFrame == null)
    {
        rootFrame = new Frame();

        rootFrame.NavigationFailed += OnNavigationFailed;

        if (e.PreviousExecutionState == ApplicationExecutionState.Terminated)
        {
            // TODO: Load state from previously suspended application
        }

        Window.Current.Content = rootFrame;
    }

    if (e.PrelaunchActivated == false)
    {
        if (rootFrame.Content == null)
        {
            rootFrame.Navigate(typeof(MainPage), e.Arguments);
        }
        Window.Current.Activate();
    }
}

void OnNavigationFailed(object sender, NavigationFailedEventArgs e)
{
    throw new Exception("Failed to load Page " + e.SourcePageType.FullName);
}
```

Views in the UWP apps, including the MainPage view, are composed of two distinct parts:

- **XAML declarations**   These are contained in the *.xaml file and declare a visual layer of the view.

- **Code-behind**   This is stored in the *.xaml.cs file, which implements the logic associated with a view.

The code-behind contains source code that handles events fired by the user after he or she uses any control on the visual layer. In the simplest case, this logic uses values entered by the user and updates the app state accordingly. To simplify this process and to create a clean separation between the presentation, logic, and data layers, you use data binding and the MVVM software architectural pattern.

Data Binding and the Model–View–ViewModel Software Architecture Pattern

Data binding is a mechanism for binding source and target properties. Usually, the source property is a field or method from the code-behind, while the target property is a specific part of the visual layer—for example, text in a text box, an item selected in a combo box, or the state of a checkbox. The idea behind data binding is to eliminate statements responsible only for rewriting values from source to target properties. UWP offers comprehensive support for data binding through the Model–View–ViewModel (MVVM) software architectural pattern.

MVVM separates the presentation layer from the logic and data layers. This offers several advantages. Most importantly, it lets you declare UI and logic independently. By explicitly decoupling logic from presentation, you make your code reusable. It can be shared across various apps and developed independently. Additionally, this separation results in improved maintainability and testability.

The MVVM pattern has three main elements (see Figure 4-2):

- **Model** This represents the application data model and contains all related logic.

- **View** This defines the visual controls employed by the user to view data or enter input.

- **ViewModel** This is an intermediate object, between the view and the model.

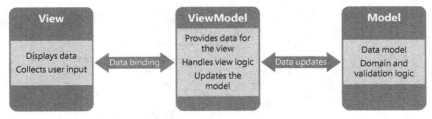

FIGURE 4-2 Components of the MVVM pattern.

The relationship between these components can be summarized as follows:

- Before the view is presented to the user, it obtains data from the ViewModel through data binding.

- The ViewModel receives data from the model through the use of dedicated methods, interfaces, or data adapters.

Every time the user performs an action on visual controls, such as typing text into a text box or selecting an item from a list, the associated target property in the ViewModel is updated.

This information is subsequently propagated to the model to synchronize the application state with the data store. This scheme represents a standard interaction between the code-behind and UI but clearly separates each layer so you can easily replace or reuse specific app elements.

Implementing Data Binding

Let's see how MVVM works in practice. To begin, create a blank UWP app, UWP.Basics, that references the MixedReality.Common library (as explained in Chapter 3). Then declare the main view of the app as shown in Figure 4-3. (You can find the complete XAML declaration in the companion code for this book in this folder: Chapter_04/UWP.Basics/MainPage.xaml.)

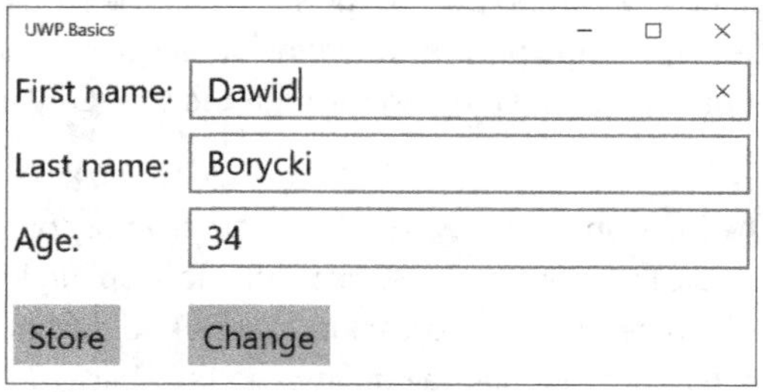

FIGURE 4-3 UI of the UWP.Basics app.

To declare the view, you proceed as you did in Chapter 3. As shown in the right pane in Figure 4-4, you use the MainPage.xaml file to declare all your controls. (The full code listing is omitted here, but you can obtain it from companion code or in Listing 4-6.)

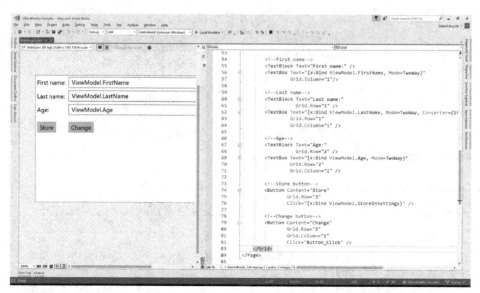

FIGURE 4-4 Visual Studio showing the view and corresponding XAML declarations of the UWP.Basics app developed in this chapter.

Notice that the view is composed of three labels, three text boxes, and two buttons. The user employs the text boxes to enter personal data (first and last name and age) and clicks the Store button to persist these values into the app settings. When this data is stored in the settings, it will be restored whenever the app is run. (The other button, Change, will be used later.) So, in this example, you can treat the app settings as the model. This model is updated through the ViewModel associated with the view whenever the user types data in the text boxes and confirms his or her changes by clicking the Store button.

Conforming to the MVVM pattern, values from text boxes are bound to properties of the ViewModel. In the UWP.Basics app, this is implemented through the `PersonViewModel` class. (See the companion code in Chapter_04/UWP.Basics/PersonViewModel.cs.) As Listing 4-5 shows, this class has three public auto-implemented properties: `FirstName`, `LastName`, and `Age`.

LISTING 4-5 A fragment of the `PersonViewModel` definition

```
public class PersonViewModel
{
    public string FirstName { get; set; }
    public string LastName { get; set; }
    public int Age { get; set; }

    // The rest of the class definition
}
```

The properties of the ViewModel are two-way bound with the text boxes of the UI. As Listing 4-6 shows, to define the binding, you use an `{x:Bind}` markup extension. (See http://bit.ly/x-bind for more information.) This requires you to provide the path to the source property. Here, this path points to the corresponding property of the ViewModel. You can also specify the binding mode with a `Mode` attribute. There are three available binding modes, each represented by the appropriate value declared in the `Windows.UI.Xaml.Data.BindingMode` enumeration:

- **OneTime**   This indicates that the target property is updated when the binding is created. All subsequent updates of the source property will not modify the target property.

- **OneWay**   This specifies that the target property is updated whenever the value of the source property changes.

- **TwoWay**   This indicates that the binding is bidirectional, which means that the source property is modified by updating the target property.

LISTING 4-6 Binding control properties with the ViewModel using the `{x:Bind}` markup extension

```
<!--First name-->
<TextBlock Text="First name:" />
<TextBox Text="{x:Bind ViewModel.FirstName, Mode=TwoWay}"
        Grid.Column="1"/>

<!--Last name-->
<TextBlock Text="Last name:"
        Grid.Row="1" />
<TextBox Text="{x:Bind ViewModel.LastName, Mode=TwoWay}"
        Grid.Row="1"
```

```
            Grid.Column="1" />

<!--Age-->
<TextBlock Text="Age:"
           Grid.Row="2" />
<TextBox Text="{x:Bind ViewModel.Age, Mode=TwoWay}"
         Grid.Row="2"
         Grid.Column="1" />
```

Listing 4-6 uses two-way binding so that any text the user types in the text boxes (the target property) updates the source property of the ViewModel. After such a binding is established, you do not need to manually rewrite properties. Clearly, without such a binding, you would need to implement a handler for the TextBox.TextChanged event as follows:

```
private void TextBox_TextChanged(object sender, TextChangedEventArgs e)
{
    if (e.OriginalSource is TextBox textBox)
    {
        ViewModel.FirstName = textBox.Text;
    }
}
```

Importantly, using an {x:Bind} markup extension ensures that these operations are performed automatically whenever the binding is defined. Moreover, you can replace the source properties with methods invoked after a particular user action is performed. For instance, to handle a Click event of the Store button, you can use the StoreInSettings method:

```
<Button Content="Store"
        Grid.Row="3"
        Click="{x:Bind ViewModel.StoreInSettings}" />
```

A definition of the StoreInSettings method appears in Listing 4-7. To access the app settings, the ApplicationDataContainer class is used. To get its instance, the LocalSettings property of ApplicationData.Current is read. Once the instance of the ApplicationDataContainer class is achieved, you can write values to the app settings by updating the Values property, which implements a key-value pair container. Listing 4-7 declares three keys, which are stored in corresponding private fields: firstNameKey, lastNameKey, and ageKey. These keys are then used to store values from the FirstName, LastName, and Age members of PersonViewModel.

LISTING 4-7 Storing data in app settings

```
private ApplicationDataContainer localSettings =
    ApplicationData.Current.LocalSettings;

private string firstNameKey = nameof(FirstName);
private string lastNameKey = nameof(LastName);
private string ageKey = nameof(Age);

public void StoreInSettings()
{
    localSettings.Values[firstNameKey] = FirstName;
    localSettings.Values[lastNameKey] = LastName;
```

```
        localSettings.Values[ageKey] = Age;
}
```

To retrieve data from settings during runtime, you proceed similarly, but instead of writing to the `Values` collection, you read it. Typically, before reading a value, you first check if that collection contains a specified key:

```
if(localSettings.Values.ContainsKey(firstNameKey))
{
    FirstName = localSettings.Values[firstNameKey].ToString();
}
```

I used such an approach to retrieve personal data from the app settings in the `PersonViewModel` class constructor:

```
public PersonViewModel()
{
    if (IsPersonDataStoredInSettings())
    {
        FirstName = localSettings.Values[firstNameKey].ToString();
        LastName = localSettings.Values[lastNameKey].ToString();
        Age = (int)localSettings.Values[ageKey];
    }
}
```

In this code block, I use the `IsPersonDataStoredInSettings` helper method. (See Listing 4-8.) This checks whether the local application settings contain all three keys.

LISTING 4-8 Checking whether personal data is stored in local settings

```
private bool IsPersonDataStoredInSettings()
{
    string[] keys = { firstNameKey, lastNameKey, ageKey };

    var isPersonDataStoredInSettings = true;

    foreach(var key in keys)
    {
        if(!localSettings.Values.ContainsKey(key))
        {
            isPersonDataStoredInSettings = false;
            break;
        }
    }

    return isPersonDataStoredInSettings;
}
```

Run the app, type any values in the text boxes, and click the Store button. Your values will be persisted in the app settings. Afterward, try closing the app and running it again. You will see that the app restores previously typed values.

This example illustrates how to start using the MVVM pattern in your UWP apps. However, there are several other aspects of data binding you need to know. I cover them next.

Using Converters

Data binding provides a convenient mechanism for displaying data and collecting user input. As you just saw, if you data bind values from the source properties, they are automatically presented in the target properties of visual controls. Sometimes, however, you might want to have more control over how your data is presented. For instance, you might want to supplement data with some culture-specific symbols or arbitrarily format your data before presentation. Fortunately, UWP provides a dedicated tool, or converter. You use it to alter data being displayed with data binding.

To create the converter, you begin by implementing a class that conforms to `Windows.UI.Xaml.Data.IValueInterface`. This interface declares two methods, `Convert` and `ConvertBack`, which you implement in your converter class. These methods are invoked whenever your binding needs to be updated. `Convert` enables you to modify the value before it is displayed in the UI or, more generally, when the target property is updated due to changes in the source. In contrast, `ConvertBack` is invoked whenever the binding update is triggered by the target property—for example, when you type a string in the text box.

To give you an example, let's supplement the UWP.Basics project with a Converters folder. Follow these steps:

1. In Solution Explorer, right-click **UWP.Basics** and choose **Add/New Folder** from the menu that appears.

2. Right-click the **Converters** folder, choose **Add**, and select **New Class** to create new code file.

3. In the Add New Item window, name the new class **ToUpperConverter.cs**.

4. Implement the new file as shown in Listing 4-9, which presents a sample definition of the converter. `ToUpperConverter` implements the `Convert` method to modify the source string to capitalize it. Note that the back conversion does not modify the value.

LISTING 4-9 A full definition of ToUpperConverter

```
public class ToUpperConverter : IValueConverter
{
    public object Convert(object value, Type targetType,
    object parameter, string language)
    {
        var strValue = value as string;

        if (!string.IsNullOrEmpty(strValue))
        {
            strValue = strValue.ToUpper();
        }

        return strValue;
    }

    public object ConvertBack(object value, Type targetType,
    object parameter, string language)
    {
```

```
        return value;
    }
}
```

5. To associate a converter with the binding, you first declare that converter in the resource dictionary accessed by the particular view. Hence, you typically declare converters in the application-scoped resource collection defined in the App.xaml file. (See the bolded statements in Listing 4-10.)

LISTING 4-10 Declaring a converter in the application-scoped resources

```
<Application
    x:Class="UWP.Basics.App"
    xmlns="http://schemas.microsoft.com/winfx/2006/xaml/presentation"
    xmlns:x="http://schemas.microsoft.com/winfx/2006/xaml"
    xmlns:converters="using:UWP.Basics.Converters"
    RequestedTheme="Light">

    <Application.Resources>
        <converters:ToUpperConverter x:Key="ToUpperConverter" />
    </Application.Resources>
</Application>
```

After declaring a converter, you apply it to the binding with the Converter attribute of the {x:Bind} markup extension:

```
<TextBox
    Text="{x:Bind ViewModel.LastName, Mode=TwoWay,
        Converter={StaticResource ToUpperConverter}}"
    Grid.Row="1"
    Grid.Column="1" />
```

If you re-run an app that has been modified in this way, the value from the Last Name text box will be capitalized when the app is executed. (See Figure 4-5.) However, you will quickly see that the text is not capitalized when you modify the text from the Last Name text box. This is because the data-binding mechanism is not notified about changes made to the ViewModel properties. As a result, data binding does not update any properties and thus does not invoke the Convert method of the ToUpperConverter class instance.

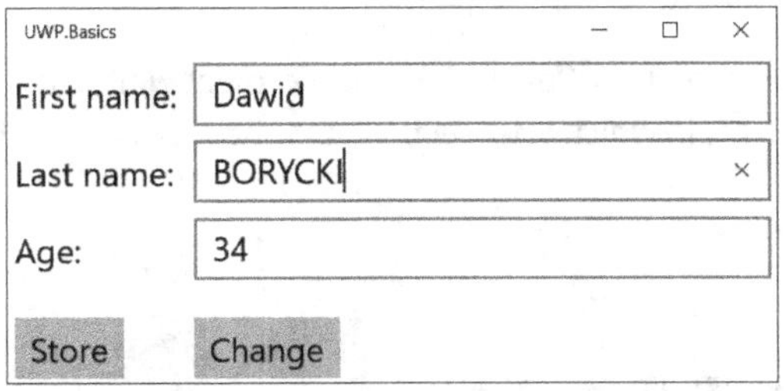

FIGURE 4-5 Using a converter to alter the string being displayed in the Last Name text box.

6. To confirm this behavior, supplement the XAML declaration of the Change button by adding a handler to the Click event (see Listing 4-11). Then implement this handler according to Listing 4-12.

LISTING 4-11 Button declaration

```
<Button Content="Change"
        Grid.Row="3"
        Grid.Column="1"
        Click="Button_Click" />
```

LISTING 4-12 Updating a viewmodel

```
private void Button_Click(object sender, RoutedEventArgs e)
{
    ViewModel.FirstName = "Nick";
    ViewModel.LastName = "Wilde";
    ViewModel.Age = 27;
}
```

Having introduced these changes, you would expect that the personal data would be modified when the user clicked the Change button, and that these changes would be reflected in the UI. However, although public members of the ViewModel are changed, values displayed in text boxes are not. This is because the data binding does not know about these updates. To solve this problem, you need to notify the binding about underlying changes to the source properties. UWP natively provides a mechanism for such notifications, based on the System.ComponentModel.INotifyPropertyChanged interface.

Notifying the Binding about Changes to Source Properties

The INotifyPropertyChanged interface contains a declaration of the PropertyChanged event. You use this event in the derived class to notify the data-binding mechanism about changes in the source properties of the ViewModel. This functionality is necessary for apps using one-way binding. To implement notifications, you typically create the base class, which derives from INotifyPropertyChanged. This class handles all the logic related to notifying data binding about changes in source properties and becomes the base class for all other ViewModels.

To give you an example, I supplemented the MixedReality.Common project with another file, BaseViewModel.cs (in the ViewModels folder), in which I define the class shown in Listing 4-13.

LISTING 4-13 A definition of the BaseViewModel class

```
public class BaseViewModel : INotifyPropertyChanged
{
    public event PropertyChangedEventHandler PropertyChanged;

    protected void OnPropertyChanged(string propertyName)
    {
```

```
        PropertyChanged?.Invoke(this, new PropertyChangedEventArgs(propertyName));
    }

    protected void SetProperty<T>(ref T property, T value,
    [CallerMemberName] string propertyName = "")
    {
        property = value;
        OnPropertyChanged(propertyName);
    }
}
```

The BaseViewModel class derives from the INotifyPropertyChanged interface and thus implements a PropertyChanged event of type PropertyChangedEventHandler. This event represents the method, which accepts two arguments:

- **sender of type object**   This stores a reference to the object, which raises an event.

- **e of type PropertyChangedEventArgs**   This is used to pass the name of the source property that was updated.

You use these arguments to raise the PropertyChanged event. Listing 4-13 fires this event in the OnPropertyChanged method. The latter accepts one argument, propertyName, which is used to instantiate PropertyChangedEventArgs. OnPropertyChanged is used to implement a generic SetProperty function, which is responsible for updating the selected property of the ViewModel and providing appropriate notification to the data binding. As Listing 4-13 shows, SetProperty accepts three arguments:

- **property**   This is the property to be updated.

- **value**   This is a new value, to be written to the property being updated.

- **propertyName**   This is an optional argument that specifies the name of the property. By default, propertyName is inferred from the property argument. However, you can use propertyName to explicitly inform the data-binding mechanism which property has changed.

You can skip the last argument, propertyName, when calling the SetProperty method. In this case, it will deduct the property name from the call to that method. This is indicated by the CallerMemberName attribute. (See http://bit.ly/callermembername for more information.)

After preparing the BaseViewModel class, use it to modify the PersonViewModel. (See Listing 4-14.) First, update the declaration of the PersonViewModel class so it derives from BaseViewModel. Next, replace three auto-implemented properties—FirstName, LastName, and Age—with new versions that explicitly implement property get and set accessors. In each case, the get accessor returns the value from the underlying private field, while the set accessor uses the base SetProperty method. This ensures that the data-binding mechanism will be notified about updates to public properties of the ViewModel.

LISTING 4-14 Notifying data binding about changes in source properties

```
public class PersonViewModel : BaseViewModel
{
    //public string FirstName { get; set; }
```

```
//public string LastName { get; set; }
//public int Age { get; set; }

public string FirstName
{
    get => firstName;
    set => SetProperty(ref firstName, value);
}

public string LastName
{
    get => lastName;
    set => SetProperty(ref lastName, value);
}

public int Age
{
    get => age;
    set => SetProperty(ref age, value);
}

private string firstName;
private string lastName;
private int age;

// The rest of class definition
}
```

After introducing these changes, re-run the app. You will see that all changes to source properties are automatically reflected in the UI and that the converter works correctly each time you modify the last name. The data-binding mechanism recognizes that `PersonViewModel` uses a `PropertyChanged` event from the `INotifyPropertyChanged` interface and automatically registers for change notifications.

Adapting a View to the Platform

Adapting the view to a specific platform is useful when you create universal UWP apps. Typically, to implement adaptive views, you use dedicated classes from the UWP API, such as `RelativePanel`, `StateTrigger`, and `AdaptiveTrigger`. Triggers are fired whenever the view layout changes—for example, due to changes to the window size. (See http://bit.ly/adaptive_layouts for more information.) Then you can handle layout updates by reorganizing controls with `RelativePanel` so they are optimally displayed onto the screen.

Sometimes, this approach may not work well, and you might want to completely replace the view for a specific platform. To do so, you supplement the app project with additional XAML files. The names of these files contain the name of the default view with different suffixes to represent each platform. For instance, if you want to use different versions of the `MainPage` view for the desktop and Mixed Reality platforms, you would add a file called MainPage.DeviceFamily-Holographic.xaml and then use this file to define the Mixed Reality view.

Let's see how this works in practice. To add the new view, follow these steps:

1. Open the Solution Explorer.

2. Open the UWP.Basics app's context menu and choose **Add/New Item**.

3. In the Add New Item dialog box, click the **Installed/XAML** tab and choose **XAML View**.

4. In the **Name** text box, type **MainPage.DeviceFamily-Holographic**. (See Figure 4-6.)
   Then click the **Add** button.

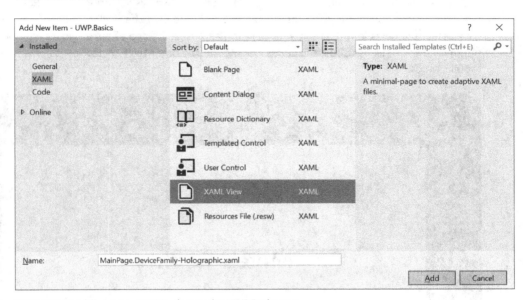

FIGURE 4-6 Adding a new XAML view to the UWP.Basics app.

After the new file is added to the project, modify it according to Listing 4-15.

LISTING 4-15 A definition of the holographic version of the MainPage

```
<Page
    x:Class="UWP.Basics.MainPage"
    xmlns="http://schemas.microsoft.com/winfx/2006/xaml/presentation"
    xmlns:x="http://schemas.microsoft.com/winfx/2006/xaml"
    xmlns:d="http://schemas.microsoft.com/expression/blend/2008"
    xmlns:mc="http://schemas.openxmlformats.org/markup-compatibility/2006"
    mc:Ignorable="d">

    <Page.Resources>
        <Style TargetType="TextBlock">
            <Setter Property="HorizontalAlignment"
                    Value="Center"/>
            <Setter Property="VerticalAlignment"
                    Value="Center"/>
            <Setter Property="FontSize"
                    Value="50"/>
```

```
            <Setter Property="FontWeight"
                        Value="Bold"/>
        </Style>
    </Page.Resources>

    <Grid Background="{ThemeResource ApplicationPageBackgroundThemeBrush}">
        <TextBlock Text="Mixed Reality"/>
    </Grid>
</Page>
```

The view declared in Listing 4-15 has a single label that displays the string "Mixed Reality." To test the view, run the app in the HoloLens emulator. (See Figure 4-7.) The UWP runtime will automatically detect the new file with the view declaration and use it instead of the original one. However, the original view will still be used if the app is executed in any other UWP platform—for example, desktop, mobile, or IoT.

FIGURE 4-7 An XAML view for the holographic platform.

Although the view for a holographic platform is loaded from a separate file, the logic is still contained in the same code-behind file, MainPage.xaml.cs. So, a platform-specific view shares the code of the general view. You can use this feature to handle any events generated in the platform-specific view with the same or different methods as in the default view. To demonstrate this, I extended the declaration of TextBlock (refer to Listing 4-15) by adding a Tapped attribute:

```
<TextBlock Text="Mixed Reality" Tapped="ViewModel.DisplayPersonData"/>
```

As shown, this declaration invokes a DisplayPersonData method from PersonViewModel:

```
public async void DisplayPersonData(object sender, TappedRoutedEventArgs e)
{
    var message = $"{FirstName} {LastName}";

    var messageDialog = new MessageDialog(message, "Person data:");

    await messageDialog.ShowAsync();
}
```

This method combines the first and last name into one string and displays it in a modal window using the Windows.UI.Popups.MessageDialog class. When you run the app in the HoloLens emulator, the FirstName and LastName properties of the PersonViewModel are null. So, this code will generate an exception. To avoid this error, you can invoke the Button_Click method (refer to Listing 4-12) within the MainPage constructor:

```
public MainPage()
{
    InitializeComponent();

    if (AnalyticsInfo.VersionInfo.DeviceFamily == "Windows.Holographic")
    {
        Button_Click(this, null);
    }
}
```

Button_Click ensures that an instance of PersonViewModel will be correctly set up so the modal window can be displayed. Note that Button_Click is invoked only if the app is running on the holographic platform. To check a platform, use the VersionInfo.DeviceFamily property of the AnalyticsInfo class, declared under the Windows.System.Profile namespace. When you run the app in the HoloLens emulator and click the text block, a modal window will be displayed. (See Figure 4-8.) So, even when you use a different view for the specific platform, you can use the same code-behind, including all ViewModels.

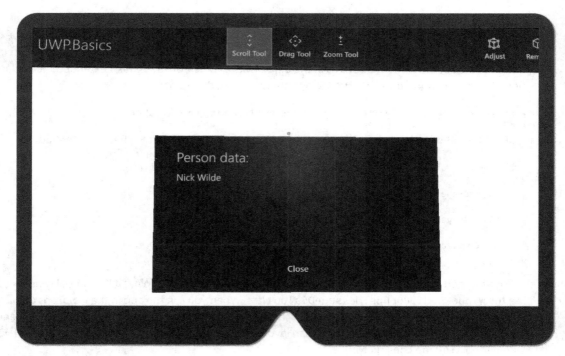

FIGURE 4-8 Presenting a modal window.

Summary

This chapter covered structuring UWP apps to achieve clean separation of visual, logic, and data layers by using data binding and the MVVM software architectural pattern. You will use these patterns in subsequent chapters to implement 2D UWP apps.

CHAPTER 5

Media Controls

This chapter shows you how to use media controls such as Image, CaptureElement, and MediaElement to render video and audio streams, including acquiring a video stream from your headset's world-facing camera. You will also learn how to detect human faces in the acquired images (see Figure 5-1). Finally, you will explore UWP speech-synthesis and speech-recognition engines and learn how to use them to support hands-free interaction between the user and the app on the Mixed Reality device. Several classes developed in this chapter will be stored in the reusable MixedReality. Common class library; you will use them to build more complex examples in next chapter.

FIGURE 5-1 Face detection in the Mixed Reality simulator.

Displaying Images

Before you acquire and display images from the camera, you'll learn how to display static images. More precisely, you'll create a UWP app containing an Image control, in which you will display a bitmap from a remote location. Again, you will follow the MVVM approach.

Start by creating a new project, MediaControls.Video, using the Blank UWP Visual C# project template. Then reference the MixedReality.Common class library and supplement the project with a new file, VideoViewModel.cs. In this file you will define a view model class, VideoViewModel, which appears in Listing 5-1. This class has one public property, Image, which is of type BitmapImage. The Image property stores a reference to a bitmap, which will be displayed in the view. In this example, the bitmap is taken from a remote resource. To obtain such an image you use a constructor of the BitmapImage class. This accepts an instance of the System.Uri class, which points to the image (in this case, http://bit.ly/ American_robin). You use this link to implement the GetImage method in Listing 5-1. Finally, you invoke GetImage in the constructor of VisionViewModel so Image will be available for the associated view.

LISTING 5-1 A definition of VideoViewModel

```
public class VideoViewModel : BaseViewModel
{
    public BitmapImage Image
    {
        get => image;
        set => SetProperty(ref image, value);
    }

    private BitmapImage image;

    public VisionViewModel()
    {
        LenaImage = GetImage();
    }

    private BitmapImage GetImage()
    {
        var uri = "http://bit.ly/american-robin";

        return new BitmapImage(new Uri(uri));
    }
}
```

After declaring the VideoViewModel class, modify the XAML declarations of the MainPage view according to Listing 5-2. You'll replace the default Grid control with a Pivot control, which implements a tab control in the UWP. Then create one tab with a single child item, Image. This represents a control for displaying images in various formats, such as BMP, PNG, GIF, and SVG. To select an image to be displayed, you use the Source attribute of the Image class. Here, this attribute is one-way bound to the Image property of the VideoViewModel class instance. In this example, you'll explicitly set the Stretch attribute. This attribute controls how the image should be resized to fill the available space (a bounding rectangle of the control). All available stretching methods are represented as appropriate values of the Windows.UI.Xaml.Media.Stretch enumeration:

- **None** The original image size is unchanged.

- **Fill** The image is resized to fill the region of the host control without preserving the original aspect ratio.

- **Uniform** This works similarly to Fill but preserves the original aspect ratio.

- **UniformToFill**   This specifies that the image is resized to fill the region of the host control while preserving the original aspect ratio. If this aspect ratio differs from the aspect ratio of the host control, the image will be clipped accordingly.

Another method for controlling how the image is resized to fit the available space is the `NineGrid` approach. (See http://bit.ly/ninegrid for more information.)

LISTING 5-2 Displaying the picture using the `Image` control

```
<Pivot Background="{ThemeResource ApplicationPageBackgroundThemeBrush}">
    <PivotItem Header="Static Image">
        <Image Source="{x:Bind viewModel.Image, Mode=OneWay}"
               Margin="10"
               Stretch="Uniform"/>
    </PivotItem>
</Pivot>
```

To complete this example, you need to instantiate the `VideoViewModel`, which you do in the MainPage.xaml.cs file:

```
public sealed partial class MainPage : Page
{
    private VideoViewModel viewModel = new VideoViewModel();

    public MainPage()
    {
        this.InitializeComponent();
    }
}
```

When you run the MediaControls.Video app, you should get the result shown in Figure 5-2.

FIGURE 5-2 Displaying the image in the HoloLens app.

Capturing Video

Now that you know how to display static images, let's move on to learn how to capture video from a webcam (desktop platform) or world-facing camera (HoloLens and Mixed Reality headset). You will also learn how to detect human faces in the acquired images using the FaceDetector class from the UWP API (refer to Figure 5-1).

Generally, to display a video sequence from a camera, you use two elements:

- **Windows.Media.Capture.MediaCapture** This class handles low-level communication with the camera to preview or record images from the camera.

- **Windows.UI.Xaml.Controls.CaptureElement** This is the control or sink for displaying images obtained with MediaCapture.

To associate these two objects, you set the Source property of the CaptureElement control to an initialized instance of the MediaCapture class.

Camera Capture

Whether you are capturing video from a webcam or a world-facing camera, you use the same API, which is also available for mobile and IoT platforms. In other words, you use the same approach to acquire video in UWP apps on all Windows 10 platforms. Therefore, the app you will develop will be compatible with all Windows 10 platforms.

To achieve this, you implement a helper class, CameraCapture, which will be used to start and stop the preview from the camera. Later, you'll see how to display these images in the UI and pass them to the face-detection module to finally achieve the result shown in Figure 5-1.

As noted, you start by implementing the CameraCapture class. This serves as the reusable helper for acquiring images from the default video device. For this reason, you should store the CameraCapture class in the MixedReality.Common class library in the Helpers folder. (See the companion code for this chapter.) Internally, the CameraCapture class uses the MediaCapture class. This class can be instantiated with a parameter-less constructor, but to start the preview from the camera, you need to perform the appropriate initialization. Listing 5-3 shows how to do this kind of initialization to obtain images from the camera. You instantiate the MediaCaptureInitializationSettings class, which is an abstract representation of the initialization settings. You can use the StreamingCaptureMode property of that class to set the capture mode. All available modes are defined in the StreamingCaptureMode enumeration. The available modes are as follows:

- **Audio** This specifies that only the audio stream will be acquired.

- **Video** This indicates that only video will be captured.

- **AudioAndVideo** This specifies that audio and video will be captured concurrently.

In this example, I've chosen the second option (Video) because we do not need audio.

Finally, after configuring settings, you pass an instance of the MediaCaptureInitialization Settings class to the InitializeAsync method of the MediaCapture class instance.

LISTING 5-3 Initializing camera capture

```
public MediaCapture MediaCapture { get; private set; } = new MediaCapture();
public bool IsInitialized { get; private set; } = false;

public async Task Initialize()
{
    if (!IsInitialized)
    {
        var settings = new MediaCaptureInitializationSettings()
        {
            StreamingCaptureMode = StreamingCaptureMode.Video
        };

        try
        {
            await MediaCapture.InitializeAsync(settings);

            IsInitialized = true;
        }
        catch (Exception)
        {
            IsInitialized = false;
        }
    }
}
```

After the MediaCapture class is configured, you can start a preview by invoking the StartPreviewAsync method. As shown in Listing 5-4, you use this method to implement CameraCapture.Start. You first check if the underlying MediaCapture object was initialized by reading the CameraCapture.IsInitialized property (see the CheckInitialization method in Listing 5-4). Then you invoke MediaCapture.StartPreviewAsync. Finally, you set the IsPreviewActive property to true. You will use this information later to update the UI. Notice that Listing 5-4 contains a custom exception of type NotInitializedException. This class derives from System.Exception and its structure is quite standard. Clearly, NotInitializedException overrides several constructors from the base Exception class. (See the companion code for this chapter at Common/MixedReality.Common/CustomExceptions/NotInitializedException.cs.)

LISTING 5-4 A definition of the Start method from the CameraCapture class

```
public bool IsPreviewActive { get; private set; } = false;

public async Task Start()
{
    CheckInitialization();

    if (!IsPreviewActive)
    {
```

```
            await MediaCapture.StartPreviewAsync();

            IsPreviewActive = true;
    }
}

private void CheckInitialization()
{
    if (!IsInitialized)
    {
        throw new NotInitializedException();
    }
}
```

To stop a preview, you proceed similarly, but replace `MediaCapture.StartPreviewAsync` with `MediaCapture.StopPreviewAsync`:

```
public async Task Stop()
{
    CheckInitialization();

    if (IsPreviewActive)
    {
        await MediaCapture.StopPreviewAsync();

        IsPreviewActive = false;
    }
}
```

You use `CameraCapture` to extend a definition of `VideoViewModel`. First, you create three public properties, as shown in Listing 5-5. You use the first property, `CameraCapture`, to store a reference to the class of the same name. The second property, `Faces`, is a collection of `Windows.UI.Xaml.Shapes.Rectangle` objects, each of which stores a bounding box of the face detected in the image. This collection is created with the `ObservableCollection` class, which implements the `INotifyPropertyChanged` interface. So, it informs the UI about any changes in that collection automatically. Accordingly, you do not need to use the `BaseViewModel.SetProperty` method here. The last property, `IsPreviewActive`, is used to inform the UI whether the camera capture is active. You use this class member to configure the state of buttons used to either start or stop the preview, depending on the current capture state.

LISTING 5-5 Additional properties of `VideoViewModel` used to handle camera capture

```
public CameraCapture CameraCapture { get; private set; }
public ObservableCollection<Rectangle> Faces { get; private set; }
    = new ObservableCollection<Rectangle>();

public bool IsPreviewActive
{
    get => isPreviewActive;
    set => SetProperty(ref isPreviewActive, value);
}
private bool isPreviewActive;
```

Next, you define two methods from Listing 5-6. The first one, `PreviewStart`, will be bound to the UI to start the camera preview. This method initializes camera capture, starts the preview, and informs the UI that the underlying `MediaCapture` class is initialized so it can be safely associated with the `CaptureElement` control. In the second method, `InitializeCameraCapture`, you manually invoke `OnPropertyChanged` right after the initialization of `CameraCapture`. Otherwise, `CaptureElement` will raise an exception during binding because its `Source` property cannot be associated with a non-initialized `MediaCapture` class instance.

LISTING 5-6 Initializing and starting camera capture

```
public async void PreviewStart()
{
    // Initialize camera capture
    await InitializeCameraCapture();

    // Start preview
    await CameraCapture.Start();

    // Update UI
    IsPreviewActive = CameraCapture.IsPreviewActive;
}

private async Task InitializeCameraCapture()
{
    CameraCapture = CameraCapture ?? new CameraCapture();

    await CameraCapture.Initialize();

    // Inform UI that CameraCapture is ready
    OnPropertyChanged("CameraCapture");
}
```

A definition of the corresponding `PreviewStop` method appears in Listing 5-7. `PreviewStop` first invokes the `Stop` method of the `CameraCapture` class instance. It then sets the `IsPreviewActive` property of the view model to update the UI state. Finally, it clears the `Faces` collection to ensure that no face rectangle is visible when the camera capture is inactive.

LISTING 5-7 Stopping camera capture

```
public async void PreviewStop()
{
    await CameraCapture.Stop();
    IsPreviewActive = CameraCapture.IsPreviewActive;
    Faces.Clear();
}
```

You now have all components of the ViewModel ready, so it's time to declare the UI. To begin, extend the MediaControls.Video app with another tab (`PivotItem`) with the header "Camera." Then, in this new tab, declare three buttons. (See Listing 5-8 and the companion code at Chapter_05/MediaControls.Video/MainPage.xaml.)

```
<PivotItem Header="Camera">
    <StackPanel>
        <StackPanel Orientation="Horizontal" >
            <Button Content="Start preview"
                    IsEnabled="{x:Bind viewModel.IsPreviewActive,
                        Mode=OneWay, Converter={StaticResource LogicalNegationConverter}}"
                    Click="{x:Bind viewModel.PreviewStart}"/>

            <Button Content="Stop preview"
                    IsEnabled="{x:Bind viewModel.IsPreviewActive, Mode=OneWay}"
                    Click="{x:Bind viewModel.PreviewStop}"/>

            <Button Content="Detect faces"
                    IsEnabled="{x:Bind viewModel.IsPreviewActive, Mode=OneWay}"
                    Click="{x:Bind viewModel.DetectFaces}"/>
        </StackPanel>

        <Canvas>
            <ItemsControl ItemsSource="{x:Bind viewModel.Faces}"/>
            <CaptureElement Source="{x:Bind viewModel.CameraCapture.MediaCapture, Mode=OneWay}"
                            Canvas.ZIndex="-1"/>
        </Canvas>
    </StackPanel>
</PivotItem>
```

The purpose of each of these buttons is as follows:

■ **Start Preview**   This is used to start camera capture, so its Click event is bound to the PreviewStart method of VideoViewModel. This button is enabled only when camera capture is inactive. To achieve this functionality, bind the Enabled property of the button with the IsPreviewActive property of the ViewModel through LogicalNegationConverter. This converter negates the Boolean values. (See the companion code at MixedReality.Common/ Converters/LogicalNegationConverter.cs.)

■ **Stop Preview**   This stops camera capture. Its Click and Enabled attributes are bound to the VideoViewModel.PreviewStop and VideoViewModel.IsPreviewActive members, respectively. The Stop Preview button is enabled only when camera capture is active.

■ **Detect Faces**   This invokes face detection on the current frame using the DetectFaces method (described in the next section). Like the Stop Preview button, the Detect Faces button is enabled only when the preview is started.

The Camera tab also has two other controls, declared within the Canvas control:

```
<Canvas>
    <ItemsControl ItemsSource="{x:Bind viewModel.Faces}"/>
    <CaptureElement Source="{x:Bind viewModel.CameraCapture.MediaCapture, Mode=OneWay}"
                    Canvas.ZIndex="-1"/>
</Canvas>
```

The first control, `ItemsControl`, is bound to the `Faces` collection and thus displays face-bounding rectangles. Rectangles appear in the UI automatically whenever they are added to the `Faces` collection. The second control, `CaptureElement`, displays a video stream from the camera. Its `Source` property is one-way bound to the corresponding property of the ViewModel.

These controls are declared within the `Canvas` control to ensure that the rectangles are drawn on top of the images displayed within `CaptureElement`. This behavior is controlled with the `ZIndex` property of the `Canvas` control. The higher the `ZIndex` value, the closer the control appears to the foreground. In the preceding code, I left the default value (0) for `ZIndex` in the `ItemsControl`, and set `ZIndex` in the `CaptureElement` to `-1`. Consequently, `CaptureElement` is closer to the foreground than `ItemsControl`.

Before testing this solution, you need two things. First, you need an empty definition of the `DetectFaces` method in the `VideoViewModel`:

```
public async void DetectFaces() { }
```

Otherwise, the code will not compile. And second, you need a declaration of the webcam capability. To declare this capability, follow these steps:

1. In Solution Explorer, expand the **MediaControls.Video** entry.

2. Double-click the **Package.appxmanifest** entry. (See Figure 5-3.)

3. Click the **Capabilities** tab and select the **Webcam** checkbox. (See Figure 5-4.)

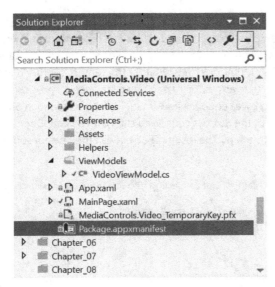

FIGURE 5-3 Solution Explorer showing the Package.appxmanifest file for the MediaControls.Video app.

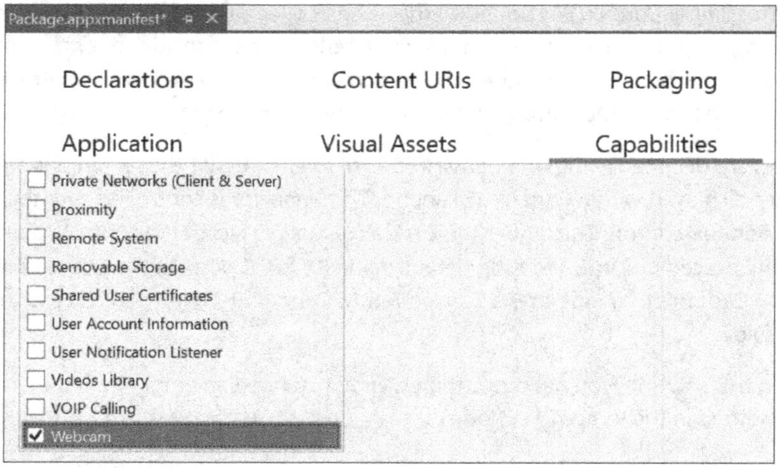

FIGURE 5-4 Declaring webcam capability.

4. To test the app on the desktop platform, click the **Privacy/Camera** tab, click **Settings**, and make sure your privacy settings do not prevent apps from accessing your camera.

After executing the MediaControls.Video app, you click the Start Preview button to enable camera capture. You will quickly see the video sequence below the buttons. (Refer to Figure 5-1.)

Face Detection

When camera capture is ready, you can extend the app by adding face-detection capabilities. To achieve this, supplement the CameraCapture class with another method, CapturePhotoToSoftwareBitmap, whose definition appears in Listing 5-9. This method verifies whether the camera capture is initialized. If so, it captures a photo to the in-memory byte array, abstracted by an instance of the InMemory RandomAccessStream class. The resulting byte sequence (raw image data) is encoded in BMP format and then converted to an instance of the SoftwareBitmap class with BitmapDecode. (See http://bit.ly/bitmapdecoder for more information.) The resulting object can then be consumed by the FaceDetector class.

LISTING 5-9 Capturing a single frame from the camera and converting it to the SoftwareBitmap class

```
public async Task<SoftwareBitmap> CapturePhotoToSoftwareBitmap()
{
    CheckInitialization();

    // Create bitmap-encoded image
    var imageEncodingProperties = ImageEncodingProperties.CreateBmp();

    // Capture photo
    var memoryStream = new InMemoryRandomAccessStream();
    await MediaCapture.CapturePhotoToStreamAsync(imageEncodingProperties, memoryStream);
```

```
    // Decode stream to bitmap
    var bitmapDecoder = await BitmapDecoder.CreateAsync(memoryStream);

    return await bitmapDecoder.GetSoftwareBitmapAsync();
}
```

A definition of the DetectFaces method of the VisionViewModel appears in Listing 5-10. DetectFaces processes a bitmap acquired with the camera to find faces and then draws face-bounding rectangles on top of the images displayed in the UI.

LISTING 5-10 Face detection

```
public async void DetectFaces()
{
    // Capture and display bitmap
    var softwareBitmap = await CameraCapture.CapturePhotoToSoftwareBitmap();

    // Detect faces
    var detectedFaces = await ProcessFaceBitmap(softwareBitmap);

    // Display face rectangles
    DisplayFaceRectangles(detectedFaces);
}
```

To detect faces, you can use a helper method, ProcessFaceBitmap, from Listing 5-11. First, create an instance of the FaceDetector class. FaceDetector doesn't implement any public constructors, so you can use the CreateAsync static method instead. Afterward, check whether the bitmap acquired with the camera has a pixel format supported by the detector. If not, you need to convert that bitmap. To that end, you can use the static Convert method of the SoftwareBitmap class. It accepts two arguments: an instance of SoftwareBitmap to convert and the target pixel format. You use the first argument to pass an input bitmap. As for the pixel format, use the first format supported by the detector. You obtain the list of supported formats from the FaceDetector.GetSupportedBitmapPixelFormats static method.

LISTING 5-11 Processing a software bitmap to find faces

```
private async Task<IList<DetectedFace>> ProcessFaceBitmap(SoftwareBitmap softwareBitmap)
{
    // Initialize face detector
    var detector = await FaceDetector.CreateAsync();

    // Ensure that bitmap format is supported by the detector
    if (!FaceDetector.IsBitmapPixelFormatSupported(softwareBitmap.BitmapPixelFormat))
    {
        softwareBitmap = SoftwareBitmap.Convert(softwareBitmap,
            FaceDetector.GetSupportedBitmapPixelFormats().First());
    }

    // Detect faces
    return await detector.DetectFacesAsync(softwareBitmap);
}
```

After the detector is instantiated and bitmap is appropriately pre-processed, you can use the DetectFacesAsync method to process a given image to find faces. DetectFacesAsync returns a collection of DetectedFace objects. DetectedFace has only one public property you can use: FaceBox, which defines a face-bounding rectangle. FaceBox is represented as a BitmapBounds struct. BitmapBounds has four public members: X, Y, Width, and Height. They specify the location of the face in the provided image. Accordingly, to draw rectangles, you iterate over the collection of detected faces and convert them to instances of the Windows.UI.Xaml.Shapes.Rectangle class so they can be added to the Faces observable collection. (See Listing 5-12.) Because this collection is bound to the UI, rectangles will be drawn automatically.

LISTING 5-12 Displaying face rectangles

```
private void DisplayFaceRectangles(IList<DetectedFace> detectedFaces)
{
    Faces.Clear();

    foreach (var detectedFace in detectedFaces)
    {
        Faces.Add(FaceBoxHelper.ToRectangle(detectedFace));
    }
}
```

To convert instances of DetectedFace to rectangles, I wrote a helper class, FaceBoxHelper. (See the companion code at Chapter_05/Helpers/FaceBoxHelper.cs.) This class has one public static method, ToRectangle, which constructs a rectangle based on the provided instance of DetectedFace. (See Listing 5-13.) To set the dimensions of the Rectangle control, use its Width and Height properties. You can just rewrite the values from the corresponding properties of FaceBox. However, the Rectangle control does not have X and Y properties, which could be used to control the location of the resulting object. So, to translate the Rectangle control, you can use the TranslateTransform class, as shown in the bottom part of Listing 5-13. This class implements a translation that you can use to arbitrarily shift a visual control. To specify a new control location, you instantiate the TranslateTransform class, set its X and Y properties, and then associate this transform with the RenderTransform property of the control. Listing 5-13 follows this approach. Finally, to set the X and Y properties of TranslateTransform you use the appropriate properties of FaceBox.

LISTING 5-13 Converting DetectedFace to Rectangle

```
public static Rectangle ToRectangle(DetectedFace detectedFace)
{
    Check.IsNull(detectedFace, "detectedFace");

    var rectangle = new Rectangle()
    {
        Width = detectedFace.FaceBox.Width,
        Height = detectedFace.FaceBox.Height,
        Stroke = new SolidColorBrush(Colors.Orange),
        StrokeThickness = 4
    };
```

```
        Translate(rectangle, detectedFace);

        return rectangle;
}

private static void Translate(Rectangle rectangle, DetectedFace detectedFace)
{
    var translateTransform = new TranslateTransform()
    {
        X = detectedFace.FaceBox.X,
        Y = detectedFace.FaceBox.Y
    };

    rectangle.RenderTransform = translateTransform;
}
```

You can now compile and execute this app in a desktop, Mixed Reality simulator, or real hardware. Then start camera capture and click the Detect Faces button. After a moment, orange rectangles representing the bounds of detected faces will be drawn. This example cannot be executed in the HoloLens emulator because this emulator doesn't simulate a world-facing camera. However, you can successfully run this example in the Mixed Reality simulator or on a desktop or mobile platform.

Audio

Now that you have learned how to display images and acquire video from the camera, let's see how to extend UWP apps by adding sound. This section will show you how to create a simple app that renders audio from the file. You will then extend this app by adding speech synthesis. Synthesized speech is rendered similarly to audio from a file. Finally, you will learn how to use the UWP API to implement speech recognition. For this implementation, you will use a new UWP app developed with MVVM.

Playing Sounds

Start by creating a new blank UWP project, MediaControls.Audio, that references the MixedReality. Common class library. Then supplement MediaControls.Audio with another file, AudioViewModel.cs, which stores a definition of AudioViewModel. This class has just one public property:

```
public Uri Source
{
    get => source;
    set => SetProperty(ref source, value);
}
private Uri source;
```

You use this property to specify an audio file to be rendered. In general, the Source property can point to any local file. You can let the user browse the file using the FileOpenPicker class. (See http://bit.ly/fileopenpicker for more information.) Here, for simplicity, set the Source property so that it points to the audio.wav file for the project. (You can find this audio.wav file in the companion code. Alternatively, you can use any other audio file in a common audio format, such as MP3, WMA, or WAV.)

```
public AudioViewModel()
{
    Source = new Uri("ms-appx:///Media/audio.wav");
}
```

With `AudioViewModel` ready, you now declare the UI. Specifically, you replace the default `Grid` control with the `Pivot` control. Then you create one tab with the header "Playback." Within this tab, you declare a `Grid` control so the label (`TextBlock`) is displayed above the `MediaElement` control. (See Listing 5-14.)

LISTING 5-14 Declaration of the Playback tab

```
<PivotItem Header="Playback">
    <Grid>
        <Grid.RowDefinitions>
            <RowDefinition Height="Auto"/>
            <RowDefinition Height="*"/>
        </Grid.RowDefinitions>
        <TextBlock Text="{x:Bind viewModel.Source, Mode=OneWay,
                        Converter={StaticResource AudioSourceToStringConverter}}"/>
        <MediaElement Grid.Row="1"
                        Source="{x:Bind viewModel.Source}"
                        AreTransportControlsEnabled="true"/>
    </Grid>
</PivotItem>
```

Both controls, `TextBlock` and `MediaElement`, are one-way bound to the `Source` property of the ViewModel. The `TextBlock` control displays the name of the audio file. In this case, the data binding is performed with the help of a converter implemented as the `AudioSourceToStringConverter` class. This converter takes an instance of the `Uri` class as an input and returns the last segment of the underlying path. (See the companion code at Chapter_05/MediaControls.Audio/Converters/AudioSourceToStringConverter.cs.) The `MediaElement` control renders an audio file pointed to by its `Source` attribute. So, this attribute is bound to the `Source` property of the ViewModel. In the preceding example, I used one more attribute of the `MediaElement` control: `AreTransportControlsEnabled`. By setting this attribute to `true`, I enabled a default pane composed of built-in controls for controlling playback, such as Play and Pause buttons.

Lastly, you must instantiate `AudioViewModel` in the code-behind (MainPage.xaml.cs):

```
public sealed partial class MainPage : Page
{
    private AudioViewModel viewModel = new AudioViewModel();

    public MainPage()
    {
        InitializeComponent();
    }
}
```

To test this app, compile and execute it. When the app becomes active, `MediaElement` automatically starts audio playback. To disable this auto-playback, you can set the `AutoPlay` attribute of `MediaElement` to `false`. Once the app is running, you can start playback with built-in transport controls. (See Figure 5-5.)

FIGURE 5-5 Playing sounds in the HoloLens emulator.

Speech Synthesis

Let's supplement the MediaControls.Audio app by adding speech synthesis, which converts a string provided by the user to artificial speech and then plays it back. To implement this functionality, you use the `Windows.Media.SpeechSynthesis.SpeechSynthesizer` class for speech synthesis and `MediaElement` to play back the resulting audio stream. You also use both objects in a helper class, `Synthesizer`, defined in the MixedReality.Common class library. (See the companion code at Common/MixedReality.Common/Helpers/Synthesizer.cs.)

The `Synthesizer` class has two public properties. (See Listing 5-15.) The first one, `Voices`, represents a collection of available speech synthesis engines. As shown in the following code, you obtain this collection by reading the `AllVoices` static property of the `SpeechSynthesizer` class. The second property, `SelectedVoice`, is used to configure the speech engine, which will be used later for synthesis.

LISTING 5-15 Properties of the Synthesizer class

```
public IReadOnlyList<VoiceInformation> Voices { get; } =
    SpeechSynthesizer.AllVoices;
public VoiceInformation SelectedVoice { get; set; } =
    SpeechSynthesizer.DefaultVoice;
```

The key element of the Synthesizer class is the Speak public method, shown in Listing 5-16. First, this method checks whether SelectedVoice is null. If so, it uses the default voice, which is obtained from SpeechSynthesizer.DefaultVoice. Otherwise, the provided voice will be used. After configuring the speech engine, the method invokes the SynthesizeTextToStreamAsync method of the SpeechSynthesizer class instance. This accepts one argument, a string to convert, and returns an instance of the SpeechSynthesisStream class. The SpeechSynthesisStream class is an abstract representation of the byte sequence, containing the synthesized speech. To play back this speech, the method uses an instance of the MediaElement class. Specifically, it sets the source to be played using a SetSource method and then plays back the speech stream by invoking a Play method.

LISTING 5-16 Speech synthesis

```
private SpeechSynthesizer speechSynthesizer = new SpeechSynthesizer();
private MediaElement mediaElement = new MediaElement();

public async Task Speak(string text)
{
    if (!string.IsNullOrEmpty(text))
    {
        // Configure voice
        speechSynthesizer.Voice = SelectedVoice ?? SpeechSynthesizer.DefaultVoice;

        // Synthesize text
        var speechStream = await speechSynthesizer.
            SynthesizeTextToStreamAsync(text);

        // Playback
        mediaElement.SetSource(speechStream, speechStream.ContentType);
        mediaElement.Play();
    }
}
```

You can then use the Synthesizer class to extend the AudioViewModel class as follows:

```
public Synthesizer Synthesizer { get; private set; } = new Synthesizer();
public string TextToSpeak { get; set; } = string.Empty;

public async void Speak()
{
    await Synthesizer.Speak(TextToSpeak);
}
```

These elements of the AudioViewModel class instance can now be bound to appropriate properties of the UI. These new controls will enable the user to choose the speech engine, enter text to be synthesized, and begin actual synthesis. Accordingly, you extend the UI of the MediaControls.Audio app by adding another tab, whose declaration appears in Listing 5-17. Here, you declare four visual controls.

The first is the label for a drop-down list (here, containing the text Select Voice). The second one is the drop-down list itself, which contains all available speech engines. To populate this list, you use the `Voices` property of the `Synthesizer` class instance. Note that the drop-down list is also two-way bound to the `SelectedVoice` property. So, whenever you choose a new item from the list, the speech engine is updated. Right below the drop-down list is a text box and, below that, a Speak button. Here, the user can type a string, which will be synthesized after he or she clicks the Speak button.

LISTING 5-17 Controls used for speech synthesis

```
<PivotItem Header="Speech Synthesis">
    <StackPanel>
        <TextBlock Text="Select voice:"
                   HorizontalAlignment="Left"
                   Margin="{StaticResource DefaultMargin}"/>

        <ComboBox SelectedItem="{x:Bind viewModel.Synthesizer.SelectedVoice,
            Mode=TwoWay, Converter={StaticResource VoiceToObjectConverter}}"
                   ItemsSource="{x:Bind viewModel.Synthesizer.Voices}"
                   DisplayMemberPath="DisplayName"/>

        <TextBox Text="{x:Bind viewModel.TextToSpeak, Mode=TwoWay}"/>

        <Button Content="Speak"
                Click="{x:Bind viewModel.Speak}" />
    </StackPanel>
</PivotItem>
```

You can test the functionality of this feature on your desktop, in the HoloLens emulator (see Figure 5-6), or in the Mixed Reality simulator. The app will work the same on each platform. However, there may be differences in the results produced by the available speech-synthesis engines.

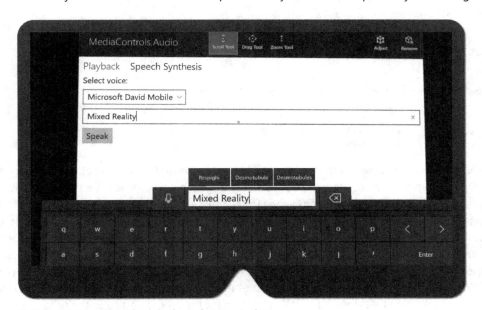

FIGURE 5-6 Speech synthesis in the HoloLens emulator.

Speech Recognition

You can extend the MediaControls.Audio app by adding a speech-recognition engine. In general, speech recognition works by processing an audio stream to extract single phonemes. (*Phonemes* are the smallest distinguishable units of speech.) It uses advanced models to map phonemes into textual words and sentences.

Windows 10's speech-recognition tool implements this scheme. You can programmatically access this tool through the `Windows.Media.SpeechRecognition.SpeechRecognizer` class. In general, methods of this class instance let you employ speech recognition in three ways (see http://bit.ly/speech_interactions):

- **One-shot recognition**   With this approach, the speech recognizer stops after it detects that speech has ended.

- **One-shot recognition with UI**   This works like one-shot recognition but uses the UI to deliver prompts and instructions.

- **Continuous dictation**   With this approach, the speech recognizer continuously analyzes incoming sound to recognize speech.

One-shot recognition is typically used in scenarios in which you collect single-user input. Instead of displaying a list of available options, you can ask the user to specify a command or choose an item. In contrast, continuous dictation constantly analyzes incoming sound in the background to recognize speech commands.

This section covers the implementation of speech recognition in continuous mode. To start, you extend the definition of `AudioViewModel` to add four members:

```
public bool IsSpeechRecognitionActive
{
    get => isSpeechRecognitionActive;
    set => SetProperty(ref isSpeechRecognitionActive, value);
}

public ObservableCollection<string> SpeechRecognitionResults =
    new ObservableCollection<string>();

private SpeechRecognizer speechRecognizer = new SpeechRecognizer();
private bool isSpeechRecognitionActive;
```

There are two public members (`IsSpeechRecognitionActive` and `SpeechRecognitionResults`) and two private members (`speechRecognizer` and `isSpeechRecognitionActive`). Let's start with the private members. The first one, `speechRecognizer`, stores an instance of the `SpeechRecognizer` class. The second one, `isSpeechRecognitionActive`, is used to define the associated public property `IsSpeechRecognitionActive`, which uses notifications through the `SetProperty` method from the underlying base ViewModel. This is done for data-binding purposes. `IsSpeechRecognitionActive` informs the UI that speech recognition is active. Specifically, it's used here to disable or enable a button the user can click to start continuous recognition. Finally, the public property, `SpeechRecognitionResults`, is an observable collection that stores information displayed to the user. In particular, this collection stores recognition results and a description of the state of the speech recognizer. The current state of the speech recognizer is represented as one of the following values from the `Windows.Media.SpeechRecognition.SpeechRecognizerState` enumeration:

- **Idle**   This indicates that the speech recognizer is inactive. It is not listening for user voice input.

- **Capturing**   This specifies that the speech recognizer is capturing an audio stream from the microphone.

- **Processing**   This indicates that the speech recognizer is processing audio input in order to recognize speech.

- **SoundStarted**   This indicates that the speech recognizer has detected that audio input has started.

- **SoundEnded**   This indicates that the speech recognizer has detected that audio input has ended.

- **SpeechDetected**   This indicates that the speech recognizer has detected human speech.

- **Paused**   This indicates that the continuous speech-recognition session is currently paused.

Next, in the `AudioViewModel` class, implement a public method that initializes continuous speech recognition:

```
public async Task InitializeSpeechRecognizer()
{
    await speechRecognizer.CompileConstraintsAsync();

    speechRecognizer.StateChanged += SpeechRecognizer_StateChanged;

    speechRecognizer.ContinuousRecognitionSession.ResultGenerated +=
        ContinuousRecognitionSession_ResultGenerated;

    speechRecognizer.ContinuousRecognitionSession.Completed +=
        ContinuousRecognitionSession_Completed;
}
```

First, this method compiles default speech-recognition constraints. These constraints are a high-level representation of the model used by the recognizer. In this example, no constraints are specified, so the speech recognizer will use its default model for recognition. (You will learn how to use custom constraints in Chapter 6.) Next, methods are associated with three events of the `SpeechRecognizer` class instance: `StateChanged`, `ContinousRecognitionSession.ResultGenerated`, and `ContinousRecognitionSession.Completed`. Listing 5-18 presents a definition of each event handler. All these handlers display information in the UI through the `SpeechRecognitionResults` observable collection. Specifically, `StateChanged` displays the current recognition state; `Continuous RecognitionSession_ResultGenerated` displays recognition results and the tool's confidence in their accuracy; and `ContinuousRecognitionSession_Completed` tells the user that the continuous recognition session has completed.

LISTING 5-18 Handling selected events in SpeechRecognizer

```
private async void SpeechRecognizer_StateChanged(
    SpeechRecognizer sender, SpeechRecognizerStateChangedEventArgs args)
{
    await ThreadHelper.InvokeOnMainThread(() =>
    {
        SpeechRecognitionResults.Add($"Recognizer state: {args.State}");
    });
}

private async void ContinuousRecognitionSession_ResultGenerated(
    SpeechContinuousRecognitionSession sender,
    SpeechContinuousRecognitionResultGeneratedEventArgs args)
{
    var result = $"{args.Result.Text} ({args.Result.Confidence})";

    await ThreadHelper.InvokeOnMainThread(() =>
    {
        SpeechRecognitionResults.Add($"Recognition result: {result}");
    });
}

private async void ContinuousRecognitionSession_Completed(
    SpeechContinuousRecognitionSession sender,
    SpeechContinuousRecognitionCompletedEventArgs args)
{
    await ThreadHelper.InvokeOnMainThread(() =>
    {
        IsSpeechRecognitionActive = false;

        SpeechRecognitionResults.Add($"Recognition completed");
    });
}
```

Each of these events is raised from the background thread because the speech recognizer acquires and analyzes audio input asynchronously. Hence, an attempt to directly update the binding from the event handler will cause an exception whose notification reads, *The application called an interface that was marshalled for a different thread.* This follows from the UWP thread model, in which all updates to visual controls can be made from the main or UI thread.

To invoke a method on the UI thread, you use the CoreDispatcher class. All UWP controls derived from the DependencyObject class (including views) have a public member, Dispatcher. You use this member to access an instance of the CoreDispatcher class. The procedure is quite straightforward when using the code-behind. In that case, you have a direct access to the view and its controls. To obtain an instance of the CoreDispatcher class in the ViewModel, you can use the Dispatcher member of MainView:

```
Windows.ApplicationModel.Core.CoreApplication.MainView.Dispatcher
```

Given an instance of the CoreDispatcher class, you use one of its methods—RunAsync or RunIdleAsync—to schedule the provided method to be executed on the UI thread. Listing 5-19 shows a common pattern for these methods. First, you check whether the dispatcher has access to the UI thread by reading the HasThreadAccess property. Then, depending on its value, you either invoke a method directly or schedule its execution on the UI thread. For example, if you invoke InvokeOnMainThread from the background thread (as in Listing 5-19), Dispatcher. HasThreadAccess will be false. This means the execution flow will be redirected under the else statement and the Dispatcher.RunAsync method will be invoked. As shown in Listing 5-19, this method calls InvokeOnMainThread again, but this time it will have access to the UI thread. (In other words, HasThreadAccess will be true.) Consequently, the action will be invoked directly.

LISTING 5-19 Invoking an action on the main or UI thread

```
public static async Task InvokeOnMainThread(Action action)
{
    if (Dispatcher.HasThreadAccess)
    {
        action?.Invoke();
    }
    else
    {
        await Dispatcher.RunAsync(CoreDispatcherPriority.Normal, async () =>
        {
            await InvokeOnMainThread(action);
        });
    }
}
```

You implement this mechanism in the ThreadHelper class under the MixedReality.Common class library (see the Helpers/ThreadHelper.cs file). In addition to the InvokeOnMainThread method, the ThreadHelper class also has one public property and a static constructor. As shown in Listing 5-20, these are used to store and obtain a reference to the CoreDispatcher class, respectively.

LISTING 5-20 Fragments of the ThreadHelper class

```
public static CoreDispatcher Dispatcher { get; private set; }

static ThreadHelper()
{
    Dispatcher = CoreApplication.MainView.Dispatcher;
}
```

In the next step, I supplement the AudioViewModel by the method, which starts a recognizer:

```
public async void StartSpeechRecognition()
{
    try
    {
        await speechRecognizer.ContinuousRecognitionSession.StartAsync();

        IsSpeechRecognitionActive = true;
    }
    catch (Exception ex)
    {
        SpeechRecognitionResults.Add($"Recognizer unavailable: {ex.Message}");
```

```
            IsSpeechRecognitionActive = false;
    }
}
```

Next, you initialize the speech recognizer in the code-behind of MainPage (MainPage.xaml.cs) right after this view is displayed. To that end, use the OnNavigatedTo event:

```
protected override async void OnNavigatedTo(NavigationEventArgs e)
{
    base.OnNavigatedTo(e);

    await viewModel.InitializeSpeechRecognizer();
}
```

Finally, you define another PivotItem control in MainPage. (See Listing 5-21.)

LISTING 5-21 Declaration of the Speech Recognition tab

```
<!--Speech recognition-->
<PivotItem Header="Speech Recognition">
    <Grid>
        <Grid.RowDefinitions>
            <RowDefinition Height="Auto"/>
            <RowDefinition Height="*"/>
            <RowDefinition Height="Auto"/>
        </Grid.RowDefinitions>

        <Button Content="Start"
            IsEnabled="{x:Bind viewModel.IsSpeechRecognitionActive, Mode=OneWay,
                    Converter={StaticResource LogicalNegationConverter}}"
            Click="{x:Bind viewModel.StartSpeechRecognition}" />

        <ListBox ItemsSource="{x:Bind viewModel.SpeechRecognitionResults}"
            Grid.Row="1"
            ItemTemplate="{StaticResource ListBoxDataTemplate}"/>

        <Button Content="Clear"
            Click="{x:Bind viewModel.SpeechRecognitionResults.Clear}"
            Grid.Row="2"/>
    </Grid>
</PivotItem>
```

These declarations add two buttons and a list to the UI. (See Figure 5-7.) The first button, Start, is bound to the StartSpeechRecognition method of the AudioViewModel instance. So, the user clicks this button to start speech recognition. When the user starts this process, the button becomes disabled, as IsSpeechRecognitionActive becomes true. When speech recognition is activated, the speech recognizer's status changes, and recognized words are presented in the list. You can clear its contents using a second button, Clear. This button's Click attribute is wired with the Clear method of the SpeechRecognitionResults observable collection. Note that no additional logic is necessary to clear the list.

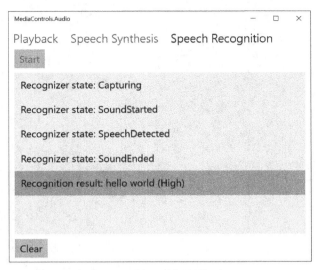

FIGURE 5-7 Speech recognition with UWP.

To test this example, you must declare microphone capability in the appx manifest. Additionally, when testing the app in a desktop environment, you must enable speech services in the Windows settings. To do so, follow these steps:

1. Choose **Update & Security**, select **Privacy**, and choose **Speech**.

2. Click the **Turn On Speech Services and Typing Suggestions** button.

3. Run the app, click the **Speech Recognition** tab, click the **Start** button, and begin speaking.

The app will capture your voice, which will be processed to identify words and sentences. The app presents recognition results in the list shown in Figure 5-7. (I used a desktop platform to create that image because it responds more quickly than a simulator.)

Summary

This chapter showed how to use media controls in UWP apps. It also explored UWP human-face detection and speech-recognition capabilities. You'll use these in the next chapter to implement human-device interaction to control the smart app, which will describe the contents of the image acquired with the camera.

CHAPTER 6

Microsoft Cognitive Services

Now that you have learned how to obtain and display images from the camera and to synthesize and recognize human speech, you will use this knowledge to build a voice-controlled app powered by artificial intelligence (AI). Specifically, in this chapter, you will learn how to create a vision assistant app, called VisionAssistant. To achieve this, you will use the cloud-based Computer Vision API and Bing Web Search API from Microsoft Cognitive Services (MCS).

VisionAssistant will help visually impaired people by describing an image captured by the camera. (See Figure 6-1.) To accomplish this, it sends the image from the camera to the MCS system for processing. The system then analyzes the image and returns a string that describes the image content. This description is displayed in the UI and is spoken to the user. VisionAssistant will also enable visually impaired people to search the web for information related to the content of the image on their screen. (See Figure 6-2.)

To obtain the results depicted in Figure 6-1, I put my mobile phone, on which an image of a bird was displayed, in front of my laptop's camera. Importantly, MCS describe the image pretty well even though it is of low quality with varying brightness.

FIGURE 6-1 A sample result of image content recognition with Microsoft Cognitive Services.

FIGURE 6-2 The VisionAssistant app showing a web page that describes the content of the image.

Exploring Microsoft Cognitive Services

Microsoft Cognitive Services (MCS), formerly known as Project Oxford, is a cloud-based AI service. You access it through the REST API (http://bit.ly/REST_Wiki).

The MCS API can be used in any app. Available intelligent systems are grouped by functionality:

- **Vision**   Vision services enable you to distill information from images, detect human emotion, and detect faces.

- **Speech**   You can use speech services for speech synthesis, speech recognition, and speaker identification.

- **Language**   Language services can enhance your app by spell-checking text and performing linguistic analyses.

- **Knowledge**   You can use knowledge APIs to implement recommendations, entity linking, or decision-making.

- **Search**   Search services provide autosuggestions, search, and entity search with Bing.

To use MCS, you can sign up for a free trial here: http://bit.ly/cognitive_services. The process is straightforward. After you set up an account, you will receive an API key and the URL of the service's endpoint. You use these to authorize and send requests to the MCS.

In this chapter, you will use two services: the Computer Vision API (http://bit.ly/mcs_cv_api) and Bing Web Search API (http://bit.ly/mcs_bing_api). To access these APIs, you can use the dedicated service clients, distributed as NuGet packages. Alternatively, you can write your own custom class clients. In this chapter, you will explore both options. Additionally, you will use the `CameraCapture` and `Synthesizer` classes developed in Chapter 5. You can find them in the MixedReality.Common project (see the Helpers folder) with the companion code.

Implementation of the Vision Assistant

When you obtain the API keys and endpoints for the Computer Vision API and Bing Web Search API, store them in the public properties of the `Settings` class. I have saved these in the MixedReality. Common class library. (See the companion code at MixedReality.Common/Helpers/Settings.cs.) Next, create a new blank UWP project named VisionAssistant. Then reference the MixedReality.Common class library and install the Microsoft.ProjectOxford.Vision NuGet package by invoking the following command in the NuGet Package Manager Console:

```
Install-Package Microsoft.ProjectOxford.Vision
```

Your next step is to supplement the project with a new file, VisionAssistantViewModel.cs, in which you implement the ViewModel class. This class, `VisionAssistantViewModel`, derives from `BaseViewModel`. `VisionAssistantViewModel` and has five public properties, which will be bound to the UI. (See the companion code at Chapter_06/VisionAssistant/ViewModels/VisionAssistantViewModel.cs.)

- **IsDescribeImageButtonEnabled** This specifies whether a Tell Me What I See button is enabled. (Refer to Figure 6-1.) I disable this button during image processing to inform the user that processing is in progress.

- **IsSearchButtonEnabled** This indicates whether a Look Up button is enabled. The user can click this button after a non-empty description is received from the Computer Vision API. At first, right after you run the app, this button will be disabled.

- **ImageDescription** This stores the image description obtained from the MCS.

- **Image** This contains a reference to the captured image.

- **WebPage** This stores an instance of the `WebPage` class. Objects of this type represent web pages returned by the Bing Web Search service. The `WebPage` property stores the web page with the highest rank relevant to the image description.

VisionAssistantViewModel also has several private members. Five of them—isDescribeImageButtonEnabled, isSearchButtonEnabled, imageDescription, image, and webPage—are related to the preceding UI-bound properties, so they do not require additional explanation.

The next two fields of VisionAssistantViewModel store references to the CameraCapture and Synthesizer modules you created in Chapter 5. You will use them to acquire images from the camera and to synthesize human speech.

```
private CameraCapture cameraCapture = new CameraCapture();
private Synthesizer synthesizer = new Synthesizer();
```

Finally, VisionAssistantViewModel has two private fields that instantiate two REST API clients. They handle bidirectional communication with MCS:

```
private VisionServiceClient visionServiceClient = new VisionServiceClient(
    Settings.VisionServiceClientKey,
    Settings.VisionServiceEndPoint);

private BingSearchServiceClient bingSearchServiceClient = new BingSearchServiceClient(
    Settings.BingSearchServiceClientKey,
    Settings.BingSearchEndPoint);
```

The first client class, Microsoft.ProjectOxford.Vision.VisionServiceClient, comes from the installed NuGet package. The second client class, VisionAssistant.BingSearch.BingSearchServiceClient, is a custom implementation of the Bing Web Search Service client.

The upcoming sections will show you how to use VisionServiceClient and how to implement the Bing Web Search API client.

Computer Vision API Client

The VisionServiceClient class instance has several methods. These enable you to analyze and describe images and to recognize handwriting and text in images. The general structure of each method follows the same pattern. Specifically, all methods of the VisionServiceClient class instance are asynchronous and require you to provide an input image. You can either provide the image URL or send raw image data, abstracted as the System.IO.Stream class.

This section shows you how to process a local image acquired from a webcam. To support this, I supplemented VisionAssistantViewModel with a private helper method: CaptureAndDipslayBitmap. (See Listing 6-1.) This method takes a snapshot from the webcam, displays it in the UI through the Image property, and returns an instance of the Stream class containing the image data.

LISTING 6-1 Capturing and displaying a bitmap

```
private async Task<Stream> CaptureAndDisplayBitmap()
{
    // Capture and display bitmap
```

```
    var softwareBitmap = await cameraCapture.CapturePhotoToSoftwareBitmap();

    // Display bitmap
    Image = SoftwareBitmapHelper.ToWriteableBitmap(softwareBitmap);

    // Return bitmap stream
    return await SoftwareBitmapHelper.GetBitmapStream(softwareBitmap);
}
```

Images from the webcam are represented as instances of the SoftwareBitmap class. To convert them to Stream objects, supplement SoftwareBitmapHelper (MixedReality.Common/Helpers/SoftwareBitmapHelper.cs) with a static GetBitmapStream method, shown in Listing 6-2. This method accepts an instance of the SoftwareBitmap as an input and converts it to a raw byte array using the BitmapEncoder class. BitmapEncoder works in the opposite way from BitmapDecoder, which you used in Chapter 5. Specifically, BitmapEncoder translates an abstract bitmap representation to a byte array, which can be then parsed by other software components. So, BitmapEncoder serializes the bitmaps represented by the SoftwareBitmap class.

Note Serialization is the conversion of a C# object to a byte array. This is necessary here because the image data is transferred to a remote REST service. Through serialization, the service can easily parse the byte array without any prior information about the original C# object structure used in the client app (VisionAssistant).

This approach helps the REST service process data from various clients, which may be running on different platforms, including UWP, iOS, Android, and so on. More precisely, each client app can use different approaches to represent bitmaps. So, by converting a bitmap to a byte array you ensure that the data becomes platform-independent.

Afterward, the REST service will deserialize the image data for internal processing purposes. This deserialization means that the REST service will convert raw byte array to an object representing a bitmap.

LISTING 6-2 Serializing an instance of SoftwareBitmap

```
public static async Task<Stream> GetBitmapStream(SoftwareBitmap softwareBitmap)
{
    Check.IsNull(softwareBitmap, "softwareBitmap");

    var bitmapImageInMemoryRandomAccessStream = new InMemoryRandomAccessStream();

    var bitmapEncoder = await BitmapEncoder.CreateAsync(
        BitmapEncoder.BmpEncoderId, bitmapImageInMemoryRandomAccessStream);

    bitmapEncoder.SetSoftwareBitmap(softwareBitmap);

    await bitmapEncoder.FlushAsync();

    return bitmapImageInMemoryRandomAccessStream.AsStream();
}
```

You send the resulting image data to the Vision Service API to obtain an image description. (See Listing 6-3.) To do so, use the DescribeAsync method of the VisionServiceClient class instance, which returns an instance of the Microsoft.ProjectOxford.Vision.Contract.AnalysisResult class. This class has multiple properties that contain information about the image provided. In general, values of these properties depend on the method of the VisionServiceClient you invoke. For example, the DescribeAsync method returns an instance of AnalysisResult, in which all properties except the Description property will be null. The Description property stores a collection of captions and tags assigned to the processed image. Listing 6-3 uses only the first caption and displays it in the label by updating an ImageDescription property of VisionAssistantViewModel. This description is also spoken to the user with the speech synthesizer. (See the NotifyUser method in Listing 6-3.)

LISTING 6-3 Describing an image with cognitive services

```
public async void DescribeImage()
{
    IsDescribeImageButtonEnabled = false;

    await NotifyUser("OK");

    // Capture bitmap
    var bitmapStream = await CaptureAndDisplayBitmap();

    // Submit an image for analysis
    var descriptionResult = await visionServiceClient.DescribeAsync(bitmapStream);

    // Retrieve the first caption
    ImageDescription = descriptionResult.Description.Captions.FirstOrDefault().Text;

    await NotifyUser($"You see: {ImageDescription}");

    // Update buttons
    IsDescribeImageButtonEnabled = true;
    IsSearchButtonEnabled = !string.IsNullOrEmpty(ImageDescription);
}

private async Task NotifyUser(string message)
{
    await synthesizer.Speak(message);
}
```

Bing Web Search API Client

After you implement the logic for obtaining an image description, you are ready to create the second MCS API client, BingSearchServiceClient. (See the companion code at Chapter_06/VisionAssistant/BingSearch/BingSearchServiceClient.cs.) Before you dig into the code, however, let's first see how to send requests to the Bing Web Search API. According to the documentation of this service, the general form of the request (in version 7.0) looks like the following string, where

`<search_query>` represents a query that will be passed to the Bing Web Search engine. (Everything before the search parameter will be denoted hereafter as the base address.)

```
https://api.cognitive.microsoft.com/bing/v7.0/search?q=<search_query>
```

The request can be further customized with additional query string parameters. For instance, to narrow the search results, you can use the count argument, and to specify the search market, you can use the mkt parameter. Accordingly, a more general request might be as follows:

```
https://api.cognitive.microsoft.com/bing/v7.0/search?q=<search_query>&mkt=en-us&count=10
```

This request will return a maximum of 10 links in the EN-US market for the search query the user provides. All other query parameters are documented here: http://bit.ly/bingwebsearch.

The Bing Web Search API requires authentication. To authenticate your requests, you need to use the subscription key provided during registration. You pass this key as the HTTP request header in the Ocp-Apim-Subscription-Key field. To programmatically send authenticated requests, you use the System.Net.HttpClient class. As shown in Listing 6-4, you create an instance of the HttpClient class within the constructor of the BingSearchServiceClient. Specifically, you first set the base address, and then add the Ocp-Apim-Subscription-Key field to the DefaultRequestHeaders collection. As a result, all requests will be authenticated with the same key.

LISTING 6-4 A constructor of the BingSearchServiceClient class

```
private HttpClient httpClient;

public BingSearchServiceClient(string apiKey, string endPoint)
{
    Check.IsNull(apiKey, "apiKey");
    Check.IsNull(endPoint, "endPoint");

    httpClient = new HttpClient
    {
        BaseAddress = new Url(endPoint)
    };

    httpClient.DefaultRequestHeaders.Add("Ocp-Apim-Subscription-Key", apiKey);
}
```

After instantiating and configuring the HttpClient class, you send the request using the GetAsync method. This method accepts a single argument: the request URL. As shown in Listing 6-5, to construct this URL, you supplement the base address with the parameterized search query. Next, you parse the response, which is represented as an HttpResponse class instance. This object has several properties and methods to help you to parse the response. One is the IsSuccessStatusCode, which lets you identify whether your request was successfully processed. If so, you can analyze the response content, represented as an HttpContent object, through the Content property of the HttpResponse class.

LISTING 6-5 Traversing the web content with Bing Search

```
public async Task<SearchResult> Search(string query)
{
    var queryString = WebUtility.UrlEncode(query);

    var getUrl = $"search?q={queryString}&mkt=en-us&count=10";

    var response = await httpClient.GetAsync(getUrl);

    if (!response.IsSuccessStatusCode)
    {
        throw new Exception("Unexpected status code");
    }

    return await response.Content.ReadAsAsync<SearchResult>();
}
```

Typically, to access the content data, you use the appropriate methods of the HttpContent class instance. For example, to retrieve the content as a byte array, you use the ReadAsByteArrayAsync method. Or, to obtain a string representation when the data is in platform-independent JSON format (http://bit.ly/JSON_Wiki), you invoke the ReadAsStringAsync method. Regardless of which method you choose, you then deserialize a response to .NET objects, so it can be further easily consumed in your code. This is a very common pattern in web and mobile programming, so there are many useful tools for automating this process. In this example, I use two such tools. One is the ReadAsAsync generic extension method for HttpContent. This extension is provided by the Microsoft.AspNet. WebApi.Client NuGet package, which you can install by entering the following command in the NuGet Package Manager Console:

```
Install-Package Microsoft.AspNet.WebApi.Client
```

The ReadAsAsync method automatically deserializes the response content to an object of a given type. In this case, content will be converted to an instance of the SearchResult class. Internally, to translate the JSON objects to C# classes, ReadAsAsync uses the Newtonsoft.Json NuGet package. This is installed with the Microsoft.AspNet.WebApi.Client package.

The second tool is the JSONUtils.com web page (https://jsonutils.com/). It is particularly useful for generating C# classes to represent the JSON objects received from web services. To use this tool, you first retrieve the response from the Bing Web Search API in string form (ReadAsStringAsync). Then do the following:

1. Copy the resulting string into the **JSON Text or URL** field on the JSONUtils web page.

2. Make sure the **C#** option button is selected.

3. Select the **Pascal Case** checkbox.

4. In the **Class Name** field, type **SearchResult**.

5. Click the **Submit** button.

The JSONUtils web page will create a set of C# classes representing the Bing Search API response. Put all these classes in separate files and store them in the BingSearch/Models subfolder of the VisionAssistant project. You can also use classes that I generated. (See the companion code at Chapter_06/VisionAssistant/BingSearch/Models.)

Generally, each class contains auto-implemented properties representing JSON objects. A detailed description of each C# class is not really necessary. Here, I'll explain only the top-level object: SearchResult. A full definition of the SearchResult class appears in Listing 6-6. This class has six auto-implemented properties:

- **Images** This property contains a list of images that were recognized as relevant to the search query.

- **RankingResponse** This property tells you where the search results should be displayed: in the main part of the search results group or in the sidebar.

- **Type** This property describes the response type.

- **QueryContext** This property stores the original query you sent to the Bing Web Search API.

- **RelatedSearches** This property is a collection of related searches made by other clients.

- **WebPages** This property stores a list of web pages relevant to the query.

Note The Type property of the SearchResult class is decorated with Newtonsoft.Json. JsonPropertyAttribute (from the Newtonsoft.Json NuGet package). This attribute instructs the internal JSON-to-C# converter to deserialize JSON members with specific names. I use this attribute in several auto-generated classes to avoid name duplicates and to improve code readability. As a result, I do not have members whose names begin with an underscore (such as the _type JSON property, for instance).

LISTING 6-6 The SearchResult class representing valid responses from the Bing Web Search API

```csharp
public class SearchResult
{
    public Images Images { get; set; }

    public RankingResponse RankingResponse { get; set; }

    [JsonProperty("_type")]
    public string Type { get; set; }

    public QueryContext QueryContext { get; set; }

    public RelatedSearches RelatedSearches { get; set; }

    public WebPages WebPages { get; set; }
}
```

After implementing the BingSearchServiceClient class, you can extend a definition of the VisionAssistantViewModel by another method, Search, whose definition appears in Listing 6-7. The Search method is bound to the Click event of the Look Up button. First, it disables the Look Up button to inform the user that search is in progress. Then it submits the search query to the Bing Web Search API using an instance of BingSearchServiceClient. To provide a detailed characterization of what the camera sees, it supplements the image description (obtained by the Computer Vision client) with a Wikipedia string. This ensures that most relevant search results will contain a link to an article explaining the camera image to the user. When the search is complete, the class takes the first item from the WebPages collection of the SearchResult. A reference to that item is stored in the corresponding property of the view model. Finally, the snippet text from the web page is spoken to the user. For Wikipedia pages, this snippet is an abstract of the article. The user can display the full article using the WebView control in the app's Web Page tab. (Refer to Figure 6-2.)

LISTING 6-7 A definition of the Search method from VisionAssistantViewModel

```
public async void Search()
{
    IsSearchButtonEnabled = false;

    var queryResults = await bingSearchServiceClient.
        Search($"{ImageDescription} + Wikipedia");

    WebPage = queryResults.WebPages.Items.FirstOrDefault();

    await NotifyUser($"Here is what I found: {WebPage.Snippet}");

    IsSearchButtonEnabled = true;
}
```

Each page found by the Bing Web Search API is represented as a WebPage class instance. A full definition of this class appears in Listing 6-8. This class is composed of several auto-implemented properties representing the web page:

- **DisplayUrl** This property displays the web page's URL.

- **DateLastCrawled** This property indicates the last time the page was crawled by the Bing Web Search engine.

- **About** This is an internally used property.

- **DeepLinks** This property assembles a collection of deep links—that is, links to other web pages that contain the page in question.

- **Name** This property stores the name of the web page. Typically, you use this property along with the Url member to create a hyperlink.

- **Id** This property is a unique identifier of the web page in the collection of web search results.

- **Snippet** This property stores a fragment of the text from the web page, which is read to the user.

- **Url** This property contains the URL for the web page, which is displayed in the app.

LISTING 6-8 A definition of the WebPage class

```
public class WebPage
{
    public string DisplayUrl { get; set; }

    public string DateLastCrawled { get; set; }

    public About[] About { get; set; }

    public DeepLinks[] DeepLinks { get; set; }

    public string Name { get; set; }

    public string Id { get; set; }

    public string Snippet { get; set; }

    public string Url { get; set; }
}
```

The VisionAssistant app uses two properties: Snippet and Url. The value of Snippet is spoken to the user, while Url displays the associated web page in the WebView control. (For more information, read on.)

UI Declaration

To create the UI shown in Figures 6-1 and 6-2, you use the XAML declarations in Listing 6-9 along with additional styles declared under the page resources. (See the companion code at Chapter_06/VisionAssistant/MainPage.xaml.)

LISTING 6-9 A fragment of the MainPage XAML declaration

```
<Pivot Background="{ThemeResource ApplicationPageBackgroundThemeBrush}">
    <PivotItem Header="Analysis">
        <Grid>
            <Grid.RowDefinitions>
                <RowDefinition Height="Auto"/>
                <RowDefinition Height="Auto"/>
                <RowDefinition Height="*"/>
            </Grid.RowDefinitions>

            <StackPanel Orientation="Horizontal">
                <Button Content="Tell me what I see"
                    Click="{x:Bind viewModel.DescribeImage}"
                    IsEnabled="{x:Bind viewModel.IsDescribeImageButtonEnabled, Mode=OneWay}"/>

                <Button Content="Look up"
                    Click="{x:Bind viewModel.Search}"
                    IsEnabled="{x:Bind viewModel.IsSearchButtonEnabled, Mode=OneWay}"/>
            </StackPanel>
```

```
                <TextBlock Text="{x:Bind viewModel.ImageDescription, Mode=OneWay}"
                           Grid.Row="1"/>

                <Image Source="{x:Bind viewModel.Image, Mode=OneWay}"
                       Grid.Row="2"/>
            </Grid>
        </PivotItem>
        <PivotItem Header="Web page">
            <WebView Source="{x:Bind viewModel.WebPage.Url, Mode=OneWay}"/>
        </PivotItem>
</Pivot>
```

The UI is organized into two tabs using the `PivotControl`. The first tab (`PivotItem`), with the Analysis header, contains four controls:

- **Tell Me What I See button**   This button is bound to the view model's `DescribeImage` method and is enabled when the view model's `IsDescribeImageButtonEnabled` property is `true`.

- **Look Up button**   This button is bound to the view model's `Search` method. Its state (enabled or disabled) is determined by the view model's `IsSearchButtonEnabled` property.

- **Image description label**   This is stored in the view model's `ImageDescription` property.

- **Image control**   This depicts an image captured by the camera.

Buttons are embedded in the `StackPanel` to lay them out horizontally.

The second tab, with the Web Page header, contains a single control: `WebView`. You use this control to render web pages inside UWP apps. As shown in Listing 6-10, you can easily display a web page by providing its URL via the Source attribute of the `WebView` control. In this example, the attribute is one-way bound to the `WebPage.Url` property. As a result, `WebView` displays the first relevant web page found by the Bing Web Search API. (Refer to Figure 6-2.)

LISTING 6-10 Configuring the Source property of the `WebView` control

```
<PivotItem Header="Web page">
    <WebView Source="{x:Bind viewModel.WebPage.Url, Mode=OneWay}"/>
</PivotItem>
```

Initializing the ViewModel

I find with my hardware that if I do not start with a preview, the first image captured by the camera always appears dark. Because this can affect the performance of the image-recognition feature, I decided to start camera preview so the device will be ready to capture images during runtime. To implement this, you initialize and start camera preview when the user views the app's `MainPage` by invoking the `Initialize` method of the `VisionAssistantViewModel` class in the `OnNavigatedTo` event handler. (See Listing 6-11.)

LISTING 6-11 Initializing the view model

```
public sealed partial class MainPage : Page
{
    private VisionAssistantViewModel viewModel = new VisionAssistantViewModel();

    public MainPage()
    {
        InitializeComponent();
    }

    protected override async void OnNavigatedTo(NavigationEventArgs e)
    {
        base.OnNavigatedTo(e);

        await viewModel.Initialize();
    }
}
```

Listing 6-12 contains the `Initialize` method of the `VisionAssistantViewModel`. Briefly, this method initializes the underlying `CameraCapture` class and then associates it with a dummy `CaptureElement`. I call it "dummy" because it is not declared in the UI; rather, it is used only as a dummy sink for the `MediaCapture` object. Once the ViewModel is initialized, you can safely capture images from the camera and send them for analysis. The only requirement to successfully run this example is to declare webcam capability under the Package.appxmanifest. Afterward, you can run the app in a Mixed Reality simulator or on a desktop platform to generate the results shown previously in Figures 6-1 and 6-2.

LISTING 6-12 A definition of the `Initialize` method of the `VisionAssistantViewModel`

```
public async Task Initialize()
{
    if (!cameraCapture.IsPreviewActive)
    {
        await cameraCapture.Initialize();

        // Dummy capture element
        var captureElement = new CaptureElement()
        {
            Source = cameraCapture.MediaCapture
        };

        await cameraCapture.Start();
    }
}
```

Supporting Voice Commands

With the VisionAssistant app's main functionality set, let's supplement it with speech recognition. This will enable app users to employ speech to issue commands rather than issuing commands using their keyboard. Because users might issue voice commands at any time, let's use the continuous speech recognition feature you explored in Chapter 5.

Speech Recognizer and Recognition Constraints

To add speech recognition to VisionAssistant, use the `Recognizer` class in the MixedReality.Common class library. (See the companion code at MixedReality.Common/Helpers/Recognizer.cs.) This class has three private fields. (See Listing 6-13.) The first one, **speechRecognizer**, stores a reference to the UWP `SpeechRecognizer` class. The second one, `voiceCommands`, stores a reference to a collection of voice commands. The third one is a list of textual representations of voice commands.

LISTING 6-13 Fields of the Recognizer class

```
private SpeechRecognizer speechRecognizer = new SpeechRecognizer();
private Dictionary<VoiceCommand, List<string>> voiceCommands;
private List<string> availableCommands;
```

Each voice command is represented as a corresponding value from the custom `VoiceCommand` enumeration. The values are as follows. (See the companion code at MixedReality.Common/Enums/VoiceCommand.cs.)

- **WhatISee** This represents a voice command that triggers image-content recognition. When the VisionAssistant app receives this command, it invokes the `DescribeImage` method of `VisionAssistantViewModel`. (Refer to Listing 6-3.)

- **LookUp** This represents a voice command that asks the app to search the web for information that relates to the image by invoking the `Search` method of `VisionAssistantViewModel`. (Refer to Listing 6-7.)

In the `Recognizer` class, write a method that associates several strings with each voice command and store this mapping in the `voiceCommands` dictionary. (See Listing 6-14.) That way, the user need not use just one strictly defined sentence to trigger a specific app function (`WhatISee` or `LookUp`). So, to obtain an image description (`WhatISee`), the user could say, "Tell me what I see," "What I see," or "Describe what I see." When the app recognizes one of these sentences, it will execute the `VisionAssistantViewModel.DescribeImage` method. And to find more information about the image (`LookUp`), the user could say, "Look this up," "Tell me more," or "Search."

LISTING 6-14 Creating a sentence-to-voice commands mapping

```
private void InitializeVoiceCommandsDictionary()
{
    voiceCommands = new Dictionary<VoiceCommand, List<string>>
    {
        {
            VoiceCommand.WhatISee,
            new List<string>()
            {
                "Tell me what I see",
                "What I see",
                "Describe what I see"
            }
        },
        {
            VoiceCommand.LookUp,
            new List<string>()
            {
                "Look this up",
                "Tell me more",
                "Search"
            }
        }
    };
}
```

 Note You can modify `InitializeVoiceCommandsDictionary` to include more sentences for each command. Just make sure none of the sentences for these commands overlap.

After you create the voice-commands dictionary, you can use it to define recognition constraints to improve performance. The UWP speech recognizer uses these constraints to narrow the phoneme-matching process to just the sentences in the dictionary, thereby speeding the recognition process. As shown in Listing 6-15, you use the `SelectMany` LINQ extension method to extract the sentences from your voice-commands dictionary. The resulting collection is then used to instantiate the `SpeechRecognitionListConstraint` class. An instance of the `SpeechRecognitionListConstraint` class represents recognition constraints and is thus added to the `Constraints` property of the `SpeechRecognizer` class instance.

LISTING 6-15 A constructor of the Recognizer class

```
public Recognizer()
{
    // Prepare voice-commands dictionary
    InitializeVoiceCommandsDictionary();

    // Prepare recognition constraints
    var availableCommands = voiceCommands.SelectMany(vc => vc.Value).ToList();

    var speechRecognitionConstraints = new SpeechRecognitionListConstraint(
        availableCommands);
```

```
speechRecognizer.Constraints.Add(speechRecognitionConstraints);

// Attach event handlers
speechRecognizer.StateChanged += SpeechRecognizer_StateChanged;
speechRecognizer.ContinuousRecognitionSession.ResultGenerated +=
    ContinuousRecognitionSession_ResultGenerated;
}
```

After the constraints are defined, you create two event handlers:

- **SpeechRecognizer_StateChanged**   This is invoked whenever the state of the recognizer is updated. Listing 6-16 shows a definition of SpeechRecognizer_StateChanged. As you can see, any changes in the state of the speech recognizer are output to the debugger console. You can use this to track the status of the speech recognizer during debugging.

- **ContinousRecognitionSession_ResultGenerated**   This is invoked whenever the speech is recognized. ContinousRecognitionSession_ResultGenerated is defined in Listing 6-17. As you can see, it first looks for the recognized text in the values of the voiceCommands dictionary. Then, a method checks whether the recognized text is associated with one of the voice commands. If so, a method retrieves the corresponding key—one of the values from the VoiceCommand enumeration—and passes it to listeners by raising the VoiceCommandRecognized event. To respond to the voice command, all you need to do is handle the VoiceCommandRecognized event, covered in the next section.

LISTING 6-16 Outputting the state of the speech recognizer to the debugger console

```
private void SpeechRecognizer_StateChanged(SpeechRecognizer sender,
    SpeechRecognizerStateChangedEventArgs args)
{
    System.Diagnostics.Debug.WriteLine(args.State);
}
```

LISTING 6-17 Decoding the voice command from recognized text

```
private void ContinuousRecognitionSession_ResultGenerated(
    SpeechContinuousRecognitionSession sender,
    SpeechContinuousRecognitionResultGeneratedEventArgs args)
{
    if (VoiceCommandRecognized != null)
    {
        if (availableCommands.Contains(args.Result.Text))
        {
            var voiceCommand = voiceCommands.First(
                c => c.Value.Contains(args.Result.Text)).Key;

            VoiceCommandRecognized.Invoke(this,
                new VoiceCommandRecognizedEventArgs(voiceCommand));
        }
    }
}

public event TypedEventHandler<object, VoiceCommandRecognizedEventArgs> VoiceCommandRecognized;
```

To run continuous speech recognition, supplement the `Recognizer` class with the `BeginVoiceCommandRecognition` method in Listing 6-18. This method asynchronously compiles recognition constraints and then starts the continuous recognition session.

LISTING 6-18 Beginning voice-command recognition

```
public async Task BeginVoiceCommandRecognition()
{
    await speechRecognizer.CompileConstraintsAsync();

    await speechRecognizer.ContinuousRecognitionSession.StartAsync(
        SpeechContinuousRecognitionMode.PauseOnRecognition);
}
```

Responding to Voice Commands

You can now use the `Recognizer` class in the VisionAssistant project so the app can be voice-controlled. To do so, modify the `VisionAssistantViewModel` class. First, instantiate the `Recognizer` class as follows:

```
private Recognizer recognizer = new Recognizer();
```

Next, extend the `VisionAssistantViewModel.Initialize` method like so:

```
public async Task Initialize()
{
    if (!cameraCapture.IsPreviewActive)
    {
        await cameraCapture.Initialize();

        // Dummy capture element
        var captureElement = new CaptureElement()
        {
            Source = cameraCapture.MediaCapture
        };

        await cameraCapture.Start();

        // Initialize speech recognizer
        recognizer.VoiceCommandRecognized += Recognizer_VoiceCommandRecognized;

        await recognizer.BeginVoiceCommandRecognition();
    }
}
```

Finally, associate the `Recognizer_VoiceCommandRecognized` method (see Listing 6-18) with the `VoiceCommandRecognized` event and run speech recognition in the background. From this point, whenever the app detects a voice command, a `Recognizer_VoiceCommandRecognized` will be invoked. As Listing 6-19 shows, this method uses a `switch` statement to handle the particular voice command. It will invoke `DescribeImage` to respond to a `WhatISee` command, and it will call `Search` when it recognizes the `LookUp` voice command. Both methods, `Describe` and `Search`, are invoked on the main thread because they update visual controls through data binding. In contrast, the

SpeechRecognizer event is raised from the background thread. Hence, to ensure that all UI updates are made with the UI thread, you use the ThreadHelper class described in Chapter 5.

LISTING 6-19 Handling voice commands

```
private async void Recognizer_VoiceCommandRecognized(object sender,
    VoiceCommandRecognizedEventArgs args)
{
    switch(args.VoiceCommand)
    {
        case VoiceCommand.WhatISee:
            await ThreadHelper.InvokeOnMainThread(DescribeImage);
            break;

        case VoiceCommand.LookUp:
            await ThreadHelper.InvokeOnMainThread(Search);
            break;
    }
}
```

To test this solution, you must first declare microphone capability. Then execute the app and say one of the sentences associated with the WhatISee command. The app should quickly respond with the OK message and then tell you what it recognized in the camera image. Next, use one of the LookUp voice commands to request a more detailed description. Notice that the constrained continuous speech recognition works much better than the default, unconstrained recognition engine.

Summary

This chapter showed you how to enhance a Mixed Reality app with artificial intelligence. You started by creating a VisionAssistant app, which sent images from the camera to the cloud-based Computer Vision API client for processing. The results of this processing were then communicated to the user via displayed text and synthesized speech. You also learned how to implement a custom REST API client for accessing MCS. This custom client could be used to search the web with Bing, return a list of retrieved search results, and present more detailed descriptions to the user. Finally, you supplemented the VisionAssistant app with the constrained speech-recognition engine to allow users to control the app via voice controls. This significantly simplifies app utilization in the Mixed Reality headset and HoloLens.

You can further extend the VisionAssistant app to support visually impaired people. The app also represents a good starting point for the creation of speech-controlled Mixed Reality apps, giving users a hands-free, AI-powered search engine.

CHAPTER 7

Communicating with Devices

In this chapter, you will learn how to create an app that communicates with other Windows 10 devices. To begin, you will develop two UWP applications. The first one, Communication.Consumer (see Figure 7-1), will run in the HoloLens emulator and will contain two visual controls: a purple circle and a rectangle, whose color will change depending on whether the circle is inside it (in which case it will be green) or outside it (in which case it will be red). The position of the circle will be modified according to messages sent from the second app, Communication.Producer. (See Figure 7-2.) This app will run in the mobile emulator to obtain accelerometer readings. These readings will then be transmitted to Communication.Consumer over the network to move the ellipse.

> **Note** To use a more typical nomenclature, the producer will play the role of the server, while the consumer will be the client. Hence, the apps you implement in this chapter will conform to a server-client communication architecture.

FIGURE 7-1 The UI of the Communication.Consumer app. The ellipse moves based on the accelerometer readings sent from the Communication.Producer app. When the ellipse is inside the rectangle, the rectangle is green (left image). Otherwise, the rectangle is red (right image).

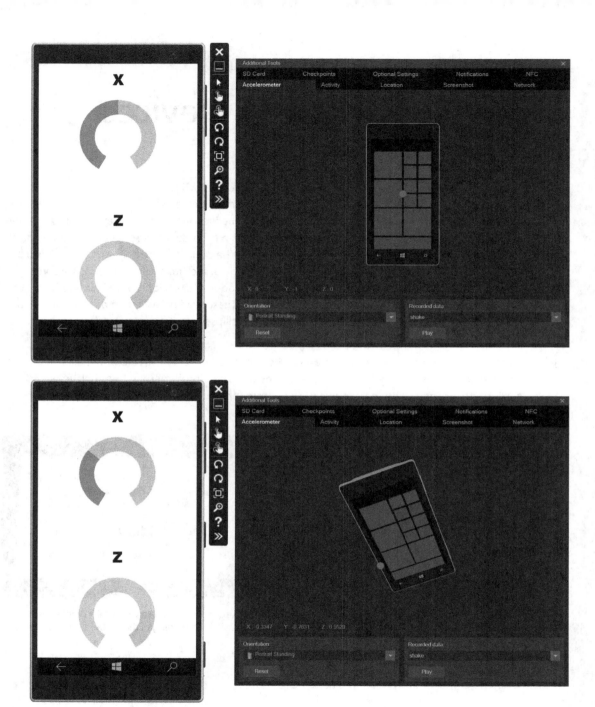

FIGURE 7-2 The UI of the Communication.Producer app. Here, two radial gauges display readings from the accelerometer, which are transmitted over the network to the Communication.Consumer app to update the position of the ellipse. The top image corresponds to the top image in Figure 7-1, where the circle is inside the rectangle. In the bottom image, the emulator has been virtually rotated, so the accelerometer readings have changed. Consequently, in the Communication.Consumer app, the circle appears in the lower-left corner of the screen.

Socket Communication

You used `HttpClient` in the previous chapter to communicate with remote web servers. According to UWP documentation (see http://bit.ly/uwp_networking), `HttpClient` is the preferred way to implement communication over the secure HTTP protocol. However, in specific cases, you must transfer data between various apps using a custom communication protocol, which requires you to send custom-defined packages of data. In such circumstances, you use socket communication.

A *socket* is defined as a communication endpoint for sending or receiving data. There are two common types of socket communication: Transmission Control Protocol (TCP) and User Datagram Protocol (UDP). Both implement low-level network communication. The main difference between the two is that TCP uses long-lived connections, while UDP does not require you to negotiate a connection and thus is better suited for fast transmission (though at the cost of reduced transfer reliability). So, TCP provides reliability but is slower, while UDP delivers faster but less reliable data transport. In this chapter, you will use UDP to transmit accelerometer data from Communication.Provider to Communication.Consumer because this transmission requires fast data transfer, and because losing some small fraction of transmitted data will not result in disaster.

As you implement the Communication.Provider and Communication.Consumer apps, you will learn how to implement UDP communication on both communication endpoints. Along the way, you will investigate the use of serialization of C# objects so they can be transmitted over platform-independent communication links as datagrams. A *datagram* is an ordered sequence of bytes transmitted between sockets via UDP. It is different from the packet used in TCP in that it requires an established connection for reliable communication.

Implementation

Start by creating two UWP applications using the Blank UWP app Visual C# project template. Set the app names to Communication.Consumer and Communication.Provider. (From now on, I will refer to these apps as the consumer and producer app, respectively.) After you create these projects, you'll reference the `MixedReality.Common` class library in both apps. Then you'll create helper objects, which will be used in both projects.

Accelerometer Reading

To set up the code to read data from the accelerometer, begin by creating a subfolder, Sensors, in the `MixedReality.Common` class library to store the `AccReading` class. Its full definition appears in Listing 7-1. As shown, `AccReading` has four public properties: X, Y, Z, and `Timestamp`. The first three properties represent accelerometer readings along each direction, while the last one stores the time when reading was obtained. `AccReading` overrides the `ToString` method, which is useful for debugging. Finally, there is one static method: `FromNativeAccelerometerReading`. Given an instance of the `Windows.Devices.Sensors.AccelerometerReading` class, this rewrites `AccelerationX`, `AccelerationY`, `AccelerationZ`, and `Timestamp` properties to corresponding members of the AccReading class. (I use a custom AccReading class here because AccelerometerReading cannot be serialized. Moreover, the IAccelerometerReading interface, which is implemented by AccelerometerReading, cannot be used as it is marked with the internal keyword.)

LISTING 7-1 A definition of the AccReading class

```
public class AccReading
{
    public double X { get; set; }
    public double Y { get; set; }
    public double Z { get; set; }
    public DateTimeOffset Timestamp { get; set; }

    public override string ToString()
    {
        return $"X: {X:F4}, Y: {Y:F4}, Z: {Z:F4}, Timestamp: {Timestamp}";
    }

    public static AccReading FromNativeAccelerometerReading(
        AccelerometerReading accelerometerReading)
    {
        Check.IsNull(accelerometerReading, "accelerometerReading");

        return new AccReading()
        {
            X = accelerometerReading.AccelerationX,
            Y = accelerometerReading.AccelerationY,
            Z = accelerometerReading.AccelerationZ,
            Timestamp = accelerometerReading.Timestamp
        };
    }
}
```

Common ViewModel

Now that you've defined AccReading, create a common ViewModel, SocketCommunicationBaseViewModel, in the ViewModels folder of the MixedReality.Common class library. The aim of this ViewModel is to allow for the serialization and deserialization of data being transmitted from provider to consumer. In this case, this data will be composed of instances of the AccReading class.

Listing 7-2 shows a full definition of the SocketCommunicationBaseViewModel class. This class derives from BaseViewModel to access common functionality related to data binding. Then, SocketCommunicationBaseViewModel defines one protected field, dataSerializer. This field is of type System.Runtime.Serialization.DataContractSerializer. You use this field to serialize the C# object to an architecture-independent XML document. This document is then transmitted over the network and deserialized at the other communication endpoint. In this case, you will serialize instances of the AccReading class in the provider and then write the resulting data to the output stream, which is an abstract representation of the communication link. (See the SendAccelerometerReading method in Listing 7-2.) The consumer will use the second method of theSocketCommunicationBaseViewModel, ReceiveAccelerometerReading, to deserialize the XML document received at the input stream to an instance of the AccReading class. Later, you will see how input and output streams are achieved. For now, just note that DataContractSerializer substantially simplifies data transmission over the network.

LISTING 7-2 A definition of the SocketCommunicationBaseViewModel class

```
public class SocketCommunicationBaseViewModel : BaseViewModel
{
    protected DataContractSerializer dataSerializer =
        new DataContractSerializer(typeof(AccReading));

    protected void SendAccelerometerReading(
        AccelerometerReading accelerometerReading,
        IOutputStream outputStream)
    {
        if (accelerometerReading != null)
        {
            var accReading = AccReading.
                FromNativeAccelerometerReading(accelerometerReading);

            dataSerializer.WriteObject(outputStream.AsStreamForWrite(),
                accReading);
        }
    }

    protected AccReading ReceiveAccelerometerReading(
        IInputStream inputStream)
    {
        var receivedObject = dataSerializer.ReadObject(
            inputStream.AsStreamForRead());

        return receivedObject as AccReading;
    }
}
```

Provider

After you prepare the common blocks, you'll begin implementing the provider app. This app will read accelerometer readings, display them locally with radial gauges (refer to Figure 7-2), and send them to the consumer app so that app updates its state accordingly (refer to Figure 7-1).

Note My development computer does not have an internal accelerometer, so I will execute the provider app in the Windows Phone emulator ver. 10.0.15063.468, which I downloaded from the Windows SDK archive (http://bit.ly/sdk_archive). Installing this emulator is similar to installing the HoloLens emulator. Although the Windows Phone emulator does not have a real accelerometer, it includes tools that offer an easy way to synthesize accelerometer readings (refer to right part of Figure 7-2). To activate these tools, left-click the double-arrow icon in the emulator toolbar.

To start, supplement the provider app project with another file, ProviderViewModel.cs. Here, you define the ProviderViewModel class. (See the companion code at Chapter_07/ViewModels/ProviderViewModel.cs.) This class derives from SocketCommunicationBaseViewModel and has only one public property: AccelerometerReading. (See Listing 7-3.)

LISTING 7-3 A property storing values obtained from the accelerometer

```
public AccelerometerReading AccelerometerReading
{
    get => accelerometerReading;
    set => SetProperty(ref accelerometerReading, value);
}

private AccelerometerReading accelerometerReading;
```

The AccelerometerReading property is one-way bound to the UI and stores values obtained from the accelerometer. To get these readings, you use the Windows.Devices.Sensors.Accelerometer class. (See Listing 7-4.) This class has no public constructor. To obtain an instance of the Accelerometer class, you use the GetDefault static method. This method returns null when a device is not equipped with an accelerometer. Otherwise, GetDefault returns a valid reference to the Accelerometer class. To obtain accelerometer readings, you handle the ReadingChanged event. This event is raised whenever the sensor has new values, but not more frequently than specified by the ReportInterval property.

> **Note** You cannot set ReportInterval below a device-dependent minimum value, which you can read from the MinimumReportInterval property.

LISTING 7-4 A constructor of the ProviderViewModel class

```
public ProviderViewModel()
{
    accelerometer = Accelerometer.GetDefault();

    if (accelerometer == null)
    {
        throw new Exception("Cannot access accelerometer");
    }

    accelerometer.ReadingChanged += Accelerometer_ReadingChanged;
}

private Accelerometer accelerometer;
```

Before you write the handler for the ReadingChanged event, supplement the ProviderViewModel class with another private field and a public Initialize method. (See Listing 7-5.) The private field stores a reference to an instance of the DatagramSocket class. You use this class to transmit datagrams. More specifically, `DatagramSocket` implements several public methods, which you use in the client and server app. Typically, you use the `ConnectAsync` method on the client side and either `BindToServiceNameAsync` or `BindEndpointAsync` on the server side. Additionally, on the server side, you handle the `MessageReceived` event to consume incoming datagrams.

LISTING 7-5 Associating a connection with a remote UDP service

```
private DatagramSocket providerDatagramSocket = new DatagramSocket();

public async Task Initialize()
{
    await providerDatagramSocket.ConnectAsync(
        Settings.HostName, Settings.Port);
}
```

The `ConnectAsync` method has two versions. The first version accepts an instance of the `Windows.Networking.EndpointPair` object. It represents the communication endpoint pair, which can be understood as a binding between local and remote network addresses. An endpoint pair is composed of host names and port numbers or service names of both local and remote machines. The second version, shown in Listing 7-5, accepts two arguments:

- **remoteHostName**   This is of type `Windows.Networking.HostName` and represents the network name or IP address of a remote UDP server.

- **remoteServiceName**   This is a string containing either the port or the service name of the remote UDP server.

As shown in Listing 7-6, you store the remote host name and service name (or port) in the corresponding properties of the `Settings` class (from the MixedReality.Common project). For the host name, you use the IP address of the HoloLens emulator. To obtain this address, follow these steps:

1. Tap the double-arrow button on the bottom of the HoloLens emulator toolbar to open the Additional Tools dialog box. This dialog box contains several tabs: Simulation, Room, Account, Network, and Optional Settings.

2. Click the **Network** tab. (See Figure 7-3.) This tab displays a list of network adapters available to the emulator. (In general, the contents of this list depend on your network settings.)

3. Click the **Emulator Adapter #1** entry. This adapter is used here to transmit datagrams between the provider and consumer. As shown in Figure 7-3, its IP address is 172.16.80.2. You use this value in Listing 7-6. For the port number, I chose 9898, but you can also use other values.

Note In this example, both emulators (HoloLens and Mobile) are within the same local network. If you intend to test this solution using real devices, you would need to ensure they can access the same network; otherwise, you may face routing issues.

LISTING 7-6 A fragment of the Settings class used to implement UDP communication

```
public static class Settings
{
    #region Cognitive services

    // Properties, which store keys and endpoints for cognitive services

    #endregion

    #region Communication

    public static HostName HostName { get; } = new HostName("172.16.80.2");
    public static string Port { get; } = "9898";

    #endregion
}
```

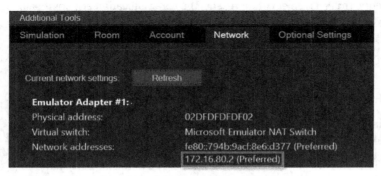

FIGURE 7-3 Network settings of the HoloLens emulator.

After configuring the UDP parameters, you implement the handler for the ReadingChanged event of the Accelerometer class instance. A definition of this event handler appears in Listing 7-7. As shown, the event handler obtains two arguments:

- **sender**   This is an instance of the Accelerometer class, which raised the event.

- **args**   This is an instance of the AccelerometerReadingChangedEventArgs. This class has a public property, Reading, which contains actual sensor readings along three axes: X, Y, and Z.

In Listing 7-7, only the second argument is used to obtain sensor readings. These readings are rewritten to the AccelerometerReading property of the view model to update the UI. Afterward, sensor readings are transmitted to the consumer using the SendAccelerometerReading method of the base class (refer to Listing 7-2). Note that the output stream, which abstracts a byte array to be sent through the data link, is obtained from the OutputStream property of the DatagramSocket class instance.

LISTING 7-7 Accelerometer readings are displayed in the UI and then sent to the consumer

```
private async void Accelerometer_ReadingChanged(Accelerometer sender,
    AccelerometerReadingChangedEventArgs args)
{
    await ThreadHelper.InvokeOnMainThread(() =>
    {
        AccelerometerReading = args.Reading;
    });

    SendAccelerometerReading(AccelerometerReading,
        providerDatagramSocket.OutputStream);
}
```

Creators of the `DatagramSocket` class strongly advise that you dispose of this class when it is no longer needed to ensure that any unmanaged resources used by that class will be released. To implicitly delete resources used by the `DatagramSocket` class instance, you write a finalizer for the `ProviderViewModel` class:

```
~ProviderViewModel()
{
    providerDatagramSocket.Dispose();
}
```

With the ViewModel ready, it's time to define the UI. Basically, the UI consists of two radial gauges and two associated labels: X and Z. (Refer to Figure 7-2.) To create the gauges, you use the UWP Community Toolkit, which you install by entering the following command in the NuGet Package Manager Console:

`Install-Package Microsoft.Toolkit.Uwp.UI.Controls`

To import the namespace with the UWP Toolkit controls into `MainPage`, modify the MainPage.xaml file by supplementing the Page declaration as highlighted in Listing 7-8.

LISTING 7-8 Importing the `UI.Controls` namespace from the UWP Toolkit

```
<Page
    x:Class="Communication.Provider.MainPage"
    xmlns="http://schemas.microsoft.com/winfx/2006/xaml/presentation"
    xmlns:x="http://schemas.microsoft.com/winfx/2006/xaml"
    xmlns:controls="using:Microsoft.Toolkit.Uwp.UI.Controls"
    xmlns:d="http://schemas.microsoft.com/expression/blend/2008"
    xmlns:mc="http://schemas.openxmlformats.org/markup-compatibility/2006"
    mc:Ignorable="d">
```

Next, create anonymous styles to modify the appearance of the radial gauges and the X and Z labels. You can find these styles in the companion code under the Page.Resources dictionary (Chapter_07/Communication.Provider/MainPage.xaml). Finally, put the labels and gauges together as shown in Listing 7-9.

LISTING 7-9 UI declaration of the provider

```
<StackPanel Background="{ThemeResource ApplicationPageBackgroundThemeBrush}">
    <TextBlock Text="X"/>
    <controls:RadialGauge Value="{x:Bind viewModel.AccelerometerReading.AccelerationX,
                          Mode=OneWay,
                          Converter={StaticResource ScaleConverter},
                          ConverterParameter=1000}"
                   TrailBrush="HotPink"/>

    <TextBlock Text="Z"
               Margin="0,50,0,0"/>
    <controls:RadialGauge Value="{x:Bind viewModel.AccelerometerReading.AccelerationZ,
                          Mode=OneWay,
                          Converter={StaticResource ScaleConverter},
                          ConverterParameter=1000}"
                   TrailBrush="Gold"/>
</StackPanel>
```

Values obtained from the accelerometer are given in g units (1 g = 9.81 m/s²) and are within a range of –1 g to +1 g. In contrast, radial gauges from the UWP Toolkit display integral numbers. Therefore, the default sensor values do not display properly in the radial gauges. To address this issue, you use the value converter, which multiplies raw sensor readings by 1,000 to display them as an aliquot of g (mg). Thanks to this scaling, the radial gauges can easily handle resulting values.

To implement the value converter, supplement the provider project with a Converters subfolder. In this subfolder, create a ScaleConverter.cs file, in which you define the class shown in Listing 7-10. This class, like any other converter, implements the IValueConverter interface. So, ScaleConverter has two public methods:

- **Convert** This method multiplies a received value by a scale factor that is passed as the converter parameter. To obtain this factor, you use a helper private method, GetScaleFactor. It converts the converter parameter, which is of type object, to a number of type double.

- **ConvertBack** This method divides the incoming value by the scale factor. In other words, it is the opposite of the Convert method.

To pass the converter parameter, use the ConverterParameter attribute of the x:Bind markup extension. (Refer to Listing 7-9.) In both bindings defined in Listing 7-9, I set the converter parameter to 1000.

LISTING 7-10 A definition of ScaleConverter

```
public class ScaleConverter : IValueConverter
{
    public object Convert(object value, Type targetType, object parameter, string language)
    {
        return (double)value * GetScaleFactor(parameter);
    }

    public object ConvertBack(object value, Type targetType, object parameter, string language)
    {
```

```
        return (double)value / GetScaleFactor(parameter);
    }

    private double GetScaler(object parameter)
    {
        var result = 1.0;

        if (Double.TryParse(parameter.ToString(), out double scaleFactor))
        {
            result = scaleFactor;
        }

        return result;
    }
}
```

Finally, create and initialize the view model. To initialize an instance of the `ProviderViewModel`, override the `OnNavigatedTo` event of `MainPage` (the MainPage.xaml.cs file of the Communication. Provider project):

```
private ProviderViewModel viewModel = new ProviderViewModel();

protected override async void OnNavigatedTo(NavigationEventArgs e)
{
    base.OnNavigatedTo(e);

    await viewModel.Initialize();
}
```

Consumer

Having created the provider, let's implement the consumer. The consumer updates the position of the purple circle according to accelerometer readings transmitted from the provider app. Initially, the circle is located inside the square, which is green. The rectangle's color changes when the circle moves outside the rectangle due to changing accelerometer readings. So, when you virtually rotate the phone emulator, you effectively control the position of the ellipse in the consumer app.

> **Note** To create the circle and square in the UI, you use controls that implement more general geometrical shapes: `Ellipse` and `Rectangle`, respectively. Therefore, the code snippets refer to ellipses and rectangles instead of circles and squares.

As before, you start by implementing the ViewModel, defined as the `ConsumerViewModel` class. (See the companion code at Chapter_07/Communication.Consumer/ViewModels/ConsumerViewModel.cs.) Again, `ConsumerViewModel` derives from `SocketCommunicationViewModel` and has several properties, which are bound to the UI:

- **EllipseTransform** This is an instance of the `TranslateTransform` class, which controls the position of the circle within the view. This property changes during runtime and is therefore two-way bound to the UI.

- **EllipseSize** This is an instance of the `Windows.Foundation.Size` struct, which defines the size of the circle. This property does not change during the runtime, so it is one-way bound to the UI.

- **RectangleBrush** This is an instance of the `Windows.UI.Xaml.Media.Brush` class, controlling the color of the square. This property changes during the runtime.

- **RectangleSize** This property is analogous to `EllipseSize` but controls the size of the square instead of the circle.

- **RectangleStrokeThickness** This property determines the thickness of the square. It does not change during runtime.

These properties have associated private members, which define the initial appearance of the circle and square.

Then, in the `ConsumerViewModel` class, you create the `DatagramSocket` object, which is configured within the asynchronous `Initialize` method. (See Listing 7-11.)

LISTING 7-11 Creating and configuring the `DatagramSocket` class

```
private DatagramSocket consumerDatagramSocket = new DatagramSocket();

public async Task Initialize()
{
    consumerDatagramSocket.MessageReceived += ConsumerDatagramSocket_MessageReceived;

    await consumerDatagramSocket.BindServiceNameAsync(Settings.Port);

    UpdateRectangleBrush();
}
```

First, the `Initialize` method associates a method with the `MessageReceived` event of the `DatagramSocket` class. This event is raised whenever a datagram is received from the provider. Next, you invoke the `BindServiceNameAsync` method of the `DatagramSocket` class. This starts the UDP server listening for incoming datagrams on the previously specified port, 9898.

The `Initialize` method also invokes a helper method, `UpdateRectangleBrush`. (See Listing 7-12.) This method checks whether the circle is contained within the square. If so, the color of the rectangle, controlled by the `RectangleBrush` property, is set to a lighter shade of green (`Colors.YellowGreen`). Otherwise, the square will be red (`Colors.Red`). To determine whether the circle is within the square, you first calculate the difference between the width of the rectangle and that of the circle. Then subtract the thickness of the line used to draw the square. The resulting value is divided by a factor of 2 and stored in the `horizontalMargin` variable. An analogous calculation is performed using square and circle heights (`verticalMargin`). When you have the horizontal and vertical margins, you check whether they are larger than the X and Y properties of `EllipseTransform`, representing a translation of the circle with respect to origin (X = Y = 0). If so, the rectangle color is set to green; if not, it's set to red.

LISTING 7-12 Updating the rectangle color depending on the circle position

```
private Brush greenBrush = new SolidColorBrush(Colors.YellowGreen);
private Brush redBrush = new SolidColorBrush(Colors.Red);

private void UpdateRectangleBrush()
{
    var horizontalMargin = (rectangleSize.Width - ellipseSize.Width
        - rectangleStrokeThickness) / 2.0;

    var verticalMargin = (rectangleSize.Height - ellipseSize.Height
        - rectangleStrokeThickness) / 2.0;

    if (Math.Abs(EllipseTransform.X) <= horizontalMargin
        && Math.Abs(EllipseTransform.Y) <= verticalMargin)
    {
        RectangleBrush = greenBrush;
    }
    else
    {
        RectangleBrush = redBrush;
    }
}
```

The X and Y members of EllipseTransform are modified according to the accelerometer readings obtained from the provider. These readings are achieved through the DatagramSocket. MessageReceived event handler, shown in Listing 7-13. This event handler has two objects:

- **sender** This is an instance of the DatagramSocket class, which raises the MessageReceived event.

- **args** This is an instance of the DatagramSocketMessageReceivedEventArgs class, representing data for the event.

LISTING 7-13 Updating the consumer application state to conform to accelerometer readings received from the provider

```
private async void ConsumerDatagramSocket_MessageReceived(
    DatagramSocket sender,
    DatagramSocketMessageReceivedEventArgs args)
{
    try
    {
        var accReading = ReceiveAccelerometerReading(args.GetDataStream());

        await UpdateEllipseTransform(accReading);

        await ThreadHelper.InvokeOnMainThread(UpdateRectangleBrush);

        Debug.WriteLine(accReading);
    }
    catch (Exception ex)
    {
        Debug.WriteLine(ex.Message);
    }
}
```

An instance of `DatagramSocketMessageReceivedEventArgs` has three public members, which you use to obtain information about the UDP connection:

- **LocalAddress**   This represents the local IP address where the datagram was received.

- **RemoteAddress**   This specifies the remote IP address of the datagram sender.

- **RemotePort**   This contains the UDP port of the remote network.

`DatagramSocketMessageReceivedEventArgs` implements two public instance methods, which let you obtain received data:

- **GetDataReader**   This returns an instance of `Windows.Storage.Streams.DataReader`, which you use to read incoming data. In this case, you would need to manually invoke appropriate methods of `DataReader` to parse the received datagram.

- **GetDataStream**   This returns an instance of `Windows.Storage.Streams.IInputStream`. The resulting object is a sequence of bytes, representing the incoming datagram.

Here, you pass an object returned by the `GetDataStream` method to the `ReceiveAccelerometerReading` method of the base class. The underlying deserializer automatically converts the datagram to an instance of the `AccReading` class. This object is composed of sensor readings, which you then use to update the app state. First, you invoke the `UpdateEllipseTransform` method, whose definition appears in Listing 7-14.

LISTING 7-14 Updating the ellipse position

```
private const double shiftScaleFactor = 50.0;

private Rect frameBounds = new Rect();

private async Task UpdateEllipseTransform(AccReading accReading)
{
    // Z accelerometer reading is used to update Y component
    // of the ellipse transform
    var horizontalShift = accReading.X * shiftScaleFactor;
    var verticalShift = accReading.Z * shiftScaleFactor;

    await ThreadHelper.InvokeOnMainThread(() =>
    {
        if (Math.Abs(EllipseTransform.X + horizontalShift)
            <= (frameBounds.Width - ellipseSize.Width) / 2.0)
        {
            EllipseTransform.X += horizontalShift;
        }

        if (Math.Abs(EllipseTransform.Y + verticalShift)
            <= (frameBounds.Height - ellipseSize.Height) / 2.0)
        {
            EllipseTransform.Y += verticalShift;
        }
    });
}
```

UpdateEllipseTransform accepts one argument of type AccReading, whose X and Z proper-ties are used to determine the distance, expressed in pixels, the ellipse is translated. Notice that in Listing 7-14, the acceleration along the z-axis is used to update the Y property of EllipseTransform. This is because the sensor reading along the y-axis is –1 g because of the phone emulator's upright ori-entation. (Refer to the top image in Figure 7-2.) This would cause immediate shifts of the circle. To avoid this problem, you can use the z-axis reading instead. You can also rescale the received sensor readings by a constant value (the shiftScaleFactor member). This factor determines the speed of the circle, which you can adjust to your needs. Note that in UpdateEllipseTransform, you need to update the X and Y properties of EllipseTransform on the UI thread, as this will affect the visual control governed by that thread.

When you change the position of the circle, you need to ensure that the calculated shift will not place the circle off the screen. Listing 7-14 contains two logical statements that check whether the translation of the circle after the addition of a horizontal or vertical shift will cause the circle to go off the screen. Screen bounds are stored in the frameBounds field, which is of type Rect. This struct con-tains four properties that describe the rectangle: X and Y (which define the top-left corner of the rect-angle), and Width and Height (which define the rectangle size). In this example, only the Width and Height members of the struct are used. Then, the calculated horizontal and vertical shifts are added to the X and Y properties of EllipseTransform, after which a check occurs to determine whether the resulting value is smaller than or equal to half the difference between the frame width (or height) and ellipse width (or height).

Note You use the half value of that difference because the circle is in the center of the screen when the app starts. Therefore, the maximum translation along each direction is half the difference between frame and ellipse lengths along that direction.

The screen bounds may change during runtime, especially if the consumer app is executed on a desktop computer. Therefore, you must supplement the ConsumerViewModel class with the Update method. (See Listing 7-15.) This method accepts one argument, frameBounds, of type Rect. The value of this argument is simply rewritten to the private field of the same name.

LISTING 7-15 Updating the frame bounds

```
public void Update(Rect frameBounds)
{
    if (frameBounds != null)
    {
        this.frameBounds = frameBounds;
    }
}
```

The Update method is invoked in two places in the MainPage code-behind for the consumer project. (See the companion code at Chapter_07/Communication.Consumer/MainPage.xaml.cs.) First, the Update method is invoked in the OnNavigatedTo event handler. Then, in the OnNavigatedTo event handler, the view model is initialized, and the Update method is associated with the SizeChanged event for the app window. (See Listing 7-16.) The method handling this event passes the new size of the app window to the view model through the ConsumerViewModel.Update function. (See Listing 7-17.)

LISTING 7-16 Updating and initializing the view model

```
protected override async void OnNavigatedTo(NavigationEventArgs e)
{
    base.OnNavigatedTo(e);

    Window.Current.SizeChanged += Current_SizeChanged;

    viewModel.Update(Window.Current.Bounds);

    await viewModel.Initialize();
}
```

LISTING 7-17 Updating the view model when the size of the app window has changed

```
private void Current_SizeChanged(object sender, WindowSizeChangedEventArgs e)
{
    viewModel.Update(Window.Current.Bounds);
}
```

After implementing this logic, you define the UI for the consumer app. As shown in Figure 7-1, the UI consists of two controls: a square (created with the Rectangle control) and a circle (created with the Ellipse control). In Listing 7-18, these are embedded in the grid. Moreover, all control properties (except the color of the circle, which is defined using an anonymous style) are either one-way or one-time bound to properties of the ViewModel. Accordingly, all aspects of the visual appearance of the rectangle and the ellipse are controlled through the ViewModel using the methods we discussed earlier.

LISTING 7-18 Declaration of the consumer UI

```
<Grid Background="{ThemeResource ApplicationPageBackgroundThemeBrush}">
    <Ellipse RenderTransform="{x:Bind viewModel.EllipseTransform, Mode=OneWay}"
            Width="{x:Bind viewModel.EllipseSize.Width}"
            Height="{x:Bind viewModel.EllipseSize.Height}"/>

    <Rectangle Width="{x:Bind viewModel.RectangleSize.Width}"
            Height="{x:Bind viewModel.RectangleSize.Height}"
            Stroke="{x:Bind viewModel.RectangleBrush, Mode=OneWay}"
            StrokeThickness="{x:Bind viewModel.RectangleStrokeThickness}"/>
</Grid>
```

Testing the Solution

To test this solution, follow these steps:

1. Declare two capabilities for the producer and consumer apps: Private Networks (Client & Server) and Internet (Client & Server).

2. Run two instances of Visual Studio.

3. Use the first instance of Visual Studio to execute the consumer app in the HoloLens emulator.

4. Check the IP address of the emulator and verify that the same value is stored in the `HostName` property of the `Settings` class. If not, update this value according to what you see in the HoloLens emulator settings. (See Figure 7-3.)

5. Use the second instance of Visual Studio to execute the producer app in any mobile emulator you want.

6. With both apps running, tap the double-arrow icon in the mobile emulator toolbar, tap the **Accelerometer** tab, and tap the orange dot to virtually rotate the phone. This will change the accelerometer readings and, in turn, move the circle in the consumer app.

7. When the ellipse goes outside the rectangle, the color of the rectangle changes from green to red. Try to move the ellipse back inside the rectangle using your virtual phone.

Summary

In this chapter, you learned how to implement UDP communication to control the HoloLens app from a mobile emulator. You also learned how to serialize C# objects to platform-independent streams, which are transmitted over the network and deserialized at the other communication endpoint. Finally, you learned how to use radial gauges from the UWP Community Toolkit. This chapter ends the second part of this book, covering topics related to 2D app development. In Part III, you will start creating 3D apps.

Developing 3D Apps

CHAPTER 8

3D Graphics Fundamentals

This chapter provides a quick introduction to 3D graphics, which you will use to develop 3D apps in Windows Mixed Reality. It omits mathematical details and instead focuses on providing general definitions of terms that will be used throughout Chapters 9 through 15. The chapter starts by defining coordinate systems used to represent pixels and voxels. It then describes vertices, primitives, and polygons, followed by transformations, quaternions and rotations, shaders and lighting, textures and materials, and particle systems. The chapter ends with a brief glossary of terms.

Pixels, Voxels, and Coordinate Systems

A pixel is an individual point in an image displayed on a screen. The position of the pixel is identified by coordinates in a two-dimensional (2D) Cartesian coordinate system. (See the left image in Figure 8-1.) A Cartesian coordinate system has two perpendicular axes (x and y), along which a pixel can be positioned. In such a system (which is employed by Unity), x values increase from right to left, and y values increase from bottom to top, with the origin of the coordinate system in the bottom-left corner of the screen. However, most 2D graphics computer software sets the origin in the top-right corner of the bitmap or screen, with x values increasing from left to right and y values increasing from top to bottom. This type of coordinate system is typically referred to as a computer coordinate system.

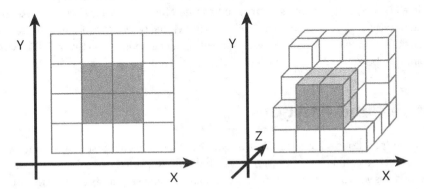

FIGURE 8-1 A 2D and 3D Cartesian coordinate system.

In 3D graphics, pixels are generalized to voxels, which represent individual points in the 3D space. Think of a voxel as a small cube within a larger one, as in the right image in Figure 8-1. Consequently, each voxel is represented using three coordinates (x, y, z) in a 3D Cartesian coordinate system. Again, the x and y values increase from left to right and from bottom to top, respectively. The z axis, however, can be oriented in two possible ways: pointing into the screen or out of it. In the first case, which is defined as a right-handed coordinate system, z values increase as they move toward you (assuming you are sitting in front of the screen). In the second case, called a left-handed coordinate system, z values increase as they move away from you.

3D graphics use several types of coordinate systems, among which the following five are most important:

- **World coordinate system**   This is a reference coordinate system along which all other systems, and consequently all objects (or models), are positioned within the scene. This system is sometimes called a model or universe coordinate system, or, as in Windows Mixed Reality, a spatial coordinate system, as it is used to determine positions of both virtual and real objects.

- **Object coordinate system**   This type of coordinate system is typically associated with individual objects. Its origin is anchored to a specific voxel of a 3D object.

- **Viewpoint or camera coordinate system**   The origin of this type of coordinate system is tied to the observer's or camera's position. This coordinate system translates as the user moves around the scene.

- **Screen coordinate system**   This 2D coordinate system represents pixels on the screen. The extent of this system is determined by the display's resolution.

- **Viewport coordinate system**   This is a 2D subset of the screen coordinate system used to represent images displayed within a single window or part of the screen.

Pixels and voxels are represented in computer memory as arrays of integers or floating numbers. Specifically, a pixel in a 2D screen coordinate system is represented by two numbers, while a voxel is represented by three numbers. In general, the location of an individual pixel or voxel can be described with integral vertices due to finite resolutions. However, points of a line connecting two pixels or voxels require floating-point numbers.

Vertices, Primitives, and Polygons

A vertex is a common endpoint of rays or lines, while a primitive is a figure composed of connected vertices. These vertices can be connected in various ways. The simplest primitive is a line segment, which connects two vertices with a straight line. To represent curves, line segments are divided into smaller segments that are connected at different angles to smoothly approximate the curve. The more of these smaller segments, the better curve approximation.

When line segments are connected in such a way as to form a closed loop, the resulting figure is a polygon. Polygons serve as the building blocks for polygonal meshes that represent the shape of a complex object. Polygons approximate shapes in much the same way line segments approximate curves; the smaller the polygon, the better approximation of a specific surface. In Chapter 12, you will see that the HoloLens uses this type of polygon approximation to represent real objects in the user's environment.

Viewing

Viewing is the process of preparing a 3D scene to be displayed or rendered on a 2D screen such that all objects will appear naturally, much as photography converts a 3D scene to a 2D picture. Even though the images are 2D, we can still determine that some objects are closer than others, and even recognize that they were originally 3D.

The quality of a photo (and hence the viewing process) depends on multiple factors, including your position and lighting conditions. To capture a good image, you first position your camera—in other words, you establish the viewing position within the world coordinate system. Then, you configure your flash, or lighting, adapt the zoom, and focus (optically or digitally, depending on the camera's capabilities). In this way you set the size and sharpness of the objects in the final image. The lens acts as a projector, projecting the 3D scene to a 2D image, which is represented in the screen coordinate system. You then capture the image and eventually crop it to contain only the portion of the image you want to see. This is your viewport transformation.

A similar approach is used in 3D graphics, but here, everything (including light) is computer-generated. Specific algorithms (like ray tracing) use a model of a light source to analyze the propagation of light rays reflected from scene objects. This is used to determine which rays can be seen by the observer and thus which objects should be displayed within the viewport. There are several transformations involved during the viewing process:

- The vertices are transformed by a viewing transformation, which depends on the observer's position and field of view, and on light conditions.

- The vertices are projected by a perspective transformation onto a 2D screen and eventually cropped if only a portion of the screen displays the scene.

After all the transformations are applied, the models are rendered such that the polygons approximating the surface are drawn using textures and shaders. The following sections discuss these transformations and renderings in more detail.

Transformations

Examples of transformations include changes to a model's position, rotation, and scale. These are represented by the transformation matrix (**T**). Because vertices can be arranged into vectors (**v**), the process of transforming models can be performed with the matrix multiplication (**Tv**). This multiplication can be easily implemented in the 3D modeling and rendering software, including various engines for 3D game and app programming.

Generally, you do not need to manually modify each entry of the transformation matrix. Instead you specify the translation, rotation, and scale along each direction. The engine uses these values to construct the T matrix and perform all calculations accordingly. In practice, this means that when you change the x value of the translation by, say, 20 pixels, the model will move accordingly in the scene preview.

Matrices are used not only to represent model transformations, but also to represent projection transformations. These transformations are responsible for projecting the 3D model onto the 2D screen. There are two common projection transformations:

- **Perspective projection**   This causes objects that are farther from the observer to appear smaller on the screen.

- **Orthographic projection**   This does not change the relative size of objects.

> **Note** In next chapter, you will see that you can use Unity Editor to quickly switch between perspective and orthographic projections to preview the scene under different conditions.

Quaternions and Rotations

Quaternions are commonly used in 3D graphics to represent rotations. They are represented as a 4x4 matrices used to derive the rotation matrix (**R**). This can be merged with other transformations (like translation or scale) by matrix multiplication, leading to the affine transform. This transformation is a composition of translation, rotation, scale, and shear.

In Unity and UrhoSharp you need not directly set particular entries for quaternions or rotation matrices. Instead, you use the editor to manipulate rotation angles along each direction or use appropriate methods from the programming interface that will instantiate the rotation matrix for you. Later chapters contain specific instructions for rotating models using Unity Editor, C# Unity scripts, and the C# API of UrhoSharp.

Shaders and Lighting

Picture quality depends strongly on lighting conditions. Objects look different when they are backlit than they do in direct light. Indeed, many photographers use light to alter the final appearance of an object and to control the shade in an image. Typically, light affects not only the object's brightness in the image but also the viewer's 3D perception.

To emulate various lighting conditions, computer graphics software uses shaders. Shaders control the brightness and color of individual pixels composing the surface of the model. For example, to render a 3D cube, the computer software applies different shades of a specific color to each side of the cube.

> **Note** One of the first realistic shading models was developed in 1973 by Bui Toung Phong. His model, known as Phong interpolation, is used in 3D graphics to realistically approximate the shading of smooth surfaces.

In practice, a shader is a piece of code that dynamically calculates the color that should be applied to a pixel during rendering. As in classical photography, shading 3D graphics depends strongly on the lighting conditions. Such effects are emulated in 3D graphics using various lighting models. Shaders use these models along with material configurations (see the next section) to determine what color should be used to display a pixel on the screen.

There are several types of light. These include the following:

- **Point light** This type of light originates from a point-like source and emerges in all directions.

- **Spot light** This is like a point light in that it originates from a point, but it emerges in a cone shape rather than in all directions.

- **Directional light** This type of light illuminates all objects equally from a specific direction, much like the sun. Directional light is automatically added to all scenes in Unity.

- **Ambient light** This type of light is emitted in all directions and affects all objects in the scene in the same way. In other words, when the intensity of the ambient light changes, the brightness of all objects will change accordingly.

> **Note** For more on these various types of light, all of which are used by Unity, see http://bit.ly/light_types.

Unity and UrhoSharp contain several built-in shaders that are usually sufficient for app development, meaning you need not have a detailed knowledge of the mathematics behind them. You will apply shaders to models and eventually control their parameters in upcoming chapters. However, this book does not cover creating custom shaders manually or programmatically.

Textures and Materials

A texture is a 2D image applied to a surface before shading. Typically, textures are used to render relatively large surfaces. For example, without textures, rendering a tree would mean drawing thousands of small surfaces on a tree-shaped object, each containing a specific number of pixels of a uniform color. Textures enable you to approximate the tree by creating a larger and simpler two-dimensional surface and applying it to a tree-shaped object.

In practice, textures are made of bitmap images, so they can be easily ported between various apps. The process of applying a texture to a surface is called texture mapping. In this process, a two-dimensional texture is wrapped around an object to precisely match its shape and orientation in the 3D space.

In Unity and UrhoSharp, you do not explicitly control texture mapping. Rather, you apply textures through a material. You then associate the material with the model to perform the rendering. This means the model cannot be rendered without a material. Hence, in Unity, primitive 3D models are automatically associated with a default material when you add them to the scene. The material includes not only a reference to the texture but also all the information required to render the surface, including shader configuration. In this part of the book, you will use materials to format 3D objects, which will act as holograms in your Windows Mixed Reality apps.

Particle Systems

So far, the 3D graphics concepts discussed in this chapter have pertained to static objects that do not move during runtime. This is in contrast to dynamic objects, whose motion depends on size, external forces, and possible interactions, such as collisions, with other objects.

Mathematically modeling the movements of large individual objects can be done relatively easily. However, modeling the movement of many small particles composing an atmosphere or fluid is a real challenge. To approximate the dynamics of such objects, 3D graphics software uses particle systems. A particle system is a group of small simple images or meshes (particles) that move collectively to create the impression that they constitute a complete system.

Particle systems are typically defined by two parameters:

- **Emission**   This refers to when a given particle was generated.

- **Lifetime**   This refers to how long the particle will be present in the system and thus visible in the scene.

Each emitted particle has an associated velocity vector that specifies where and how quickly the particle is moving. This vector may be affected by gravity, obstacles, or wind. Gravity attracts a particle to the ground, while obstacles and wind change the direction of the particle's motion. In Chapter 10 you will learn how to use particle systems to create reliable explosion effects.

Glossary of Terms

For your reference, here is a glossary of the most important terms to remember from this chapter:

Line segment   A straight line that connects two vertices.

Material   A full rendering definition including shader and textures information.

Mesh   A collection of vertices that define the shape of a 3D object.

Model   A representation of a 3D object based on the mesh. The model extends the mesh by a material and, eventually, animations.

Pixel   A single point in a 2D image or on a screen.

Polygon   A figure made of line segments.

Primitive   A figure formed by connected vertices.

Shader   An algorithm that defines how to render the pixels of a surfaces.

Texture   A two-dimensional array of data that can be applied to surfaces before shading.

Vertex   A common endpoint of lines. Vertices are fundamental elements that compose primitives in 3D graphics.

Voxel   A single point in a 3D scene.

Summary

This chapter provided a brief and concise introduction to 3D computer graphics concepts that will be used in Chapters 9 through 15 to develop 3D apps for Windows Mixed Reality. The chapter omits full mathematical descriptions because this book does not cover the creation of models or shaders from scratch. Rather, to control the scene, you will use predefined objects, shaders, materials, and various Unity or UrhoSharp components.

CHAPTER 9

Unity Basics

This is the chapter where you start developing 3D apps for Windows Mixed Reality. To that end you will first explore the Unity Editor. After reviewing the main elements of this editor, you will learn how to create scenes with primitive and advanced 3D objects. Specifically, you will create simple objects such as planes, spheres, cubes, and cylinders, and more advanced elements like trees and characters.

To create an animated character, you will use the Unity Editor Ragdoll Creator. You will also explore using the Ragdoll Creator to control that character in a realistic way. Namely, this chapter will show you how to make your ragdoll fall down onto other objects in the scene. You will see that Unity provides mechanisms to make this vertical drop truthful. You will also learn how to use materials and prefabs to adjust the visual appearance of objects in the scene.

Finally, you will investigate how to build and deploy the app to achieve the result shown in Figure 9-1. This app comprises several objects. These include a plane, which represents the ground; 3D text; and a character (cyan humanoid model) that falls down and lands on a custom 3D object made from a cylinder, a cube, and a sphere. There are also trees, which sway like real trees in the wind.

FIGURE 9-1 The final form of the app we will build in this chapter.

The Unity Editor

This chapter starts by covering some important Unity concepts. After you grasp these, you will learn how to set up and use the Unity Editor to create your first scene.

Understanding Game Objects and Components

In Unity, every element in a scene, including lighting, terrain, and characters, is defined as a game object. A game object does not have any particular properties or perform any specific function until you supplement it with a component. Components define visual and functional properties for game objects. Every game object has a default transform component, which determines the position and dimensions of the game object in the scene.

> **Note** Because you will use Unity to create apps for Windows Mixed Reality, the objects you use will not be limited to typical game objects. Therefore, this chapter uses the terms *scene object* (or simply *object*) and *game object* interchangeably.

Configuring Your Unity ID and Signing In

When you run the Unity Editor, the Sign Into Your Unity ID dialog box opens. (See Figure 9-2.) Before you can use the Unity Editor, you must create a Unity ID. To do so, click the Create One link at the top of the Sign Into Your Unity ID dialog box. (Alternatively, use this link: http://bit.ly/unity_id.) Then, in the dialog box that appears, provide the information requested to create a Unity ID. This includes your name, a valid email address, and the user name and password you want to use. You must also agree to the terms of use. (For step-by-step instructions, including screenshots, see http://bit.ly/unity_activation.)

FIGURE 9-2 The Sign Into Your Unity ID dialog box.

After you create your Unity ID, you choose a license. Unity offers three license tiers:

- **Personal** Unity offers this license free of charge, provided "your company currently does not make more than $100k in annual gross revenues or has not raised funds in excess of $100k."

This version contains all core modules. However, you cannot modify the splash screen the user sees when your app launches. (This license was used in the writing of this book.)

- **Plus** This license costs $35 per month. You can use this license if your company earns "up to $200k in annual gross revenues." In addition to giving you access to all the core modules, this version also provides several packs, which enhance core Unity functionality, and lets you modify the splash screen.

- **Pro** This license costs $120 per month but allows for an "unlimited revenue or fundraising capacity." This version extends the capabilities of the Plus version by including additional services, such as analytics and visualizations, and premium support.

After you create your Unity ID and choose a license, you use your Unity ID to sign into Unity. You'll see a welcome screen like the one in Figure 9-3. This screen has two tabs:

- **Projects** Click this tab to create a new project (by clicking the New link in the upper-right corner of the screen) or to open an existing one (by clicking the Open link next to the New link and selecting the project you want to open).

- **Learn** Click this tab to access links to tutorials, tutorial projects, and resources that can help you jump-start developing apps with Unity.

FIGURE 9-3 The Projects tab of the Unity welcome window.

Creating a New Project

To create a new project, follow these steps:

1. Click the **New** link in the Projects tab.

2. Type a name for the project in the **Project Name** box. In this case, type **UnityBasics**.

3. Select the **3D** option button.

4. Enter a location for the project's source code in the **Location** box.

5. Click the **Create Project** button.

After a moment, the Unity Editor will be open. (See Figure 9-4.) The main components of the Unity Editor are as follows:

- Toolbar
- Hierarchy window
- Scene view
- Inspector window
- Project window

The following sections cover each of these components.

Note The window also features a menu bar, located above the toolbar. This component is self-explanatory and is not covered in more detail in the sections that follow.

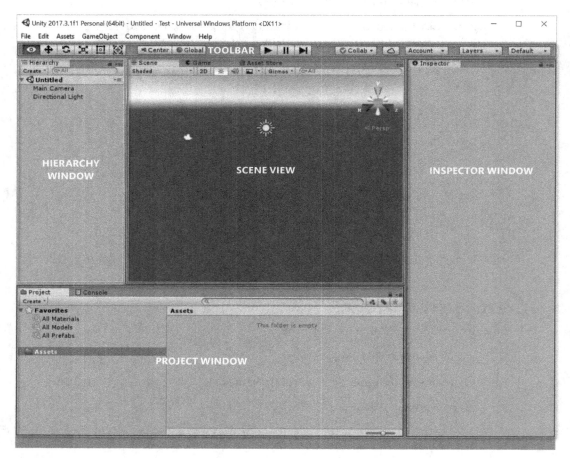

FIGURE 9-4 The default view of the Unity Editor.

> **Note** You can change the layout of the Unity Editor screen to suit your needs by dragging the Hierarchy, Inspector, and Project windows. This chapter assumes these windows are arranged in the default layout.

The Toolbar

The toolbar contains buttons that give you quick access to the Unity Editor's most important features. Let's briefly review them, starting with the controls located on the left:

- **Drag, Move, Rotate, Scale, and RectTransform**   You use these buttons to position objects in the scene. (For more information, see http://bit.ly/positioning_objects.)

- **Gizmo toggles**   These buttons, labeled Center and Local in Figure 9-4, enable you to toggle the gizmo handle position. You use these to define the center of a transform. (See http://bit.ly/positioning_objects for more information.)

- **Play, Pause, and Step**   You use these buttons to control the execution of your app in the editor's play mode. You use this mode to preview your app in Unity editor.

- **Collab**   When you click this button, a pop-up window opens, which you use to manage Unity Collaboration. Unity Collaboration is a cloud-based service that enables you to store your project in the cloud so other members of your team can quickly see your changes and synchronize their work with yours.

- **Cloud**   When you click this button, a pop-up window opens, where you can configure Unity services like Unity Ads, Unity Analytics, Unity Cloud Build, and others. (See http://bit.ly/unity_services for more details.)

- **Account**   Clicking this button opens a menu that gives you access to tools to manage your account and license.

- **Layers**   Clicking this button opens a menu containing layers to be displayed in the Scene view

- **Layout**   Clicking this button—labeled Default in Figure 9-4—opens a menu with predefined layout options. Use this list to quickly rearrange windows of the Unity Editor. To restore the default arrangement, select the Default option.

The Hierarchy Window

The Hierarchy window (sometimes simply called the Hierarchy) presents a list of all objects in the current project. The Hierarchy is like Solution Explorer in Visual Studio but shows a list of objects composing the scenes instead of source code files composing projects. So, you use the Hierarchy window in much the same way you use the Solution Explorer.

By default, the Hierarchy window contains only two objects: a main camera object and a directional light object. To add new objects, you use the Hierarchy window's context menu. As shown in Figure 9-5, this menu contains a list of built-in objects, which you can use to extend the default scene. You will learn about these objects later in this chapter.

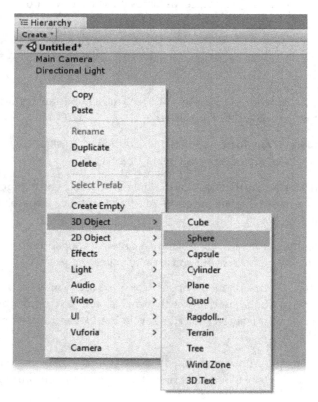

FIGURE 9-5 Adding new objects to the scene from the Hierarchy window.

Scene View

The Scene view is an interactive component in which you place and position all objects to compose your app. Typically you proceed as follows:

1. You add objects using the Hierarchy window.

2. You select the object using the Hierarchy window or through the Scene view.

3. You position and transform the object using toolbar buttons or with the Inspector window. (See the next section.)

If you compare the Unity Editor workflow with the Visual Studio workflow, Scene view is like a Visual Designer that enables you to use a drag-and-drop approach to define the visual layer of your app.

By default, the Scene view contains three tabs. (Actually, they are separate windows, which you can move freely, but I will refer to them as tabs here.)

- **Scene**   This tab displays the scene preview mode, which contains a Scene gizmo (in the top-right corner) and a control bar (along the top) to help you preview the scene. You'll learn more about each of these tools in the following sections.

- **Game View**   You use this tab to preview and test your final app—for example, whether your scripts work and if controlled objects behave as expected. (You can also click the Play button in the control bar to access this view.)

- **Asset Store**   This tab opens the Assets Store. Here, you can download various assets (free or for purchase) to jump-start building comprehensive environments for Windows Mixed Reality apps. (You'll learn how to use the Asset Store in Chapter 10.)

The Scene Gizmo

As shown in Figure 9-6, the Scene gizmo looks like a gray cube with six conical arms that extend from the middle of each side of the cube. You use the Scene gizmo to modify the viewing angle and projection mode. To change the viewing angle, click one of the conical arms. Alternatively, right-click the Scene gizmo and choose the desired viewing angle from the context menu that appears. (See Figure 9-7.) (To restore the default viewing angle, right-click the Scene gizmo and choose **Free**.) To switch perspective modes, right-click the Scene gizmo and uncheck the Perspective option to enable Orthographic mode (also known as Isometric) in the context menu. You can also switch perspective modes by clicking the **Persp** or Iso option under the Scene gizmo. (Again, see Figure 9-6.)

FIGURE 9-6 The Scene gizmo.

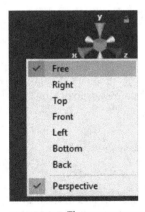

FIGURE 9-7 The context menu of the Scene gizmo.

Tip In addition to using the Scene gizmo to change your viewing angle, you can use your mouse (or touchpad). To do so, press and hold down the Alt key as you click and drag the cursor. You can also use your mouse (or touchpad) to change the zoom, by using the scroll function. To move around the scene, you can use the keyboard arrows. Alternatively, click the Drag button in the toolbar (it features a hand icon) or press the Q key on your keyboard to use the Drag tool.

The Control Bar

The control bar, shown in Figure 9-8, includes several settings for controlling the scene preview.

FIGURE 9-8 The control bar with the Draw Mode settings displayed.

The control bar includes access to the following settings:

- Draw Mode
- View, lighting, and audio
- Effects
- Gizmos

Draw Mode settings The Draw Mode settings are divided into several groups. The most important ones for our purposes are the Shading Mode, Miscellaneous, and Global Illumination groups.

The Shading Mode group has the following options (see Figure 9-9):

- **Shaded** Click this option to view the surfaces and textures of the selected object.
- **Wireframe** Click this option to view a wireframe rendering of the selected object.
- **Shaded Wireframe** Click this option to view the surfaces and textures and a wireframe rendering of the selected object.

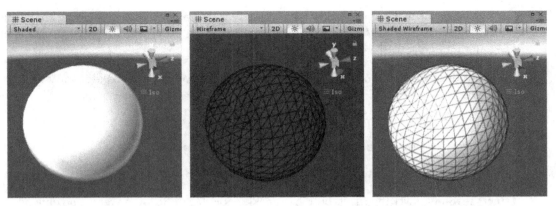

FIGURE 9-9 A comparison of shading modes used to render a sphere: Shaded (left), Wireframe (middle), and Shaded Wireframe (right).

The Miscellaneous group has the following options (see Figure 9-10):

- **Shadow Cascades**   Choose this option to display directional light shadow cascades.

- **Render Paths**   Choose this option to show the color-encoded rendering path. Blue denotes deferred shading, green denotes deferred light, and yellow denotes forward rendering.

- **Alpha Channel**   Choose this option to render opacity (alpha). Brighter objects have less opacity.

- **Overdraw**   Choose this option to render transparent envelopes of scene objects. The intensity of each point in the rendered scene increases with the number of overlapping objects.

- **Mipmaps**   Choose this option to denote color-encoded texture sizes. Blue indicates that the texture size could be larger, while red denotes that the texture size is too large.

- **Sprite Mask**   Choose this option to display sprite masks.

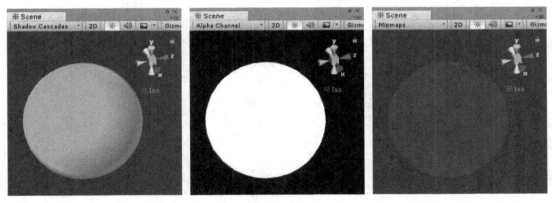

FIGURE 9-10 A comparison of selected drawing modes from the Miscellaneous group: Shadow Cascades (left), Alpha Channel (middle), Mipmaps (right).

The Global Illumination group provides several options to help you visualize global scene illumination, including UV Systems, Albedo, Irradiance, and Directionality. Visit http://bit.ly/GI_visualization to learn more about global illumination.

View, lighting, and audio options   Next to the Draw Mode option in the control, you'll see three buttons:

- **2D/3D**   This button toggles between 2D and 3D views of the scene.

- **Lighting**   Use this button to disable or enable scene lighting.

- **Audio**   Use this button turn on or off any audio effects.

Effects settings   Click the Effects button to enable or disable the following rendering options:

- **Skybox**   Clicking this option enables or disables rendering of the skybox texture.

- **Fog**   Use this option to enable or disable the fog effect.

- **Flares**   This option enables or disables the display of lens flares of light.

- **Animated Materials**   Choose this option to enable or disable the animation of materials.

- **Image Effects**   This option lets you enable or disable all effects at once.

The Gizmos menu   The Gizmos menu, shown in Figure 9-11, contains many additional options for controlling the rendering of objects in the scene. These options are documented here: http://bit.ly/gizmos_menu.

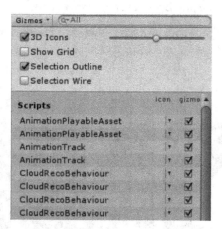

FIGURE 9-11 A fragment of the Gizmos menu.

 Note   Options in the Gizmos menu alter the scene preview. They do not affect the final app.

The Inspector Window

The Inspector window (sometimes simply called the Inspector) shows a list of configurable properties of the object selected in the Hierarchy window or Scene view. As an example, Figure 9-12 shows the Inspector window displaying properties of the main camera object.

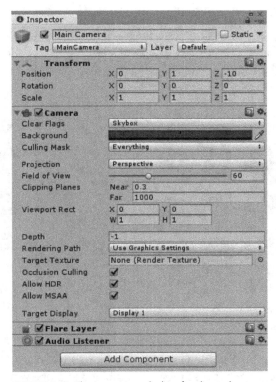

FIGURE 9-12 The Inspector window for the main camera object.

The Inspector window divides properties into several groups. Different object types have different groups of properties. However, some groups apply to many objects, such as the following:

- **Identity** This group, located at the top of the Inspector window, includes an Object Name box; an Object Tag drop-down list; a Layer drop-down list, which you can use to associate the object with a particular scene layer; and a Static checkbox, which you can use to inform the Unity engine that the object will not move during app execution (and thereby enable Unity to optimize physics simulation to improve app performance).

- **Transform** This group is located right below the Identity group. You use the boxes in this group to define the object's position in the scene as well as its rotation angle and scale along each direction. Modifying Transform properties in the Inspector is a convenient way to position and resize objects in the scene.

- **Component** You use this group, located on the bottom of the Inspector window, to associate components with the game object.

The Project Window

By default, the Project window contains two tabs:

- **Console** This tab displays warnings, errors, and other messages generated by Unity. You typically use this tab for debugging and building (to investigate eventual build errors). The Unity Console tab is like the Debug window in Visual Studio.

- **Project** You use this tab to display and manage assets in the current project. This tab has a pane on the left that shows a hierarchical list of all the assets and asset folders. When you choose a folder in the pane, its contents are displayed on the right. (See Figure 9-13.) You typically use the Project tab to search for assets and add them to the scene.

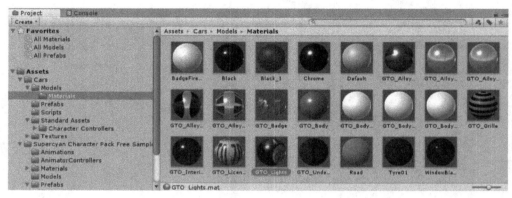

FIGURE 9-13 The Project tab displays a project's assets.

Note The Console and Project tabs can also be displayed as separate windows and placed wherever you like. I describe them together here because they are combined into one window in the default layout of the Unity Editor.

Creating Scenes

Now that you've explored the interface of the Unity Editor, you're ready to learn how to modify a default scene created by the Unity Editor. In this section, you'll start by reviewing primitive 3D objects with default materials. Then you'll learn how to use more advanced objects like terrain, trees, and ragdolls. After that you'll find out how to create and edit materials, use prefabs, and how to create a wind zone. This will give you a comprehensive overview of how to extend a default scene.

Working with 3D Objects

There are multiple ways to add a 3D object to a scene:

- By right-clicking in the Hierarchy window, choosing **3D Object** in the menu that appears, and selecting the type of object you want to create from the list that appears (refer to Figure 9-5)

- By clicking the **Create** button in the upper-left corner of the Hierarchy window, choosing **3D Object** from the menu that appears, and selecting the type of object you want to create in the menu that appears

- By opening the **GameObject** menu in the menu bar, choosing **3D Object**, and selecting the type of object you want to create

You can create six types of primitive 3D objects—cube, sphere, capsule, cylinder, plane, and quad—as well as several complex 3D objects, including terrain, tree, ragdoll, wind zone, and 3D text.

Exploring Primitive 3D Objects

Figures 9-14 and 9-15 show examples of primitive 3D objects added to a scene.

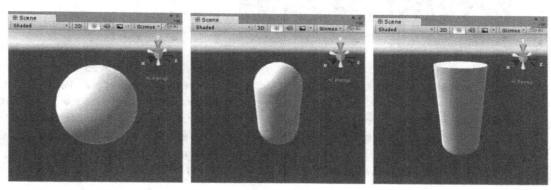

FIGURE 9-14 Primitive 3D objects: sphere (left), capsule (middle), and cylinder (right).

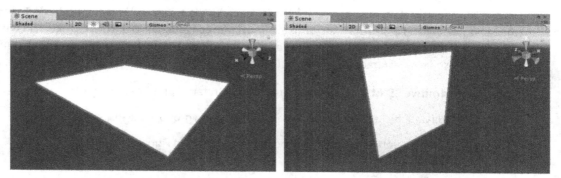

FIGURE 9-15 Primitive 3D objects: plane (left) and quad (right).

Let's start by learning how to work with primitive 3D objects using a cube. Go ahead and add one to the scene. Afterward, your scene should look like the one in Figure 9-16—just a single solid object.

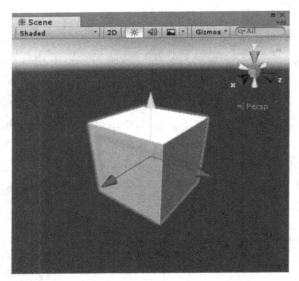

FIGURE 9-16 A cube added to the scene.

Positioning a primitive 3D object   By default, this new object will be positioned at the origin of the coordinate system associated with the scene (When you change the scene preview area, new objects will be placed approximately in the center of the currently displayed region of the scene.) The coordinate system uses three component vectors (X, Y, Z) to uniquely represent object position in the scene. To check the current position of the object in the scene, you select the object (in this case, the cube) and switch to the Inspector. The Position settings in the Transform group will indicate the position: 0, 0, 0. If you change these values, the cube will be repositioned accordingly.

You can also move the object using its Move gizmo handle. A gizmo handle is a visual tool that helps you transform an object. You can see the cube's Move gizmo handle in Figure 9-16. It features three color-coded coordinate arrows: red for the X axis, green for the Y axis, and blue for the Z axis. To use the Move gizmo handle, you drag and drop the arrow that corresponds to the desired axis. This is useful when you want to adjust an object's position along only a single axis. During this process, the Unity Editor ensures that object translation does not reflect involuntary mouse or touchpad movements.

Rotating a primitive 3D object   There are two ways to rotate a primitive 3D object:

- By modifying the Rotation properties in the Transform group in the Inspector

- By clicking the Rotate button in the toolbar (highlighted in Figure 9-17)

FIGURE 9-17 The toolbar buttons used to access Unity Editor's object-manipulation tools. The button for the Rotate tool is selected.

When you click the Rotate button, a Rotate gizmo handle with several spheres surrounds the selected object. (See Figure 9-18.) Like the arrows in the Move gizmo handle, the active spheres in this gizmo handle are color-coded: the red sphere corresponds to the X axis, the green sphere to the Y axis, and the blue sphere to the Z axis. Simply click the sphere representing the axis along which you want to rotate the object and drag the cursor.

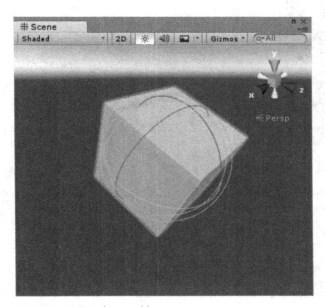

FIGURE 9-18 Rotating an object.

Note When you rotate an object, the Rotation properties in the Inspector's Transform group display the rotation angles.

Scaling a primitive 3D object   Scaling an object is very similar. You can either use the Scale properties in the Transform group of the Inspector or you can click the Scale button in the toolbar (located to the right of the Rotate button; refer to Figure 9-15). This activates the Scale gizmo handle. (See Figure 9-19.) Each scaling axis is represented by a line with a color-coded cube on one end. You click and drag a cube to scale the object along the corresponding direction. (Again, red corresponds to the X axis, green to the Y axis, and blue to the Z axis.) Again, all changes will be automatically reflected in the Scale properties of the Transform group in the Inspector.

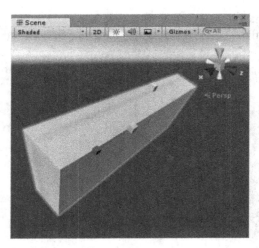

FIGURE 9-19 Scaling an object.

Using the RectTransform tool The RectTransform tool combines the Move, Rotate, and Scale tools into a single gizmo. To access it, click the RectTransform button in the toolbar (the rightmost button shown in Figure 9-17). As shown in Figure 9-20, a rectangle with small blue dots in each corner and a small doughnut-shaped icon in the center will surround the selected object. Do one of the following:

- To move the object, click anywhere inside the rectangle and drag in the desired direction.

- To rotate the object, click just beyond the corner. Then, when the cursor icon changes, click and drag the icon in the desired direction.

- To scale the object, position the cursor on one corner of the rectangle (to scale along two directions simultaneously) or on an edge (to scale along a single direction). Then, when the cursor icon changes, click and drag inward or outward.

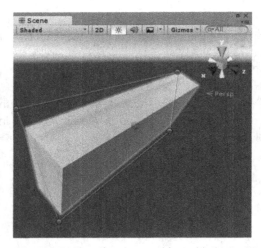

FIGURE 9-20 Transforming an object with the RectTransform tool.

Again, all changes done with the tool will be reflected in the Transform group in the Inspector.

> **Tip** You can also select the various transform tools using keyboard hot keys. Press W to select the Move tool, press E to select the Rotate tool, press R to select the Scale tool, and press T to select the RectTransform tool. At first, you will probably prefer to use the toolbar, but in the long run you will likely want switch to using these hot keys.

Adding More Objects

When you're adding a new object, deselect any existing objects in the Hierarchy. Otherwise, the new object will automatically become a descendant of the selected object. (For more on this, see the section "Object Parenting.")

Using Primitive 3D Objects to Create Items for Your Scene

Typically, you do not use primitive 3D objects as is. Instead, you transform them and apply materials to them to create real world–type objects. For example:

- **Cubes**   Use these to build walls, steps, buildings, and so on.

- **Spheres**   Use these to create balls, planets, and the like.

- **Capsules**   These can be used to replace sharp-edged cubes to build walls and such.

- **Cylinders**   These work well for creating posts and rods.

- **Planes**   You can use these to create flat surfaces.

- **Quads**   These are good for displaying images and creating simple user interfaces in the scene. A quad is like a plane, but its surface is oriented in the XY plane. This means you need to change the viewing angle to see its surface. (Refer to Figure 9-15 and compare the Scene gizmos in each image.)

Object Parenting

You can combine primitive 3D objects to create complex 3D models. When working with such items, you often use *parenting*. An object's parenting describes its location in the scene's hierarchy. The top item is the parent, and all items below it are defined as child objects or descendants. In general, this hierarchy contains multiple levels. In the default scene you created earlier, the untitled scene was the parent of two objects: main camera and directional light. (Refer to Figure 9-5.)

Object parenting is also very helpful when you want to manipulate multiple objects at once. For instance, you can move, rotate, or scale a group of objects simultaneously rather than adjusting the properties of each individual object independently.

To make one object (let's call it object A) the descendant of another object (object B), you use the Hierarchy window. Simply click object A and drag it to object B. When you release the mouse button, object B will become the parent of object A. From now on, any transformations you make to the parent will also apply to its descendants.

Let's see how this works in practice. Follow these steps:

1. Remove the cube object from the scene by right-clicking it in the Hierarchy and choosing **Delete** from the menu that appears.

2. Add a new cube, a cylinder, and a sphere. Make sure all of them are positioned at the origin (0, 0, 0).

3. Click the cube to select it. Then, in the **Scale** properties in the **Transform** group of the Inspector, change the **X** setting to **1.5**, the **Y** setting to **0.1**, and the **Z** setting to **1.5**.

4. Click the sphere to select it. Then, in the **Position** properties in the **Transform** group of the Inspector, change the **Y** setting to **1**.

5. Leave the cylinder transform unchanged. Then, in the Hierarchy, drag the cylinder and sphere objects to the cube.

6. Right-click in the Hierarchy, choose **Save Scene As**, and set the scene name to **MyScene**. Your saved scene should look like the one shown in Figure 9-21.

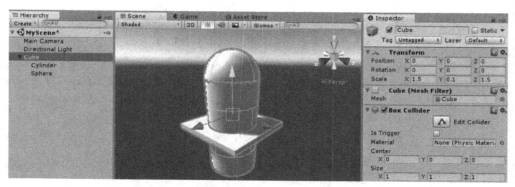

FIGURE 9-21 An object created from a cube, a cylinder, and a sphere.

With this scene, whenever you select the cube, all its descendants will be also become active. So, you can transform them together using the Scene view and the toolbar or by manually changing the Transform group properties in the Inspector. To transform a descendant object independently, select it in the Hierarchy. Any changes you make to it will *not* apply to the parent or to any other objects on the same hierarchy level.

Applying Terrain

You can use terrain—or more precisely, the terrain engine—to develop landscapes in a scene. You add terrain in the same way as you add primitive 3D objects: via the Hierarchy window context menu or the 3D Object submenu of the GameObject menu.

After you add terrain to a scene, you can use brushes that appear in the Inspector to draw landscape elements. (See Figure 9-22.) Here's how:

1. Terrain occupies a lot of space in a scene, so start by reducing the zoom.

2. In the Inspector, choose the brush you want to use and adjust its settings as desired.

3. In Scene view, drag the cursor along three dimensions to create or more precisely draw the landscape.

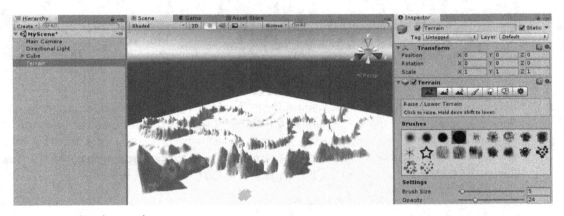

FIGURE 9-22 Creating terrain.

You can quickly define the entire landscape for your app. Note, however, that you use terrains only to build virtual reality (VR) experiences. In augmented reality (AR) applications, the terrain, or landscape, is composed of real objects (trees, mountains, lakes, and so on), so it is not necessary to make virtual terrain. (For more info on creating terrains, see http://bit.ly/terrain_engine.)

Adding Trees

You add a tree to a scene the same way you add any other 3D object. When you do, the tree will open in the Tree Editor. At first, the tree will have a single branch. (See Figure 9-23.)

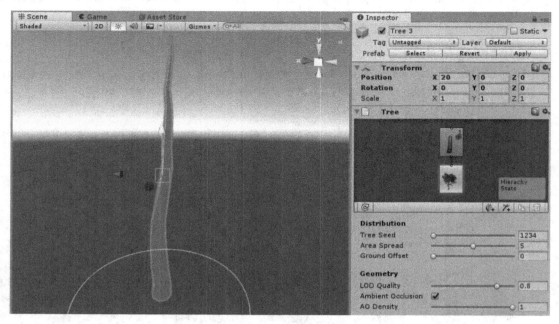

FIGURE 9-23 Creating a tree.

To create new branches and leaves, you edit the tree hierarchy using the Tree group in the Inspector. (Refer to Figure 9-23.) As shown in Figure 9-24, the tree hierarchy in the Tree group contains two elements by default: a Tree Root node (bottom icon) and a Branch Group (top icon). The Tree group also contains four buttons in the bottom-right corner. From left to right these are the Add Leaf Group button, the Add Branch Group button, the Copy button, and the Delete button.

FIGURE 9-24 A default tree hierarchy.

Tip Your tree will be added to your project's assets—meaning you can reuse it. You'll learn how to do this later in this chapter.

To add a new branch to the tree, follow these steps:

1. Click the **Branch Group** node.

2. Click the **Add Branch Group** button. The new branch is created.

3. To modify the branch to make it look more realistic, experiment with the **Distribution**, **Geometry**, and **Shape** parameters in the Inspector. (See Figure 9-25).

4. Add more branches as you see fit.

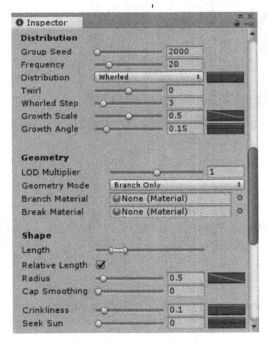

FIGURE 9-25 Modifying the tree branch.

To add leaves to the tree, follow these steps:

1. Click the branch to which you want to add leaves. (In this example, I selected the top branch.)

2. Click the **Add Leaf Group** button. (Refer to Figure 9-24.)

3. At first, the leaves will appear as rectangular planes. (See Figure 9-26.) For them to look like actual leaves, you'll need to apply a material to them. (You'll learn how to add materials to leaves later in this chapter.) For now, in the Inspector, increase the value for the **Frequency** parameter in the Distribution group to add more leaves.

4. Experiment with the other leaf properties. (For more on these properties, see http://bit.ly/tree_editor.)

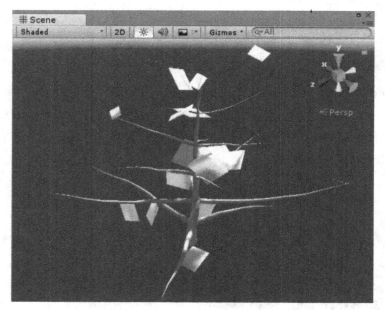

FIGURE 9-26 A tree generated in the Tree Editor.

Adding 3D Text

The 3D text object displays strings of letters, numbers, or symbols. This string can appear on a single line or can be multi-line. After you add a 3D text object to the scene—which you do in the same way you add any other type of object—you can change its appearance by modifying its parameters in the Inspector. Options include the following:

- **Text** This is where you enter the text to be displayed in the 3D text object. Provided the Rich Text checkbox is selected, the rendering engine will format your string based on the following tags:

  - **...** These tags format the 3D text object with a bold font. For example, the string Mixed Reality results in a 3D text object with the text Mixed Reality in bold font.

  - **<i>...</i>** These tags format the 3D text object with an italic font. For example, the string <i>Hello, World!</i> results in a 3D text object with the text Hello, World! in italic font.

  - **<size=x>...</size>** These tags set the font size to x pixels. For example, the string <size=45>Big Text</size> results in a 3D text object with the text Big Text set to 45 pixels.

- **<color=#rrggbbaa>...</color> or <color=color_name>...</color>** These tags set the font color to the given hexadecimal code or color name. For example, the strings <color=#ff0000ff>Red</color> and <color=red>Red</color> both produce the same result: a 3D object containing the word Red in red text.

- **OffsetZ** This parameter indicates the distance from the origin of the Z axis that the text should be rendered.

- **Character Size** This parameter sets the size of each character.

- **Line Spacing** This parameter sets the spacing between each line.

- **Anchor** This parameter marks the beginning point of the transform. If you change the value for this parameter, the transform properties (position, rotation, and scale) will start from the new point.

- **Alignment** This parameter sets the text alignment.

- **Tab Size** This parameter sets the size of the text indent in the 3D text object. (To create an indent, type \t.)

- **Font, Font Size, Font Style, and Color** These parameters specify the font, font size, font style, and font color. You can use these instead of tags to change the appearance of your text.

Figure 9-27 shows the result of a 3D text object with the text Hello, Mixed Reality, in which the bold font was set using tags (as described in the Text bullet in the preceding list) and the text color and size were defined using the corresponding properties in the Inspector.

FIGURE 9-27 A 3D text object displaying the text Hello, Mixed Reality.

Adding a Ragdoll

A ragdoll is a tool that automatically implements the physics needed to make a character move and interact with objects in a scene in a realistic manner. Before you can create a ragdoll, you need to assemble the various elements that will constitute its body, including its feet, legs, hips, pelvis, arms, elbows, hands, head, and spine. You can model these objects in 3D software to include skinned meshes. This is time-consuming, however. To speed things up, this chapter uses the Ethan character included in the character package of standard Unity assets.

To import the character package and extract the Ethan character, follow these steps:

1. Open the **Assets** menu, choose **Import Package**, and select **Characters**. The Import Unity Package window opens, showing a list of included assets.

2. Click the **All** button to select all the assets.

3. Click the **Import** button.

4. When the import operation is finished, the Project window appears. Open the **Assets/ Standard Assets/Characters/ThirdPersonCharacter/Models** folder, as shown in Figure 9-28. (Alternatively, type **Ethan** in the search box.) Then click the **Ethan** item and drag it to the Scene view. (Click **OK** in any dialog boxes that appear.)

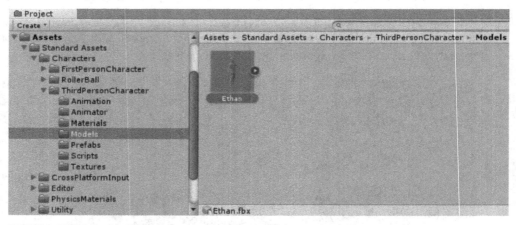

FIGURE 9-28 The Project window showing the Ethan model.

Next, you'll add a plane and several objects to the scene, including the Ethan character, a tree, and some 3D text. First, make sure your tool handles are in Global mode—that is, with the gizmo toggles set to Center and Local. After you add the objects, set the Position and Rotation parameters in the Inspector's Transform group as described in Table 9-1.

TABLE 9-1 Position and Rotation Parameter Settings

Object	Position parameter setting	Rotation parameter setting
Plane	X: 0 Y: −1 Z: 1	X: 0.6 Y: −1 Z: 1
Ethan	X: 0 Y: 3 Z: −0.1	X: 0 Y: 180 Z: 0
Tree	X: 10 Y: −2 Z: 10	X: 0 Y: 0 Z: 0
3D text	X: −20 Y: −1 Z: 25	X: 0 Y: −45 Z: 0
Main camera	X: 0 Y: 3 Z: −7	X: 15 Y: 0 Z: 0
Directional light	X: 0 Y: 3 Z: 0	X: 50 Y: −30 Z: 1

To gain a better understanding of the ragdoll, click the Play button in the toolbar. You'll see the Ethan character positioned above some 3D text, a tree, a cube and its descendants (which compose the object you created earlier; refer to Figure 9-21), and the plane, as shown in Figure 9-29.

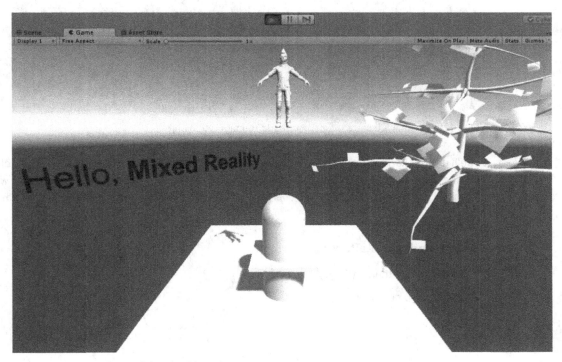

FIGURE 9-29 A scene containing the Ethan character.

Notice that even in Play mode, the Ethan character does not move. This is because you have not yet applied a ragdoll object to the Ethan character. You'll do that next.

1. Click the **Start** button to exit Play mode.

2. Expand the **Ethan** object in Hierarchy window to display its child items. (See the left screen in Figure 9-30.) Make sure all other objects in the window are deselected.

3. Right-click in the Hierarchy, choose 3D Object from the menu that appears, and select Ragdoll to open the Ragdoll Creator. (See the right screen in Figure 9-30.)

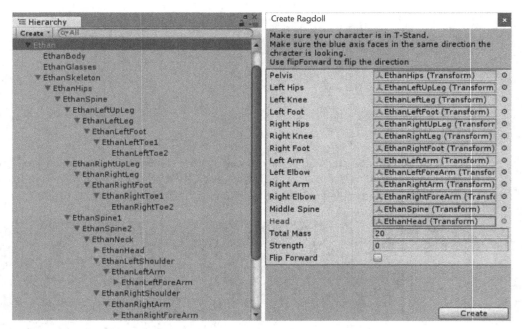

FIGURE 9-30 Ethan's hierarchy (left) and ragdoll configuration (right).

4. You'll use the Ragdoll Creator to associate Ethan's child items with the corresponding ragdoll items as follows. (Leave any other settings at their default values.) To associate a child item with a ragdoll item, you drag it from the Hierarchy to the corresponding box in the Ragdoll Creator.

- **Pelvis** EthanHips

- **Left Hips** EthanLeftUpLeg

- **Left Knee** EthanLeftLeg

- **Left Foot** EthanLeftFoot

- **Right Hips** EthanRightUpLeg

- **Right Knee** EthanRightLeg

- **Left Arm** EthanLeftArm

- **Left Elbow** EthanLeftForeArm

- **Right Arm** EthanRightArm

- **Right Elbow** EthanRightForeArm

- **Middle Spine** EthanSpine

- **Head** EthanHead

5. Click the **Create** button.

6. Click the **Start** button in the toolbar to run the app again. This time, when the app starts, Ethan will begin to fall (see Figure 9-31) until he finally lands on the plane (see Figure 9-32). Note that his movement appears very realistic because he bounces off of all obstacles.

7. Change Ethan's initial position. Notice that his movement changes accordingly.

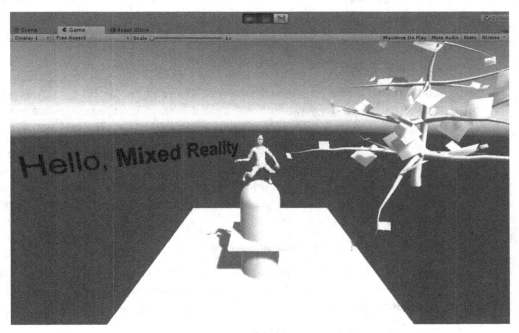

FIGURE 9-31 The Ethan ragdoll hits the custom 3D object.

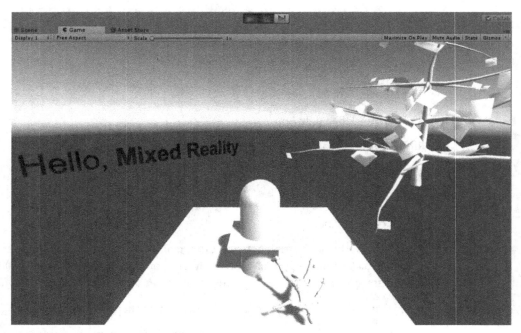

FIGURE 9-32 The Ethan ragdoll falls on the plane.

Using Materials

So far, you've created several 3D objects. However, all these objects—except the 3D text object—are the same color. This is because they all use their default material. You can apply a different material to an object to change how its surfaces are rendered.

Let's explore materials by creating some to apply to the leaves on the tree object you assembled earlier in this chapter. To start, you need to import the appropriate textures for these materials into Unity. In this example you'll use textures from the environment package in the standard Unity assets. To import this package, open the Assets menu, choose Import Package, and select Environment. Then import all elements from that package.

Your next step is to create the materials. Here's how:

1. Create a new folder for the materials you are about to create. To do so, open the Project window and right-click the **Assets** folder. Then, in the menu that appears, choose the **Create** option and select **Folder**.

2. Name the new folder **Custom Materials**.

3. Click the **Custom Materials** folder to select it.

4. Open the **Assets** menu, choose **Create**, and select **Material**. This adds a new material to the Custom Materials folder.

5. Name the new material **LeavesMaterial**.

6. In the Inspector for the LeavesMaterial material, open the **Shader** drop-down list, and choose **Nature/Tree Creator Leaves Fast**.

7. In the Inspector, click the **Select** button on the texture slot (highlighted in blue) to open a Select Texture window. (See Figure 9-33.)

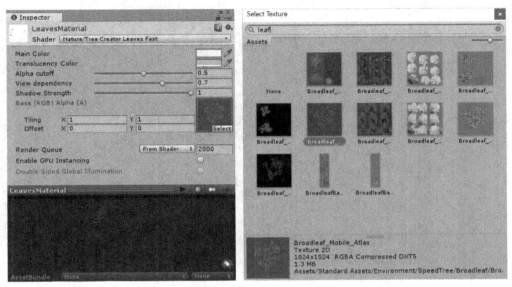

FIGURE 9-33 Creating a material for leaves using the Inspector for the material (left) and the Select Texture options (right).

8. In the Select Texture window, select the leaf texture you want to use. (I chose Broadleaf_Mobile_Atlas.)

9. Drag and drop the **LeavesMaterial** material onto your tree in the Scene view.

10. Optionally, adjust the number of leaves according to your preferences.

To make your tree look even more realistic, you can create a material for the bark. Follow these steps:

1. Select the **Assets/Custom Materials** folder in the Project window.

2. Open the **Assets** menu, choose **Create**, and select **Material** to create new material.

3. Name the new material **BarkMaterial**.

4. In the material's Inspector, change the **Shader** setting to **Nature/Tree Creator Bark**.

5. Select a base texture for the material. (I chose ConiferBark.)

6. Drag and drop the **BarkMaterial** material on the tree branches in the Scene view. Figure 9-34 shows the final version of my tree.

FIGURE 9-34 A tree with materials applied.

Your scene is starting to look pretty good. Let's make it even prettier by applying materials to other objects as follows:

1. Change the plane object to look like the ground. To do so, create a new material named **GroundMaterial**, change its **Shader** setting to **Unlit/Texture**, set its texture to **GrassRockyAlbedo**, and apply it to the plane.

2. Add a new material for your custom object (made from a cylinder, cube, and sphere) and name it **ObstacleMaterial**. Change its **Shader** setting to **Unlit/Texture**, set its texture to **MudRockyAlbedoSpecular**, and apply it to all elements composing the custom object.

3. Modify the material already applied to Ethan to change its color. To do so, open the Project window and type **EthanWhite** in the search box. Unity filters the list of assets to display only one. Click this item, switch to its Inspector, click the color box next to the **Albedo** setting, and choose any color you like from the color picker that appears. I've made Ethan cyan. (See Figure 9-35.)

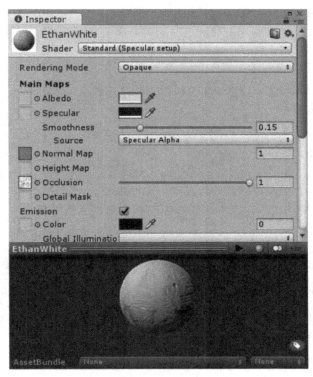

FIGURE 9-35 Properties of the modified Ethan material.

Applying Prefabs

Now that you've learned how to create and edit materials, let's investigate how to quickly reuse custom objects using prefabs. Unity defines *prefab* as a game object with associated components and properties. A tree, like the one you created earlier, is a good example of an object that can be converted into a prefab that you can use to quickly create a little forest. Here's how to do it:

1. In the Project window, open the **Assets** folder and create a new folder inside it called **Custom Prefabs**.

2. Open the Custom Prefabs folder.

3. Open the **Assets** menu, choose **Create**, and select **Prefab** to create a new prefab. It will appear under the Assets in the Project window.

4. Name the new prefab **Tree Prefab**.

5. Drag the tree object from the Hierarchy onto the **Tree Prefab** in the Project window. The prefab icon will change to show a miniature of the tree.

6. Drag the two instances of the new prefab from the Project window into the scene. The scene should now contain three trees.

7. Change the **Position** setting for the two new trees as follows:

    - **X: 8, Y: 0, Z: 1**

    - **X: 2, Y: 0, Z: 7**

8. Extend the plane so it will look like a larger area of ground. To do so, set the plane's **Scale** setting to **X: 5**, **Y: 5**, **Z: 5**.

Adding a Wind Zone

To make the scene even more exciting, try adding a wind zone. A wind zone is an object that makes trees sway in a realistic manner in the wind. (For more information, see http://bit.ly/wind_zone.) To see how the wind zone works, add one to your scene, just as you would any other object.

After you add the wind zone object to your scene, you can use the Inspector to set various parameters. (See Figure 9-36.) One such parameter is Mode, which enables you to set the wind mode. Options include the following:

- **Directional**   Choose this if you want the wind to appear to blow in a single direction.

- **Spherical**   Select this if you want the wind to appear to blow inside the sphere of a given radius (set via the Radius parameter).

You can also set the wind strength using the following parameters:

- **Main**   This setting refers to the primary wind force, which changes slowly over time.

- **Turbulence**   This setting creates a wind force that changes rapidly.

- **Pulse Magnitude**   You use this setting to specify the amplitude of wind changes over time. The larger the value here, the more the trees sway.

- **Pulse Frequency**   This setting determines the frequency of wind changes over time. The smaller the frequency, the faster the trees will sway.

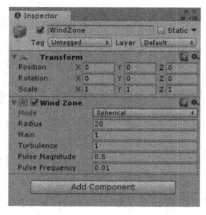

FIGURE 9-36 The Inspector for the wind zone object.

Tip Try experimenting with these parameters and adjusting them to your needs. To see real-time updates of the wind parameters, click the Start button to enter preview mode. Then use the Inspector to modify parameters and see how they affect the way your trees sway.

Physical Reality versus Performance Tradeoffs

Typically, the more realistic the physical simulation of an object is, the higher the computational needs. So be patient when adjusting parameters of various components. Generally, improving app performance means slightly decreasing the app's level of realism.

Building and Deploying the Project

With your scene ready, you can now build your project, UnityBasics, and deploy it to a Windows Mixed Reality device—either the HoloLens emulator or a Windows Mixed Reality headset. In general, the build process involves two steps. First, you build the project in the Unity. This creates a Visual Studio solution. Then, you compile this solution and deploy to the selected target device. With the use of some additional tools, discussed later in this chapter, you can simplify this general build process.

Building the Project

To build a project in Unity, open the File menu and choose Build Settings or press the Ctrl+Shift+B keyboard shortcut to open the Build Settings window. (See Figure 9-37.) Then, in the Build Settings window, follow these steps:

1. Click the **Add Open Scenes** button. This ensures your scene will be included in the build.

2. In the **Platform** list, click **Universal Windows Platform**. Then click the **Switch Platform** button to change the current platform to UWP.

3. Ensure that the **Build Type** drop-down list is set to **D3D**.

4. Ensure that the **SDK** drop-down list is set to **Latest Installed**.

5. Click the **Player Settings** button to open the PlayerSettings Inspector window. (See Figure 9-38.)

6. Click the **Other Settings** option to expand it and, in the Configuration group, click the **Scripting Backend** drop-down list. The scripting backend is a framework you use to implement logic. When developing for UWP, you can choose from two scripting backends:

   - **.NET** This uses the Microsoft .NET Framework and produces the Visual C# UWP project.

   - **IL2CPP** This extends the capabilities of the .NET scripting backend. IL2CPP converts the IL code into C++ code. So, it produces the Visual C++ UWP project.

   In this case, choose the **.NET** option. (See the left screen in Figure 9-38.)

7. Click the **XR Settings** option to expand it and select the **Virtual Reality Supported** checkbox.

 Note XR stands for X Reality. This is a slightly more general term than Mixed Reality (MR). XR includes all technologies, both hardware and software, that enable the creation of VR, AR, and MR experiences. Sometimes XR is defined as an umbrella term for VR, AR, and MR.

8. Make sure the **Virtual Reality SDKs** list contains a **Windows Mixed Reality** entry. If not, click the **plus** button and choose **Windows Mixed Reality** to add it. (See the right screen in Figure 9-38.) The Windows Mixed Reality SDK enables a stereoscopic preview and head tracking. In other words, you do not need to implement stereoscopy or head tracking separately.

9. Click the **Build** button in the Build Settings window.

10. Select a folder to contain the build—for example, the **UnityBasicsBuild** folder—and click **Select Folder**. The build process starts. The app may take a while to build.

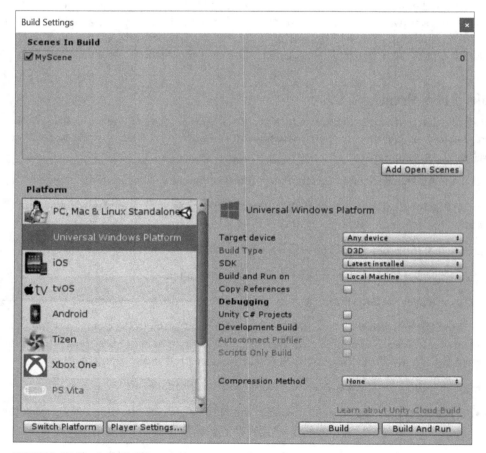

FIGURE 9-37 The Build Settings window.

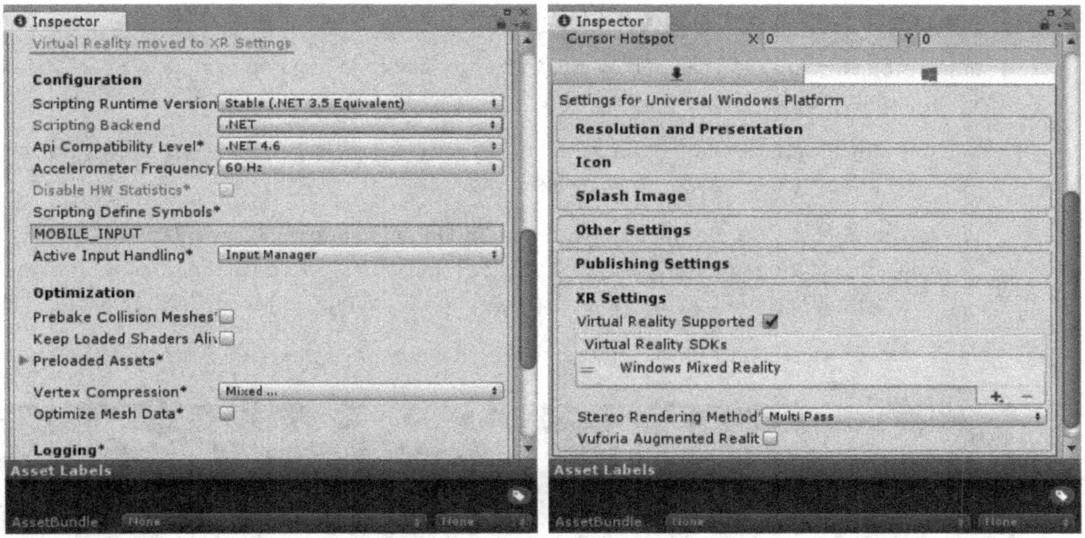

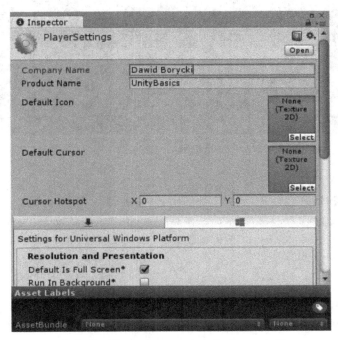

FIGURE 9-38 Two views of the PlayerSettings Inspector window.

The PlayerSettings Inspector window enables you to configure many more app details. Specifically, you can set the company and product name, default icon, splash screen, app capabilities, and so on. (See Figure 9-39.)

FIGURE 9-39 Setting the company and product name in the PlayerSettings Inspector window.

Deploying to Immersive Headsets

After the project is built, you can deploy it to the target device. When deploying to immersive head-sets, you have two options for executing the app:

- Click the Play button in the Unity Editor. This will open the Windows Mixed Reality portal where, after a short while, your app will be executed.

- Open the Visual Studio solution generated by Unity, change the target platform to either x86 or x64, and set the target device to the local machine. Then proceed in the same way as when you deployed 2D apps—by opening the app through the Windows Mixed Reality portal.

Regardless of which method you choose, the result will be the same. (See Figure 9-40.)

FIGURE 9-40 The UnityBasics app running in the Mixed Reality simulator.

Deploying to a HoloLens

You use Visual Studio to deploy to a HoloLens emulator. First, change the platform to x86 and then choose HoloLens Emulator from the drop-down list. Then build and run the app. The app will be executed in the emulator. (See Figure 9-41.)

FIGURE 9-41 The UnityBasics app running in the HoloLens emulator.

Unity generates a Visual C# UWP project, so you can easily deploy the app to any other UWP device. Figure 9-42 shows the UnityBasics app running in the Mobile emulator.

FIGURE 9-42 The UnityBasics app in the Mobile emulator.

When you run the app in the HoloLens emulator, you will notice two issues related to the default camera settings:

- The default skybox is visible and will hide real objects if the app is executed in a real device with see-through display (HoloLens).

- The field of view is much smaller than with the immersive headset simulator, so you can only see a small part of the scene. To see more elements of the scene, press the D key on the keyboard to move the viewer back.

To address the first issue, you change the following camera settings in the Inspector. (See Figure 9-43.)

- Change the **Clear Flags** setting to **Solid Color**.

- Click the Background color option to open a color picker and set all the color components (R, G, B, and A) to 0.

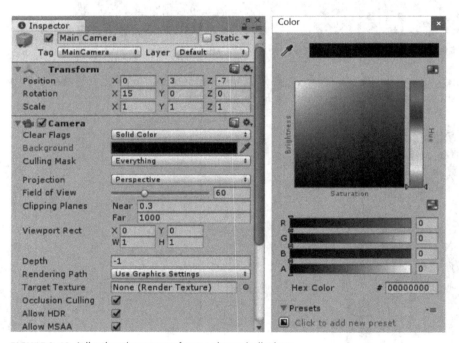

FIGURE 9-43 Adjusting the camera for see-through displays.

Note You'll learn how solve the second issue, related to FoV, later in this chapter.

Using Holographic Emulation

You can adjust the camera position iteratively, but this is time-consuming and inefficient. Instead, use holographic simulation, part of the Unity Editor's holographic emulation feature. Holographic emulation reduces the iterative build process for HoloLens because it enables you to preview your app directly in the Unity Editor or to automatically deploy it to real a device. (For more information, see http://bit.ly/holographic_emulation.) When you click the Play button, the app is executed in the Game view (holographic simulation) or in the real device (holographic remoting).

To enable and employ holographic emulation, follow these steps:

1. Open the **Window** menu in the Unity menu bar and choose **Holographic Emulation** to open the Holographic window.

2. The Holographic window contains an Emulation Mode setting. (See Figure 9-44.) The options for this setting are as follows. (Note that when you choose an option for the Emulation Mode setting other than None, the Holographic window changes to include additional parameters.)

    • **None**   Select this option to disable holographic emulation.

    • **Remote to Device**   When you choose this option, the app will be executed in the HoloLens device. To enable this mode, you must install and run Remoting Player on the headset. (For more information, see http://bit.ly/remoting_player.) Then, in the Holographic Emulation window, enter the IP for your device and click the Connect button.

    • **Simulate in Editor**   When you choose this option, the app will be executed in the Unity Editor in the same way as in the HoloLens emulator. To configure this mode, choose one of the available rooms from the Room list and select the Right Hand option for the Gesture Hand setting. The Room list enables you to choose one of the available spatial mapping meshes (see Chapter 12 for more details), while the Gesture Hand setting lets you define which hand is used to simulate air gestures.

3. Choose **Simulate in Editor**.

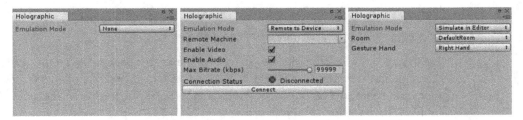

FIGURE 9-44 Configuring holographic emulation in Unity.

4. To use holographic simulation to view the app, click the **Play** button. The Game view will show a preview of the app. Notice that the time it takes to display the app is much less than when deploying an app through Visual Studio.

You can now use this mode to investigate what happens to the camera settings when the app is executed in holographic simulation mode. Follow these steps:

1. Stop the preview mode.

2. Click the **Main Camera** entry in the Hierarchy.

3. After ensuring that the Inspector shows the properties of the main camera object, click the **Play** button. Notice that several camera properties, including Transform and Field of View, change during the runtime. Specifically, the Field of View value is reduced from 60 to 17.

4. Stop the preview mode and change the value for the **Field of View** setting to **17**.

5. Adjust the Transform value. After a bit of trial and error, I settled on the following parameters:

   - **Position**   X: 4.5, Y: 6, Z: –20

   - **Rotation**   X: 15, Y: –12, Z: 0

6. Rebuild the app in Unity and rerun it in the HoloLens simulator through Visual Studio. (You will need to reload the solution.) Notice that the initial view now shows more elements of the scene. (Refer to Figure 9-1.)

Mixed Reality Toolkit for Unity

Chapter 2 introduced the Mixed Reality Toolkit. This chapter shows you how to install it in Unity. You'll use this toolkit in the chapters that follow.

To install the Mixed Reality Toolkit for Unity, follow these steps:

1. Download the toolkit package from http://bit.ly/mrtk_release. At the time of this writing, the current version of this package was HoloToolkit-Unity-2017.2.1.4. (It is attached to the companion code in the Chapter_09/MixedRealityToolkit folder.)

2. In Unity, open the **Assets** menu, choose **Import Package**, and select **Custom Package**.

3. Select the package you just downloaded for import.

4. The Import Unity Package window opens. Unity parses the package and displays a list of its components in the window. (See Figure 9-45.) Make sure all the components are selected and then click the **Import** button. When the package is imported, the Mixed Reality Toolkit for Unity will be ready for use in your projects.

FIGURE 9-45 Installing the Mixed Reality Toolkit for Unity.

3D Models

Unity lets you import 3D models created with various modeling software, including the following:

- 3D Builder
- 3D Studio Max
- Blender
- Maya
- Cinema 4D
- 3ds Max
- Cheetah3D
- Modo
- Lightwave
- SketchUp

You can also import models from various online repositories. This section shows you how to import 3D models from a 3D Builder library of models provided by Microsoft and from CGtrader.com.

To import models from the 3D Builder library, follow these steps:

1. Create a new Unity project named **ExternalModels**.

2. Open the 3D Builder library of models, available at http://bit.ly/3DBuilder_models.

3. Select and download any model you like. (I chose the Shuttle model, from the featured group.)

4. You cannot import the downloaded file, which has a .3mf file extension, directly to Unity. Before you can import it, you use 3D Builder to save the file with an .obj extension. To do so, open the file in 3D Builder. Then click the **File** menu (it looks like a hamburger) and choose **Save As**.

5. The Save As dialog box opens; choose a folder in which to store your file and change the **Save as Type** setting to **OBJ Format**. Then click **Save**.

6. Now you can import the model into Unity. In the Unity Editor, open the **Assets** menu, choose **Import New Asset**, locate and select the model (with the .obj extension), and click **Import**. Unity adds the model to the assets of whatever project you have open.

7. Drag the model into the Scene view. (See Figure 9-46.)

FIGURE 9-46 A 3D Builder model imported to the Unity scene.

To import models from CGtrader.com, you must first sign up for an account with the site. You can do so here: http://bit.ly/cgtrader_registration. CGtrader.com provides models in several different formats, including 3D Studio Max, Autodesk FBX, and OBJ. If you select the OBJ format, you can import the model directly into Unity and add it to the scene as you did in steps 6 and 7 in the preceding numbered list. To import and work with one of these models, follow these steps:

1. Decide which model you want to import. I chose the SciFiFighter model (http://bit.ly/SciFiFighter_model).

2. Click the **Free Download** button.

3. If prompted, sign in to your account. After you do, the download process will begin.

4. The downloaded file will be an RAR archive, containing a model (OBJ file) and textures (three JPEG files). Import all these files to Unity as assets.

5. Add the model to the scene as you would any other object.

6. Use the Unlit/Texture shader to create the materials. Your model should be similar to that shown in Figure 9-47.

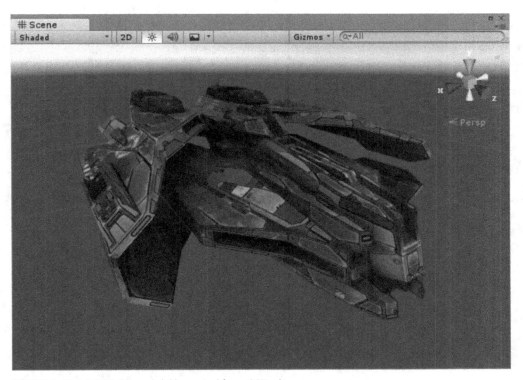

FIGURE 9-47 A SciFiFighter model imported from CGTrader.com.

Summary

This chapter discussed using Unity to create 3D scenes for Windows Mixed Reality apps. You learned about fundamental Unity concepts and elements, including game objects, components, transforms, and primitive and complex 3D objects. Then you investigated how to control the visual appearance of the objects in a scene by using materials and how to apply ragdoll physical effects to a character so it can move. This chapter also covered the deployment of 3D apps to a HoloLens emulator and an immersive headset simulator. Finally, it presented approaches for importing complex models created in 3D modeling software. In the next chapter, you will learn how to write scripts and manually implement physics to make your scenes dynamic.

CHAPTER 10

Physics and Scripting

Chapter 9 explored various 3D objects available in Unity. In this chapter, you'll learn how to turn those objects into elements that can interact with each other. The Unity physics engine—built on top of Nvidia PhysX—governs the interaction of elements. With the Unity game engine, all game objects move and collide realistically. Without realizing it, you used the Unity physics engine in Chapter 9 to create a ragdoll.

In this chapter, you will investigate how to put 3D objects under the control of the physics engine using Rigidbody components. After that, you will learn how to create colliders so rigid bodies can obstruct each other. Then, you'll use the Physic Material to create bouncy rigid bodies. You'll also learn how to create custom components with C#. You'll use these scripts to control game objects. In particular, you'll create a HitTheCanGame app. (See Figures 10-1 and 10-2.) This app contains several 3D elements, including a plane, a pyramid made of cola cans created with primitive cylinders, and two cubes with spike balls on top of them. It also uses a script that responds to user input. Every time the user presses the touchpad, presses the thumbstick on a Windows Mixed Reality motion controller, or makes a select gesture, he or she will throw a ball toward the scene, which will eventually either break the pyramid or, if it hits one of the cubes containing a spike ball, explode. (See Figure 10-2.) Along the way, you'll learn about collision detection, triggers, and explosions, as well as how to handle input from interaction sources such as voice, gesture, and motion controllers. Finally, you'll analyze the Unity API to determine how to detect the headset model and to explore debugging techniques.

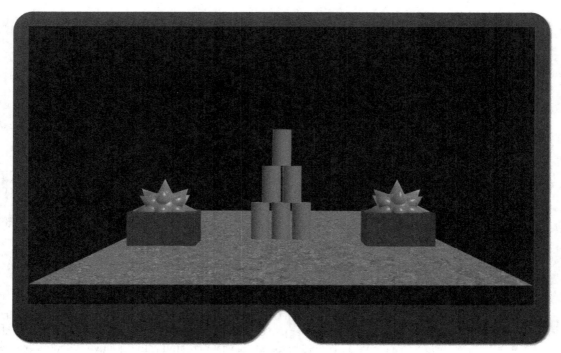

FIGURE 10-1 Initial view of the HitTheCanGame app in the HoloLens emulator.

FIGURE 10-2 The HitTheCanGame app running in the Windows Mixed Reality simulator.

Rigidbody

Rigidbody is a Unity component that controls the position of a game object through physics simulation. This component can quickly turn your static game objects into a dynamic element that can interact with the environment in which it is embedded. For example, if you add a Rigidbody component to a sphere, it will behave like a ball and bounce around the scene. In Chapter 9, you unknowingly used Rigidbody components when you created a ragdoll. In this section, you will learn how to manually add a Rigidbody to the game object. To do this, first create a new 3D Unity project named HitTheCanGame. Then open the Inspector for the main camera object and adjust its properties for the HoloLens emulator as outlined in Table 10-1.

TABLE 10-1 Settings for the Main Camera Object

Inspector group	Setting name	Setting value
Transform	Position	X: 0 Y: 0 Z: 0
Transform	Rotation	X: 0 Y: 0 Z: 0
Transform	Scale	X: 0 Y: 0 Z: 0
Camera	Clear Flags	Solid Color
Camera	Background	R: 0 B: 0 G: 0 A: 0
Camera	Field of View	17
Camera	Clipping Planes	Near: 0.85 Far: 1000

After you configure the camera, let's start building the scene. In general, when you build an app, you can use assets from the Asset Store. However, due to license restrictions, I cannot take screenshots of an app utilizing those assets.

To import a 3D model from the Asset Store, follow these steps:

1. Open the **Window** menu and choose **Asset Store** or click the **Asset Store** tab in the Scene view to open the Asset Store.

2. Type **can** in the search box and then use the Price slider to find **Free Only** assets.

3. A list of free can models appears. (See Figure 10-3.) Locate and select the **Cola Can** package.

4. A full description of the package appears. (See Figure 10-4.) Click the **Import** button. Then, in the Import Unity Package window, select all elements in the package and click **Import** again.

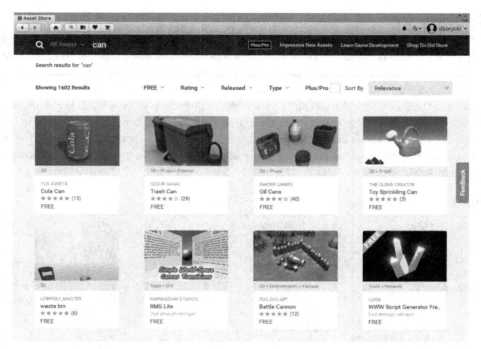

FIGURE 10-3 Can models in the Unity Asset Store.

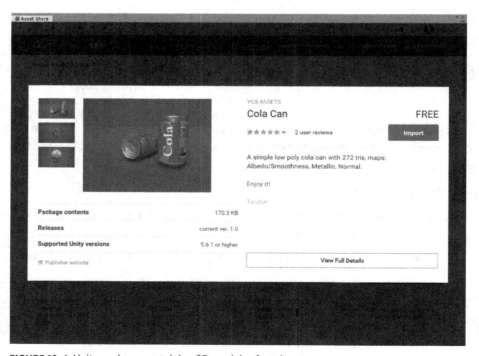

FIGURE 10-4 Unity package containing 3D models of a cola can.

To add the imported can model to the scene, follow these steps:

1. In the search box in the Project window, type **can t:Model** to view assets whose names contain the word can and are of type model.

2. The search returns just one model: cola_can. Click the **cola_can** model and drag it onto the scene.

As you proceed, you can use this cola_can model. However, due to the restrictions I mentioned earlier, I will use a plain cylinder instead.

> **Note** If you decide to use the cola_can model, you will need to eventually use different X, Y, and Z values for object transforms. This is because the primitive cylinder has different dimensions than the cola_can model.

Now I will tell you how to add the cylinder, format it, and then use it to create a Rigidbody.

1. Use the Hierarchy to add the cylinder to the scene.

2. Using the Inspector, change the cylinder's name to **cola_can**.

3. Modify the **X**, **Y**, and **Z Position** components in the **Transform** group to **0**, **0.5**, and **3**, respectively.

4. Set the **Scale** component to **0.06** along each direction.

5. In the **Project** window, right-click **Assets**, choose **Create**, and select **Folder** to create a new folder. Change the folder's name to **Materials**.

6. Click the **Assets** menu and expand the **Create** list.

7. Locate and select the **Material** entry and change its name to **Red**.

8. Click the material you just created and open its **Inspector**.

9. Select the **Albedo** color box. In the Color pop-up that appears, set the **R**, **G**, **B**, and **A** color components to **255**, **0**, **0**, and **255**, respectively.

10. Drag the **Red** material from the Project window onto the cylinder.

11. The object is ready, but it is still static. To set it up to move, you need to add a Rigidbody component. To do so, click the **Add Component** button in the Inspector of the cylinder.

12. A drop-down menu with a hierarchical list of available components opens. Do one of the following:

    - Locate and select the **Rigidbody** component in the **Physics** category.

    - Type **rigid** in the search box at the top of the menu and select the Rigidbody component in the list of search results. (See Figure 10-5.)

FIGURE 10-5 Adding a Rigidbody component to the cola_can object.

The Rigidbody component is added to the cola_can model and its configurable parameters are displayed in the inspector. As Figure 10-6 shows, these include the following:

- **Mass** This is the mass of the object, expressed in kilograms. This parameter determines how the object will collide with other objects.

> **Note** According to the Unity documentation, the size of an object is more important than its mass. If you notice that an object does not move naturally, you will most likely need to adjust its size.

- **Drag** This controls the air resistance when the object is moved by force (push). The larger the value, the higher the air resistance—and the more the object will slow down. If you set Drag to 0 the object will face no air resistance and will not slow down at all.

- **Angular Drag** This controls the air resistance when the object is rotating due to torque. As with the Drag setting, the larger the Angular Drag value, the higher the air resistance.

- **Use Gravity** This specifies whether the object will be affected by gravity. If you select this option, the object will behave like any physical object according to Newton's law of universal gravitation. When an object falls, its Y-axis value decreases.

- **Is Kinematic** This specifies whether the object is kinematic. The kinematic body is the game object, whose position is controlled by the physics engine. Kinematic bodies can also collide with other game objects.

- **Interpolate** This specifies how the physical effects are smoothed. Options are as follows:

- **None**   No interpolation is applied.

- **Interpolate**   The object's transform will be smoothed based on the transform from the previous frame.

- **Extrapolate**   The object's transform will be smoothed based on the estimated transform for the next frame.

- **Collision Detection**   This specifies the collision-detection mode. You use this setting to prevent fast-moving objects from passing through other objects. Options are as follows:

  - **Discrete**   This option—the default—offers the fastest collision detection. However, collisions are evaluated at fixed time intervals, which means fast-moving objects could pass through rigid bodies with mesh colliders.

  - **Continuous**   With continuous collision detection, collisions are detected for any static mesh geometry. In this mode, fast-moving objects will not pass through rigid bodies with static mesh geometry.

  - **Continuous Dynamic**   Continuous dynamic collision detection requires extensive physical computation and is therefore the slowest collision-detection mode. This mode is recommended only for those objects that require the most realistic effects possible. It extends continuous collision detection by preventing rigid bodies from passing through other rigid bodies that have continuous collision detection enabled.

- **Constraints**   This setting enables you to disable movement (Freeze Position) or rotation changes (Freeze Rotation) applied by the physics engine along selected axes.

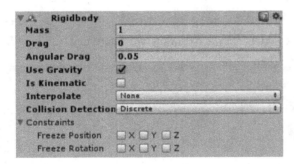

FIGURE 10-6 Default settings of the Rigidbody component.

Let's investigate how these properties work in practice:

1. Select the **Use Gravity** checkbox.

2. Click the **Start** button. In Game view, the cola can falls and disappears because there is no obstacle to stop it.

In the next section, you will add a plane to the scene and learn how to use colliders to stop the can. Once these are configured, you will also be able to investigate other properties of the Rigidbody component.

Colliders

Colliders are Unity components that simulate physical collisions. These invisible components define the shape that determines how an associated object will obstruct the movement of other game objects. Quite often, a collider has a much simpler shape than the object with which it is associated. This is to improve performance. The fact that it is a rough approximation of the object's shape is usually undetectable during runtime.

3D Primitive Colliders

Unity provides the following types of 3D primitive colliders:

- **Box**   This is a cube-shaped collider. To configure this collider, you can change its center position and size (along each direction) in the associated object's local space.

- **Sphere**   This is a sphere-shaped collider. You configure it much as you do a box collider, but a sphere collider has a uniform size along each direction, determined by the radius property.

- **Capsule**   This collider is shaped like a cylinder with two half-spheres on either end. In addition to the Center property (which works the same as for the box and the sphere), you can use the following parameters to control a capsule collider:

  - **Radius**   This specifies the width of the collider.

  - **Height**   This sets the height of the collider.

  - **Direction**   This specifies the orientation of the collider in the object's local space. It can be along the x-axis, the y-axis, or the z-axis.

In addition, each of the preceding colliders has the following two properties:

- **Is Trigger**   This indicates whether the collider is raising events instead of registering collisions. If so, the collider will be ignored by the Unity physics engine.

- **Material**   This specifies the Physic Material, which further adjusts the friction and bounciness of the collider.

Mesh Colliders

Primitive colliders might not work well for complex objects. In such cases it's better to use a mesh collider. A mesh collider is constructed based on the mesh of the object, so it precisely matches the object's shape. Like primitive colliders, you can configure mesh colliders using the Is Trigger and Material properties. In addition, mesh colliders have two other configurable options:

- **Mesh**   This specifies the mesh representing a collider.

- **Convex**   This determines whether the collider is convex. You use this property to enable collisions with other mesh colliders.

Using Colliders

The cylinder already has a primitive capsule collider assigned to it (refer to Figure 10-5), so let's explore how to use mesh colliders. Follow these steps:

1. Add a plane to the scene.

2. Using the plane's Inspector, configure the plane's Transform settings as follows:

    - **Position**   X: 0, Y: −0.25, Z: 3.5

    - **Rotation**   X: 0, Y: 0, Z: 0

    - **Scale**   X: 0.1, Y: 0.1, Z: 0.3

3. Let's change the material applied to the plane to the SandAlbedo texture. To start, you must import the texture. Open the **Assets** menu, choose **Import Package**, and select **Environment**. Then, in the Project window, type **SandAlbedo t:Texture** in the search box. Finally, locate and select the SandAlbedo texture in the list of results and drag it onto the plane. The plane will look like sandy ground.

4. Open the **Shader** drop-down list in the **SandAlbedo** component in the Inspector and choose Unlit/Texture. (See Figure 10-7.) This way, the texture will not use lighting.

FIGURE 10-7 The plane Inspector with the Transform and SandAlbedo components expanded.

From Figure 10-7 you see that that the plane object has an associated mesh collider component. If you open the Inspector of the cola_can object, you will see that it has an associated capsule collider (refer to Figure 10-5). So, both objects will collide. The cola_can imported from the Asset Store does not have associated colliders. In this case the can will pass through the plane. To fix this, you need to add a mesh collider to the cola_can object. To do so, follow these steps:

1. Open the Inspector for the cola_can object.

2. Click the **Add Component** button and locate and select the **Mesh Collider** option.

3. In the mesh collider's Inspector, set the **Convex** property to **True**. (Otherwise, the cola_can object will pass through the plane, as both objects use a mesh collider.)

You can now click Play to verify that the cola_can object is stopped by the plane. (See Figure 10-8.)

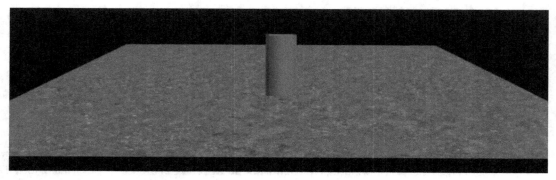

FIGURE 10-8 The cola can on the plane.

> **Tip** At this point it is also instructive to play with the parameters for the Rigidbody component associated with the cola_can object to see how they affect how the can falls.

To conclude this section let's compare the mesh collider with the primitive box collider. Follow these steps:

1. Open the Inspector for the plane object and deselect the **Mesh Collider** checkbox.

2. Click the **Add Component** button and choose **Box Collider** from the drop-down list.

3. Click **Play**. Notice that nothing really changes because the box collider effectively approximates the plane.

4. Change the box collider's **Y Size** setting to **3** and click **Play**. Notice that the physics change significantly, with the can stopping far above the plane. Although the box collider is invisible, the physics engine treats it as an obstacle for the can.

5. To undo these changes, revert the **Y Size** component to **0**, disable the box collider, and re-enable the mesh collider.

Physic Material

You just learned how to use colliders to stop the can's gravity-induced fall. Notice, however, that the can lands hard on the plane. From everyday experience, you know that a can should lightly bounce after it hits the ground. To emulate these effects, Unity provides the Physic Material feature. In this section, you will apply the Physic Material to the can so it will land softly.

Note Unity omits the "s" in Physic to distinguish Physic Material (which works in 3D) from its 2D Physics Material feature.

Physic Material can emulate two effects:

- **Bounciness** Bounciness describes elasticity of the surface. For instance, a ball is more elastic than a stone. Hence, a ball should bounce more after being occluded by another rigid body.

- **Friction** Friction prevents relative motion between objects. Unity defines two types of friction and allows you to adjust the levels of both:

  - **Dynamic** This type of friction applies when objects are moving. For example, it slows down objects when they collide.

  - **Static** This type of friction applies when objects are not moving. For example, high static friction will prevent movement of two stacked ice blocks.

To create the Physic Material for the can, proceed as follows:

1. Create a new folder in the Assets folder of the Project window. Name the new folder **Physic Materials**.

2. Select the **Physic Materials** folder, open the **Assets** menu, and choose **Physic Material**. A new material appears in the Project window.

3. Name this new material **Can Physic Material**.

4. Click the **Can Physic Material** item to view its settings in the Inspector. As shown in Figure 10-9, it has the following configurable properties:

   - **Dynamic Friction** This specifies the level of dynamic friction. A value of 0 means no friction (for objects with polished surfaces—for example, ice), while 1 means maximum friction (for rough objects).

   - **Static Friction** This sets the level of static friction. Again, values range from 0 (none) to 1 (maximum).

   - **Bounciness** This determines the elasticity of the object. A value of 0 works for non-elastic objects (such as a stone), while a value of 1 applies for elastic objects (such as a ball).

   - **Friction Combine and Bounce Combine** These options establish how the friction and bounciness of two colliding objects will be combined to achieve the resultant value. There are four choices:

     Average When you select this option, the values for the two objects are averaged.

     Minimum When you select this option, the smaller of the two values is used.

     Maximum When you select this option, the larger of the two values is used.

     Multiply When you select this option, the values for the two objects are multiplied.

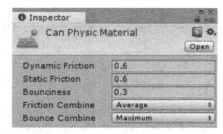

FIGURE 10-9 The Inspector for the Can Physic Material.

By default, the Dynamic Friction and Static Friction values for a new Physic Material are set to 0.6, the Bounciness value is set to 0, and the Friction Combine and Bounce Combine values are set to Average.

5. Change the **Bounciness** setting to **0.3**.

6. Change the **Bounce Combine** setting to **Maximum**.

7. To associate the Physic Material with the capsule collider for the cola_can object, open the cola_can Inspector. Then in the **Capsule Collider** group, click the icon (a small circle with dot in the middle) to the right of the **Material** box.

8. The Select PhysicMaterial window appears. (See the left screen in Figure 10-10.) Click the **Can Physic Material** entry. Notice that the Material setting in the Capsule Collider group in the Inspector changes accordingly. (See the right screen in Figure 10-10.)

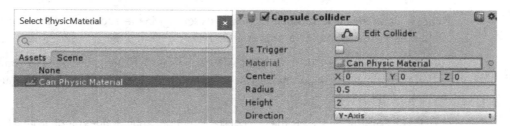

FIGURE 10-10 Associating the Physic Material with the capsule collider.

9. Click **Start**. Notice that the can hits the plane and bounces for a while before it stabilizes.

10. Experiment with the Can Physic Material's **Bounciness** value to see how it affects the can's behavior. A high value (0.9 or 1) will likely cause the can to fall off the plane after a few bounces.

Scripting

So far, you've learned how to create many interesting physical effects without writing even a single line of code. Everything was controlled by the Unity physics engine and configured with adjustable parameters. In this section, you'll learn how to create scripts to implement custom components to control the interaction between various objects in the scene. First, however, you'll build a pyramid of cola_can models. This pyramid will serve as the basis for the HitTheCanGame app.

Creating the Can Pyramid

To create the can pyramid, you will restore the original cylinder scale because that will make it easier to position the various cylinders that represent cans. Then, you will group all the cans together and rescale them at once. Along the way you will also learn the difference between the capsule collider and the mesh collider when they are applied to the cylinder.

Follow these steps to create the can pyramid:

1. Click the **cola_can** object in the Hierarchy.

2. In the **Transform** group of the Inspector, set the **Position** properties as follows:

   - **X: 0**
   - **Y: 0.75**
   - **Z: 3**

3. Set the scale uniformly for each direction (X, Y, Z) from **0.06** to **1**.

4. In the **Capsule Collider** group, click the icon to the right of the **Material** box to open the Select PhysicMaterial window. Then, in the Select PhysicMaterial window, choose **None**.

5. Add the mesh collider component and disable it by deselecting the checkbox to its left in the Hierarchy. (You will restore it later.)

6. In the Hierarchy, create five duplicates of the cola can, so you have six in all.

   To create a duplicate, you have several options:

   - Right-click the can and choose **Copy** and **Paste**.
   - Right-click the object and choose **Duplicate.**
   - Select the can and use the **Ctrl+C** and **Ctrl+V** shortcut keys.

   The duplicate cans will automatically be named cola_can (1), cola_can (2), and so on.

7. Change the **Position** property in the **Transform** group for each can as follows:

   - **Cola_can (1)**   X: 1.10, Y: 0.75, Z: 3
   - **Cola_can (2)**   X: –1.10, Y: 0.75, Z: 3
   - **Cola_can (3)**   X: 0.55, Y: 2.75, Z: 3
   - **Cola_can (4)**   X: –0.55, Y: 2.75, Z: 3
   - **Cola_can (5)**   X: 0, Y: 4.75, Z: 3

8. Right-click in the Hierarchy and choose **Create Empty** from the menu that appears.

9. Using the Inspector, rename this new object **CanPyramid** and set its position so **X** is **0**, **Y** is **0**, and **Z** is **0**.

10. Go back to Hierarchy, select all **cola_can** objects, and drag them below the **CanPyramid** object. The Hierarchy should look as shown in Figure 10-11.

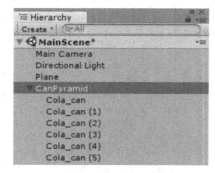

FIGURE 10-11 The Hierarchy for HitTheCanGame.

11. Click the **CanPyramid** object and, in the **Transform** group of the Inspector, set its position as follows:

   - **X: 0**

   - **Y: –0.25**

   - **Z: 3**

12. In the Scale group of the Inspector, set each property to **0.06**.

13. Click **Play**. Your scene should look like the one shown in Figure 10-12.

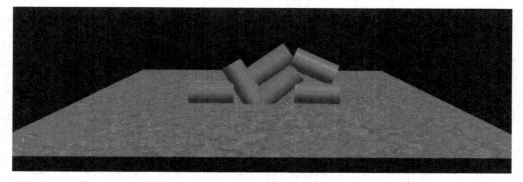

FIGURE 10-12 The can pyramid does not behave as expected.

After you click Play, the can pyramid is demolished. This is because the capsule collider does not precisely match the shape of the cylinder. To fix this you need to disable the capsule collider for each cola_can object and then enable and configure the mesh collider. Proceed as follows:

1. Select all **cola_can** objects in the Hierarchy.

2. In the Inspector, deselect the Capsule Collider option.

3. Select the **Mesh Collider** option and select the corresponding **Convex** checkbox.

4. Click **Play**. You will see that can pyramid is now stable. (See Figure 10-13.)

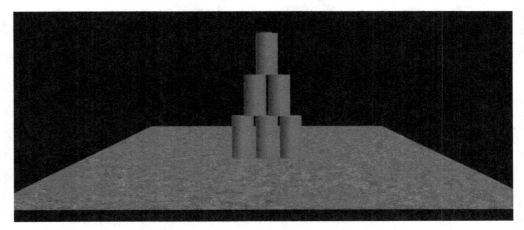

FIGURE 10-13 The can pyramid becomes stable after choosing the right collider.

Creating a Script

The script component, also known as simply the script, is a custom component that you can implement with C# or UnityScript. (UnityScript is a JavaScript-inspired custom programing language for Unity.) You can also invoke external code from .NET class libraries. In this section, you will learn how to create the script for the main camera object. (Later, you will implement this script to create the functionality described earlier: hitting the cans with balls.) Follow these steps:

1. Create a new folder in the Assets folder of the Project window. Name the new folder **Scripts**.

2. Select the **Scripts** folder. Then open the **Assets** menu, choose **Create**, and select **C# Script**.

3. Name the new script **HitTheCan**.

4. To associate the HitTheCan script with the main camera, first click the **Main Camera** entry in the Hierarchy.

5. Click the **Add Component** button in the Inspector for the main camera, type **hit**, and choose the **Hit The Can** component in the list. (See Figure 10-14.)

FIGURE 10-14 Associating the script component with the main camera object in the Inspector.

Script Structure

So far, you've created the script and associated it with the camera object. To edit the script, double-click the script in the Project window. Visual Studio 2017 will open. Use it to edit your script.

Note If you didn't install the Visual Studio Tools for Unity, double-clicking the script will open the source code editor. If you did install the Visual Studio Tools, but Visual Studio 2017 did not open when you double-clicked the script, open the **Edit** menu and choose **Preferences** to open the Preferences dialog box. Then click the **External Tools** tab and review the **External Script Editor** setting. If the value for this option is not Visual Studio, select it in the menu.

The Solution Explorer shows the structure of the HitTheCanGame solution, which contains several projects. It also displays the contents of the HitTheCan script. Listing 10-1 contains the default form of this script. Notice that the Unity script is the C# class (of the same name as the script) that derives from the UnityEngine.MonoBehaviour class. This is the base class for every Unity script and provides many methods for controlling game objects.

LISTING 10-1 Default C# HitTheCan script

```
using UnityEngine;

public class HitTheCan : MonoBehaviour
{
```

```
    // Use this for initialization
    void Start()
    {
    }

    // Update is called once per frame
    void Update()
    {
    }
}
```

Unlike traditional applications, Unity scripts do not have an entry point from which the app is sequentially executed. Instead, functions implemented in Unity scripts are invoked during runtime. Listing 10-1 has two prototypes of such functions:

- **Start**   Unity invokes this right before the app begins. So, you typically use this method for any initialization.

- **Update**   Unity invokes this every time it renders a frame. You use this method to provide functionality for your component. To check when an Update method was last invoked, you read the deltaTime property of the Time class.

Declarations of these methods are provided by default, as they are most frequently used. However, MonoBehaviour also has several other methods you can use:

- **FixedUpdate**   Unlike Update, this method is called at fixed time intervals. You typically use FixedUpdate for controlling Rigidbody components.

- **LateUpdate**   This is invoked at fixed time intervals after all other Update methods. You can use this method to perform final adjustments.

- **OnGUI**   This is used to safely update values presented in UI controls.

Unity scripts can also use several physics events invoked during collisions. You'll learn about these later in this chapter in the "Collision Detection, Triggers, and Explosions" section. For now, you'll just use the FixedUpdate method with ray casting.

Ray Casting

Ray casting is a method of detecting objects in a scene with a virtual light beam. This works a bit like echolocation. Some animals use echolocation to assess the distance of various objects. With echolocation, the animal emits a sound wave and then listens for frequency changes as that sound wave bounces off nearby objects and returns to the animal. These frequency changes tell the animal how far away it is from these objects. Similarly, with ray casting, you send a virtual light ray to the scene. This virtual beam propagates the scene and can be virtually backscattered by objects in the scene.

Understanding Ray Casting

To cast the ray, you use the `Physics.Raycast` method. This method has several overloaded versions, but most of them accept the `UnityEngine.Ray` structure as the first input argument. Instances of the Ray structure represent light rays. A ray is an infinite line originating from a given point in 3D space toward the specified direction. Therefore, you can instantiate the Ray structure by providing two public arguments:

- **origin**   This indicates the point from which the ray originates.

- **direction**   This specifies the ray direction.

Both of these arguments are of type `UnityEngine.Vector3`, being abstract representations of three-dimensional vectors and points.

Often, you cast rays from the camera plane. In such situations, you will use one of the following static methods of the `Camera` class:

- **Camera.ScreenPointToRay**   This creates a ray that originates from a given point in the camera plane. Coordinates of this point are expressed in pixels.

- **Camera.ViewportToRay**   This also creates a ray that originates from a camera plane. However, in this case, the coordinates of this point are normalized—meaning they have values ranging from 0 (bottom left) to 1 (top right).

After you create the ray, you pass it to the `Physics.Raycast` method. This returns a Boolean value that indicates whether the ray hit any colliders in the scene. To obtain information about a given collider, you use the `hitInfo` argument of the `Physics.Raycast` method. This argument is of type `UnityEngine.RaycastHit`, and is marked by an `out` keyword. This means you need to declare a variable of type `RaycastHit` before passing it to the `Physics.Raycast` method as a reference. `RaycastHit` is a struct whose properties enable you to identify and interact with the collider. In most cases, you will use the following members of this struct:

- **point**   This indicates the impact location—where the ray hit the collider.

- **distance**   This specifies a distance between the ray origin and the impact location.

- **collider**   This is an instance of the collider that was hit.

- **rigidbody**   This is an instance of the Rigidbody associated with the collider.

- **transform**   This is the transform of the Rigidbody. This property stores the position, rotation, and scale (the same values you can edit with the Inspector) of the Rigidbody associated with the collider.

`Physics.Raycast` enables you to detect only one collider. If you want to detect more colliders, you use the `Physics.RaycastAll` method, which returns a collection of `RaycastHit` objects.

Using Ray Casting to Detect Cans in the Scene

This section shows you how to use ray casting to detect the cans in your scene. You will also add a virtual force to them so that after they are detected, they will move. To achieve this, you must extend the definition of the HitTheCan script with the helper method, called AddForceToHitTarget, in Listing 10-2.

LISTING 10-2 Adding force to the Rigidbody found by ray casting

```
void AddForceToHitTarget(Ray ray, float forceScaleFactor)
{
    RaycastHit hitTarget;

    if (Physics.Raycast(ray, out hitTarget))
    {
        var rigidbody = hitTarget.rigidbody;

        if (rigidbody != null)
        {
            rigidbody.AddForce(transform.forward * forceScaleFactor);
        }
    }
}
```

As you can see, this method accepts two arguments:

- **ray**   This is an in instance of the Ray structure.

- **forceScaleFactor**   The is the amount of force to be added to the hit target. The larger this factor, the more force will be added.

Given these arguments, AddForceToHitTarget proceeds as follows:

1. The ray is casted with the Physics.Raycast method.

2. Information about the hit target is retrieved and stored in the hitTarget local variable.

3. It reads the rigidbody property of the collider that was hit. If rigidbody is not null, it invokes the AddForce instance method to add force. This will move the can with the force given.

4. To define the force, you create a vector. The vector's orientation specifies force direction and its magnitude determines the force strength. In this case, the force orientation is the same as the camera orientation (the blue z-axis of the camera transform in the world space). Therefore, the script uses the forward property of the Transform class associated with the camera.

5. The forward property is of type Vector3 but now it represents the vector components. To get the Transform, the script reads the transform property of the current component, which is the camera (because the script is associated with the camera).

6. To control the vector magnitude, the script multiplies the resulting vector by the forceScaleFactor.

`Rigidbody.AddForce` has an additional, optional argument, which specifies the force mode. This is represented by one of the following values declared in the `UnityEngine.ForceMode` enumeration:

- **Force** This indicates that the force will be added continuously.

- **Acceleration** This specifies that the Rigidbody will be accelerated.

- **Impulse** This indicates that the force will be added instantly.

- **VelocityChange** This specifies that an instant velocity change will be added to the Rigidbody.

> **Note** Depending on the force mode, the physics engine will ignore (`Acceleration` and `VelocityChange`) or not ignore (`Force` and `Impulse`) the mass of the Rigidbody to perform physics simulations.

To invoke the `AddForceToHitTarget` method, you implement `FixedUpdate` from the HitTheCan script as shown in Listing 10-3.

LISTING 10-3 Creating a ray originating from the camera toward the pointer position

```
void FixedUpdate()
{
    if (Input.GetMouseButton(0))
    {
        var ray = GetComponent<Camera>().ScreenPointToRay(Input.mousePosition);

        AddForceToHitTarget(ray, 10);
    }
}
```

This script first uses the static `GetMouseButton` method of the `Input` class to check whether a mouse button is being pressed and returns `true` if so. Mouse buttons are represented by the following numbers, which you pass to the `GetMouseButton` method:

- **0** Left mouse button

- **1** Right mouse button

- **2** Middle mouse button.

If the left mouse button is pressed (argument 0 of the `GetMouseButton` method), the script creates the Ray structure using the `Camera.ScreenPointToRay` method. To set the Ray orientation, it also reads the `mousePosition` property of the `Input` class. This reveals the location of the cursor in the scene; the ray will go from the camera position toward that point. Hence, you can choose the can to which the force will be added when you play back the scene.

To obtain an instance of the Camera class, which represents the camera component associated with the current game object, the script uses the generic GetComponent method. GetComponent also has another non-generic version, which accepts the string with the component name.

To test this script, save it in Visual Studio and return to the Unity Editor. Click Play, place the mouse cursor over one of the cans, and press and hold the left mouse button. As force is applied to the can, it will start to shake, and will eventually fall if you hold the mouse button long enough. (See Figure 10-15.)

FIGURE 10-15 Adding force to Rigidbodies detected with ray casting.

You can apply the force to the can even after it falls. You can even move the fallen can outside the plane. I encourage you to play around a bit with the script. Try changing the forceScaleFactor value and supplementing the Rigidbody.AddForce method with additional arguments to try different force modes.

Projectiles

Let's create the ball the user will throw to hit the cans. These types of effects are commonly called projectiles. To start, you create a ball prefab, which will be instantiated from the script. Follow these steps:

1. Open the **Assets** menu, choose **Import Package**, and select **Prototyping** to import the Prototyping Unity asset.

2. Add a sphere to the scene.

3. Change the screen's **Scale** setting to **0.1** along each direction.

4. Add a Rigidbody component to the sphere.

5. Let's apply the YellowSmooth material to the sphere. To do so, type **YellowSmooth t:Material** in the Project window's search box. Then drag the **YellowSmooth** material onto the sphere.

6. Change the sphere's **Position** setting to **0** along each direction.

7. Open the **Assets** menu, choose **Create**, and select **Prefab** to create a prefab, and name it **Ball**.

8. Drag the **sphere** from the Hierarchy window to the **Ball.prefab** entry in the Project window. Your prefab should look like the one in Figure 10-16. If it does, remove the sphere from the scene.

FIGURE 10-16 The Project window showing the Ball.prefab item.

This prefab will serve as a ball that the user will throw toward the can pyramid. To dynamically create balls, you instantiate the prefab in the script in response to user input—in this case, a left mouse button press.

To access other game objects from the script, you declare the public members. These members will be automatically shown in the object's Inspector. You'll use this approach to associate Ball.prefab with the Ball property of the HitTheCan class. Switch to Visual Studio and modify the HitTheCan.cs file as shown in Listing 10-4.

LISTING 10-4 Creating the editable script field

```
public class HitTheCan : MonoBehavior
{
    public GameObject Ball;

    // The rest of class definition
}
```

When you save the script, the `Ball` property will appear as an editable field in the main camera Inspector in the Unity Editor. (See Figure 10-17.) To set that field to Ball.prefab, click the small icon to the right of the Ball box to open the Select GameObject window. Then click the Ball.prefab. The Ball box will now contain the value Ball.prefab.

FIGURE 10-17 The Inspector for the main camera showing the editable field you created.

To proceed further, switch to Visual Studio to extend a definition of the `HitTheCan` class by another private method, `ThrowTheBall`. (See Listing 10-5.)

LISTING 10-5 Throwing the ball

```
private void ThrowTheBall(Ray ray, float speed)
{
    if (Ball != null)
    {
        var ball = Instantiate(Ball, transform.position, Quaternion.identity);

        var rigidbody = ball.GetComponent<Rigidbody>();

        if (rigidbody != null)
        {
            rigidbody.velocity = ray.direction * speed;
        }
    }
}
```

The `ThrowTheBall` method accepts two arguments:

- **ray** You use this argument to obtain the ray direction, toward which the ball will be thrown.

- **speed** This argument specifies the velocity of the ball.

To create the ball, the script uses the `Object.Instantiate` method. It works like the Duplicate option in the Unity Editor's Hierarchy window, letting you copy an object. `Object.Instantiate` has several overloaded versions but all of them accept an original object to be cloned. In this case, the original object was selected through the Inspector and points to Ball.prefab.

Other arguments of Object.Instantiate include the following:

- **parent**   This indicates the parent object, which will be assigned to the instantiated object.

- **position**   This specifies the position of the new object.

- **rotation**   This defines the rotation of the new object.

- **instantiateInWorldSpace**   This specifies whether the new object will be positioned absolutely in the world space (true) or relatively to its parent position (false).

Listing 10-5 uses three arguments. First, it instantiates the Ball prefab, then it sets its position such that the initial Ball position is the same as the camera position. Finally, the rotation argument is set to Quaternion.identity. Quaternion is the struct, which Unity uses to represent rotations; identity means no rotation at all.

After instantiating the ball, the script in Listing 10-5 obtains its Rigidbody component and sets its velocity. This is done in much the same way as applying the force. You pass a vector whose orientation specifies the movement direction, and the magnitude determines the speed. Here, the ball direction depends on the ray orientation, while the speed depends on the scale factor, which in this case is fixed to 10. (See Listing 10-6.) You can arbitrarily modify its value to change the speed of the ball.

After implementing the ThrowTheBall method, it helps to comment out or remove the FixedUpdate method so the force will not be added to cans and then implement the Update method (see Listing 10-6). First, invoke the Input.GetMouseButtonDown method to check whether the left mouse button was pressed during the frame rendering. Then, if so, create a ray oriented toward the mouse cursor and pass the resulting object to ThrowTheBall. (You'll use Update instead of FixedUpdate because you do not need to throw the ball at fixed time intervals.)

LISTING 10-6 ThrowTheBall is invoked when the user presses the left mouse button

```
void Update()
{
    if (Input.GetMouseButtonDown(0))
    {
        var ray = GetComponent<Camera>().ScreenPointToRay(Input.mousePosition);

        ThrowTheBall(ray, 10);
    }
}
```

After you implement this functionality, click the Play button and press the left mouse button. The ball will be thrown and, if it hints one of the cans, will topple the can pyramid. (See Figure 10-18.) Note that the physics simulation is very realistic.

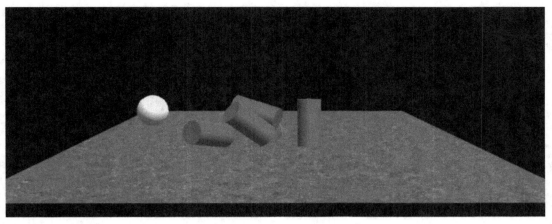

FIGURE 10-18 The can pyramid after being hit by the ball.

Collision Detection, Triggers, and Explosions

Earlier I mentioned that Unity engine implements several physics events that are raised when colliders or rigid bodies are in contact. There are three such events:

- **OnCollisionEnter** This is invoked when a collision begins.

- **OnCollisionStay** This is invoked when the colliders or rigid bodies are still in contact during the frame rendering.

- **OnCollisionExit** This is invoked when the collision is finished and the colliders or rigid bodies are not in contact anymore.

These events are provided with the Collision argument type. This class represents the collision, and thus has the following non-deprecated public properties:

- **relativeVelocity** This is the relative velocity between colliders.

- **rigidbody** This is an instance of the Rigidbody class associated with the object that was hit.

- **collider** This is an instance of the Collider class, representing the colliding object.

- **transform** This is an instance of the Transform class, associated with the object that was hit.

- **gameObject** This is an instance of the game object whose collider was hit.

- **contacts** This is a collection of ContactPoint structs, each representing the point where colliders and Rigidbodies are in contact.

- **impulse** This specifies the total impulse (calculated by the physics engine) that was applied to the contact point.

Another group of physics events is related to triggers. As mentioned, a trigger is a special kind of collider that, instead of registering a collision, raises an `OnTriggerEnter`, `OnTriggerExit`, or `OnTriggerStay` event. These are similar to collision events but are provided with an instance of the `Collider` class instead of the `Collision` argument type. So, you typically use triggers and their events to detect whether a collider has gone through or touched another collider and you don't want the physics engine to let them collide.

Adding Spike Balls to the Scene

Let's use collision-detection events to enhance the HitTheCanGame project. Specifically, let's add spike balls to the scene. These spike balls will cause the projectile (yellow ball) to explode when the two collide. You'll obtain these balls from the Ball Pack package, accessible from the Asset Store. As for the explosion effect, you'll take that from the standard Unity package.

> **Note** Due to Asset Store restrictions, screenshots in this section feature a spike model I created with 3D Builder by sticking several cones to a sphere. You can find it in the companion code here: Chapter_10/Models. My model is slightly different from the spike ball from the Ball Pack package.

Follow these steps to create spike exploders:

1. Open the Asset Store and import the Ball Pack package. (See Figure 10-19.)

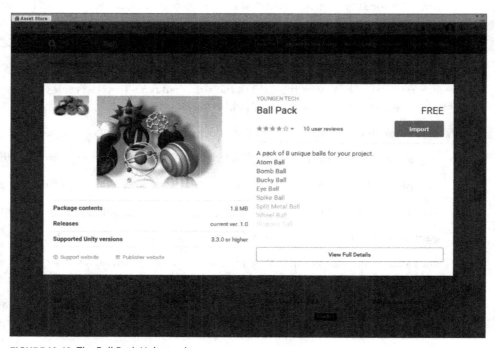

FIGURE 10-19 The Ball Pack Unity package.

2. Open the **Assets** menu, choose **Import Package**, and select **Particle Systems** to import the Particle Systems Unity package.

3. Add a cube to the scene and name it **Exploder L**.

4. In the cube's Inspector, change the **Position** settings in the **Transform** group so that **X** is **–0.35**, **Y** is **–0.2**, and **Z** is **3**.

5. Ensure the **Rotation** settings in the **Transform** group are all set to **0**.

6. Change the **Scale** settings in the **Transform** group so that **X** is **0.2**, **Y** is **0.1**, and **Z** is **0.2**.

7. Open the Project window and in the search box type **t:Material NavySmooth**.

8. Drag the **NavySmooth** material onto the cube.

9. Your next step is to add the spike ball. In the search box in the Project window, type **SpikeBall t:Model**.

10. Drag the **SpikeBall** model onto the Hierarchy so that it becomes a child of Exploder L.

11. In the Inspector for the SpikeBall, change the **Position** settings in the **Transform** group so that **X** is **0**, **Y** is **0.5**, and **Z** is **0**.

12. Change the **Rotation** settings in the **Transform** group so that **X** is **0**, **Y** is **0**, and **Z** is **0**.

13. Change the **Scale** settings in the **Transform** group so that **X** is **0.5**, **Y** is **1**, and **Z** is **0.5**. The cube and spike ball, or the exploder, should look similar to the one shown in Figure 10-20 (note that I'm using my own spike ball model).

FIGURE 10-20 A model of the exploder.

14. In the Hierarchy, create a duplicate of Exploder L, and name it **Exploder R**.

15. In the Inspector for Exploder R, change the **Position** settings in the **Transform** group so that **X** is **0.35**. Figure 10-21 shows the complete scene.

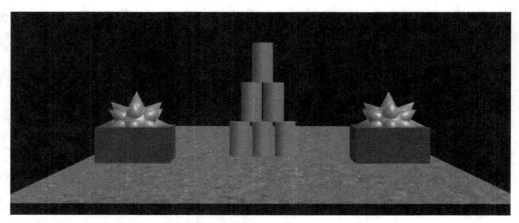

FIGURE 10-21 The final scene of the HitTheCanGame app.

Creating a Script to Blow Up the Projectile

Your next move is to create the script to blow up the projectile. This script will use an `OnCollisionEnter` event and will be associated with the exploder objects. To begin, open the Scripts folder in the Project window and create a new C# script named ExploderCollision. Then open this new script in Visual Studio to modify it as shown in Listing 10-7.

LISTING 10-7 The exploder collision script

```
using UnityEngine;

public class ExploderCollision : MonoBehaviour
{
    public GameObject ExplosionEffect;

    private void OnCollisionEnter(Collision collision)
    {
        if (ExplosionEffect != null)
        {
            var explosion = Instantiate(ExplosionEffect, transform);
            Destroy(explosion, 0.5f);
        }

        Destroy(collision.gameObject);
    }
}
```

The `ExploderCollision` class has one public member, `ExplosionEffect`, of type `GameObject`. This member is used to select the explosion effect through the Unity Editor. The explosion effect will be played when the ball hits the exploder. To detect this collision, this script uses the `OnCollisionEnter` event. The script duplicates the explosion effect, making it a child of the exploder object, and then executes it to simulate blowing up the ball. After that, the script invokes the `Object.Destroy` method, which removes the explosion effect from the Hierarchy at runtime. In general, `Object.Destroy` accepts two arguments:

- **obj** This is an object to be destroyed.

- **t** This is the delay time, expressed in seconds, after which destruction occurs.

Listing 10-7 delays the destruction by 500 ms so the animation associated with explosion will be displayed. The final statement of `OnCollisionEnter` destroys the ball so it disappears after the ball hits the exploder.

After you create the script, you need to associate it with the exploder objects. Follow these steps:

1. Click the **Exploder L** object in the Hierarchy.

2. In the Inspector, click the **Add Component** button, type **Exploder** in the search box, and select **Exploder Collision**. (See the left screen in Figure 10-22.)

3. An Exploder Collision (Script) group is added to the Inspector. (See the right screen in Figure 10-22.) Click the small icon next to the **Explosion Effect** box.

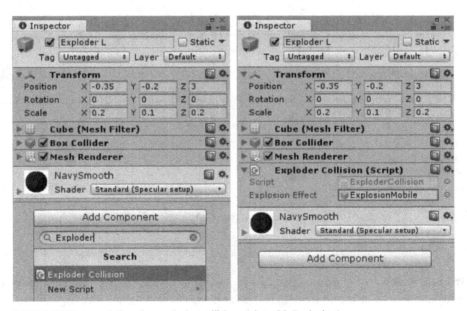

FIGURE 10-22 Associating the exploder collision script with Exploder L.

4. The Select GameObject window opens. Locate and select the **Explosion Mobile** object.

5. Repeat these steps for the Exploder R object. Both exploders will cause the yellow ball to explode.

The ExplosionMobile game object derives from the Unity Particle Systems feature, found in the standard Unity assets. Therefore, you can find the ExplosionMobile object in the Project window by typing **ExplosionMobile** in the search box. Only one item appears in the search results; click it to view the properties of the ExplosionMobile object in the Inspector. In addition to the Transform component, an ExplosionMobile object has two script components:

- **ExplosionPhysicsForce** This class adds an explosion force to neighboring Rigidbodies.

- **ParticleSystemMultiplier** This attribute is used to scale and control the lifetime of the particle system.

Listing 10-8 contains a full definition of the ExplosionPhysicsForce class.

LISTING 10-8 The ExplosionPhysicsForce class

```
public class ExplosionPhysicsForce : MonoBehaviour
{
    public float explosionForce = 4;

    private IEnumerator Start()
    {
        yield return null;

        float multiplier = GetComponent<ParticleSystemMultiplier>().multiplier;

        float r = 10*multiplier;
        var cols = Physics.OverlapSphere(transform.position, r);
        var rigidbodies = new List<Rigidbody>();

        foreach (var col in cols)
        {
            if (col.attachedRigidbody != null && !rigidbodies.Contains(col.attachedRigidbody))
            {
                rigidbodies.Add(col.attachedRigidbody);
            }
        }

        foreach (var rb in rigidbodies)
        {
            rb.AddExplosionForce(explosionForce*multiplier, transform.position,
                r, 1*multiplier, ForceMode.Impulse);
        }
    }
}
```

This class has one public member: explosionForce. It controls the strength of the force applied to all Rigidbodies, which are attached to the colliders found inside the sphere of a given center and radius. This functionality is implemented within the Start method of ExplosionPhysicsForce. The first statement of ExplosionPhysicsForce (yield return null) waits until the frame rendering ends. This is because some explosion effects generate additional objects, which must be moved by the physics engine. Afterward, the actual processing begins, in which the multiplier attribute of ParticleSystemMultiplier is obtained and used to determine the sphere radius (r). This radius is then passed to Physics.OverlapSphere. This method returns the collection of colliders inside or on the border of the sphere. Because the origin of this sphere overlaps with the position of the game object with the `ExplosionPhysicsForce` component, `Physics.OverlapSphere` will return a collection of colliders in the local neighborhood of that game object. Subsequently, the `foreach` loop iterates over the resulting collection of colliders to find associated Rigidbodies. These are stored within the generic list, where each object is an instance of the `Rigidbody` class. Finally, another `foreach` loop is used to add an explosion force to each Rigidbody. This force is applied using the `Rigidbody.AddExplosionForce` method, which, depending on the overloaded version, accepts up to five arguments:

- **explosionForce** This sets the force of the explosion.

- **explosionPosition** This specifies the center of the sphere. The sphere represents a region in which the explosion occurs. In practice, all Rigidbodies in that sphere will be affected by the explosion.

- **explosionRadius** This sets the radius of the aforementioned sphere.

- **upwardsModifier** This is a special parameter that adjusts to the apparent position of the explosion effect so that the explosion affects neighboring objects.

- **mode** This is the force mode used to apply the force to Rigidbodies.

A definition of the second script, `ParticleSystemMultiplier` appears in Listing 10-9.

LISTING 10-9 The `ParticleSystemMultiplier` script

```
public class ParticleSystemMultiplier : MonoBehaviour
{
    public float multiplier = 1;

    private void Start()
    {
        var systems = GetComponentsInChildren<ParticleSystem>();

        foreach (ParticleSystem system in systems)
        {
            ParticleSystem.MainModule mainModule = system.main;

            mainModule.startSizeMultiplier *= multiplier;
            mainModule.startSpeedMultiplier *= multiplier;
            mainModule.startLifetimeMultiplier *= Mathf.Lerp(multiplier, 1, 0.5f);

            system.Clear();
            system.Play();
        }
    }
}
```

This script also has just one attribute, `multiplier`, and implements a `Start` method. This method, using `Component.GetComponentsInChildren`, collects all components of type `ParticleSystem` associated with the current game object or any of its descendant objects. The `ParticleSystem` component represents a module used to simulate various effects with numerous small objects, called particles. Here, the particle system simulates an explosion. You can envision this explosion as the quick emission of several small particles from a given center. When the collection of these objects is retrieved, the foreach loop is used obtain the main property of each ParticleSystem. This property is of type MainModule and represents all configurable properties of the system. The ParticleSystemMultiplier script modifies only three of these properties:

- **startSizeMultiplier**   This sets the factor by which the initial size of particles emitted by the system is multiplied.

- **startSpeedMultiplier**   This sets the factor by which the speed of the emitted particles is multiplied during their lifetime.

- **startLifetimeMultiplier**   This sets the lifetime multiplier.

All these properties are of type float and are multiplied by the multiplier attribute. Only start Lifetime is modified using the Mathf.Lerp method. This method implements a linear interpolation between a and b (which are the first two arguments) by the third argument (t). In practice, Mathf.Lerp calculates the weighted average: a * (1-t) + b * t.

When the properties of each particle system are adjusted, the last two statements of the foreach loop in Listing 10-9 restart the system by invoking Play followed by the Clear method of the ParticleSystem class instance.

Note that both of these scripts use an attribute of type float. Like attributes of type GameObject, float attributes also appear in the Inspector of the Unity Editor. For such numeric attributes (of type float, int, and so on) you can restrict the attribute range using RangeAttribute. For example:

```
[Range(-10, 10)]

public float myCustomAttribute = 1;
```

This code will allow only values between –10 to 10 to be entered in the Inspector of the Unity Editor for myCustomAttribute.

Let's get back to the HitTheCanGame app. Click Play to test the app. You will quickly see that the ball and cola cans are destroyed whenever they collide with an exploder. Additionally, any object that hits the exploder will trigger the explosion effect. Note, however, that the explosion is too strong. To reduce its strength, you can adjust explosionForce and multiplier attributes of the ExplosionPhysicsForce and ParticleSystemMulitplier components. After a bit of trial and error, I settled on the following values for these parameters:

- **explosionForce**   1
- **multiplier**   0.01

Click Play again to rerun the app. You should now see a realistic explosion effect. (See Figure 10-23.)

Tip When you are editing properties of the `ExplosionMobile` component, be sure its position is set to 0 along each direction. Otherwise the explosion effect will appear at the incorrect location.

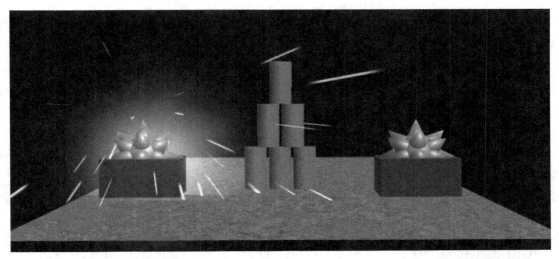

FIGURE 10-23 An explosion effect, which is played whenever the yellow ball or a can hits an exploder object.

To conclude this section, let's improve the `ExploderCollision` script so that the delay time before the object occluding the exploder is destroyed will precisely match the duration of the explosion effect. To achieve this, you simply need to implement one more method to read the `duration` property of the `MainModule` of the particle system associated with the explosion effect. First, obtain an instance of the particle system by using the generic `Object.GetComponentsInChildren<ParticleSystem>` method. Then, read the `main.duration` property. Listing 10-10 offers the complete code for such an implementation. (Notice that the listing code replaces the second argument of the first `Destroy` method with the result of the `GetExplosionDuration` method. This reads a duration of the first particle system associated with the `ExplosionEffect`.)

LISTING 10-10 Final version of the ExploderCollision script

```
using UnityEngine;
using System.Linq;

public class ExploderCollision : MonoBehaviour
{
    public GameObject ExplosionEffect;

    private void OnCollisionEnter(Collision collision)
    {
        if (ExplosionEffect != null)
        {
```

```
            var explosion = Instantiate(ExplosionEffect, transform);

            Destroy(explosion, GetExplosionDuration());
        }

        Destroy(collision.gameObject);
    }

    private float GetExplosionDuration()
    {
        // Default value
        var explosionDuration = 0.5f;

        var particleSystem = ExplosionEffect.GetComponentsInChildren<ParticleSystem>().First();

        if (particleSystem != null)
        {
            explosionDuration = particleSystem.main.duration;
        }

        return explosionDuration;
    }
}
```

Object Tagging

In the previous section you learned how to detect collisions and create explosion effects. You used this knowledge to destroy objects when they occlude exploder objects. During app testing, however, you probably noticed that not only does the yellow ball explode when it collides with the exploders, the cola cans do, too. To prevent this, you can use object tagging.

A tag is a string that helps you identify objects in a script. Typically, tags are used to find objects within the scene using the GameObject.FindWithTag method or to identify colliders that hit the given object. This section covers the use of object tagging for the second scenario. Specifically, in this section, you'll create a tag for the yellow ball and then use that tag in the ExploderCollision script to detect whether the object that hits the exploder is indeed the yellow ball. Follow these steps:

1. In the Project window, type **Ball t:prefab** in the search box and click the yellow ball prefab that appears in the search results.

2. In the Inspector for the yellow ball prefab, open the **Tag** drop-down list and choose **Add Tag**. (See the left screen in Figure 10-24.) The Tags & Layers window opens.

3. Click the **plus** icon to create a new tag. Then type a name for the new tag: **Yellow Ball**.

4. In the yellow ball Inspector, open the **Tag** drop-down list again. It should now contain a Yellow Ball tag. Select the **Yellow Ball** tag. (See the right screen in Figure 10-24.)

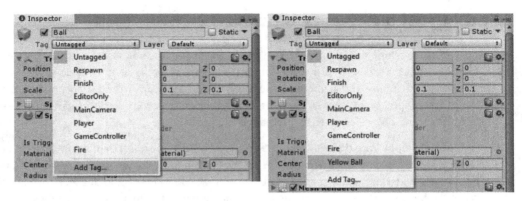

FIGURE 10-24 Creating and applying an object tag.

After the new tag is configured, you need to modify the ExploderCollision script. Open it in Visual Studio and add the IsBallHittingTheExploder method to the ExploderCollision class. Listing 10-11 contains the definition for the IsBallHittingTheExploder method.

LISTING 10-11 Using object tagging to detect whether the yellow ball hits the collider

```
private bool IsBallHittingTheExploder(Collision collision)
{
    return collision.collider.CompareTag("Yellow Ball");
}
```

As shown in Listing 10-11, to check whether the collider has an expected tag, you use the Collider.CompareTag method. It accepts a string argument with the test tag and returns a Boolean value indicating whether the tag matches that of the collider. Alternatively, you can read the Collider.tag property and then manually compare its value to the test tag.

As a last step, use the IsBallHittingTheExploder method in the OnCollisionEnter event handler as shown in Listing 10-12.

LISTING 10-12 Only the yellow ball is destroyed when it collides with an exploder

```
private void OnCollisionEnter(Collision collision)
{
    if (IsBallHittingTheExploder(collision))
    {
        if (ExplosionEffect != null)
        {
            var explosion = Instantiate(ExplosionEffect, transform);

            Destroy(explosion, GetExplosionDuration());
        }

        Destroy(collision.gameObject);
    }
}
```

Click Play to run the modified app. Notice that only the ball is destroyed after it hits the exploder.

Handling Mixed Reality Input

In all previous examples, you've only used mouse input because you test the app in Unity Play mode. You can also use a mouse to provide input for the HoloLens emulator and Windows Mixed Reality simulator if the mouse and keyboard inputs are enabled. Windows Mixed Reality headsets can also accept voice input, input from air gestures, or input from motion controllers (immersive headsets only). These are commonly referred to as interaction sources.

To handle input from different interaction sources, you can either use the common Unity APIs or the Windows Mixed Reality–specific input API for the Unity engine. In general, the Mixed Reality–specific input API provides more information about the interaction source. So, in this section, you will learn how to use the Mixed Reality–specific input API for handling input from motion controllers and select gestures (primary interaction). If you would prefer to use the common Unity APIs, you can obtain instructions from http://bit.ly/mr_input and http://bit.ly/mr_input_unity.

To access information about an interaction source, you use the `UnityEngine.XR.WSA.InteractionManager` class. This class implements the static method `GetCurrentReading` and several static events, which are raised whenever the state of the input source changes. `InteractionManager.GetCurrentReading` has two overloaded versions. The first one accepts the preinitialized array of `UnityEngineXR.WSA.InteractionSourceState` objects and returns the number of active sources. The second one does not take any input arguments and returns an array of `InteractionSourceState` objects. So, the second version is much easier to use, but the first one works well when you want to reuse the collection of `InteractionSourceState` objects. `InteractionSourceState` is a struct whose properties describe the status of the input source. Before we discuss these properties, let's briefly summarize the hardware features of motion controllers.

Motion Controllers

As shown in Figure 10-25, a motion controller is equipped with a touchpad and thumbstick. These components enable the user to both adjust an action in two dimensions over a circular range and commit the action. In both cases, the finger position on the touchpad or the stick is reported in normalized XY coordinates.

The associated coordinate system is centered at (0,0) and has four corners:

- **(−1,1)** This is the top-left corner.
- **(−1,−1)** This is the bottom-left corner.
- **(1,1)** This is the top-right corner.
- **(1,−1)** This is the bottom-right corner.

The touchpad and thumbstick can be in two logical states:

- **touched** This is when the user touches the touchpad or thumbstick to adjust an action.

- **pressed** This is when the user presses the touchpad or thumbstick to confirm an action.

A motion controller also has the following buttons:

- **Trigger/Select** This button is used for the primary interaction with an active hologram.

- **Menu** This button is used to perform secondary interactions—for example, opening the context menu.

- **Windows/Home** This button displays the Start menu. It works like the Windows key on any Windows 10 device.

- **Grab** This button is used to grasp holograms and manipulate objects. The user can also activate this function by squeezing his or her fist while holding the motion controller.

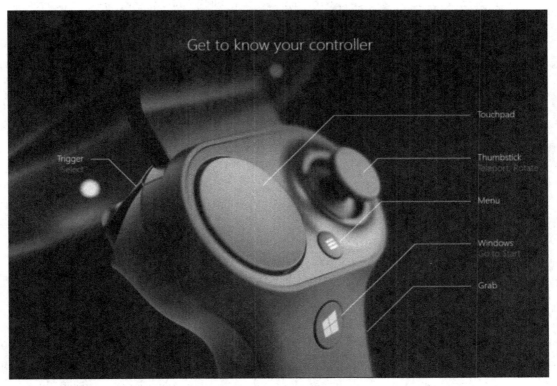

FIGURE 10-25 The motion-controller inputs. (Courtesy of developer.microsoft.com.)

InteractionSourceState

Now that you've explored the hardware features of a motion controller, let's return to the `InteractionSourceState` struct. This struct has the following public properties, which directly correspond to components of the motion controller:

- **touchpadPosition** and **thumbstickPosition**　These indicate the normalized coordinates of the user's finger on the touchpad or the thumbstick position, respectively.

- **touchpadTouched** and **touchpadPressed**　These are Boolean values that indicate whether the touchpad is touched or pressed, respectively.

- **thumbstickPressed**　This is a Boolean value that indicates whether the thumbstick is pressed.

- **grasped**　This indicates whether the controller is grasped.

- **menuPressed**　This indicates whether the menu button is pressed.

`InteractionSourceState` also contains several public members, which are common for all interaction sources. These include the following:

- **anyPressed**　This indicates whether the source is in the pressed state. This property is `true` when the touchpad, thumbstick, select button, or any other interaction action (for example, air tap) is pressed or active.

- **selectPressedAmount**　This is a floating-point value that ranges from 0 to 1. If the value is non-zero, it describes how forcefully the select button is being pressed.

- **headPose**　This is an instance of the `UnityEngine.Pose` struct, whose `Position` and `Rotation` properties contain information about the user's head pose during interaction.

- **source**　This describes the interaction source.

- **sourcePose**　This represents the pose of the interaction source.

The two last properties are represented as complex types `UnityEngine.XR.WSA.Input.InteractionSource` (source) and `UnityEngine.XR.WSA.Input.InteractionSourcePose` (sourcePose). You'll analyze these structs in more detail below.

InteractionSource

`InteractionSource` exposes five public Boolean members, representing supported capabilities of the interaction source:

- **supportsGrasp**　This indicates whether the interaction source is equipped with the grasp/grab button.

- **supportsMenu**　This property is `true` if the interaction source has a menu button.

- **supportsThumbstick** and **supportsTouchpad**　This indicates whether the interaction source has a thumbstick and touchpad, respectively.

- **supportsPointing** This property is `true` if the interaction source supports pointing pose. (Pointing pose is discussed in the next section.)

The `InteractionSource` struct also has several integral members that contain the identifier of the input source (`id`) and its version (`productVersion`), as well as product (`productid`) and vendor (`vendorId`) identifiers. To recognize the type of the interaction source, you use the kind property. It takes one of the values, defined under the `UnityEngine.XR.WSA.Input.InteractionSourceKind` enumeration:

- **Controller** This indicates that the source of the input is the motion controller.

- **Voice** This represents voice input—that is, voice commands.

- **Hand** This represents hand input—for example, air gestures.

- **Other** This indicates that input is associated with a source other than the ones just mentioned.

Finally, the `handedness` property denotes which hand was used as an input. `Handedness` is represented using a `UnityEngine.XR.WSA.Input.InteractionSourceHandedness` enumeration, defining three values:

- **Right and Left** These represent right and left hand, respectively. With a motion controller, they also correspond to the controller side (right or left).

- **Unknown** This indicates that handedness could not be detected.

InteractionSourcePose

`InteractionSourcePose` is a struct that recognizes and processes the pose of the interaction source. There are two kinds of poses:

- **Grip pose** With this pose, the user's hand is holding the motion controller (immersive headsets) or the palm of the user's hand is detected by the HoloLens. Grip pose is typically used to render the user's hand or to overlay the hologram on the hand, as described here: http://bit.ly/controller_visualization.

- **Pointer pose** With this pose, the tip of the controller points forward. This pose is typically used as the origin for a ray cast.

To obtain the position and rotation of the interaction source, you use the `InteractionSourcePose:TryGetPosition` and `TryGetRotation` methods. As you'll see shortly, these methods obtain this information using out-like method arguments, meaning you obtain position and rotation through method arguments passed by the reference (and not by the method return value). Additionally, the `TryGetPosition` and `TryGetRotation` methods accept an optional second argument node. This node argument indicates the pose through values defined in the `UnityEngine.XR.WSA.Input.InteractionSourceNode` enumeration. These values are as follows:

- **Grip** This corresponds to the grip pose.

- **Pointer** This represents the pointer pose.

InteractionSourcePose implements a few other methods, which you can use to determine the velocity (TryGetVelocity), the angular velocity (TryGetAngularVelocity), and the forward (TryGetForward), up (TryGetUp) or right vectors (TryGetRight) of the interaction source. They work like TryGetPosition/TryGetRotation.

Finally, InteractionSourcePose has a public member, positionAccuracy. It represents the tracking accuracy of the interaction source. The position is tracked by sensors on the headset. Hence, performance of the tracking decreases when the user's hands or motion controllers are outside the headset's field of view—and can be lost completely when they are outside the headset's field of view for long periods. Hence, positionAccuracy is represented by one of the following values, defined in the UnityEngine.XR.WSA.Input.InteractionSourcePositionAccuracy enumeration:

- **None** This indicates that the tracking system is unable to detect the 3D position of the input source.

- **Approximate** This indicates that the position accuracy is approximated based on previous trajectories.

- **High** This indicates that the position accuracy is high, as the input source is within the headset's field of view.

The Mixed Reality–specific input API offers even more functionality by predicting the likelihood that the tracking system will not be able to follow the input source. To do so, it uses relevant members of the UnityEngine.XR.WSA.Input.InteractionSourceProperties struct. You can obtain an instance of this object using the properties member of the InteractionSourceState.

InteractionManager Events

Now that you've learned about the states, sources, and poses of Mixed Reality inputs, you're ready to explore the events raised by the InteractionManager class in response to user interactions. These interactions can cause the following events:

- **SourceDetected** This is raised when a new interaction source (a hand, motion controller, or voice command) is detected.

- **SourceLost** This is raised when the interaction source becomes unavailable.

- **SourcePressed** This occurs when the interaction source enters the pressed state.

- **SourceReleased** This is raised when the interaction source exits the pressed state.

- **SourceUpdated** This is raised whenever the state of the interaction source changes.

You can handle all these using the appropriately defined event handler, which you wire in the script's Awake or Start methods and unwire in the Destroy method. Event handlers dedicated to InteractionManager events accept one argument, which depends on the event. For example, SourcePressed uses the UnityEngine.XR.WSA.Input.InteractionSourcePressed EventArgs struct.

Although these structs have different names, their general structure is quite common. All of them have a `state` property of type `InteractionSourceState`, which you already learned about. Only the `InteractionSourcePressedEventArgs` and `InteractionSourceReleasedEventArgs` have an additional member, `pressType`. The `pressType` property uses `UnityEngine.XR.WSA.Input.InteractionSourcePressType` to represent the thing (gesture, button, touchpad, thumbstick) that triggered the press state. Thus, the `InteractionSourcePressType` defines the following values:

- `Thumbstick`
- `Touchpad`
- `Grasp`
- `Menu`
- `Select`
- `None`

Having concluded this long theoretical description of the Mixed Reality–specific input API, let's use this knowledge to handle interaction source input in the HitTheCanGame project. Specifically, you will use the `SourcePressed` event to detect whether the interaction source was pressed. Then, you will learn how to use an instance of the `InteractionSourceState` struct to infer whether the press state was triggered by the touchpad, thumbstick, or select gesture. Finally, you will use the interaction source pose to set the origin and direction of the ray used to throw the yellow ball.

Putting It All Together

Let's put all this together. First, open the HitTheCan.cs file in Visual Studio. You'll make all code modifications to this file. Then, import the `UnityEngine.XR.WSA.Input` namespace by adding the following statement to the header of the HitTheCan.cs file:

```
using UnityEngine.XR.WSA.Input;
```

Finally, set up the event handler for the `InteractionManager.InteractionSourcePressed` event using `Awake` (to wire the event handler) and `OnDestroy` (to unwire the handler) as shown in Listing 10-13.

LISTING 10-13 Handling the `InteractionSourcePressed` event

```
private void Awake()
{
    InteractionManager.InteractionSourcePressed +=
        InteractionManager_InteractionSourcePressed;
}

private void OnDestroy()
{
    InteractionManager.InteractionSourcePressed -=
        InteractionManager_InteractionSourcePressed;
}
```

Listing 10-14 shows the definition of the `InteractionManager_InteractionSourcePressed` method, which is invoked whenever the interaction source is in the pressed state. The main goal of this method is to configure the ray object. The origin of this ray represents the location from which the ball is thrown. Then the ball moves toward the ray direction.

LISTING 10-14 The ray, which dictates the direction the ball is thrown, depends on the state of the interaction source

```
private void InteractionManager_InteractionSourcePressed(
    InteractionSourcePressedEventArgs obj)
{
    if (obj.state.anyPressed)
    {
        // Configure ray
        var ray = new Ray()
        {
            origin = GetRayOrigin(obj),
            direction = GetRayDirection(obj)
        };

        // ... and then throw the ball
        ThrowTheBall(ray, 10);
    }
}
```

Ray origin and direction are determined using two helper methods: `GetRayOrigin` (see Listing 10-15) and `GetRayDirection` (see Listing 10-16). Both accept one argument of type `InteractionSourcePressedEventArgs`. An instance of this struct is provided to the `InteractionManager_InteractionSourcePressed` event handler, and then supplied to `GetRayOrigin` and `GetRayDirection` (refer to Listing 10-14). `GetRayOrigin` attempts to obtain the pointer pose position of the interaction source and then returns this as the ray origin. To obtain this position and pose, `GetRayOrigin` invokes the `TryGetPosition` method of the `InteractionSourcePose` struct with the second argument set to `InteractionSourceNode.Pointer`. An instance of the `InteractionSourcePose` struct is obtained from the `state.sourcePose` property of the `InteractionSourcePressedEventArgs` struct. `InteractionSourcePose.TryGetPosition` returns a Boolean value, indicating whether the pointer pose position can be obtained. The code in Listing 10-15 uses this information to return the camera position if the pointer pose position cannot be determined.

LISTING 10-15 Gathering the ray origin

```
private Vector3 GetRayOrigin(InteractionSourcePressedEventArgs obj)
{
    // Ray origin is inferred from the interaction source pose if available.
    // Otherwise the ray origin is set to the camera position
    Vector3 interactionSourcePose;

    if (obj.state.sourcePose.TryGetPosition(out interactionSourcePose,
        InteractionSourceNode.Pointer))
    {
        return interactionSourcePose;
    }
```

```
    else
    {
        return transform.position;
    }
}
```

The `GetRayDirection` method (see Listing 10-16) returns the ray direction depending on the state of the interaction source. When the touchpad or thumbstick is pressed, `GetRayDirection` uses its XY position to construct the XYZ direction of the ray. In all other cases, the direction is set based on the forward vector of the camera. To get the head pose, you can use the `state.headPose` property of the `InteractionSourcePressedEventArgs` struct.

LISTING 10-16 Determining the ray direction

```
private Vector3 GetRayDirection(InteractionSourcePressedEventArgs obj)
{
    if (obj.state.touchpadPressed)
    {
        // Ray direction is set according to the touchpad position
        return Position2DToRayDirection(obj.state.touchpadPosition);
    }
    else if (obj.state.thumbstickPressed)
    {
        // Ray direction is set according to the thumbstick position
        return Position2DToRayDirection(obj.state.thumbstickPosition);
    }
    else
    {
        // Ray direction is set according to the camera orientation along z-axis
        return transform.forward;
    }
}
```

You obtain the touchpad and thumbstick positions from the corresponding properties of the `InteractionSourceState` struct, gathered from the state property of the `InteractionSource` `PressedEventArgs` struct. Touchpad and thumbstick positions are represented using the `Vector2` struct. `Vector2` is an abstract representation of the pointer pose position in two dimensions (X and Y) or two-component vectors. To convert these 2D positions to the ray origin, represented as `Vector3`, you use the helper method `Position2DToRayDirection` (see Listing 10-17). This method takes the `Vector2` object as an input argument, and then uses this object to set x and y properties of the new `Vector3` struct. The last component of that 3D vector is set to 1 using the `Vector3.forward` property, which generates the 3D vector, whose elements are (0,0,1). Thus, the resultant vector points in the direction of the view (z) and is oriented toward x and y components of either the touchpad or thumbstick positions, if they are pressed.

LISTING 10-17 Converting the thumbstick or touchpad XY position to Vector3

```
private Vector3 Position2DToRayDirection(Vector2 position2D)
{
    var result = Vector3.forward;

    if (position2D != null)
```

```
    {
        result.x = position2D.x;
        result.y = position2D.y;
    }

    return result;
}
```

Testing the App

Let's use the Windows Mixed Reality simulator to test the solution you've developed. Follow these steps:

1. In the Unity Editor, open the **File** menu and choose **Build Settings**. Then change the **Platform** setting to **Universal Windows Platform** and click the **Switch Platform** button.

2. In the player settings, click **Other Settings** and find the **Configuration** group. Then change the **Scripting Runtime** setting to **Stable (.NET 3.5 Equivalent)** and the **Scripting Backend** setting to **.NET**.

3. Click the **XR Settings** tab, select the **Virtual Reality Supported** checkbox, and ensure that **Windows Mixed Reality SDK** is available. If not, add it.

4. Click the **Play** button. The app will start in the Windows Mixed Reality simulator. (See Figure 10-26.) Notice that the app looks different. This is because the simulator's field of view is much larger (approximately 94 degrees) than the one you set for the HoloLens emulator (17 degrees). You'll learn how to solve this problem in the next section.

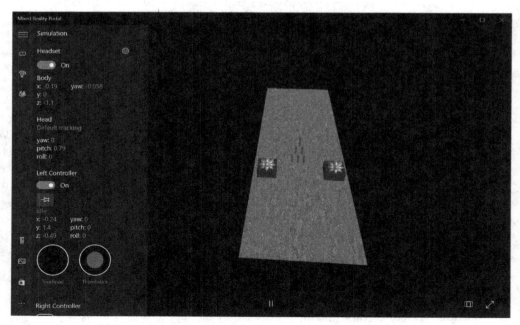

FIGURE 10-26 The HitTheCanGame app in the Windows Mixed Reality simulator.

5. Let's verify the functionality of the ball. First, if the **Headset** setting in the Simulation panel on the left of the simulation window is set to Off, press **Win+Y** to ensure that keyboard and mouse input will be directed to the simulator.

6. Make sure controller simulation is available by clicking the **Left Controller** or **Right Controller** setting in the Simulation panel to turn it to **On**.

7. Right-click in the **Touchpad** or **Thumbstick** circle in the Simulation pane to throw a ball. The spot where you click in the circle will affect the direction in which the ball is thrown. (That is, if you click the upper-right part of the circle, the ball will be thrown upward and to the right.)

8. To test the settings using your mouse, scroll down in the Simulation panel to locate the Input Settings section. (See Figure 10-27.) Then select the **Use Mouse for Simulation** checkbox.

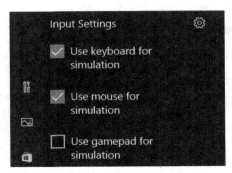

FIGURE 10-27 Input Settings of the Windows Mixed Reality simulator.

9. To change the ray origin, click the left mouse button and move the mouse. This will change the camera direction in the simulator. Choose the desired viewing angle. Then right-click to throw the ball.

 Note You can also use your keyboard for simulation. First, select the **Use Keyboard for Simulation** checkbox. (Refer to Figure 10-27.) Then use the **W**, **A**, **S**, **D**, and **arrow** keys to change the camera direction.

Dynamic Scene Adjustment

In this section, you'll find out how to dynamically adjust the scene and camera settings in the Windows Mixed Reality simulator. This will enable you to make the app universal for both the HoloLens and Windows immersive headset simulator. You can also use this technique to develop multiplatform AR and VR apps.

Before you can dynamically adjust the scene and camera settings, you must be able to detect the device type on which the app is running. You can obtain this information by reading the properties of the UnityEngine.XR.XRDevice static class. The XRDevice class implements the model property, which returns a string that describes the headset—whether it's a Microsoft HoloLens or a Windows Holographic device. So, to detect whether the app is running in a HoloLens, you could use the following statement:

```
if(UnityEngine.XR.XRDevice.model.Contains("HoloLens"))
{
    // Perform HoloLens-specific actions
}
```

XRDevice also has another property, fovZoomFactor, which you can use to dynamically zoom the field of view. Zooming the field of view is particularly useful if you want to scale all scene objects without manipulating individual game objects. For example, you can use the following code snippet to increase the field of view zoom for immersive headsets by a factor of 2.5:

```
if(!UnityEngine.XR.XRDevice.model.Contains("HoloLens"))
{
    UnityEngine.XR.XRDevice.fovZoomFactor = 2.5f;
}
```

This code snippet sets the fovZoomFactor to an empirically adjusted value. However, in general, you can calculate the zoom factor using the camera's current field of view. To obtain a field of view value, you use the fieldOfView property of the Camera component like this:

```
GetComponent<Camera>().fieldOfView.
```

Zooming the field of view will not be enough to dynamically adjust the HitTheCanGame app for immersive headsets. This is because the plane with the can pyramid and the two exploders is on the ground—meaning the user will need to be able to look downward. To place this plane closer to the user's head you need to lift it (and all the other game objects) up. Follow these steps:

1. Right-click a blank area in the Hierarchy and choose **Create Empty** from the menu that appears.

2. Name this new object **Platform**.

3. In the Inspector, change the platform object's **Position** settings so that **X** is **0**, **Y** is **0**, and **Z** is **0**.

4. In the Hierarchy, drag the **Plane**, **CanPyramid, Exploder L**, and **Exploder R** objects under the **Platform** object. (See Figure 10-28.)

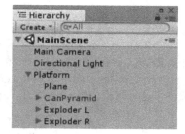

FIGURE 10-28 The hierarchy of HitTheCanGame app scene.

5. In Visual Studio, implement the AdjustSettings method as shown in Listing 10-18. You'll invoke this method during scene initialization. (See the Start method in Listing 10-18). Note that to implement this method, you'll need to import the UnityEngine.XR namespace. So, go ahead and include the following statement in the HitTheCan.cs file: using UnityEngine.XR;

LISTING 10-18 Dynamic scene adjustment for the Windows Mixed Reality simulator

```csharp
private void AdjustSettings()
{
    if (!XRDevice.model.Contains("HoloLens"))
    {
        XRDevice.fovZoomFactor = 2.5f;

        GameObject.Find("Platform").transform.position +=
            new Vector3(0.0f, 1.25f, 0.0f);
    }
}

private void Start()
{
    AdjustSettings();
}
```

The AdjustSettings method uses previously described techniques to detect whether the app is running on the immersive headset. If so, the fovZoomFactor value for XRDevice will be rescaled by a factor of 2.5. Then, the GameObject.Find method obtains a reference to the Platform object. Once this is done, the position of the Platform object and all its descendants will be lifted by 1.5 meters. Accordingly, the Platform object will appear much closer to the user's head, as you can see when you click Play. (See Figure 10-29.)

FIGURE 10-29 The HitTheCanGame app after the field of view is zoomed, and the platform is lifted. (Compare this with Figure 10-26.)

Debugging

There are several tools for debugging Unity apps. The most important is the `UnityEngine.Debug` class provided by Unity. This class exposes several static methods that help track script execution (Log), assert conditions (`Assert`), log assertions (`LogAssertion`), errors (`LogError`), and exceptions (`LogException`) to the Unity console. For example, to log information about the headset during Play in the Unity console, import the `UnityEngine` namespace in the HitTheCan.cs file and extend the definition of the `AdjustSettings` method using the bolded statement in Listing 10-19. Listing 10-20 shows the use of `Debug.Log` in the `ThrowTheBall` method.

LISTING 10-19 Debugging the headset model

```
private void AdjustSettings()
{
    Debug.Log("XRDevice.model = " + XRDevice.model);

    if (!XRDevice.model.Contains("HoloLens"))
    {
        XRDevice.fovZoomFactor = 2.5f;

        GameObject.Find("Platform").transform.position +=
            new Vector3(0.0f, 1.25f, 0.0f);
    }
}
```

LISTING 10-20 Debugging the ray used to throw the ball

```
private void ThrowTheBall(Ray ray, float speed)
{
    if (Ball != null)
    {
        var ball = Instantiate(Ball, transform);

        var rigidbody = ball.GetComponent<Rigidbody>();

        if (rigidbody != null)
        {
            rigidbody.velocity = ray.direction * speed;
        }

        Debug.Log("Throw the ball. Origin: "
            + ray.origin + ", Direction: " + ray.direction);
    }
}
```

After you make these modifications, click Play and open the Unity Editor Console window to see output generated by `Debug.Log`. (See Figure 10-30.) Notice that each time `Debug.Log` is invoked, a defined message (for example, information about the headset) appears in the upper part of the Console window. Click the message to see contextual information in the bottom part of the Console window. In this case, you see the call stack with detailed information about all the methods, and their locations in the script, that were invoked before `Debug.Log`.

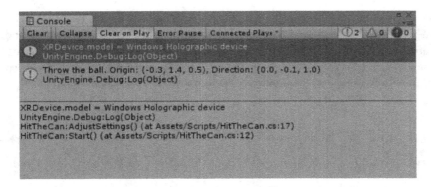

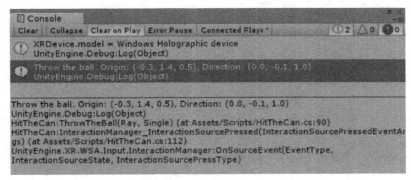

FIGURE 10-30 Sample output of the UnityEngine.Debug.Log method.

> **Note** The other methods of the Debug class can be used in a similar way. In the next section, you'll investigate the Debug.DrawRay method, which you can use to debug ray casting.

Drawing Rays

The UnityEngine.Debug class implements a static DrawRay method, which you can use to visualize rays in the Unity Editor's Scene view. This function is useful when you need to debug ray casting. The Debug.DrawRay method has several overloaded versions. Its most general version accepts five arguments:

- **start** This is the 3D position, or the origin of the ray.

- **dir** This is a three-dimensional vector that represents the ray direction.

- **color** This is the color of the line drawn in Scene view to represent the ray.

- **duration** This indicates how long (in seconds) the ray will be visible.

- **depthTest** This indicates whether the ray line should be obscured by objects located closer to the camera.

To see how Debug.DrawRay works, let's employ it to display rays used to throw the ball. To do so, modify the ThrowTheBall method as shown in Listing 10-21. To draw the ray, you use the origin and direction properties of the Ray struct. Then, you set the color to green and display time to 3.0 (seconds). When you're finished, click Play and switch to Scene view. Each time you throw the ball (using one of the supported interaction sources), the corresponding ray will be drawn as shown in Figure 10-31.

LISTING 10-21 Debugging ray casting

```
private void ThrowTheBall(Ray ray, float speed)
{
    if (Ball != null)
    {
        var ball = Instantiate(Ball, transform);

        var rigidbody = ball.GetComponent<Rigidbody>();

        if (rigidbody != null)
        {
            rigidbody.velocity = ray.direction * speed;
        }

        Debug.Log("Throw the ball. Origin: "
            + ray.origin + ", Direction: " + ray.direction);

        Debug.DrawRay(ray.origin, ray.direction, Color.green, 3.0f);
    }
}
```

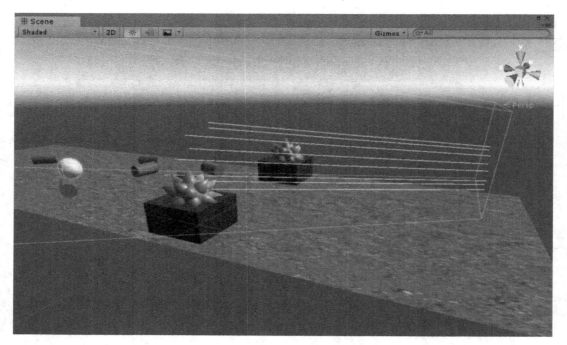

FIGURE 10-31 Drawing rays used to throw the ball. Notice that all rays originate from the camera plane.

Attaching the Visual Studio Debugger to Unity

Visual Studio Tools for Unity provide a mechanism that enables you to debug Unity scripts directly from Visual Studio using standard debugging tools. To use this mechanism, open the Attach to Unity drop-down list (which replaces the Debugging Target drop-down list when you use Visual Studio to implement C# apps) and choose one of the following. (See Figure 10-32.)

- **Attach to Unity** This attaches the Visual Studio debugger to the active Unity Editor. In this case you need to manually click Play to start debugging.

- **Attach to Unity and Play** This works like the previous option but starts playback automatically.

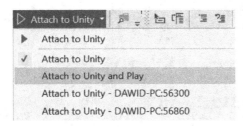

FIGURE 10-32 Attaching the Visual Studio debugger to Unity.

Note The number of items in the Attach to Unity drop-down list varies depending on how many Unity instances are running. In Figure 10-32, I have two local Unity instances running: DAWID-PC:56300 and DAWID-PC:56860.

To see this debugging in action, set a breakpoint in the AdjustSettings method of the HitTheCan class. (See Figure 10-33.) Then open the Attach to Unity drop-down list and choose Attach to Unity and Play. The app will start and will quickly hit the breakpoint. Starting from this point, you can use Visual Studio's built-in debugging tools. For example, in Figure 10-33, I used a data tip to preview values of the XRDevice class properties.

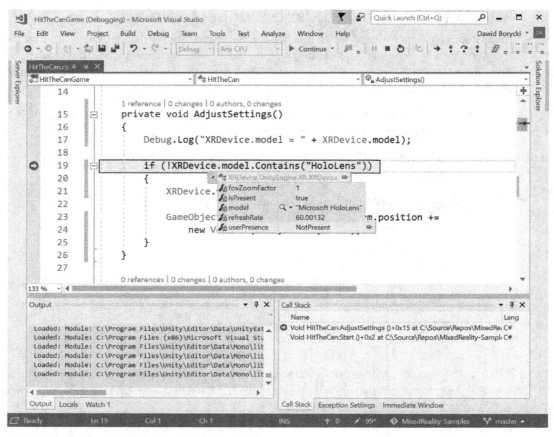

FIGURE 10-33 Debugging a Unity script in Visual Studio.

Unity C# Projects

Normally, when you build a Unity project, the resulting solution will not include the C# scripts you create in Unity Editor. However, you might need these scripts for debugging or to enhance the development process by decreasing the number of times you build the project in Unity and then deploy it to the device from Visual Studio. In this case, you will use Unity C# Projects. To access these C# scripts, select the Unity C# Projects checkbox in the Debugging group in the Build Settings dialog box. (See Figure 10-34.)

FIGURE 10-34 Setting up the build settings to generate Unity C# projects.

Let's see how this works in the HitTheCanGame app. Follow these steps:

1. Open the Build Settings dialog box in Unity Editor and select the **Unity C# Projects** checkbox.

2. Click the **Build** button and select the build output location.

3. When the build is complete, open the HitTheCanGame.sln file in Visual Studio. The resulting solution is made up of three projects:

    - **Assembly-CSharp-firstpass**   This is a class library with C# scripts from standard Unity assets.

    - **Assembly-CSharp**   This is a class library with the C# scripts you created, including HitTheCan.cs and ExploderCollision.cs.

    - **HitTheCanGame**   This is the application project. It references two Assembly-CSharp-firtspass and Assembly-CSharp class libraries.

4. Open the **HitTheCan.cs** file (from the built Unity project).

Because Unity Editor uses a different C# compiler than Visual Studio, Visual Studio displays productivity tips for using recent C# features. For example, Figure 10-35 shows a productivity tip over the `hitTarget` variable that suggests replacing the following statements:

```
RaycastHit hitTarget;
if (Physics.Raycast(ray, out hitTarget)) {}
```

with a simpler construction:

```
if (Physics.Raycast(ray, out RaycastHit hitTarget)){}
```

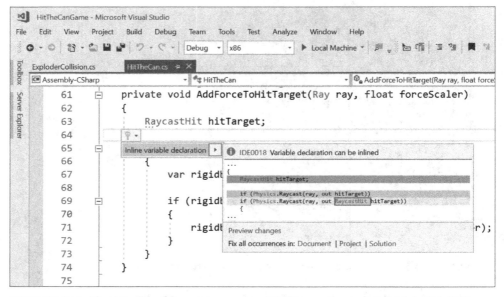

FIGURE 10-35 In Visual Studio, you can use more recent C# features than are available in Unity Editor.

You can, of course, apply this change. The project will still work in Visual Studio but will not be compatible with Unity. If you run it in Unity, you'll see the following error:

```
error CS1644: Feature 'declaration expression' cannot be used because it is not part of the C#
4.0 language specification.
```

Deploying the Project to the Hololens Emulator

After you've built the HitTheCanGame project in Unity Editor, you can deploy it to the HoloLens emulator to achieve the results shown in Figure 10-1. To test the app in the HoloLens emulator, you need to enable mouse and keyboard input by pressing the F5 key or the keyboard icon in the HoloLens emulator toolbar.

Summary

In this chapter, you took a deep dive into using Unity objects to create physics effects and learned how to create custom components called scripts. You started by associating Rigidbody components to 3D models of the cola can. Then, you learned how to use colliders to detect collisions, to use Physic Material, to perform ray casting, to tag objects, and to handle input from interaction sources such as motion controllers and simple air gestures. After that, you investigated using the Unity API to dynamically adjust an app to a particular device. Finally, you learned how to debug scripts. All these aspects were discussed in terms of the custom HitTheCanGame app you created here. In the next chapter, you will analyze animations and then use them to further extend the HitTheCanGame app.

CHAPTER 11

Animations and Navigation

This chapter shows you how to use Unity's animation and navigation systems. In this chapter, you'll create an app called AnimatedHumanoid (see Figure 11-1) that features an animated version of Ethan, the humanoid model from Chapter 9. The app's scene will contain a floor, platform, and steps. You will create an animation to enable Ethan to walk across the floor and even use audio clips that synchronize with Ethan's footsteps while he is walking. You will then apply a navigation system to enable Ethan to climb the steps and avoid other obstacles. After you create the AnimatedHumanoid app, you will learn how to create custom animations. You will use these to extend the HitTheCanGame app so the exploders rotate. (See Figure 11-2.) By the time you complete this chapter you'll be able to use Unity's animation and navigation systems in your Mixed Reality apps.

FIGURE 11-1 The AnimatedHumanoid app.

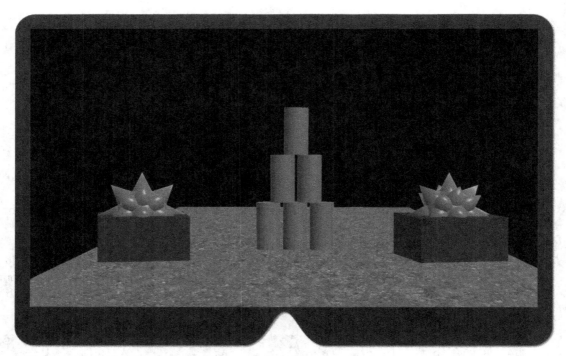

FIGURE 11-2 The HitTheCanGame app with custom animations.

Animations

The goal of an animation is to make a game object move. To achieve this you must modify one or more of the object's properties in time. For example, to translate an object, you modify the X, Y, and/or Z settings in the Transform component.

Unity has a built-in system called Mecanim that helps you create, use, and control animations. To animate game objects, Mecanim uses animation clips. These clips contain information about how specific object properties should change over time. You can import animation clips from external sources as assets or create them in Unity. Once you have your animation clips ready you can arrange and control them using an animation controller. You can apply various parameters to animation controllers and control them using scripts.

In this section you will build the AnimatedHumanoid app to learn how to import and create animation clips and control them using an animation controller.

Adding Assets and Creating the Scene

Start by creating the new Unity 3D project named AnimatedHumanoid. Then import two packages from the standard Unity assets by doing the following:

1. In the Unity Editor, open the **Assets** menu, choose **Import Package**, and select **Characters**.

2. The Import Unity Package windows open. Click the **Import** button to import all assets from that package.

3. Open the **Assets** menu, choose **Import Package**, select **Prototyping**, and click **Import** in the Import Unity Package window to import all assets from that package.

Character and Animation Assets

This chapter uses standard Unity assets to animate a humanoid model. Alternatively, you could use humanoid models and associated animations from various online services, such as Mixamo (www.mixamo.com). At the time of this writing, all Mixamo characters and animations were available free of charge for users with an active Adobe ID.

After you log on to Mixamo, click the Characters link along the top of the screen to see the list of available characters. When you download a character you specify a file format. To import a character into Unity, choose FBX for Unity (.fbx). This is the same type of file as the Ethan humanoid model in the standard Unity assets.

Mixamo also contains animations for humanoid models. To access these animations, click the Animations link (to the right from the Characters link). A list of available animations appears on the left, while an animation preview for the selected character appears on the right, enabling you to easily preview an animation before downloading it. Again, to use animations in Unity projects, download them as FBX for Unity files.

After you import the required assets, you can start designing the scene. Follow these steps:

1. First, you'll create the floor. In the Project window, type **Floor t:Model** in the search box.

2. From the list of matching items, select **FloorPrototype08x01x08**, and drag it onto the scene or to the Hierarchy.

3. In the Inspector, rename this new object **Floor**.

4. Position the Floor object at the origin by setting all the **Position** components in the **Transform** group to **0**.

5. To rescale the Floor object, set the **X** and **Y Scale** components in the **Transform** group to **2**, and the **Z** component to **4**.

6. Now you can place the Ethan humanoid model on top of the floor. In the Project window, type **Ethan t:Model** in the search box.

7. Drag the matching **Ethan** element onto the scene.

8. Set the **X** and **Y Position** components in the **Transform** group to **0**, and the **Z** component to **–7.5**. (See Figure 11-3.)

FIGURE 11-3 A scene composed of the floor and the Ethan humanoid model.

Creating and Configuring the Animator Controller

In this section you'll learn how to apply animations to the Ethan model.

> **Note** In this chapter I follow Unity's Editor nomenclature and call the controller of the animation as animator controller.

Creating an Animator Controller

Start by creating an animator controller, which you will use to arrange and control two animation clips. These clips will be used to switch Ethan between two modes: idle and walking. To get started, follow these steps:

1. Create an **Assets/Animations** folder in the Project window.

2. Right click the **Assets/Animations** folder, choose **Create**, and select **Animation Controller**.

3. Name the new controller **EthanAnimatorController**.

4. To associate the controller with the Ethan humanoid model, first switch to the Hierarchy and click the **Ethan** entry.

5. The Inspector opens with the Animator group displayed. Click the small circular icon next to the **Controller** box (see the left screen in Figure 11-4) to open the Select RuntimeAnimatorController window (see the right screen in Figure 11-4). Then select the **EthanAnimatorController** entry.

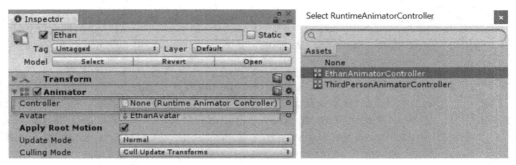

FIGURE 11-4 Configuring the animation controller.

The Animator Window

Next, you will configure the EthanAnimatorController animation controller. You do this from the Animator window. (See Figure 11-5.) To open this window, double-click **EthanAnimatorController** in the Project window. The Animator window (or Animator for short) enables you to define animation layers and event parameters and to arrange and define transitions between animation states.

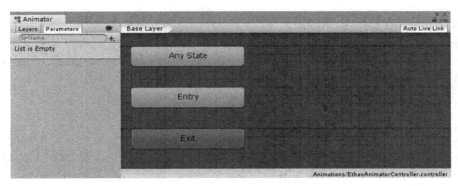

FIGURE 11-5 The Animator window.

As shown in Figure 11-5, the Animator contains two panes:

- **The Layers and Parameters pane** The left pane has two tabs: Layers and Parameters. These represent the layers and parameters widgets, respectively. You use the layer widget to define layers, which are typically employed to manage complex animations with many states and clips. You use the second widget to define animation parameters.

In Figure 11-5 no parameters are defined, and there is just one default layer, Base Layer. To create new layers or parameters you click the small plus (+) button in the top-right corner of the pane. You can create four types of parameters:

- **Int**   This is a parameter that accepts integral numbers.

- **Float**   This is a parameter that can accept fractional numbers.

- **Bool**   This is a logical-valued parameter that can be either true or false.

- **Trigger**   This is like a Bool parameter but is reset to its default value after the transition completes.

■ **The Animation State Machine (ASM) visualization pane**   This pane contains a collection of rectangular objects representing animation states. These states are also defined as the nodes of the Animation State Machine (ASM). The ASM combines states and the transitions between them to control the animation flow. Nodes can be connected via arrows, which define transitions between the states and by extension the flow of the animation.

There are three default ASM state nodes:

■ **Entry**   The Entry node represents the ASM's original state or the state at which it begins to transition to another state.

■ **Exit**   The Exit node indicates the state of the ASM at the point when the animation is finished.

■ **Any State**   This is the node used to define the transition to be performed to override the original flow of the ASM.

Extending the Animator Controller with an IsWalking Parameter

Let's extend the default animator controller by adding an IsWalking Boolean parameter. This parameter will be used to switch the ASM between two standard Unity asset animation clips: HumanoidIdle and HumanoidWalk. Follow these steps:

1. Click the **Parameters** tab in the Animator window.

2. Click the **plus** (+) icon and choose **Bool** from the menu that appears.

3. Name the new Bool parameter **IsWalking** and deselect the parameter's checkbox to set its initial value to **False**. This way, Ethan will not be walking when the application starts.

 Note You use a checkbox to set the Bool parameter's initial value. For the Int and Float parameters you use a text box, and you use an option button for the Trigger parameter.

4. Now you're ready to associate the HumanoidIdle and HumanoidWalk clips with the EthanAnimatorController animation controller's IsWalking parameter. To start, open the Project window and type **HumanoidIdle t:Animation** in the search box.

5. Drag the **HumanoidIdle** entry in the list of matching animations to the ASM visualization pane in the Animator window.

 Tip If the Project window does not display full animation names, click an entry in the search results to see its name and other properties in the top part of the Inspector.

6. Type **HumanoidWalk t:Animation** in the Project window search box and drag the **HumanoidWalk** entry to the ASM visualization pane. (See Figure 11-6.)

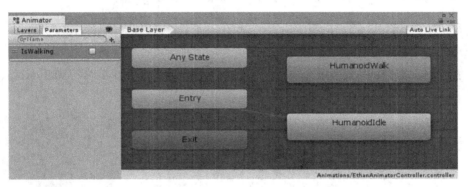

FIGURE 11-6 The ASM visualization pane with two animation clips added.

Notice the yellow arrow connecting the HumanoidIdle animation clip to the Entry node. This defines the default entry transition. Let's define two more transitions to connect the HumanoidIdle and HumanoidWalk states.

7. Right-click the **HumanoidIdle** node and choose **Make Transition** from the menu that appears. A white arrow pointing from the HumanoidIdle node to the HumanoidWalk node will displayed.

8. Right-click the **HumanoidWalk** node, choose **Make Transition**, and drag the arrow onto the **HumanoidIdle** state. Your ASM visualization pane should look like the one shown in Figure 11-7.

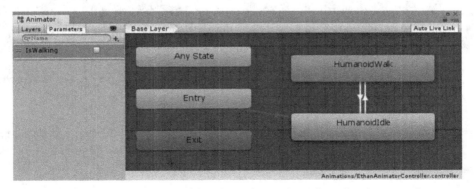

FIGURE 11-7 The final configuration of the EthanAnimatorController animation controller.

Setting the Transition Condition

Now it's time to set the transition condition. By default, when you run the app, the ASM enters the HumanoidIdle animation—meaning that Ethan is stomping his feet in place because the IsWalking parameter is false. You can change this parameter dynamically using transition condition. This indicates that when the IsWalking parameter is true, the animation state will change from HumanoidIdle to HumanoidWalk. When the IsWalking parameter is false, the Ethan model will stop walking and again start stomping his feet without moving forward. To create this transition condition, follow these steps:

1. Click the transition arrow pointing from the **HumanoidIdle** node to the **HumanoidWalk** node.

2. Open the Inspector and scroll down to the **Conditions** group.

3. Click the small **plus** (**+**) icon on the right. Two drop-down lists appear.

4. Open the left drop-down list and choose the **IsWalking** parameter.

5. Open the right drop-down list and choose **True**. (See Figure 11-8.) This will activate the HumanoidIdle-to-HumanoidWalk transition when the IsWalking is true.

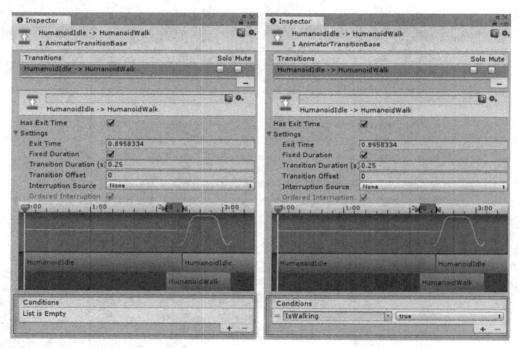

FIGURE 11-8 Transition settings.

6. Repeat steps 1 through 5 to specify the opposite condition for the HumanoidWalk-to-HumanoidIdle transition, where the **IsWalking** parameter is set to **False** in the Inspector.

7. Click the **Play** button to test the conditions and activate Game view to observe the results. Notice that the Ethan character stomps his feet. Again, this is because the HumanoidIdle animation clip is being played.

8. To make Ethan walk instead of stomp, select the **IsWalking** checkbox in the Parameters tab in the Animator window.

9. After a short while, Ethan starts walking. (See Figure 11-9.) Notice that the ASM visualization pane in the Animator shows the progress of the clip. (See Figure 11-10.)

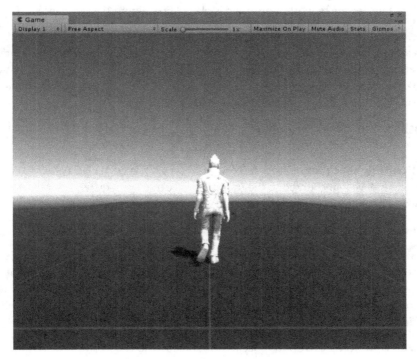

FIGURE 11-9 The Ethan figure begins walking.

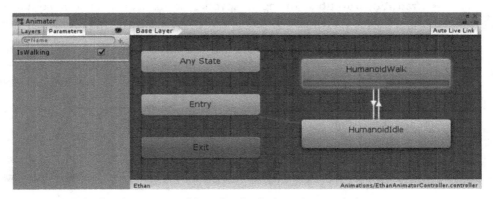

FIGURE 11-10 Viewing the progress of the animation in the Animator window.

Applying Transition Settings

To improve the animator controller such that Ethan starts walking immediately after the IsWalking parameter becomes true you use transition settings.

You access all transition settings in the Transitions group in the Inspector. (Refer to Figure 11-8.) This group contains the following options and settings:

- **Available transitions**   At the top of the Transitions group is a list of all available transitions. You can also rearrange items in the Transitions group to set the priority and order of execution. The top item has the highest priority and is played first. Figure 11-8 contains just one option: HumanoidIdle -> HumanoidWalk.

- **Solo and Mute**   Each transition listed in the Transitions group has two corresponding checkboxes: Solo and Mute. These options are typically used in complex transitions with many animation states to either disable the selected state (mute) or disable all other states (solo) from the transition.

- **Transition name box**   Below the list of transitions is a box that you can use to name the selected transition.

- **Has Exit Time checkbox**   Select this checkbox only if you want a delay before the transition. In this case leave it unchecked so the transition will occur immediately after the value of the IsWalking parameter is changed and Ethan will start walking right away.

- **Settings**   Expand this option to access the following settings:

  - **Exit Time**   This option is available only when the Has Exit Time checkbox is selected. It specifies the time when the transition should occur in normalized units between 0 and 1, where 0 denotes the beginning and 1 the end. So, a value of 0.5 will correspond to an exit time at the middle of the total transition time. You can preview the transition and its time using the timeline editor at the bottom of the Settings options.

  - **Fixed Duration**   This option specifies whether the transition time is given in seconds (unchecked) or as a fraction of the normalized time (as a percentage) of the source state.

  - **Transition Duration**   This option specifies the transition duration in seconds (when the Fixed Duration setting is disabled) or in the normalized time of the source state otherwise.

  - **Transition Offset**   This option indicates the fraction of the total transition duration that will be skipped when playing the animation. For instance, if Transition Offset is set to 0.25, the target state animation will be executed starting from 25% of its total duration time.

  - **Interruption Source**   This option defines how the transition can be interrupted. Interruption source can take one of the following values:

    - **None**   Transitions cannot be interrupted.

    - **Current State**   Transitions can be interrupted by triggers on the source state.

- **Next State** Transitions can be interrupted only by the next state—that is, the state with the next-lower priority than the current one.

- **Current State Then Next State** Transitions can be interrupted depending on the current and then next states.

- **Next State Then Current State** Transitions can be interrupted depending on the next and then current state.

> **Tip** See this article for more details on the Interruption Source setting: http://bit.ly/transition_interruptions.

- **Ordered Interruption** When this option is checked, the current transition can be interrupted by other transitions regardless of their order. This setting is unavailable when Interruption Source is set to None or Next State.

■ **Preview** This displays a preview of the animation performed during the transition. (See Figure 11-11.) Because the animation controller is associated with the Ethan model, all animation clips are applied to this object instead of the default one. (Refer to Figure 11-6.)

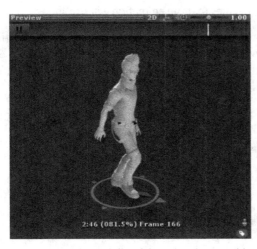

FIGURE 11-11 The preview of the animation transition shows Ethan walking.

Animator Properties

Figure 11-4 in the section "Creating an animator controller" showed settings in the Inspector's Animator group for the Ethan model. You've already worked with the Controller setting in that group. In this section you'll explore the other settings. As shown in Figure 11-12 these settings are as follows:

■ **Avatar** This setting allows you to specify an avatar for the humanoid model you are animating. The avatar defines the model's bone structure or rig. Unity matches the character's bone structure to the avatar structure for humanoid animations. In this example this option was automatically set to EthanAvatar.

- **Apply Root Motion** This setting specifies whether the humanoid movement will be controlled by the dedicated script (true) or through the animation (false).

- **Update Mode** This setting indicates when the Animator is updated. It has three options:

  - **Normal** This synchronizes the Animator with the `Update` method. Because this method is not always invoked at fixed time intervals, animations may be slowed to match their execution with the `Update` event.

  - **Animate Physics** This synchronizes the Animator with the `FixedUpdate` method so it is updated at fixed time intervals. This update mode is dedicated for animations in which the humanoid model interacts with rigid bodies.

  - **Unscaled Time** This synchronizes the Animator with the `Update` method but without slowing down the animation.

- **Culling Mode** You can use this setting to specify what happens when the animated humanoid model is off the screen. It has three options:

  - **Always Animate** This setting specifies that the animation will continue.

  - **Cull Update Transforms** This setting specifies that inverse kinematics, animation retargeting, and updates to transforms are disabled when the animated object is off the screen. (See http://bit.ly/unity_ik and http://bit.ly/unity_retargeting for more on inverse kinematics and animation retargeting, respectively.)

  - **Cull Completely** This setting disables the animation.

FIGURE 11-12 The Animator group settings for the Ethan model.

Animation Clips

The animation clips and the Ethan model are stored as FBX files. In general, FBX is a file format used to exchange 3D data between various applications. FBX has hierarchical, adaptable structure. It can store various structures representing 3D objects, including models, rigs, animations, and materials. You can import these elements into Unity using a dedicated importer. Follow these steps to view the import settings:

1. Click any animation clip in the Project window. In this example select the **HumanoidWalk** clip.

2. Click the **Edit** button in the top-right corner of the Inspector.

    An import window opens. It contains four tabs—Model, Rig, Animation, and Materials, each with various import settings—because Unity can import each of these types of items from FBX files. (For information about these settings, see http://bit.ly/FBX_Importer.)

3. Click the **Animation** tab.

Figure 11-13 shows all the settings for the HumanoidWalk animation clip. You can divide these settings into animation-specific and clip-specific properties.

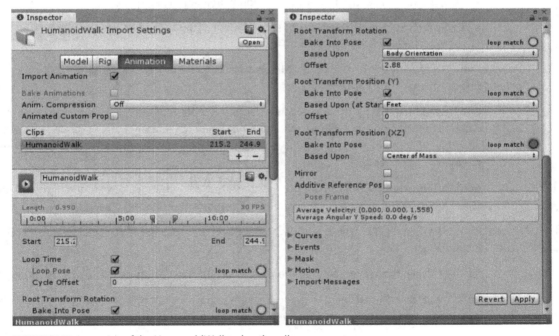

FIGURE 11-13 Inspector of the HumanoidWalk animation clip

Animation-specific settings, starting in the top-left part of Figure 11-13, apply to all clips in the FBX file. They are as follows:

- **Import Animation** This setting specifies whether the animation should be imported. If not, the animation saved in the FBX file will be ignored.

- **Bake Animations** This setting allows you to bake (plot) the animation. It is only available for animations exported from Maya, 3dsMax, and Cinema4D files.

- **Animation Compression** This setting specifies the method of animation compression during import. There are three options:

  - **Off** No compression will be applied.

  - **Keyframe Reduction** Unnecessary keyframes will be removed.

  - **Optimal** Unity will decide whether compression is required and apply keyframe reduction if needed.

- **Animated Custom Properties** This setting indicates whether custom animatable properties will be imported.

  You can adjust clip-specific settings separately for each clip from the FBX file by modifying the following properties:

  - **Start and End** These settings specify the start and end frame of the animation clip.

  - **Loop Pose** This setting smooths the motion animation on replay.

  - **Cycle Offset** This setting specifies the number of frames before the animation restarts when looping is enabled.

Mecanim uses three kinds of mathematical objects to achieve smooth and natural character movements:

- **Body transform (BT)** This defines the character's center of mass. This is a special point in a game object. If a force is applied to the center point, the object will move toward the force's direction without any rotation. So, the center of mass provides the most stable displacement model for the character.

- **Body orientation (BO)** This defines the character's orientation relative to the model's T-pose. (The T-pose is when the character is standing straight with spread-eagle arms.)

- **Root transform (RT)** This is a projection of BT on the Y plane. RT is calculated at runtime to move the game object.

You can use the clip properties to parameterize the calculation of RT using the following settings:

- **Root Transform Rotation** These settings determine how the object's rotation will be modified during animation. The settings are as follows:

  - **Bake Into Pose** When you select this setting, the animation clip will not rotate the game object. The corresponding Loop Match icon indicates whether the animation clip is a good candidate for baking (green) or not (red).

- **Based Upon**   This sets the orientation of the clip. There are three options:

  - **Body Orientation**   Choose this to orient the animation clip—or more precisely the direction toward which the object's rotation will be modified during animation—to follow the forward vector of the game object.

  - **Original**   Choose this to use the clip's original orientation.

  - **Offset**   This setting specifies the value to be added to control the object's rotation during animation.

- **Root Transform Position (Y)**   This setting determines how the vertical position of the model will change during animation:

  - **Bake Into Pose**   This setting specifies, whether the Y component of the motion should be fixed during animation. Again, the Loop Match icon indicates whether the animation clip is a good candidate for baking.

  - **Based Upon**   This setting sets the method for controlling the height. The height can be changed based on the center of mass or by feet, or you can use the original value from the animation clip. If you select Feet, the Y position will match the lowest foot of all frames.

  - **Offset**   This setting specifies the value to be added to control the Y position of the model.

- **Root Transform Position (XZ)**   This setting determines how the horizonal position of the model will change during animation. The options are Bake Into Pose and Based Upon, and are analogous to corresponding Root Transform Position (Y) settings.

> **Note** In addition to all these are settings to configure parameters related to curves, events, and masks, or to define custom motion.

Script

Now that you've configured the animation and understand all the settings, you're ready to create a script that will dynamically alter the IsWalking parameter whenever the user clicks the left mouse button during runtime. Follow these steps:

1. In the **Project** window, create a **Scripts** folder inside the **Assets** folder.

2. Right-click the **Scripts** folder, choose **Create**, and select **C# Script** to create a new script file.

3. Rename the script file **EthanScript**.

4. In the Inspector, click **Add Component** and choose **EthanScript** to associate the script with the Ethan object.

5. Double-click the script file and add the script in Listing 11-1. This script contains the full definition of the EthanScript class and references to necessary namespaces.

LISTING 11-1 A full definition of the EthanScript class

```
using UnityEngine;

public class EthanScript : MonoBehaviour
{
    private Animator animator;
    private bool isWalking = false;

    private void Start()
    {
        TryGetComponent(ref animator, "Animator is unavailable");
    }

    private void Update()
    {
        if (Input.GetMouseButtonDown(0))
        {
            UpdateAnimatorParameter();
        }
    }

    private void TryGetComponent<T>(ref T field, string errorMessage)
    {
        field = GetComponent<T>();

        if(field == null)
        {
            Debug.LogError(errorMessage);
        }
    }

    private void UpdateAnimatorParameter()
    {
        if (animator != null)
        {
            isWalking = !isWalking;

            animator.SetBool("IsWalking", isWalking);
        }
    }
}
```

The EthanScript class is composed of two fields and four methods:

- **animator** This field is of type UnityEngine.Animator and stores a reference to the Animator component.

- **isWalking** This field stores the current value of the IsWalking transition parameter. Hence, the initial value of the isWalking field is false.

- **Start** When the rendering starts, EthanScript invokes the Start method, in which the reference to the Animator component is obtained using the TryGetComponent helper method.

- **TryGetComponent**   This is a generic method that tries to obtain a reference to a component of a given type (in this case, `Animator`) stored in the specified field. If the reference to the given component cannot be obtained, the Unity console displays an error message, and the `IsWalking` transition parameter cannot be changed. This method appears in several other places in this chapter.

- **UpdateAnimatorParameter**   During every call to the `Update` method, the script checks whether the user has clicked the left mouse button. If so, this method will be invoked. This method changes the value stored in the `isWalking` field and then uses it with the `Animator.SetBool` method to update the `IsWalking` transition parameter.

- **Animator.SetBool**   As mentioned, the `UpdateAnimatorParameter` method works with the `Animator.SetBool` method to update the `IsWalking` transition parameter. `Animator.SetBool` accepts two arguments: the ID or name of the transition parameter and the new value for that parameter.

The `Animator` class implements three other methods to update transition parameters of integer, float, and trigger type: `Animator.SetInteger`, `Animator.SetFloat` and `Animator.SetTrigger`.

To see how the script in Listing 11-1 works, click **Play**. When the app preview is activated, the Ethan model will be stomping his feet. If you click the mouse, the `IsWalking` parameter will change to `true`, and Ethan will start walking.

In-Place Animations

The script in Listing 11-1 works very well. Ethan is translated because the animation clip updates his position (Root Transform XZ is enabled and not baked). However, sometimes an imported animation—for instance, from the Mixamo service—has disabled Root Transform XZ. In such cases you must use the script to control the model's position by implementing a `MonoBehavior.OnAnimatorMove` callback. This callback is invoked at each frame after the animation has been evaluated. You use it to change the model position before the subsequent animations (which aim at repositioning the character) are executed. To implement this functionality, you typically extend the script as shown in Listing 11-2.

LISTING 11-2 Moving the in-place animated character

```
private void OnAnimatorMove()
{
    if (animator && isWalking)
    {
        var zOffset = animator.speed * Time.deltaTime;
        transform.position += new Vector3(0, 0, zOffset);
    }
}
```

`OnAnimatorMove` in Listing 11-2 updates the Z property of the model transform so the character will be translated at each animation frame. The translation distance is calculated based on the speed at which the animation is played (`animator.speed`) and the time that passed since the last frame has been completed. This time represents the delay between two consecutive calls to the `Update` method. To obtain this delay you use the deltaTime property of the UnityEngine.Time class. This class exposes several static properties, providing various information about time in Unity. For instance, apart from deltaTime, the Time class also has a fixedDeltaTime property, representing the interval between calls to the FixedUpdate method. So, you typically use fixedDeltaTime for physics-related applications.

Audio Effects

In this project you will use audio effects to play an audio clip of footsteps whenever Ethan is walking. You obtain the footsteps audio samples from the Unity standard assets. This section also covers how to create spatial 3D sound effects, which you can use to implement spatial sound for the HoloLens headset.

To use audio effects in Unity you typically need two components: Audio Source and Audio Listener. Audio Source generates sound, while Audio Listener receives it. Audio Source and Audio Listener are used to simulate real-world or spatial sound experience, in which audio sources or listeners can move relatively to each other, which changes their perception of the sound. People experience this every day. For example, at a train station, as a train approaches the platform, the volume and frequency of the sound of the incoming train changes.

To learn how to use Audio Source and Audio Listener, follow these steps:

1. Select the Ethan object in the Hierarchy.

2. In the Inspector click **Add Component** and choose **Audio Source**. The Inspector should look like Figure 11-14.

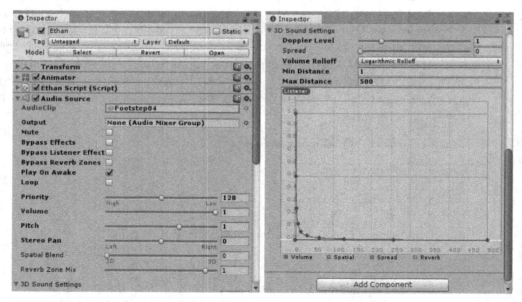

FIGURE 11-14 Inspector for the Ethan object with Audio Source settings expanded.

3. To choose an audio clip, click the small circular icon to the right of the AudioClip box.

4. The Select AudioClip window appears. Select one of the Footstep audio clips. (I chose **Footstep04.wav**.)

   By default, Audio Listener is attached to the camera object. It has no configurable properties. It merely acts as a virtual sound recording device that receives sound from the source and plays it to the user through a device's speakers.

   To play the audio clip when Ethan is walking, you extend the `EthanScript` class. But first you need to change two settings in the Inspector. (Refer to Figure 11-14.)

5. Deselect the **Play On Awake** checkbox so the audio clip won't play when the app starts. (You don't want to hear footsteps when Ethan is stomping.)

6. Select the **Loop** checkbox so the footsteps clip will be played continuously.

7. Extend the definition of the `EthanScript` class by adding the following field:

```
private AudioSource audioSource;
```

This field stores a reference to the `AudioSource` component.

8. Define two helper methods as outlined in Listing 11-3.

   LISTING 11-3 Obtaining a reference to the AudioSource component

```
private void UpdateAudioClip()
{
    if(audioSource != null)
    {
        if (isWalking)
        {
            audioSource.Play();
        }
        else
        {
            audioSource.Stop();
        }
    }
}
```

   This method uses a reference to the Audio Source component to either play the audio clip (`isWalking` is `true`) or stop it (`isWalking` is `false`). To do this, you use appropriate properties of the `AudioSource` class instance.

9. To obtain an instance of the `AudioSource` class, use the `TryGetComponent` method, which you invoke in the `Start` method of `EthanScript`:

```
private void Start()
{
    TryGetComponent(ref animator, "Animator is unavailable");
    TryGetComponent(ref audioSource, "AudioSource is unavailable");
}
```

10. Use `UpdateAudioClip` in the `Update` method as shown in Listing 11-4.

LISTING 11-4 Modified version of the `Start` and `Update` methods from the `EthanScript` class

```
private void Update()
{
    if (Input.GetMouseButtonDown(0))
    {
        UpdateAnimatorParameter();

        UpdateAudioClip();
    }
}
```

11. Click **Play**. After a moment you will see Ethan stomping.

12. Click the left mouse button.

Ethan starts walking and footsteps are audible. However, the volume of the footsteps does not decrease when Ethan moves away from the Audio Listener attached to the camera. This effect does not seem natural. To solve this problem, you can use the following two Unity parameters:

- **Spatial Blend** This transforms 2D sounds (left and right audio channel) into a 3D sound.

- **Volume Rolloff** This simulates the real perception of the sound. Unity's 3D sound engine can emulate audio attenuation according to distance (volume roll-off) and direction.

You configure the Spatial Blend function using the Spatial Blend slider (refer to the left side of Figure 11-14). The Spatial Blend value can range from 0 to 1. This value indicates how much the sound will be spatially blended or how much the 3D engine will affect the audio source. The larger the value, the more obvious the effect.

There are three controls to configure the Volume Rolloff function, located in the 3D Sound Settings group in the Inspector. (Refer to the right side of Figure 11-14.)

- **Volume Rolloff** This drop-down list contains three rolloff modes, which change the volumes between the minimum and maximum distances.

- **Min Distance** Use this box to set the distance at which the volume will begin to be attenuated. The volume will not be attenuated until the audio source is farther from the listener than this distance.

- **Max Distance** Use this box to set the distance at which the volume will stop being attenuated.

You can configure the specific volume attenuation using the various Volume Rolloff options, which determine how the sound volume decreases as the audio source moves. The options are as follows. (See Figure 11-15.)

- **Logarithmic Rolloff** If you select this option the volume will be decreased logarithmically with distance. So, the most rapid volume decrease will be for smaller distances.

- **Linear Rolloff** This option decreases the volume linearly (at constant steps) with distance.

- **Custom Rolloff** This option enables you to manually configure a custom rolloff function. To do so you modify the curve displayed in the bottom part of Audio Source properties by clicking and dragging the endpoints or the whole curve. (Note that for this option only the Max Distance box is available.)

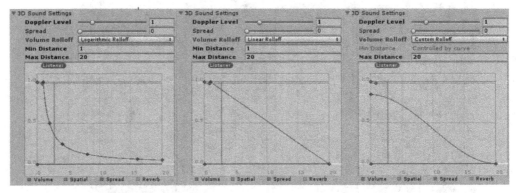

FIGURE 11-15 Volume Rolloff functions.

To enable 3D sound for the app, follow these steps:

1. Set the **Spatial Blending** slider to **1**.

2. Set the **Min Distance** to **1**.

3. Set the **Max Distance** to **20**.

4. Open the **Volume Rolloff** drop-down list and choose **Linear Rolloff**. (Later I recommend that you experiment with other possible volume roll-off functions.)

5. Click **Play**. Notice that the volume of the footsteps audio clip decreases when Ethan moves away.

Navigation and Pathfinding

Let's extend the app so the Ethan model will walk through the scene. In this section, you will improve the HumanoidAnimation project in two ways:

- By adding scene objects, including steps, which the model can walk up (see Figure 11-16)
- By specifying a destination point in the scene that the model will approach

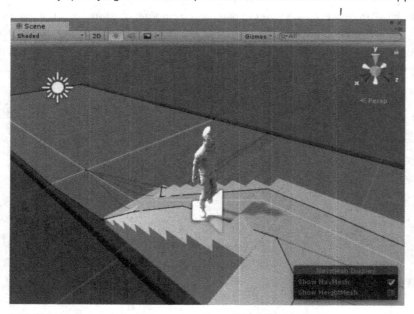

FIGURE 11-16 Scene view of the app we will create in this subsection.

To find the optimal path between the origin and destination points of the model's path, you will use Unity's pathfinding mechanism. This approach is based on the A* algorithm. (For more information, see http://bit.ly/A_star.) The goal of this procedure is to find the shortest path between two points. This is fairly straightforward when there are no obstacles between path endpoints. However, the app scene contains several areas that could be defined as non-walkable for the model, which the model should avoid. Hopefully, Unity's pathfinding algorithm can take these areas into account when identifying the shortest path that avoids them.

To start, add the steps to the scene. Follow these steps:

1. Open the Project window and type **steps t:Model** in the search box.

2. In the search results, select **StepsPrototype04x02x02**, and drag it onto the scene.

3. Change the step model's name to **Steps L**.

4. In the Inspector, change the Steps L model's **Position** settings in the **Transform** group as follows:

- **X: 0**

- **Y: 0**

- **Z: −4**

5. Apply the RollerBallWhite material to the Step L model. To do so, type **RollerBallWhite t:Material** in the search box in the Project window. Then drag the material onto the **Steps L** object in the Hierarchy or Scene view.

6. Click **Play** and then click the left mouse button.

The Ethan model starts walking. However, as shown in Figure 11-17, rather than climbing the steps, it blends with the steps. You'll fix this problem in the next section.

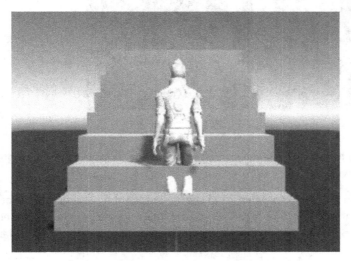

FIGURE 11-17 Ethan does not yet know how to climb the stairs.

The Nav Mesh Agent Component

To enable the Ethan model to walk through the area, called the navigation mesh, you must add a Nav Mesh Agent (or Agent for short) component. In addition to enabling the model to walk through the mesh, the Agent component also endows the model with intelligence so it can avoid both static and moving obstacles.

To add the Agent component to the Ethan model, follow these steps:

1. Select the **Ethan** object in the Hierarchy or by clicking it in the Scene view.

2. In the Inspector, click the **Add Component** button, type **Nav Mesh Agent** in the search box, and select **Nav Mesh Agent** in the list.

A collision cylinder representing the Nav Mesh Agent component appears around the Ethan model. (See Figure 11-18.) This collision cylinder serves as a virtual representation of the model, which Unity uses to avoid obstacles.

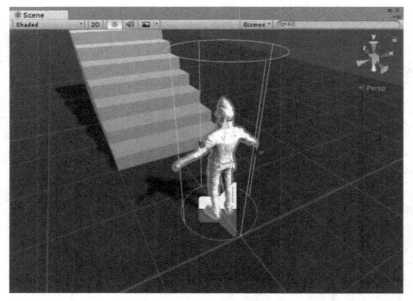

FIGURE 11-18 Scene view showing the cylinder.

You can use the Inspector to configure the properties of the Agent component. (See Figure 11-19.) Options include the following:

- **Agent Type** You use this drop-down list to choose the agent type. Different agent types have different characteristics (like radius and height) that approximate the associated object. By default, this drop-down list has a single option: Humanoid. You'll learn how to define more agent types later.

- **Base Offset** This represents the offset for the collision cylinder from the agent pivot point (the center of the cylinder).

- **Speed** This is the maximum linear speed of the agent, expressed in world units (usually meters) per second. The default value of 3.5 meters per second is equivalent to approximately 12 kilometers per hour or 7.8 miles per hour.

- **Angular Speed** This defines the maximum rotational speed, expressed in degrees per second.

- **Acceleration** This defines the acceleration of the agent, expressed in world units per second squared.

- **Stopping Distance**   This is used to specify the acceptable distance variation. This value is used when the agent is approaching its destination. When the difference between the actual and destination position is below the stopping distance, the model stops moving.

- **Auto Braking**   This indicates whether the model should slow down as it approaches its destination.

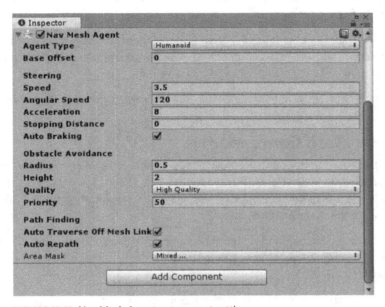

FIGURE 11-19 Nav Mesh Agent component settings.

The Inspector for the Nav Mesh Agent also contains Obstacle Avoidance and Path Finding settings. You use the Obstacle Avoidance settings to specify how the model will avoid obstacles. Each obstacle is defined as an object that prevents the model from moving through it. These settings are as follows:

- **Radius and Height**   The larger these values, the larger the margin between the model and an obstacle will be.

- **Quality**   The larger this value, the more precise the pathfinding calculations will be. This may look better but it will decrease overall app performance.

- **Priority**   Use this parameter to specify how important the Agent component is. This parameter accepts values between 0 and 99. The lower the number, the higher the priority. Agent components with a lower priority than the current one will be ignored during obstacle avoidance.

You use the Path Finding settings to configure the agent's behavior when it reaches the end of the path or reaches non-walkable areas. These settings are as follows:

- **Auto Traverse Off**   This specifies whether the agent should automatically traverse off-mesh links. The off-mesh link is the navigation shortcut.

- **Auto Repath**   This indicates whether the agent will try to find a new walkable path when it reaches the end of a partial path.

- **Area Mask**   This specifies the type of regions that the Agent component will consider during mesh preparation. There are several predefined masks, including walkable masks and non-walkable masks.

For now, leave all the parameters at their default values. You will experiment with them later.

The Navigation Mesh Component

After you configure the Agent component, you need to specify the walkable areas for the model. To do so, you create a Navigation Mesh (NavMesh) component. This component defines the regions the model can traverse. In the case of VR development, the Navigation Mesh component can also define the virtual world in which the user can move.

You define the NavMesh component using the Navigation dialog box. (To open this dialog box, open the **Windows** menu in Unity and choose **Navigation**.) This dialog box contains four tabs. (For more about each tab, read on.)

- **Agents**   Use this tab to create new and edit existing agent types.

- **Areas**   Use this tab to define areas, which you then use to configure an area mask.

- **Bake**   Use this tab to create a navigation mesh.

- **Object**   Use this tab to select and configure objects to be included in the calculation of the navigation mesh.

Typically, the process of creating the navigation mesh proceeds as follows:

1. You use the Agents and Areas tabs to define your agents and areas. Everything you define in these tabs will appear in the Agent Type and Agent Mask fields of the Nav Mesh Agent Inspector, respectively. (Refer to Figure 11-19.)

2. You use the Object tab to choose game objects to be included in the navigation mesh.

3. You use the Bake tab to start calculations. Once they are finished you can test your solution.

The Agents Tab

Figure 11-20 shows the Agents tab of the Navigation dialog box. This tab contains a list of already-defined agent types. You can create or remove agent types by clicking the small plus (+) and minus (–) icons, respectively. Below the list is a light blue cylinder, which is the visual representation of the agent.

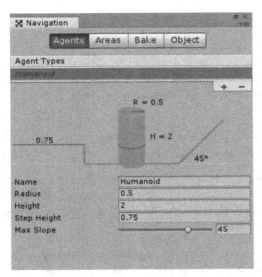

FIGURE 11-20 The Agents tab of the Navigation dialog box.

You can configure five options to describe the agent:

- **Name**   This specifies the agent name. This name appears in the Agent Type drop-down list in the Inspector for the Nav Mesh Agent component.

- **Radius**   This specifies the radius of the cylinder representing the agent. This value is also denoted by the R in the blue cylinder preview.

- **Height**   This specifies the cylinder height. This value is also denoted as the H in the cylinder preview.

- **Step Height**   In general, the agent can walk on platforms or steps that are positioned at different heights. So, this setting specifies the height difference for which different navigation meshes (platforms or steps) are considered connected. This way, the agent can easily navigate between them.

- **Max Slope**   The navigation mesh calculation will ignore all surfaces with a slope higher than this value.

This example shows just one agent type, Humanoid. It was defined with the following default values:

- **Radius: 0.5 m**

- **Height: 2 m**

- **Step Height: 0.75 m**

- **Max Slope: 45°**

The Areas Tab

Figure 11-21 shows the Areas tab of the Navigation dialog box. This tab consists of a table with three columns:

- Column 1 contains a color and a corresponding area type (either built-in or user-defined). Unity uses the color to draw the navigation mesh in the Scene view.

- Column 2 shows the area name. The names of built-in areas are Walkable, Not Walkable, and Jump. (Note that you cannot modify Not Walkable areas.) To add a user-defined area simply type a name in this column for any User row. In Figure 11-21, I created a custom area by typing New Area in column 2 of the User 3 row.

- Column 3 displays the area cost. This describes how difficult it is for the model to move through an area. The higher the cost, the more difficult (or the more time is needed) for the model to pass through the area.

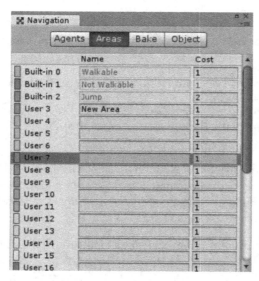

FIGURE 11-21 The Areas tab of the Navigation dialog box.

The Object Tab

Figure 11-22 shows the Object tab of the Navigation dialog box. This tab does not contain any configurable options until you select an appropriate object in the Hierarchy or in the Scene view. To access the settings shown in Figure 11-22 I selected the Steps L object in the Hierarchy. Steps L has a Mesh Renderer component, so you can use it to define the navigation mesh. (Only terrains or objects associated with mesh renderers can be included in the navigation mesh.)

FIGURE 11-22 The Object tab of the Navigation dialog box.

This tab contains three configurable options:

- **Navigation Static** Use this checkbox to indicate whether the object should (selected) or should not (deselected) be included when the navigation mesh is baked.

- **Generate OffMeshLinks** Use this checkbox to enable or disable the generation of off-mesh links. These links can connect meshes on different levels. For example, you could create one mesh for the bottom level of the scene and one for the top level. An off-mesh link could then connect these two meshes to enable the model to jump between levels.

- **Navigation Area** This drop-down list is populated with items defined in the Areas tab. You use it to select the navigation area.

To proceed, use the Object tab to ensure that both the Steps L and Floor objects are marked as navigation static and are associated with the Walkable navigation area.

The Bake Tab

Figure 11-23 shows the Bake tab of the Navigation dialog box. You click the Bake button in this tab to calculate the navigation mesh.

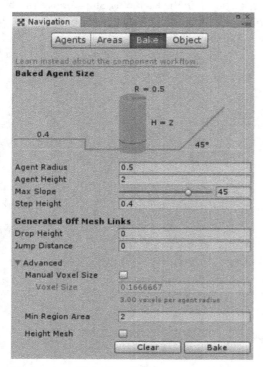

FIGURE 11-23 The Bake tab of the Navigation dialog box.

Before you calculate the navigation mesh, you can adjust various settings in this tab. These include the following:

- **Baked Agent Size settings** This group of settings includes Agent Radius, Agent Height, Max Slope, and Step Height parameters. These are the same as the parameters in the Agents tab.

- **Generated Off Mesh Links settings** This group of settings includes the following parameters:

  - **Drop Height** Use this box to specify the height threshold below which off-mesh links will be created for adjacent navigation meshes.

  - **Jump Distance** Use this box to specify the horizontal distance threshold below which off-mesh links will be created for adjacent navigation meshes.

- **Advanced** This group of settings includes the following:

  - **Manual Voxel Size** Select this checkbox to set the voxel size manually. (A voxel is the 3D equivalent of a pixel.)

- **Min Region Area**   This specifies the area threshold. Regions smaller than this threshold will be discarded when the navigation mesh is created.

- **Height Mesh**   Select this checkbox for accurate character placement on the navigation mesh. Without this option, the character is moved along an approximate surface.

Baking the Navigation Mesh

To bake the navigation mesh, click the Bake button in the Bake tab. How long it takes to bake depends on how many game objects are included in the navigation mesh. Here, we have only two objects (Steps L and Floor), so baking is quick. After the baking process is complete, the Scene view should look like Figure 11-24.

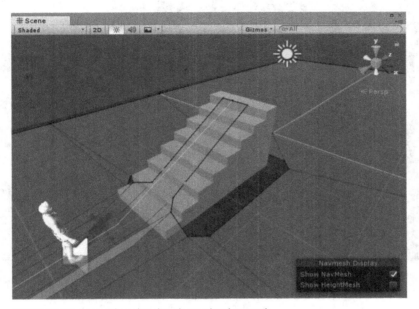

FIGURE 11-24 Scene view showing the navigation mesh.

Notice the small Navmesh Display window in the bottom-right corner of the screen. This window contains two checkboxes:

- **Show NavMesh**   Use this checkbox to display or hide the navigation mesh.

- **Show HeightMesh**   Use this checkbox to display the height mesh.

When the Show NavMesh option is enabled, the Unity editor displays light blue rectangles that represent walkable areas. (Refer to Figure 11-24.) In this case these rectangles indicate that the Ethan model can walk around the floor and climb the steps. Other kinds of areas are represented by other colors (defined in the Areas tab).

To view the results, click Play, and then click the left mouse button. Based on the defined walkable areas, you will see Ethan approach the steps and then climb them. (See Figure 11-25.) However, when Ethan approaches the last step, he starts walking in place. This is because there is no more walkable area, and we have not programmatically stopped Ethan from continuing to move. You'll fix this in the next section.

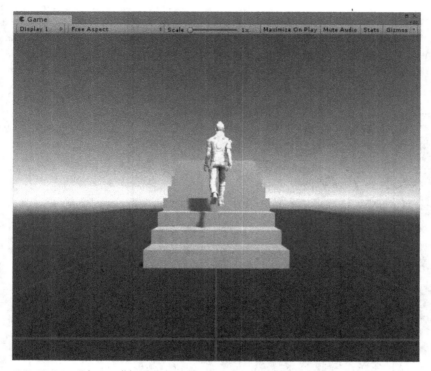

FIGURE 11-25 Ethan walking up the stairs.

Pathfinding

In this section you'll add more steps and two platforms to the scene. As shown in Figure 11-26, the first platform will connect the stairs, while the second platform will serve as an obstacle for the Ethan character. After you set up the scene, you will create the navigation path for the Ethan model that will connect two points on the opposite sides of the obstructing platform. To avoid the obstruction, Ethan will have to climb the first set of stairs, walk across the upper platform, and descend the second set of stairs.

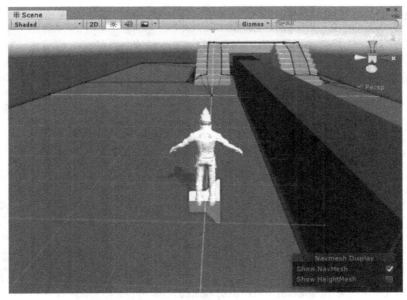

FIGURE 11-26 The scene with additional steps, two platforms, and an obstacle.

To add the steps and two platforms to the scene, follow these steps:

1. In the Hierarchy, click the **Steps L** object.

2. In the **Transform** group of the Inspector, under **Position**, change the **Z** setting from **–4** to **5**.

3. In the Project window, add the following objects to the scene:

    -   **PlatformPrototype04x01x04**

    -   **PlatformPrototype08x01x08**

    -   **StepsPrototype04x02x02**

4. In the Inspector, configure the **StepsPrototype04x02x02** object as follows:

    -   **Name: Steps R**

    -   **Position:**

        X: 5

        Y: 0

        Z: 5

    -   **Material: RollerBallGrey**

5. In the Inspector, configure the **PlatformPrototype04x01x04** object as follows:

- **Name: Platform**
- **Position:**

    X: 2.5

    Y: 2

    Z: 9

- **Scale:**

    X: 1.75

    Y: 0.5

    Z: 1

- **Material: RollerBallGrey**

6. In the Inspector, configure the **PlatformPrototype08x01x08** object as follows:

- **Name: Obstacle**
- **Position:**

    X: 2.5

    Y: 1

    Z: –2

- **Scale:**

    X: 0.2

    Y: 1

    Z: 3.5

- **Material: Default (NavyGrid)**

Now let's create the navigation mesh. Follow these steps:

7. In the Hierarchy, click **Steps R**.

8. In the Navigation dialog box, click the **Object** tab.

9. Select the **Navigation Static** checkbox.

10. Click the **Navigation Area** drop-down list and choose **Walkable**.

11. Repeat steps 1–4 for the **Platform** object.

12. In the Hierarchy, click **Obstacle**.

13. In the **Object** tab of the Navigation dialog box, select the **Navigation Static** checkbox.

14. Click the **Navigation Area** drop-down list and choose **Not Walkable**.

15. Click the **Bake** tab and click the **Bake** button to create the navigation mesh. Your scene should look like the one in Figure 11-26.

Now you're ready to implement the script that will set the navigation path so that Ethan goes to the other side of the obstacle using the steps and one of the platforms. Open EthanScript.cs (in the Assets/Scripts/EthanScript folder) and do the following:

1. Use the following command to import the **UnityEngine.AI** namespace:

```
using UnityEngine.AI;
```

2. Add the following two fields to the EthanScript class:

```
private NavMeshAgent navMeshAgent;
private bool isPathSet = false;
```

3. In the EthanScript class, define the two methods in Listing 11-5:

LISTING 11-5 Setting the navigation path and checking whether the agent destination has been reached

```
private void SetPath(Vector3 destination)
{
    if (navMeshAgent != null && !isPathSet)
    {
        var navMeshPath = new NavMeshPath();

        if (NavMesh.CalculatePath(transform.position,
            destination, NavMesh.AllAreas, navMeshPath))
        {
            navMeshAgent.SetPath(navMeshPath);

            isPathSet = true;
        }
        else
        {
            Debug.Log("The path cannot be determined");
        }
    }
    else
    {
        navMeshAgent.isStopped = !isWalking;
    }
}

private void CheckIfDestinationWasReached()
{
    if (navMeshAgent != null)
    {
        if (navMeshAgent.remainingDistance <= navMeshAgent.stoppingDistance && isWalking)
        {
            UpdateAnimatorParameter();
```

```
            UpdateAudioClip();
        }
    }
}
```

4. Modify the Update method as shown in Listing 11-6.

    LISTING 11-6 Update method of the EthanScript class

    ```
    void Update()
    {
        if (Input.GetMouseButtonDown(0))
        {
            UpdateAnimatorParameter();

            UpdateAudioClip();

            SetPath(new Vector3(5, 0, -7));
        }

        CheckIfDestinationWasReached();
    }
    ```

Click Play and click the left mouse button. Ethan will start walking toward the destination point specified by the argument of the SetPath method (refer to Listing 11-5). Specifically, he will attempt to reach the following location: X: 5, Y: 0, Z: –7. This point is on the opposite side of the Obstacle object. Because this Obstacle was marked as Not Walkable, Ethan cannot move through it. So, he will climb the steps on the left, walk across the platform, and then descend the steps on the right. He will stop moving, when he reaches his destination.

To calculate the navigation path, you use the CalculatePath static method of the UnityEngine .AI.NavMesh class. Unity implements two overridden versions of the CalculatePath method. They return a Boolean value, indicating whether the path was successfully identified. Both CalculatePath versions accept the following four arguments. (The only difference is in the third argument, filter or areaMask.)

- **sourcePosition**   This is the position of the path from which Ethan will start moving.

- **targetPosition**   This is the final position on the path—Ethan's destination.

- **filter** or **areaMask**   When using the filter, use this argument to specify the cost of the navigation areas. When using an area mask, use this argument as a bitfield to specify which navigation areas can be passed when calculating a path.

- **path**   This argument stores the calculated path as an instance of the UnityEngine.AI .NavMeshPath class.

In this example, sourcePosition is set to Ethan's current position, while targetPosition is set to a new instance of the Vector3 struct with the following x, y, z properties, respectively: 5, 0, –7. Moreover, I set areaMask to the NavMesh.AllAreas constant so all areas will be included. Note that this NavMesh.AllAreas constant is –1. To create a custom area mask you need to combine indexes of navigation areas using the bitwise or operator |. To get the integral value representing the specified area, you use NavMesh.GetAreaFromName. This method accepts the single argument of type string, which is the area name. For example, NavMesh.GetAreaFromName("Not Walkable") returns index 1, representing the Not Walkable area. (Refer to column 1 in Figure 11-21.)

The animation path generated by the CalculatePath function is composed of numerous straight lines. Locations where lines of different directions connect are defined as corners or waypoints. You can preview any path in Scene view using the DrawLine method from the Debug class (discussed in Chapter 10). To display the whole path, you can use the DebugPath method from Listing 11-7.

LISTING 11-7 Debugging the navigation path

```
private void DebugPath(NavMeshPath navMeshPath)
{
    for (var i = 0; i < navMeshPath.corners.Length - 1; i++)
    {
        Debug.DrawLine(navMeshPath.corners[i],
            navMeshPath.corners[i + 1], Color.red);
    }
}
```

As Listing 11-7 shows, DebugPath accepts one argument, which is an instance of the NavMeshPath class. This object represents the path determined by the CalculatePath method. This object has a corners property. This is a collection of 3D vectors that represent the waypoint. DebugPath iterates over the corners collection to draw the path using Debug.DrawLine. At each iteration, DebugPath uses two corners to create a red line. So, you can invoke DebugPath in the SetPath method to preview the calculated path in the Scene view.

When the path is determined, it is passed to the SetPath instance method of the NavMeshAgent class. This method associates the path with a given agent. As a result, the Ethan model will start following this path. He will continue to move until he reaches targetPosition or you click the mouse. To check whether Ethan has reached the destination, I used the CheckIfDestinationWasReached method. (Refer to Listing 11-5.) This method checks whether the distance remaining to a destination is smaller than or equal to the stoppingDistance property of NavMeshAgent. StoppingDistance indicates the threshold below which the agent should be stopped. If the logical condition used by the CheckIfDestinationWasReached method is satisfied, the UpdateAnimatorParameter and UpdateAudioClip methods are invoked to switch animation from HumanoidWalk to HumanoidIdle and disable the footsteps audio clip.

If you click the mouse while Ethan is moving, the SetPath method will be invoked one more time. As shown in Listing 11-5, isPathSet will be true, so the control will be redirected under the else statement. So, the isStopped property of the NavMeshAgent class instance will be set to !isWalking. This is to inform Unity that the agent should not be moving when the isWalking parameter is false. Otherwise, the animation will be changed, and the audio clip will be disabled, but Ethan will be translated by the navigation system.

You can now build the AnimatedHumanoid project for the UWP platform, deploy the solution to HoloLens, and achieve the result shown in Figure 11-1.

Custom Animations

In the previous sections you learned how to add and control animation clips through the animation controller. However, all the animations you used came from standard Unity assets. In this section you will learn how to create your own custom animation clips. Specifically, you will create an animation clip that rotates the exploders you created for the HitTheCanGame. Follow these steps to get started:

1. Open the **HitTheCanGame** project in the Unity Editor.

2. Open the **Window** menu and choose **Animation** to open the Unity Editor Animation window.

3. Click the **Exploder L** object in the Hierarchy.

Your Animation window should look like the one shown in Figure 11-27. This window contains two panes: a property list on the left and an animation timeline on the right. You can display this timeline in two different views: Dopesheet (the default) and Curves. Currently, both these panes are empty. You'll see how to use them after you create the animation clip.

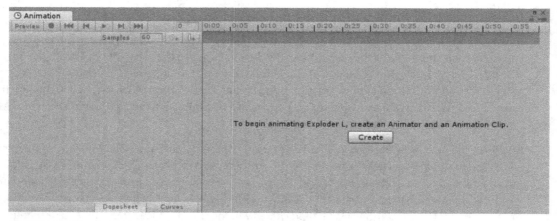

FIGURE 11-27 The Animation window, which you use to define custom animation clips.

Creating a Custom Animation Clip

To create an animation clip, follow these steps:

1. In the Animation window's timeline pane, click the **Create** button.

2. In the Create New Animation dialog box—similar to the standard Windows Open dialog box—create a new folder named **Animations**, type **ExploderAnimation** in the **File Name** box, and click **Save**.

Unity adds a new folder to the Assets folder that contains an ExploderAnimation.anim file and the Animation window view changes as shown in Figure 11-28. Notice that the timeline now contains a graphical representation of animation frames, called a dope sheet. This timeline view is called Dopesheet view. An animation frame is a discrete time position in your animation.

The animation is not composed of continuously displayed frames. Rather, the frames are separated by a fixed time constant (which must be smaller than the flicker fusion threshold). This process is called *sampling*. The value in the Samples box dictates how Unity samples your animation. The default sample rate is 60 frames per second (FPS). So, a new animation frame will be displayed approximately every 16.67 milliseconds.

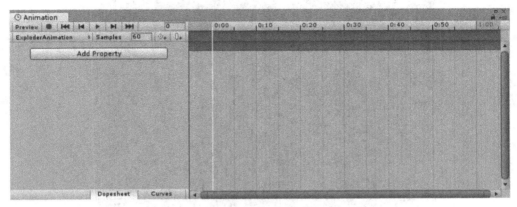

FIGURE 11-28 The Animation window containing the ExploderAnimation clip.

3. Click the **Add Property** button. A list of animatable properties, grouped similarly to properties in the Inspector, appears next to the button.

4. Expand the **Transform** group and click the small **plus** (+) icon next to **Rotation** entry.

   The property list displays the Rotation property's X, Y, and Z components, and several diamonds representing property keys appear in the timeline. These property keys are the control points that your animation curve passes through. The animation curve is a function that tells Unity how to animate the property. A frame containing a curve with a key is called a keyframe.

5. Click the **timeline header** (it displays the animation time) and move the cursor to the very end of the animation. The white line indicating the position will overlap with five diamonds on the left.

6. Type **360** in the box next to the **Rotation.y** setting in the property list. (See Figure 11-29.)

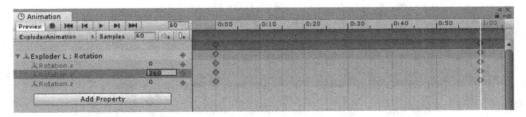

FIGURE 11-29 The Animation window with a modified Rotation.y key property.

7. Click **Play** in the toolbar in the Animation window and open the Scene view to preview the animation. The exploder should perform a full rotation around the Y axis. (See Figure 11-30.)

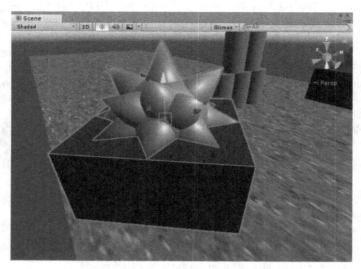

FIGURE 11-30 Preview the animation can in Scene view.

Animation Toolbar

Before going further, let's quickly discuss the controls available in the top-left corner of the Animation window. (See Figure 11-31.) These include the following (from left to right):

- **Preview**   Click this to enable or disable the animation preview in the Scene view.

- **Record**   Click this to enable or disable keyframe recording mode. When this mode is enabled, Unity records all changes you make to the animatable properties of the selected object. For example, you can translate, scale, or rotate the selected object using either the Scene view or Inspector, and Unity will automatically add those changes as keyframes to the Animation clip.

- **Go to Beginning**   Click this to move to the first animation frame. Frame position in the animation clip is indicated by the white line in the timeline and by the value displayed in the box to the right of the buttons toolbar. (Refer to Figure 11-29.)

- **Go to Previous Keyframe**   Click this to move to the previous keyframe.

- **Play**   Click this to play the animation clip.

- **Go to Next Keyframe**   Click this to move to the next keyframe.

- **Go to End**   Click this to move to the last frame in the animation clip.

FIGURE 11-31 Animation window toolbar.

FPS and Curves

When you preview the exploder animation, you'll probably notice that at first the exploder rotates slowly. Then, the angular speed increases for a while until it reaches the maximum value, which persists throughout most of the rest of the rotation animation. Finally, right before the rotation ends, the angular speed decreases until the exploder stops. So, it looks like the exploder needs to stop rotating before the subsequent rotations can happen. You will resolve these issues in this section.

To make the exploder rotate more slowly, you can either move keyframes to later times on the timeline or simply reduce the animation FPS. To decrease the FPS, simply type **30** in the **Samples** box. (See Figure 11-32.) This extends the timeline (in Dopesheet view) from 1 second to 2 seconds and moves the animation keys accordingly. If you don't see the keys at the end of the animation, press the A key on the keyboard to rescale the timeline to display all keys. You can now enable animation preview to see that the exploder is rotating much more slowly.

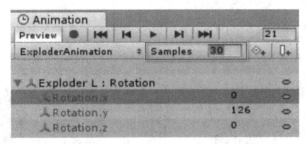

FIGURE 11-32 Reducing the animation speed to 30 FPS.

You resolve the second issue by adjusting the animation curve. Each animation property has an associated curve. This curve provides a visualization of how the property will change during the animation. To view these curves, you click the Curves tab in the bottom-left corner of the Animation window. When you do, the timeline pane changes to Curves view. (See Figure 11-33.) Again, if the entire curves are not displayed, press the A key on the keyboard to view them in their entirety.

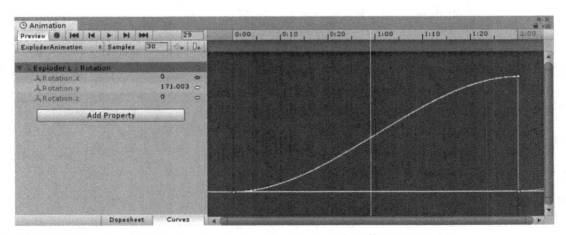

FIGURE 11-33 The Curves timeline view showing the animation curves for different properties.

As shown in Figure 11-33, animation curves are color-coded. In this case the Rotation.y curve is yellow and the Rotation.z curve is cyan. (A third curve, the Rotation.x curve, is purple. This curve is not visible in Figure 11-33 because it is identical to the Rotation.z curve, and because curves are drawn in the order in which their corresponding properties appear in the property list, the Rotation.z curve obscures the Rotation-x curve.)

The curves shown in the right part of Figure 11-33 indicate that the Rotation.x and Rotation.z properties will not be changed during animation. These properties are represented as lines on the 0 ordinate. In contrast, the Rotation.y property will change during animation, as represented by the sigmoid function. This also explains changes in the angular speed of the exploder observed previously.

To make the angular speed constant over the duration of the animation clip, you simply need to make the yellow curve linear. First, however, it helps to know that each animation key has two tangents: left and right. These control the ingoing (to the left of the key) and outgoing (to the right of the key) slopes of the curve. So, you create a linear curve as follows:

1. Right-click the end key of the **Rotation.y** property, click **Left Tangent**, and select **Linear**. (See Figure 11-34.) The portion of the animation curve near the end key will become linear.

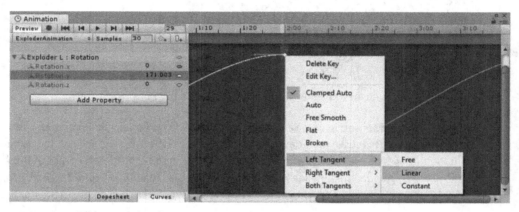

FIGURE 11-34 Editing an animation curve.

2. Right-click the beginning key of the **Rotation.y** property, choose **Right Tangent**, and select **Linear**. As shown in Figure 11-35, the entire animation curve will now be linear, meaning the exploder will rotate smoothly and continuously.

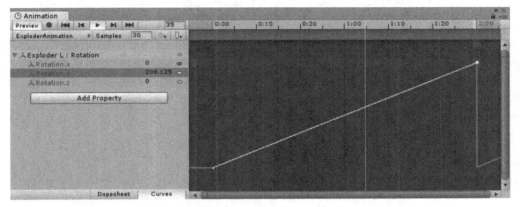

FIGURE 11-35 The curve of the Rotation.y property is now linear.

 Tip If you prefer, you can manually modify the left and right tangents. To do so, right-click a keyframe, choose **Left Tangent** or **Right Tangent**, and select **Free**. Then click the small curve that appears (it represents tangent) and drag it as desired.

 Tip You can use the animation curve to arbitrarily change the way in which the animatable property is changed during animation.

Adding Custom Animations to Other Objects

Along with the ExploderAnimation clip you created at the beginning of this section, Unity generated an Exploder L animation controller associated with the Exploder L object's Animator object. Because the animation controller was created as an asset, you can reuse it for the Exploder R object. Here's how:

1. Click the **Exploder R** object in the Hierarchy.

2. In the Inspector, click the **Add Component** button, type **Animator** in the search box, and select the **Animator** option to create an Animator component.

3. Click the small circular icon to the right of the **Controller** box.

4. The Select RuntimeAnimatorController window opens. Select the **Exploder L** object. The Exploder R object's Inspector should look as shown in Figure 11-36.

FIGURE 11-36 The Exploder R object's Inspector.

5. Rebuild HitTheCanGame and deploy it to the HoloLens emulator to obtain the result shown in Figure 11-2.

Note Because the ExploderAnimation clip has an associated animation controller, you can use all techniques described previously to extend the controller with additional animation clips and control transitions using parameters and scripts.

Summary

In this chapter, you learned how to make, use, and control animations to create a walking humanoid model. You then used navigation and pathfinding to make this humanoid model "intelligent" so he could autonomously move throughout the scene. Along the way you investigated how to define navigation areas, use them to build a navigation mesh, create a path within that mesh, and associate that path with the humanoid model.

This chapter diverged from strictly covering MR aspects to discuss Unity's components for creating animations, sound, and navigation. The next chapter is devoted to HoloLens-specific features, including interacting with holograms and spatial mapping (which is used to detect real objects in the scene and to apply boundaries for the character's movement). So, after you finish Chapter 12, you will be able to extend your MR apps by adding animatable holograms and implementing spatial sound.

Understanding HoloLens-Specific Features

This chapter explores the fundamental capabilities of the HoloLens apps. You will investigate input methods based on gaze, voice commands, and gestures. Then, you will learn how to use spatial mapping to create holograms that can interact with the real environment. Along the way you will also learn how to use the Mixed Reality Toolkit package for Unity to speed up mixed-reality development with prefabs. Most of the topics presented in this chapter (including gestures and spatial mapping) are related to HoloLens only because only that headset is equipped with sensors that understand the environment.

The main goal of this chapter is to fill a gap in the official Mixed Reality Academy documentation (http://bit.ly/mixed_reality_academy). Although this documentation contains plenty of sample apps and full source code, it assumes you are already familiar with Unity development. If your coding experience is based mostly in desktop, web, or mobile programming, it might be difficult to start with the Mixed Reality Academy documentation. Hence, this chapter tells you step-by-step how to use basic Unity tools to handle input. After that, it explores more advanced material using Mixed Reality Toolkit for Unity.

Note This chapter does not discuss spatial sound because that was covered in Chapter 11.

Configuring Gaze Input

Gaze indicates the direction in which the user is looking. This is a very important form of input. In the real environment, before interacting with an object, you typically look at it first.

Usually, the cursor indicates the gaze direction. The appearance of the cursor is updated when the gaze intersects the virtual object (hologram) in the scene. In this section you will learn how to implement such a cursor by extending the AnimatedHumanoid app from Chapter 11. (See Figure 12-1.)

Note The HoloLens does not track your eyes to pinpoint the direction of your gaze. Instead, it uses sensors to track your head movement.

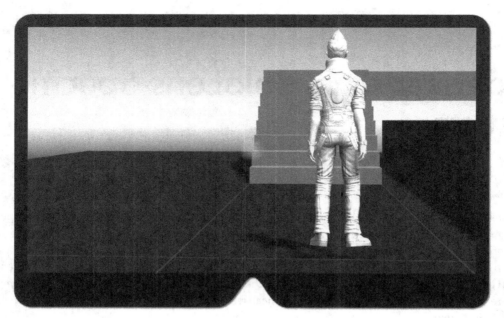

FIGURE 12-1 The AnimatedHumanoid app extended by the gaze cursor.

The cursor will be composed of a semi-transparent object made with a point light. Inside the cursor you will place a small pink solid sphere. This sphere will become visible whenever the gaze intersects with the hologram. (See Figure 12-2.) To detect the hologram, you will use ray casting, which you learned about in Chapter 10.

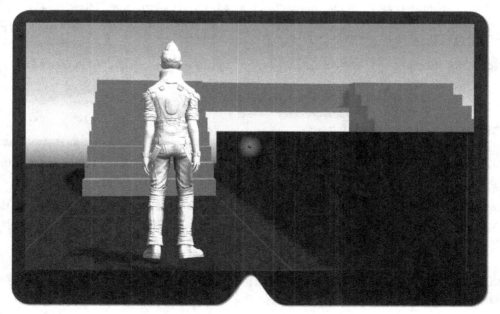

FIGURE 12-2 A small solid pink sphere becomes visible when the cursor points to the hologram.

Creating the Cursor

To create the cursor, follow these steps:

1. Open the **AnimatedHumanoid** project in the Unity Editor.

2. Click the **Create** button in the Hierarchy and choose **Create Empty** from the drop-down list that appears.

3. Name this new object **Cursor**.

4. Right-click the **Cursor** object, choose **3D Object**, and select **Sphere**.

5. In the Inspector, name the sphere **Cursor Dot**.

6. In the Cursor Dot Inspector, right-click **Sphere Collider** and choose **Remove Component** to remove it so it will not be detected by ray casting. (Alternatively, you could define a new layer that would be ignored by ray casting.)

7. Right-click the **Cursor** object in the Hierarchy, choose **Light**, and select **Point Light**.

8. In the Inspector, name the point light **Cursor Halo**. Your Hierarchy should appear as shown in Figure 12-3.

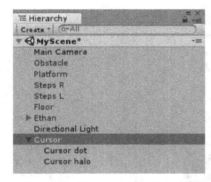

FIGURE 12-3 Hierarchy of the AnimatedHumanoid app

Configuring the Cursor

To configure the cursor, you add a material to the Cursor Dot object. Follow these steps:

1. Open the Project window and type **Pink t:Material** in the search box.

2. The search results should contain two entries: PinkGrid and PinkSmooth. Drag the **PinkSmooth** entry onto the **Cursor Dot** object.

3. In the Inspector for the Cursor Dot object, in the **Scale** settings under the **Transform** group, set the **X**, **Y**, and **Z** components to **0.05**.

4. In the Inspector for the Cursor Halo object, change the **Range** setting to **0.15**.

5. Click the **Color** box to open the Color Picker and set the **R**, **G**, **B**, and **A** properties to **255**, **0**, **255**, and **255**, respectively.

6. Change the **Intensity** setting to **5**.

7. Select the **Draw Halo** checkbox. The Inspector should appear as shown in Figure 12-4. The cursor is now ready and should appear in the Scene view, as show in Figure 12-5.

FIGURE 12-4 Configuring the Cursor Halo object

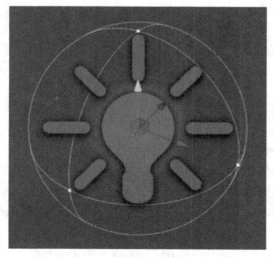

FIGURE 12-5 The cursor.

Implementing the Gaze Script

You're now ready to implement the gaze logic. To do so, you'll create a new script: GazeHandler. This script will move the cursor along the user's gaze, enabling him or her to easily navigate the scene to interact with holograms. The script will also employ the user's gaze to control the Ethan model's movement. That is, when the user looks at Ethan for a specified amount of time, Ethan will start walking.

You create the GazeHandler script as you would any other script: by right-clicking the **Scripts** folder in the Project window, choosing **Create**, and selecting **C# Script**. After you create the script, you associate it with the Camera component by clicking **Add Component** in the Inspector, typing **GazeHandler** in the search box, and clicking it in the search results.

To implement GazeHandler, start by adding two public properties, Cursor and CursorDot, as shown in Listing 12-1. Both properties, which are of type GameObject, will be used to select objects to create cursor elements. These objects will be configurable through the Inspector. If the Cursor and CursorDot properties are not selected in the Inspector, the GazeHandler script cannot work properly.

LISTING 12-1 Public properties of the GazeHandler script

```
[Tooltip("Gaze cursor")]
public GameObject Cursor;

[Tooltip("An indicator that becomes active when the user is looking at the collider")]
public GameObject CursorDot;
```

In Listing 12-1, both declarations are supplemented by a Tooltip attribute. This attribute enables you to specify a text string to offer contextual help. This string will appear in the Inspector when the user places the cursor on the property name. (See Figure 12-6.) While you're in the Inspector, take a moment to set the Cursor property to the Cursor object and the CursorDot property to the Cursor Dot object, both of which you created earlier.

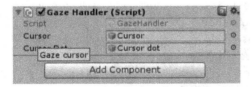

FIGURE 12-6 GazeHandler script configuration.

Now implement the Start method of GazeHandler. (See Listing 12-2.) The Start method will be responsible for updating the CursorDot position as the user gazes around the scene.

LISTING 12-2 Configuring initial state of the cursor dot

```
private float gazeTime;

private void Start()
{
    UpdateCursorDot(false);
    ResetGazeTimer();
```

```
    }

    private void UpdateCursorDot(bool isActive)
    {
        CursorDot.SetActive(isActive);
    }

    private void ResetGazeTimer()
    {
        gazeTime = 0.0f;
    }
```

This functionality is achieved using two helper methods:

- **UpdateCursorDot** This method accepts one argument: isActive. Depending on the value of this parameter, the method either activates or deactivates the CursorDot game object. This means CursorDot will be either visible (isActive = true) or hidden (isActive = false). To programmatically activate or deactivate the game object, you use the GameObject.SetActive method (see the UpdateCursorDot method from Listing 12-2). To statically deactivate an object, you can use Inspector to disable a checkbox labeled with the object's name. (See Figure 12-7.)

- **ResetGazeTimer** This method sets the value of the gaze timer (gazeTime field) to 0. You will use this timer to measure how long the user gazes at the hologram.

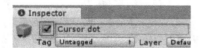

FIGURE 12-7 You can statically deactivate an object using its associated checkbox in the Inspector.

Next you implement another public property, GazeTriggerTime, with the CheckGazeTime method. (See Listing 12-3.) GazeTriggerTime defines the time threshold (in seconds) after which a message to the observed object will be sent. A private CheckGazeTime method increments a gaze timer based on the amount of time that has passed since the previous frame was rendered. CheckGazeTime then compares the value of the gazeTime field with the GazeTriggerTime property and returns a Boolean value representing the result of this comparison. Based on this information you implement the Update method. (See Listing 12-4.)

LISTING 12-3 Measuring gaze time

```
[Tooltip("Indicates the time (in seconds) after which a message will be sent to the gazed
    object")]
public int GazeTriggerTime = 10;

private bool CheckGazeTime()
{
    gazeTime += Time.deltaTime;

    return gazeTime >= GazeTriggerTime;
}
```

LISTING 12-4 Handling gaze input

```
private void Update()
{
    var gazeRay = CreateGazeRayAndUpdateCursorPosition();

    RaycastHit hitInfo;

    if (Physics.Raycast(gazeRay, out hitInfo))
    {
        UpdateCursorDot(true);

        CorrectCursorPosition(hitInfo);

        UpdateFocusedObject(hitInfo.collider.gameObject);

        if (CheckGazeTime())
        {
            SendMessageToFocusedObject("GazeEntered");
        }
    }
    else
    {
        UpdateCursorDot(false);

        SendMessageToFocusedObject("GazeExited");

        UpdateFocusedObject(null);
    }
}
```

The Update method proceeds as follows:

1. It invokes the CreateGazeRayAndUpdateCursorPosition helper method. (See Listing 12-5.)

2. The CreateGazeRayAndUpdateCursorPosition method creates an instance of the Ray struct, which represents a virtual light beam originating from the camera plane toward the gaze direction.

3. The ray origin is set to the current camera position. This position is obtained by reading the position property of the camera's transform. Similarly, the ray direction is set to forward the property of this transform. This property represents the camera's forward vector (in which only the Z component is not zero).

    The GazeHandler script is attached to the main camera so you can read the current game object's Transform properties. Alternatively, you can use the following statement to access the main camera's Transform properties:

    ```
    var gazeOrigin = Camera.main.transform.position;
    ```

    In Unity, the main camera is identified by the MainCamera tag. You check this using the Tag drop-down menu in the camera Inspector.

4. An instance of the Ray struct is used to position the cursor at the point where the user is looking. To determine this location, you use the Ray.GetPoint method. This method accepts one argument, distance, and returns an instance of the Vector3 struct. The struct represents the point along the ray at a specified distance from the ray origin. Here, the distance is stored in a private field: maxCursorDistance.

LISTING 12-5 Creating the gaze ray to update the cursor position

```
private float maxCursorDistance = 5.0f;

private Ray CreateGazeRayAndUpdateCursorPosition()
{
    // Get gaze origin and direction
    var gazeOrigin = transform.position;
    var gazeDirection = transform.forward;

    // Create the gaze ray
    var gazeRay = new Ray(gazeOrigin, gazeDirection);

    // Position the cursor along the gaze ray
    Cursor.transform.position = gazeRay.GetPoint(maxCursorDistance);

    // Return the gaze ray to be used for ray casting
    return gazeRay;
}
```

The gaze ray created in Listing 12-5 is also used to detect colliders with ray casting. Specifically, the ray is casted onto the scene using the Physics.Raycast method. This method returns true if the ray hits a collider. In that case, the following will occur (refer back to Listing 12-4):

1. The Cursor Dot object will become active because the UpdateCursorDot(true) method is invoked.

2. The cursor will be positioned on the collider if the collider is closer to the camera than the cursor. This is implemented by the CorrectCursorPosition method in Listing 12-6.

3. The game object associated with the observed collider will be stored in the focusedObject field. (See the UpdateFocusedObject method from Listing 12-6.)

4. The GazeEntered message is sent to the observed game object if the observation time is longer than the specified threshold.

LISTING 12-6 Correcting the cursor position and storing the game object of the observed collider

```
private void CorrectCursorPosition(RaycastHit hitInfo)
{
    if (hitInfo.point.z <= Cursor.transform.position.z)
    {
        Cursor.transform.position = hitInfo.point;
    }
}
```

```
        private GameObject focusedObject;

        private void UpdateFocusedObject(GameObject gameObject)
        {
            if(gameObject != focusedObject)
            {
                ResetGazeTimer();

                focusedObject = gameObject;
            }
        }
```

You send messages to game objects using the **SendMessage** method. (See Listing 12-7.)

LISTING 12-7 Sending a message to an object in the user's focus

```
public void SendMessageToFocusedObject(string methodName)
{
    if (focusedObject != null)
    {
        focusedObject.SendMessage(methodName,
            SendMessageOptions.DontRequireReceiver);
    }

    ResetGazeTimer();
}
```

The SendMessage function enables you to trigger events in target scripts. SendMessage has four overloaded versions, but the most general version accepts the following three arguments:

- **methodName**   This specifies the name of the method (from the target script class) to be invoked.

- **value**   This is an optional parameter to be passed to the invoked method.

- **options**   This conveys sending options. Possible values for this argument as defined in the UnityEngine.SendMessageOptions enumeration include RequireReceiver and DontRequireReceiver. If the first value is used, Unity will report an error (through the console) that the target script does not implement a given method. For SendMessageOptions.DontRequireReceiver this error will not be reported.

Later, you will extend another script, called EthanScript, to support two additional methods: GazeEntered and GazeExited. They will handle messages received from the GazeHandler script.

SendMessageToFocusedObject is public because you will use it later to extend the AnimatedHumanoid app to support voice commands. Specifically, SendMessageToFocusedObject will be invoked from a separate script responsible for handling these types of commands.

Let's get back to the Update method and analyze what happens when the ray cast does not hit a collider. When this occurs, the script invokes three methods under the else clause (refer to the bottom part of Listing 12-4) that deactivate the Cursor Dot object, send a GazeExited message to the receiver, and finally clear the focusedObject field.

To test this solution, you need to add mesh colliders to the following game objects in the scene:

- Steps L and Steps R
- Platform
- Floor
- Obstacle
- Ethan

To add these components, simply click the **Add Component** button in the Inspector and choose **Mesh Collider** from the menu that appears. For all objects except the Ethan object, the mesh colliders will be configured automatically. You must configure the Ethan object manually. Follow these steps:

1. In the Inspector, click the small icon to the right of the **Mesh** box in the Mesh Collider group.

2. The Select Mesh dialog box opens. Select the **EthanBody** object. (See Figure 12-8.)

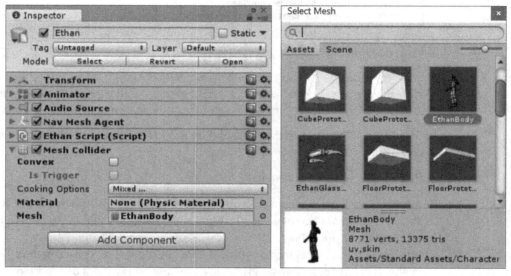

FIGURE 12-8 Configuring the Ethan object's mesh collider.

After everything is configured, you build the app and deploy it to the HoloLens emulator. You will then achieve the result shown earlier in Figures 12-1 and 12-2. When you emulate head movements, the cursor position will be updated accordingly. Moreover, the small sphere inside the cursor will become visible when the ray hits the collider.

Tip You can further extend this app with a gaze stabilizer, as explained in Microsoft Docs (http://bit.ly/mr_gaze).

Handling Messages

Let's extend the EthanScript to handle GazeEntered messages sent by GazeHandler. To do so, open the EthanScript.cs file and implement the two methods shown in Listing 12-8:

- **GazeEntered**   This method will be invoked whenever the message from the GazeHandler script is received.

- **UpdateEthanState**   When GazeEntered is invoked, UpdateEthanState is executed. As shown in Listing 12-8, this method updates the animator parameter (UpdateAnimatorParameter), launches or stops an audio clip (UpdateAudioClip), and sets the Ethan object's path (SetPath). Ethan will then either start or stop walking, depending on his current state.

LISTING 12-8 Handling GazeEntered messages

```
private void GazeEntered()
{
    UpdateEthanState();
}

private void UpdateEthanState()
{
    UpdateAnimatorParameter();

    UpdateAudioClip();

    SetPath(new Vector3(5, 0, -7));
}
```

In Chapter 11 you used the preceding functions to implement the EthanScript.Update method. You can now replace them with a single call to the UpdateEthanState function, as shown in Listing 12-9.

LISTING 12-9 Simplifying the Update method for EthanScript

```
private void Update()
{
    if (Input.GetMouseButtonDown(0))
    {
        UpdateEthanState();

        //UpdateAnimatorParameter();
        //UpdateAudioClip();
        //SetPath(new Vector3(5, 0, -7));
    }

    CheckIfDestinationWasReached();
}
```

Redeploy the app to the HoloLens emulator. After the app is executed, look at Ethan for at least 10 seconds. This will activate the SendMessageToFocusedObject method, which in turn sends the GazeEntered message to the EthanScript component. As a result, the GazeEntered method from Listing 12-8 will be invoked. So, Ethan starts walking.

Supporting Voice Commands

Having explored gaze input, let's extend the AnimatedHumanoid app by implementing support for voice commands. In this section, you will create two voice commands: walk and stop. As you have probably guessed, when they are issued, Ethan will start or stop walking, respectively.

The Unity speech-recognition system is based on the intrinsic UWP speech-recognition capabilities you learned about in Chapter 5 and Chapter 6. Unity scripts use three main "recognizer" classes for speech recognition, all defined in the `UnityEngine.Windows.Speech` namespace:

- **KeywordRecognizer** This analyzes user voice input and compares phrases uttered to a list of registered keywords. If one of the keywords is recognized, an `OnPhraseRecognized` event is invoked. You typically use this recognizer for short, well-defined voice commands.

- **GrammarRecognizer** This recognizer extends the `KeywordRecognizer` class by adding the ability to specify recognition constraints based on an XML grammar file. This file must conform to the World Wide Web Consortium (W3C) Speech Recognition Grammar Specification (SRGS) Version 1.0.

- **DictationRecognizer** This recognizer works like the continuous dictation you used in Chapter 5. It analyzes voice input and in response generates a series of events (`DictationHypothesis`, `DictationResult`, `DictationComplete`, and `DictationError`) that you can use to obtain recognized phrases and handle eventual errors.

`KeywordRecognizer` and `GrammarRecognizer` derive from the common abstract class `PhraseRecognizer`. This section discusses using `KeywordRecognizer` to handle voice commands. To implement this you'll create a new script. This script will send messages to Ethan through GazeHandler; that way Ethan will respond to voice commands only when the user is gazing at him.

Creating a Singleton Class

In many scenarios, it would be good to have shared access to a single instance of some specific script. This usually happens when you have a script (for example, GazeHandler) that is responsible for handling specific input (like gaze). Because there is only one gaze input per app, you should have a single instance of such a script. Then, instead of creating a new instance of GazeHandler, all other scripts should access the single instance. A common approach to providing shared access to a single instance is to use a singleton software design pattern.

In this section, you will apply the singleton pattern to EthanScript and GazeHandler. You start by creating a common generic class: `Singleton`. This class will serve as a new base class for all scripts that use the singleton pattern (including `EthanScript` and GazeHandler).

To implement the `Singleton` class, follow these steps:

1. In the Unity Editor Project window, right-click the **Scripts** folder, choose **Create**, and select **C# Script**.

2. Name the new script **Singleton**.

3. Define the Singleton class in the new script as shown in Listing 12-10.

LISTING 12-10 Definition of the Singleton class

```
public class Singleton<T> : MonoBehaviour where T : Singleton<T>
{
    private static T instance;

    public static T Instance
    {
        get
        {
            if (instance == null)
            {
                instance = FindObjectOfType<T>();
            }

            return instance;
        }
    }
}
```

Singleton is a generic class that derives from UnityEngine.MonoBehaviour. The use of the Singleton class is restricted to the types that derive from it. This limitation is specified by the following constraint from the class declaration:

```
where T : Singleton<T>
```

As Listing 12-10 shows, the Singleton class has one private static field: instance. It is used to store the instance of the object of a generic type T. An instance of that object is obtained within the public static property Instance using the MonoBehaviour.FindObjectOfType method. This method retrieves the object of a given type only when the instance field is null. This ensures that the class pointed to by the generic parameter T will be created only once. All subsequent calls to Instance will return a previously created instance.

Given the Singleton class, you can now modify declarations of GazeHandler and EthanScript as shown in Listing 12-11 to replace MonoBehavior with Singleton<T>. Then extend the definition of EthanScript by adding a public property IsWalking. (See Listing 12-12.) You will use this property later to determine whether the message should be sent to Ethan.

LISTING 12-11 Updated definitions of the GazeHandler and EthanScript classes

```
public class GazeHandler : Singleton<GazeHandler>
public class EthanScript : Singleton<EthanScript>
```

```
public bool IsWalking
{
    get { return isWalking; }
}
```

Building the Recognizer

Now you're ready to create the script that will recognize voice commands. Follow these steps:

1. In the Unity Editor Project window, right-click the **Scripts** folder, choose **Create**, and select **C# Script**.

2. Name the script **VoiceInputHandler**.

3. Select the main camera in the Unity Editor.

4. In the Inspector, click the **Add Component** button and choose **VoiceInputHandler** to associate the camera with the script.

5. To implement VoiceInputHandler, import the necessary namespaces in the file header:

    *   `using System`

    *   `using System.Collections.Generic`

    *   `using System.Linq`

    *   `using UnityEngine`

    *   `using UnityEngine.Windows.Speech`

6. Define the following two private fields (see Listing 12-13):

    *   **keywordRecognizer** This stores a reference to the KeywordRecognizer class.

    *   **voiceCommands** This defines phrases along with corresponding methods.

    These methods will be invoked when a keyword is recognized, as with the voice-commands dictionary you created in Chapter 6.

    LISTING 12-13 Fields in VoiceInputHandler

    ```
    private KeywordRecognizer keywordRecognizer;
    private Dictionary<string, Action> voiceCommands;
    ```

7. Implement the following three helper methods (see Listing 12-14):

- **InitializeVoiceCommandsDictionary** This method creates an instance of the Dictionary class with keys of type string and values of type action. The dictionary contains two important elements. The first element has a Walk key and an associated WalkCommandHandler method (see Listing 12-14). The second element has a Stop keyword and uses the StopCommandHandler method.

- **WalkCommandHandler** This method is invoked when the Walk keyword is detected. When this happens, StartCommandHandler sends an UpdateEthanState message, provided Ethan is not walking—in other words, EthanScript.Instance.IsWalking is false.

- **StopCommandHandler** This method is executed when the phrase Stop is recognized. Unlike WalkCommandHandler, this method sends the UpdateEthanState message when Ethan is walking.

LISTING 12-14 Initializing voice commands dictionary

```
private void InitializeVoiceCommandsDictionary()
{
    voiceCommands = new Dictionary<string, Action>();

    voiceCommands.Add("Walk", () => WalkCommandHandler());
    voiceCommands.Add("Stop", () => StopCommandHanlder());
}

private void WalkCommandHandler()
{
    if (!EthanScript.Instance.IsWalking)
    {
        GazeHandler.Instance.
            SendMessageToFocusedObject("UpdateEthanState");
    }
}

private void StopCommandHanlder()
{
    if (EthanScript.Instance.IsWalking)
    {
        GazeHandler.Instance.
            SendMessageToFocusedObject("UpdateEthanState");
    }
}
```

8. Use the code in Listing 12-15 to implement the logic for KeywordRecognizer. There are two methods:

- **ConfigureAndStartRecognizer** This method initializes a new instance of the KeywordRecognizer class, adds an event handler for OnPhraseRecognized, and starts speech recognition.

- **KeywordRecognizer_OnPhraseRecognized** This method is invoked whenever one of the keywords is detected.

LISTING 12-15 Configuring keyword recognizer and handling phrase recognition

```
private void ConfigureAndStartRecognizer()
{
    keywordRecognizer = new KeywordRecognizer(
        voiceCommands.Keys.ToArray(), ConfidenceLevel.Medium);

    keywordRecognizer.OnPhraseRecognized +=
        KeywordRecognizer_OnPhraseRecognized;

    keywordRecognizer.Start();
}

private void KeywordRecognizer_OnPhraseRecognized(
    PhraseRecognizedEventArgs args)
{
    Action voiceCommandHandler;

    if (voiceCommands.TryGetValue(args.text,
        out voiceCommandHandler))
    {
        voiceCommandHandler.Invoke();
    }
}
```

9. Create an instance of KeywordRecognizer using the class constructor. There are two con-
    structors available—one that accepts two arguments and one that accepts one argument. The
    two arguments for the first constructor are as follows:

    - **keywords**   This the string array that contains the list of recognizable phrases. Here, this
      array is created using the Keys property of the voiceCommands dictionary.

    - **minimumConfidence**   This specifies the minimum recognition confidence level. Recognition
      with a lower score than that specified will be ignored. As in Chapter 5, the confidence level is
      represented by a value defined in the UnityEngine.Windows.Speech.ConfidenceLevel
      enumeration: High, Medium, Low or Rejected. In Listing 12-15, the minimum confidence
      level is Medium.

    The second constructor of the KeywordRecognizer class accepts only one argument:
    keywords. It has the same meaning as explained above.

    According to Listing 12-15, the keyword recognition engine invokes the KeywordRecognizer_
    OnPhraseRecognized event handler whenever a walk or stop voice command is detected.
    The event handler is provided with an instance of the UnityEngine.Windows.Speech.
    PhraseRecognizedEventArgs class. This class has the following five read-only properties,
    which describe recognized phrases:

    - **confidence**   This is the recognition confidence level.

    - **semanticMeanings**   This an array of semantic meanings associated with the
      recognized phrase.

- **text** This is a string containing recognized text.

- **phraseStartTime** This indicates the time when the user started to say the phrase.

- **phraseDuration** This represents the phrase duration.

Listing 12-15 shows the `text` property used to obtain the action associated with the keyword. This action is then invoked to execute logic for the given phrase.

10. Use `InitializeVoiceCommandsDictionary` and `ConfigureAndStartRecognizer` to implement the `Start` method of VoiceInputHandler, as shown in Listing 12-16.

LISTING 12-16 Start method of VoiceInputHandler

```
private void Start()
{
    InitializeVoiceCommandsDictionary();

    ConfigureAndStartRecognizer();
}
```

Before testing the app, let's summarize the structure of the current implementation. As shown in Figure 12-9, there are three scripts: EthanScript, VoiceInputHandler, and GazeHandler. When a keyword is recognized, VoiceInputHandler reads the `IsWalking` property of EthanScript to determine whether Ethan is currently walking. Then, depending on the keyword, VoiceInputHandler uses GazeHandler to send a message to EthanScript.

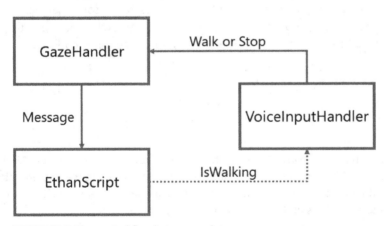

FIGURE 12-9 The control flow between scripts.

Follow these steps to test the app—that is, to make sure Ethan starts walking in response to the voice command:

1. Comment out the `UpdateEthanState` statement in the `GazeEntered` method in EthanScript.

2. Open the **File** menu and choose **Build Settings** or press **Ctrl+Shift+B** to open the Build Settings window. Then click **Player Settings**.

3.   Navigate to **Publishing Settings**, locate the **Capabilities** group, and select the **Microphone** checkbox. (See Figure 12-10.)

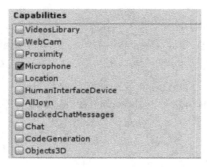

FIGURE 12-10 Enabling microphone capability.

4.   Build the app and deploy it to the HoloLens emulator.

5.   When the app starts, gaze at Ethan and say "walk." He should start walking. (The gaze is necessary here because messages are sent only to the focused object.)

6.   While still gazing at Ethan, say "stop." He should stop walking.

> **Tip** When designing voice commands, try to provide easily distinguishable keywords. This ensures that the speech recognizer will not confuse phrases. This is the reason I used walk and stop commands instead of start and stop commands. My initial tests showed the latter pair of keywords were quite similar—so much so that the keyword recognizer could barely distinguish them.

Gestures

In this section, you will create a new app to investigate gesture input. This app, shown in Figure 12-11, will extend input capabilities by adding support for handling gestures. To accelerate the implementation of this app, you will use the Mixed Reality Toolkit. As mentioned in Chapter 3, this toolkit provides materials, prefabs, scripts, and extensions for Unity Editor to simplify common tasks.

Gesture input is available only for HoloLens. HoloLens supports two core gestures:

- **Air tap**   You use this gesture to confirm an action, as you would click the left mouse button in a conventional computing system. In the HoloLens device, you perform the air-tap gesture by raising your index finger to the "ready position" and then pressing your finger down.

- **Bloom**   This is the home gesture. It activates the HoloLens Start menu. You perform this action by holding out your hand palm up, with your fingertips together, and then separating your fingers.

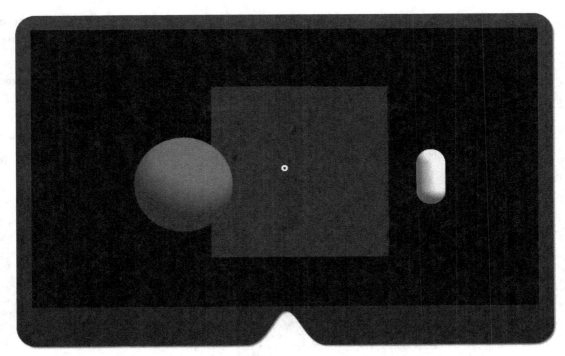

FIGURE 12-11 Gestures app executed in the HoloLens emulator.

HoloLens can also recognize the following composite gestures:

- **Tap and hold** To do this gesture, you keep the downward finger position of the air tap—similar to holding down the left mouse button after clicking it.

- **Manipulation** This gesture starts with the tap and hold. Any subsequent changes in your hand position are then interpreted as manipulation. You typically use this gesture to resize or rotate a hologram.

- **Navigation** This gesture starts with the tap and hold. You then move your hand within the normalized 3D cube centered around the location where you started the gesture. You use this gesture to navigate between UI elements.

In this section you will use manipulation and navigation gestures to interact with holograms. First, however, you will learn how to use the Mixed Reality Toolkit for Unity.

Configuring the Scene and Project Settings with the Mixed Reality Toolkit

Before you can configure the scene and project settings with the Mixed Reality Toolkit, you need to import the Mixed Reality Toolkit for Unity (MRTKu) package. Follow these steps:

1. Create a new Unity project and name it **Gestures**.

2. Import the MRTKu package from the following website: http://bit.ly/mrtk_release. (For more information on importing the MRTKu, refer to Chapter 3.) This chapter uses version 2017.2.1.4 of the package. It is included in the companion code for this book in the Tools folder.

3. In Unity Editor, open the **Assets** menu, choose **Import Package**, and select **Custom Package**. The Import Package dialog box appears.

4. Browse for and select the Mixed Reality Toolkit Unity package you downloaded in step 2. (If you use the version attached to the companion code, the full file name is HoloToolkit-Unity-2017.2.1.4.)

5. Unity decompresses the package and the Import Unity Package dialog box appears. (See Figure 12-12.) Click the **All** button to import all elements in the package and then click **Import** to begin the import operation. (Be patient. It may take a while.)

FIGURE 12-12 Importing the Mixed Reality Toolkit for Unity package.

6. If the Make Meta Files Visible dialog box appears, click the **Enable Visible Meta Files** button.

After the package is imported, you need to replace the Main Camera object with a HoloLensCamera prefab from the MRTKu and configure it. Follow these steps:

1. In the Hierarchy, delete the **Main Camera** object.

2. In the Project window, type **HoloLensCamera** in the search box.

3. Drag the **HoloLensCamera** entry in the search results onto the Hierarchy.

4. To configure the HoloLensCamera object, open the **Mixed Reality Toolkit** menu in Unity, choose **Configure**, and select **Apply Mixed Reality Scene Settings**.

5.   The Apply Mixed Reality Scene Settings dialog box opens. (See Figure 12-13.) Select the following checkboxes:

- **Move Camera to Origin**   This ensures that each position component of the HoloLensCamera prefab will be equal to 0.

- **Add the Input Manager Prefab**   This imports the script for handling input events.

- **Add the Default Cursor Prefab**   This imports the default cursor that indicates where the user is gazing.

 Note You leave the first setting (Add the Mixed Reality Camera Prefab) unchecked because the app will target HoloLens only.

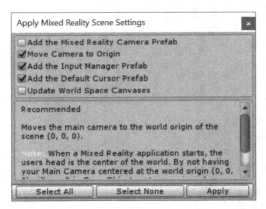

FIGURE 12-13 Applying Mixed Reality scene settings.

6.   Click the **Apply** button.

Next, you'll configure the app build settings. Follow these steps:

1.   Click the **Mixed Reality Toolkit** menu, choose **Configure**, and select **Apply Mixed Reality Toolkit Project Settings**.

2.   The Apply Mixed Reality Project Settings dialog box appears. (See Figure 12-14.) Select the following checkboxes:

- **Target Windows Universal UWP**   This is equivalent to setting the build platform to UWP using the Unity Editor Build Settings dialog box. (Refer to Figure 9-37.)

- **Enable XR**   This setting enables XR support. It is a shortcut for enabling virtual reality support with Windows Mixed Reality SDK through the Player Settings.

- **Build for Direct3D**   Sets the build type to D3D. This setting corresponds to the Build Type drop-down list in the Build Settings dialog box. (Again, refer to Figure 9-37.)

- **Enable .NET Scripting Backend** This a shortcut for enabling the .NET scripting backend. It is equivalent to the options in the Other Settings group in the Player Settings.

> **Note** The Mixed Reality Project Settings dialog box has three other settings, which we disabled here. The first is Target Occluded Devices. You use this option when deploying for Mixed Reality headsets. This adjusts quality settings for opaque HMD displays. The second is Enable Sharing Services. You use this to enable sharing, which lets you develop Mixed Reality apps spanning multiple devices. (For more information, see http://bit.ly/sharing_services.) The third is Use Toolkit-specific InputManager axes. This enables input from an Xbox controller.

FIGURE 12-14 Applying Mixed Reality project settings.

3. Click the **Apply** button.

After you apply these settings, you can add holograms to the scene. Follow these steps:

1. Add a capsule, a cube, and a sphere to the scene.

2. Set the **X**, **Y**, and **Z Scale** components in the **Transform** group to **0.25**.

3. Position the holograms as follows:

    - **Capsule: X: 0.75, Y: 0, Z: 3.5**

    - **Cube: X: 0, Y: 0, Z: 3**

    - **Sphere: X: –0.5, Y:0, Z: 2.5**

4. Let's apply a material to each hologram. To start, open the **Assets** menu, choose **Import Package**, and select **Prototyping**.

5. In the Project window, type **t:Material** in the search box. The search results will contain a list of material assets.

6. Drag the **YellowSmooth** material onto the Capsule hologram.

7. Drag the **PinkSmooth** material to the Sphere hologram.

8. Drag the **NavySmooth** material to the Cube hologram. Your scene should look like the one in Figure 12-15.

FIGURE 12-15 The scene you just created.

Adding the GazeManager Script

Now that you've configured the scene and project settings are finished, you're ready to implement the logic. Start by adding the GazeManager script from the MRTKu package. To do so, type **GazeManager** in the search box in the Project window. Then, drag the **GazeManager** entry in the search results onto the HoloLensCamera.

The GazeManager script will handle the gaze-related logic to position the cursor according to the user gaze direction. The internal structure of the GazeManager script is similar to the GazeHandler script developed earlier in this chapter. GazeManager uses the main camera to determine the gaze origin and direction. Then, it constructs the ray, which is cast to the scene to detect the colliders. GazeManager also uses the GazeStabilizer class to minimize the effect of involuntary movements when the app is running on a real device.

If you open GazeManager in Visual Studio, you will see that the actual code responsible for updating the gaze ray is contained in the UpdateGazeInfo method, shown in Listing 12-17.

LISTING 12-17 Updating gaze info for GazeManager

```
public Ray Ray { get; private set; }

private void UpdateGazeInfo()
{
    if (GazeTransform == null)
    {
        Ray = default(Ray);
    }
    else
    {
        Vector3 newGazeOrigin = GazeTransform.position;
        Vector3 newGazeNormal = GazeTransform.forward;

        // Update gaze info from stabilizer
        if (Stabilizer != null)
        {
            Stabilizer.UpdateStability(newGazeOrigin, GazeTransform.rotation);
            newGazeOrigin = Stabilizer.StablePosition;
            newGazeNormal = Stabilizer.StableRay.direction;
        }

        Ray = new Ray(newGazeOrigin, newGazeNormal);
    }

    UpdateHitPosition();
}
```

UpdateGazeInfo uses the position and forward vectors of the gaze transform to instantiate the Ray struct. The gaze transform is achieved through the FindGazeTransform helper method in Listing 12-18. You can configure the gaze transform through the Inspector by setting the GazeTransform public property. If you do not explicitly set this property, GazeManager will use Camera.main.transform instead.

LISTING 12-18 Obtaining the gaze transform

```
public Transform GazeTransform;

private bool FindGazeTransform()
{
    if (GazeTransform != null) { return true; }

    if (CameraCache.Main != null)
    {
        GazeTransform = CameraCache.Main.transform;
        return true;
    }

    Debug.LogError("Gaze Manager was not given
        a GazeTransform and no main camera exists to default to.");

    return false;
}
```

UpdateGazeInfo also uses the `UpdateHitPosition` helper method to determine the point where the gaze ray intersects the hologram. (See Listing 12-19.)

LISTING 12-19 Updating the hit position

```
private float lastHitDistance = 2.0f;

private void UpdateHitPosition()
{
    HitPosition = (Ray.origin + (lastHitDistance * Ray.direction));
}
```

GazeManager invokes `UpdateGazeInfo` in the `UpdatePointer` public method. (See Listing 12-20.) That method is then used in another MRTKu script called FocusManager.

LISTING 12-20 Updating the gaze pointer

```
public void UpdatePointer()
{
    UpdateGazeInfo();
}
```

FocusManager handles input from various pointing sources, including gaze (HoloLens) and motion controllers (immersive headsets). To explore the implementation of FocusManager, type **FocusManager** in the search box in the Project window and double-click the **FocusManager** entry in the search results. Notice that FocusManager uses an instance of GazeManager to register the pointing source, which is stored in the `gazeManagerPointingData` field. (See the `Start` method in Listing 12-21). After the pointer source is configured, FocusManager uses the `Update` method to adjust the cursor position and update focused objects. (See the `Update` method in Listing 12-21.)

LISTING 12-21 A fragment of the FocusManager script

```
private PointerData gazeManagerPointingData;

private void Start()
{
    if (gazeManagerPointingData == null)
    {
        if (GazeManager.IsInitialized)
        {
            gazeManagerPointingData =
                new PointerData(GazeManager.Instance);
        }
    }
    else
    {
        Debug.Assert(ReferenceEquals(
            gazeManagerPointingData.PointingSource,
            GazeManager.Instance));
    }

    if ((pointers.Count == 0)
        && autoRegisterGazePointerIfNoPointersRegistered
```

```
        && GazeManager.IsInitialized)
    {
        RegisterPointer(GazeManager.Instance);
    }
}

private void Update()
{
    UpdatePointers();
    UpdateFocusedObjects();
}
```

You can now build and deploy an app to the HoloLens emulator. Notice that the cursor follows the gaze. Moreover, when the gaze intersects one of the holograms, the cursor is overlaid on the hologram. This effect is best visible with the sphere. (See Figure 12-16.)

FIGURE 12-16 Gaze handling with Mixed Reality Toolkit.

Note To summarize, both `GazeManager` and `FocusManager` derive from the `HoloToolkit.Unity.Singleton` class. This class implements a singleton pattern. It works like the `Singleton` class implemented earlier but extends the simple implementation to include additional methods.

Adding the GestureHandler Script and GestureRecognizer Class

Now that the gaze logic is ready, you can supplement the Gestures app by adding the GestureHandler script. This script will handle manipulation and navigation gestures to enable the user to use hand gestures to move and resize the capsule, cube, and sphere during runtime. To create the GestureHandler script, follow these steps:

1. In the Project window, create a **Scripts** folder inside the **Assets** folder.

2. Right-click the **Scripts** folder, choose **Create**, and select **C# Script**.

3. Name the new script **GestureHandler**.

4. In the Inspector, associate the **GestureHandler** script with the **HoloToolkitCamera** object.

The GestureHandler script contains a GestureRecognizer class. The general approach to using this class works as follows:

1. You use a default parameter-less constructor to instantiate the class. You can invoke this constructor in the script's Awake or Start method.

2. You use the GestureRecognizer.SetRecognizableGestures method to specify which gestures should be recognized. This method accepts one argument, newMaskValue, of enumeration type UnityEngine.XR.WSA.Input.GestureSettings. The enumeration type defines all available gestures.

3. If you want to recognize multiple gestures simultaneously, you use bit masking. For example, to detect Tap and ManipulationTranslate gestures, you use the following statement:

```
GestureRecognizer.SetRecognizableGestures(
    GestureSettings.Tap | GestureSettings.ManipulationTranslate)
```

If you do not explicitly invoke GestureRecognizer.SetRecognizableGestures, the recognizer will respond to only the following gestures:

- GestureSetttings.None

- GestureSetttings.Tap

- GestureSetttings.Hold

- GestureSetttings.NavigationX

- GestureSetttings.NavigationY

- GestureSetttings.NavigationZ

Note that manipulation and navigation gestures cannot be recognized simultaneously through a single instance of the GestureRecognizer. Hence, in the Gestures app, you will use two instances of that class—one devoted to manipulation and the other to navigation gestures.

4. When an instance of the `GestureRecognizer` class is ready and configured, you associate methods with recognizer events, which are raised whenever the corresponding gesture is detected. For example, for a simple tap gesture, the recognizer raises only one event: Tapped. For the hold gesture, the recognizer fires three events:

- **`GestureRecognizer.HoldStarted`** This is raised when the user starts the hold gesture. You typically use this event to implement the logic that should be executed when the gesture starts—for instance, to reset your fields related to gesture handling.

- **`GestureRecognizer.HoldCompleted`** This is raised when the hold gesture has ended. You use this event to finalize logic related to the gesture.

- **`GestureRecognizer.HoldCanceled`** This is raised when the user cancels the hold event using a hand gesture or a voice command. You use this event to break execution or reset the state of any code you executed in the `HoldStarted` event handler.

For manipulation and navigation gestures, you can use the following events:

- **`GestureRecognizer.ManipulationStarted`** and **`GestureRecognizer.Navigation Started`** These events are fired when the user starts a manipulation or navigation gesture. As with `HoldStarted`, you use these events to prepare your code to handle manipulation or navigation gestures.

- **`GestureRecognizer.ManipulationUpdated`** and **`GestureRecognizer.Navigation Updated`** These events are invoked when the user's hand position changes during the gesture. You use these events to invoke the actual statements that should respond to the gesture.

- **`GestureRecognizer.ManipulationCanceled`** and **`GestureRecognizer.Navigation Canceled`** These events are fired when the user cancels the manipulation or navigation gesture.

- **`GestureRecognizer.ManipulationCompleted`** and **`GestureRecognizer.Navigation Completed`** These events are fired when the manipulation or navigation gesture is finished.

Apart from these events, each recognizer also supports the following three events:

- `GestureRecognizer.RecognitionStarted`

- `GestureRecognizer.RecognitionEnded`

- `GestureRecognizer.GestureError`

These are invoked when recognition starts, recognition ends, or the recognizer issues a warning about gesture recognition, respectively.

5. To start gesture recognition, invoke the **`GestureRecognizer.StartCapturingGestures`** method. The Unity engine will capture selected gestures until you call the **`GestureRecognizer.StopCapturingGestures`** method.

Manipulation

Let's now see how to use `GestureRecognizer` in the GestureHandler script. Follow these steps:

1. To implement the GestureHandler script, import the `HoloToolkit.Unity.InputModule` and `UnityEngine.XR.WSA.Input` namespaces. To do so, add the following statement to the file header:

```
using HoloToolkit.Unity.InputModule;
using UnityEngine.XR.WSA.Input;
```

2. Declare two private fields, as shown in Listing 12-22:

   - **manipulationRecognizer**   This stores a reference to the `UnityEngine.XR.WSA.Input.GestureRecognizer` class.

   - **previousManipulation;**   This stores the vector that represents the cumulative manipulation the user performed on the selected hologram since the gesture started.

   LISTING 12-22 Private fields used to handle manipulation

```
private GestureRecognizer manipulationRecognizer;
private Vector3 previousManipulation;
```

3. Instantiate and configure the recognizer as shown in Listing 12-23. Specifically, you arrange the recognizer so it only captures manipulation gestures, associate methods with the `GestureRecognizer.ManipulationStarted` and `GestureRecognizer.ManipulationUpdated` events, and start the recognizer.

   LISTING 12-23 Configuring the manipulation gesture recognizer

```
private void ConfigureAndStartManipulationRecognizer()
{
    // Instantiate recognizer
    manipulationRecognizer = new GestureRecognizer();

    // Configure recognizable gestures
    manipulationRecognizer.SetRecognizableGestures(
        GestureSettings.ManipulationTranslate);

    // Wire the event handlers
    manipulationRecognizer.ManipulationStarted +=
        GestureRecognizer_ManipulationStarted;

    manipulationRecognizer.ManipulationUpdated +=
        GestureRecognizer_ManipulationUpdated;

    // Start recognizer
    manipulationRecognizer.StartCapturingGestures();
}
```

4. Implement the event handlers according to Listing 12-24. Specifically, when the manipulation starts, you set the default value of the `previousManipulation` field to `Vector3.zero`, which represents the null position change. (See the `GestureRecognizer_Manipulation Started` method from Listing 12-24.) Then, in the `GestureRecognizer_Manipulation Updated` event handler, you check the `HitObject` property of the `GazeManager` class instance to determine whether the user is gazing at any hologram. If so, you update the position of the hologram according to the value stored in the `cumulativeDelta` property of the `ManipulationUpdatedEventArgs` struct. An instance of this struct is passed to the event handler associated with the `ManipulationUpdated` event. `ManipulationUpdatedEventArgs` delivers additional info about the manipulation gesture through the following properties:

- **cumulativeDelta** This stores the total translation of the user's hand since the beginning of the gesture.

- **headPose** This represents the head pose during the gesture's update.

- **source** and **sourcePose** These represent the interaction source and its pose during the gesture update. (These elements were discussed in Chapter 10 in the context of interaction controllers.)

Here, you only use the `cumulativeDelta` property. It stores the total translation, so to correctly update the hologram position, you only need the amount of gesture translation since the last call to the `ManipulationUpdated` event. Therefore, you need to subtract the previous value of `cumulativeDelta` from the current one.

LISTING 12-24 Handling events of the manipulation gesture recognizer

```
private void GestureRecognizer_ManipulationStarted(
    ManipulationStartedEventArgs obj)
{
    previousManipulation = Vector3.zero;
}

private void GestureRecognizer_ManipulationUpdated(
    ManipulationUpdatedEventArgs obj)
{
    if (GazeManager.Instance.HitObject != null)
    {
        UpdatePosition(GazeManager.Instance.HitObject,
            obj.cumulativeDelta);
    }
}
```

5. Use the resulting difference to update the hologram position. The `UpdatePosition` method in Listing 12-25 implements this approach.

LISTING 12-25 Updating the hologram's position

```
private void UpdatePosition(GameObject hitObject,
    Vector3 cumulativeDelta)
{
    var delta = cumulativeDelta - previousManipulation;

    previousManipulation = cumulativeDelta;

    GazeManager.Instance.HitObject.transform.position += delta;
}
```

Navigation

Handling navigation gestures is similar to handling manipulation gestures. To start, you instantiate and configure an instance of the GestureRecognizer class. (See Listing 12-26.) Here, you'll respond only to the GestureSettings.NavigationZ gesture. This is because manipulation and navigation gestures are emulated in the same way in the HoloLens emulator. By limiting recognizable gestures to navigation along the Z axis, you ensure that navigation gestures along other axes will not interfere with manipulation events.

LISTING 12-26 Configuring the navigation gesture recognizer

```
private GestureRecognizer navigationRecognizer;

private void ConfigureAndStartNavigationRecognizer()
{
    navigationRecognizer = new GestureRecognizer();

    navigationRecognizer.SetRecognizableGestures(
        GestureSettings.NavigationZ);

    navigationRecognizer.NavigationStarted +=
        NavigationRecognizer_NavigationStarted;

    navigationRecognizer.NavigationUpdated +=
        NavigationRecognizer_NavigationUpdated;

    navigationRecognizer.StartCapturingGestures();
}
```

When the Unity engine recognizes a navigation Z gesture, it will raise a NavigationUpdated event. You will use this event to uniformly rescale the hologram the user is looking at. Additionally, you will use NavigationStarted to reset the previousScale field. This field stores the intermediate value representing the scaling factor obtained in the previous navigation update.

Another event handler, NavigationRecognizer_NavigationUpdated, is used to rescale the hologram the user is gazing at. To obtain the information required to rescale the hologram, you use an instance of the NavigationUpdatedEventArgs struct. (An instance of this type is passed to the NavigationUpdate event.) This struct has four properties: source, sourcePose, headPose, and normalizedOffset. The first three properties are the same as in the case of ManipulationUpdatedEventArgs. The last property, normalizedOffset, is an instance of the

Vector3 struct. Each component of that struct informs you about the navigation offset since the navigation gesture began. Here, you use only the Z component of that offset to scale the hologram uniformly along each direction. The logic responsible for this scaling is implemented in the UpdateScale method shown toward the end of Listing 12-27.

LISTING 12-27 Handling navigation events

```
private float previousScale;

private void NavigationRecognizer_NavigationStarted(
    NavigationStartedEventArgs obj)
{
    previousScale = 0.0f;
}

private void NavigationRecognizer_NavigationUpdated(
    NavigationUpdatedEventArgs obj)
{
    if (GazeManager.Instance.HitObject != null)
    {
        UpdateScale(GazeManager.Instance.HitObject,
            obj.normalizedOffset);
    }
}

private void UpdateScale(GameObject hitObject,
    Vector3 normalizedOffset)
{
    var scale = normalizedOffset.z - previousScale;

    previousScale = normalizedOffset.z;

    hitObject.transform.localScale += Vector3.one * scale;
}
```

Putting It All Together

Let's put everything together. Implement the Start method of the GazeHandler script as shown in Listing 12-28. This method invokes the two helper methods developed previously: ConfigureAnd StartManipulationRecognizer and ConfigureAndStartNavigationRecognizer. Both of these will be configured and started when the GazeHandler script starts.

LISTING 12-28 Gesture recognizers are configured and started within the script's Start method

```
private void Start()
{
    ConfigureAndStartManipulationRecognizer();

    ConfigureAndStartNavigationRecognizer();
}
```

A common approach is to release resources reserved for gesture recognizers before the script is destroyed. So, you use GazeHandler.OnDestroy to release manipulation and navigation gesture recognizers using two helpers: `ReleaseManipulationRecognizer` and `ReleaseNavigationRecognizer`. (See Listing 12-29.) They both work in the same way: The `StopCapturingGestures` method is invoked, after which event handlers are unwired using the `-=` operator.

LISTING 12-29 Releasing gesture recognizers

```
private void OnDestroy()
{
    ReleaseManipulationRecognizer();

    ReleaseNavigationRecognizer();
}

private void ReleaseManipulationRecognizer()
{
    manipulationRecognizer.StopCapturingGestures();

    manipulationRecognizer.ManipulationStarted -=
        GestureRecognizer_ManipulationStarted;

    manipulationRecognizer.ManipulationUpdated -=
        GestureRecognizer_ManipulationUpdated;
}

private void ReleaseNavigationRecognizer()
{
    navigationRecognizer.StopCapturingGestures();

    navigationRecognizer.NavigationStarted -=
        NavigationRecognizer_NavigationStarted;

    navigationRecognizer.NavigationUpdated -=
        NavigationRecognizer_NavigationUpdated;
}
```

Testing the App

Finally, let's test the Gestures app. Follow these steps:

1. Build and deploy the app to the HoloLens emulator.

2. Press **F4** to ensure that the emulation of the human input is enabled.

3. Press and hold the left or right **Alt** key (to emulate a left or right hand gesture, respectively) and right-click the mouse. The app's gaze cursor will change from a dot to a ring.

4. Move the mouse cursor to emulate a manipulation gesture. When the gaze cursor hits the hologram, the hologram will be translated around the scene according to your manipulation.

5. Use the mouse scroll wheel or **W** and **S** keyboard keys to emulate navigation. You will see the focused hologram rescale.

6. To ensure that your hand gestures are really working, you use the Additional Tools window in the HoloLens emulator. To open this window, click the **Tools** icon (marked with a double arrow) on the emulator toolbar.

7. Click the **Simulation** tab. (See Figure 12-17.) This tab conveys transformation information for the body, head, and hands. This information changes as you virtually move around the scene, rotate the head, or emulate hand gestures, respectively.

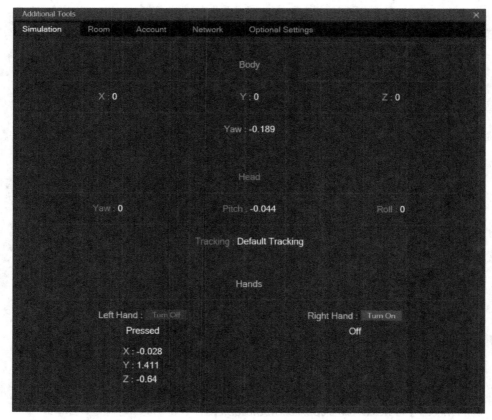

FIGURE 12-17 The Additional Tools window in the HoloLens emulator.

 Note You can arbitrarily position the holograms in relation to each other. To make them occlude, you can employ the physics engine as explained in Chapter 10.

Spatial Mapping

Spatial mapping is a key element of mixed reality. It collects data from various HoloLens sensors that understand the environment to deliver information about real objects located near the wearer of the HoloLens. Developers use spatial mapping to position holograms in real objects to provide a true mixed-reality experience in which the real and virtual environments are blended.

From a low-level point of view, spatial mapping uses two primary objects:

- **Spatial surface observer** This defines the bounding volume for which a device will provide spatial data. This data is represented as a spatial surface.

- **Spatial surface** This is a digital representation of a recognized real object.

You typically use spatial mapping in the following scenarios:

- **Placement** In this scenario, spatial data is used to anchor a hologram to a specific location in the scene. When the hologram is anchored using world coordinates, it will preserve its position. This means that even if the user moves to a different location in the near environment, when they return, the hologram will still be there.

- **Occlusion** In this scenario, you use spatial surfaces to occlude your holograms. For example, you can hide real objects behind virtual content.

- **Physics** In this scenario, the physics engine is used with spatial surfaces to implement interaction between real objects and holograms. For instance, you can throw the virtual ball around your environment, and the ball will bounce off real structures.

- **Navigation** In this scenario, you combine navigation agents with spatial data to define the navigation area in which agents can move with spatial surfaces. For example, you could use this approach to force your characters to move inside your room only.

In this section, you will learn how to use spatial mapping for physics simulations and hologram placement. You'll start by exploring two Unity scripts that can be used to draw spatial-mapping meshes (spatial-mapping renderer) and detect collisions between holograms and real objects (spatial-mapping collider). You will then see how to use the Mixed Reality Toolkit to display spatial-mapping meshes and place holograms.

Creating a Spatial-Mapping Renderer

To create a spatial-mapping renderer, follow these steps:

1. Create a new 3D project in Unity named **SpatialMapping**.

2. Import the **MRTKu** package. (Refer to the section "Configuring the Scene and Project Settings with the Mixed Reality Toolkit" for guidance.)

3. Replace the **Main Camera** object with the **HoloLensCamera** prefab object.

4. Open the **Mixed Reality Toolkit** menu in Unity, choose **Configure**, and select **Apply Mixed Reality Scene Settings**.

5. Select the following checkboxes in the Apply Mixed Reality Scene Settings dialog box and click the **Apply** button. (Refer to Figure 12-13.)

- **Move Camera to Origin**

- **Add the Input Manager Prefab**

- **Add the Default Cursor Prefab**

6. Click the **Mixed Reality Toolkit** menu, choose **Configure**, and select **Apply Mixed Reality Toolkit Project Settings**.

7. Select the following checkboxes in the Apply Mixed Reality Project Settings dialog box. (Refer to Figure 12-14.)

- **Target Windows Universal UWP**

- **Enable XR**

- **Build for Direct3D**

- **Enable .NET Scripting Backend**

8. To enable the app to access spatial mapping functionality, click the **Mixed Reality Toolkit** menu, choose **Configure**, and select **Apply UWP Capability Settings**.

9. The Apply UWP Capability Settings dialog box opens. (See Figure 12-18.) Select the **Spatial Perception** checkbox and click the **Apply** button.

> **Note** The Apply UWP Capability Settings dialog box is similar to the Apply Mixed Reality Settings and Apply Mixed Reality Scene Settings dialog boxes you used earlier. You can also use the Apply UWP Capability Settings dialog box to declare other app capabilities much more quickly than with the Player Settings. (Refer to Figure 12-10.)

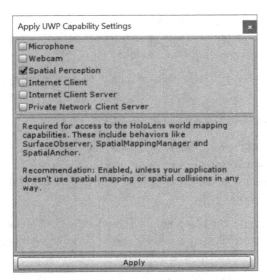

FIGURE 12-18 Declaring spatial perception capability.

10. To add the spatial mapping renderer component to the HoloLensCamera object, click the **Add Component** button in the HoloLensCamera Inspector and choose **XR**. Then select **Spatial Mapping Renderer** from the list that appears. (See Figure 12-19.)

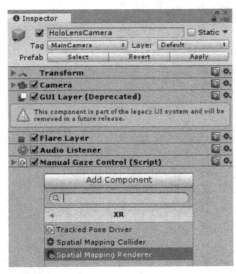

FIGURE 12-19 Adding a spatial mapping renderer to the HoloLensCamera object.

The Spatial Mapping Renderer component appears in the HoloLensCamera Inspector. (See Figure 12-20.) You can configure this component using two group of options: Render Settings and General Settings. The Render Settings options are as follows:

- **Render State** Use this drop-down list to specify how spatial meshes will be rendered. There are three possible values:

  - **None** This disables spatial mapping mesh rendering.

  - **Occlusion** This specifies that the component will render the occlusion material. The default occlusion material, SpatialMappingOcclusion, appears transparent but occludes holograms. You use this option when developing apps in which holograms should be hidden behind or under real-world objects.

  - **Visualization** This specifies that the component will render the visual material. The default material, SpatialMappingWireframe, displays a wireframe, which represents color-coded distances from the observer to real objects.

- **Occlusion Material** Use this option to specify the material that should be used for occlusion rendering.

- **Visual Material** This indicates the material to be used when visualization rendering is enabled.

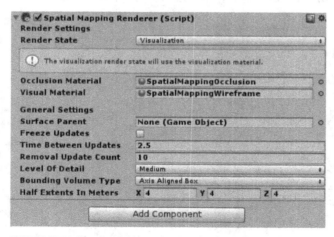

FIGURE 12-20 The Spatial Mapping Renderer Inspector.

11. Leave the **Occlusion Material** and **Visual Material** parameters at their default settings.

12. Change the **Render State** setting to **Visualization** so the spatial-mapping renderer will visualize the surfaces of real objects.

13. To enable this visualization, click the **Window** menu and choose **Holographic Emulation**.

14. The Holographic window opens. (See the top-right corner of the screen in Figure 12-21.) Open the top drop-down list and choose **Simulate in Editor**.

15. Open the **Room** drop-down list and choose any of the available rooms (except None).

16. Click **Play** and switch to Scene view. After a short while, meshes representing detected surfaces will be rendered. (See Figure 12-21.)

FIGURE 12-21 Preview spatial-mapping meshes in Scene view.

There are two things worth noting here. First, the Hierarchy contains a new object: Surface Parent. It is the parent for all detected surfaces. You can click them in the Hierarchy and they will become highlighted in the Scene view. Second, surface meshes have different colors. These colors encode distances from the observer to the real objects as follows:

- **0–1 meters (m)**   Black
- **1–2 m**   Red
- **2–3 m**   Green
- **3–4 m**   Blue
- **4–5 m**   Yellow
- **5–6 m**   Cyan
- **6–7 m**   Magenta
- **7–8 m**   Maroon
- **8–9 m**   Teal
- **9–10 m**   Orange
- **>10 m**   White

You can zoom in or out in the Scene view to decrease or increase the distance between the observer and the real objects and mesh colors will be updated accordingly.

Note Meshes representing real surfaces are also visible in Game view but are limited to the camera's FOV.

To wrap up this section, let's investigate the general settings of the spatial-mapping renderer. As you saw in Figure 12-20, these settings are as follows:

- **Surface Parent** Use this setting to choose the game object that will serve as the parent for all detected surface meshes. By default, this property is set to null, so Unity will automatically generate the parent object. This parent object is named Surface Parent *N*, where *N* is an integer.

- **Freeze Updates** Use this option to disable querying for spatial mapping updates.

- **Time Between Updates** This indicates the time (in tenths of seconds) between querying for spatial-mapping updates.

- **Removal Update Count** Use this option to specify the number of updates before the surface game object is removed from the scene.

- **Level of Detail** Use this drop-down list to set the quality level for mesh generation. Your options are Low, Medium (the default), and High. The higher the quality, the better the rendering, at the cost of increased computational needs. Conversely, the lower the quality, the worse the mesh accuracy, but the better the computational performance.

- **Bounding Volume Type** This defines the bounding volume used to define the spatial-mapping area. You can choose between a sphere or an axis-aligned box.

- **Half Extent in Meters** This indicates the size of the bounding volume.

Creating a Spatial-Mapping Collider

Let's use another Unity component for spatial mapping: the spatial-mapping collider. This Unity component enables you to quickly configure your HoloLens app such that your holograms will interact with real objects. The spatial-mapping collider works like the mesh collider but uses meshes as digital representations of real objects in the near environment. So, spatial-mapping colliders automatically serve as obstacles for all other colliders.

Let's see how this works in practice by adding a spatial-mapping collider to the SpatialMapping app and implementing a projectile (a yellow ball) as in Chapter 10. The user will be able throw the ball around the scene, and the ball will bounce off detected objects. Follow these steps:

1. Add a **Spatial Mapping Collider** component to the **HoloLensCamera** object. (Refer to Figure 12-19.)

2. Create three folders in the Project window and name them **Prefabs**, **Physic Materials**, and **Scripts**.

3. Right-click the **Prefabs** folder and choose **Import New Asset** from the menu that appears.

4. The Import New Asset dialog box appears. Import the **Ball.prefab** object you created in Chapter 10. Alternatively, import it from the companion code at **Chapter_10\ HitTheCanGame\Assets**.

5. Right-click the **Physic Material** folder, choose **Create**, and select **Physic Material**. Nar new material **Bouncy**.

6. In the Inspector, change the **Dynamic Friction** and **Static Friction** settings to **0.6**.

7. Change the **Bounciness** setting to **0.3**.

8. Change the **Friction Combine** setting to **Average**.

9. Change the **Bounce Combine** setting to **Maximum**.

10. In the HoloLensCamera Inspector, expand the **Spatial Mapping Collider** group and change the **Physic Material** setting to **Bouncy**. (See Figure 12-22.)

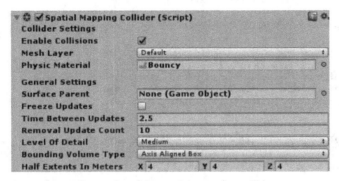

FIGURE 12-22 Properties of the spatial-mapping collider.

As shown in Figure 12-22, there are two groups of spatial-mapping collider settings: general settings and collider settings. The general settings are identical to those for the spatial-mapping renderer. The collider settings are as follows:

- **Enable Collisions** Select this checkbox to enable collisions. If this checkbox is deselected, the spatial-mapping collider will not interact with holograms.

- **Mesh Layer** Use this to specify the layer associated with the collider. This optimizes ray casting so it works only with objects associated with the designated layer.

- **Physic Material** Use this option to specify the physic material for the spatial-mapping collider.

With all the objects ready, now you can implement the projectile logic. It will work such that the yellow ball will be thrown along the gaze ray right after the user performs a double-tap gesture. To create this functionality, follow these steps:

1. In the Project window, right-click the **Scripts** folder, choose **Create**, and select **C# Script**.

2. Name the new script **ProjectileScript**.

3. Associate **ProjectileScript** with the **HoloLensCamera** object.

4. Add the following two statements to the file header to import the necessary namespaces:

```
using HoloToolkit.Unity.InputModule;
using UnityEngine.XR.WSA.Input;
```

5. In the ProjectileScript class, declare a public Ball property:

```
public GameObject Ball;
```

6. Implement the double-tap gesture recognizer as shown in Listing 12-30.

LISTING 12-30 Double-tap gesture recognizer

```
private GestureRecognizer doubleTapRecognizer;

private void ConfigureAndStartGestureRecognizer()
{
    doubleTapRecognizer = new GestureRecognizer();

    doubleTapRecognizer.SetRecognizableGestures(GestureSettings.DoubleTap);
    doubleTapRecognizer.Tapped += DoubleTapRecognizer_Tapped;
    doubleTapRecognizer.StartCapturingGestures();
}

private void DoubleTapRecognizer_Tapped(TappedEventArgs obj)
{
    ThrowTheBall(GazeManager.Instance.Ray, 15);
}

private void ReleaseGestureRecognizer()
{
    doubleTapRecognizer.StopCapturingGestures();
    doubleTapRecognizer.Tapped -= DoubleTapRecognizer_Tapped;
}
```

7. Add the ThrowTheBall method in Listing 12-31 to ProjectileScript.

LISTING 12-31 Throwing the ball

```
private void ThrowTheBall(Ray ray, float speed)
{
    if (Ball != null)
    {
        var ball = Instantiate(Ball,
            transform.position, Quaternion.identity);

        var rigidbody = ball.GetComponent<Rigidbody>();

        if (rigidbody != null)
        {
            rigidbody.velocity = ray.direction * speed;
        }
    }
}
```

8. Implement the `Start` and `Destroy` methods according to Listing 12-32.

LISTING 12-32 Start and OnDestroy methods

```
private void Start()
{
    ConfigureAndStartGestureRecognizer();
}

private void OnDestroy()
{
    ReleaseGestureRecognizer();
}
```

9. In the Unity Editor, modify the Ball prefab to set its **X**, **Y**, and **Z** components under **Scale** in the **Transform** group to **0.25**.

10. Set the **Ball** property of ProjectileScript to **Ball.prefab**.

Build and deploy the SpatialMapping app to the HoloLens emulator. After the app starts, you will need to wait approximately 10 seconds to see the meshes representing real surfaces. (See Figure 12-23.) To deploy the projectile, emulate double-tap gesture. (To do this in the emulator, simply right-click the mouse twice.) The yellow ball will be thrown along the gaze direction. You can now move around and throw the ball toward meshes. The ball will bounce off those meshes because Unity's physics engine detects collisions between the ball and the spatial mapping mesh collider. However, when you throw the ball toward an area without spatial meshes, the ball will fly freely. Its trajectory will still depend on the simulated gravity, however.

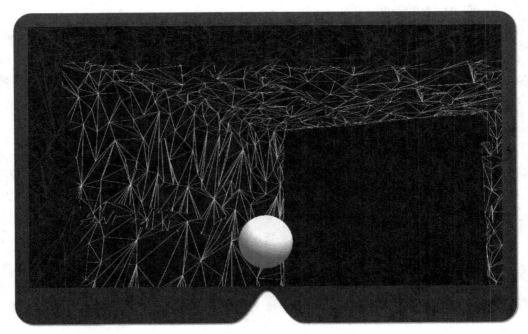

FIGURE 12-23 The SpatialMapping app executed in the HoloLens emulator.

In the HoloLens emulator, the spatial mapping meshes represent one of the simulated rooms. You can switch between rooms using the Room tab of the HoloLens Additional Tools window. (See Figure 12-24.) The name of the loaded room is displayed next to the Status label. To load another room, click the **Load Room** button and choose one of the available XEF files from the Open dialog box that appears. These files are in the following folder: %Program Files (x86)%\Microsoft XDE\10.0.14393.0\ Plugins\Rooms.

FIGURE 12-24 A portion of the Room tab of the HoloLens Additional Tools window.

As of this writing, there were five XEF files available:

- **DefaultRoom.xef**   This depicts a small living room with a TV, a coffee table, and two sofas. When you run the HoloLens emulator, this room is loaded by default.

- **Bedroom1.xef**   This depicts a small bedroom with a desk.

- **Bedroom2.xef**   This defines a bedroom with a queen-sized bed, a dresser, nightstands, and a walk-in closet.

- **GreatRoom.xef**   This defines a large open-space great room with a living area, dining table, and kitchen.

- **LivingRoom.xef**   This defines a living room with a fireplace, a sofa, armchairs, and a coffee table with a vase.

Note You can clear spatial definitions by clicking the Clear button.

In the real HoloLens device, holograms are overlaid on the real objects because the HoloLens has a see-through display. In contrast, in the HoloLens emulator, you do not see any real objects until you enable the rendering of spatial-mapping meshes.

There is yet another way to visualize spatial definition: with the 3D View option in the Device Portal. This preview can work concurrently with the spatial-mapping renderer as you execute the app in the HoloLens emulator or on a real device. To see how this works, follow these steps:

1. Click the **globe** icon on the emulator toolbar to open the Device Portal.

2. Click the **3D View** option in the left pane of the Device Portal to display the preview in the right pane. (See Figure 12-25.)

3. Follow the instructions below the preview to rotate, pan, and zoom the view.

 Note It is instructive to virtually walk around the scene in the HoloLens emulator and check that your virtual movement is reflected in the 3D view.

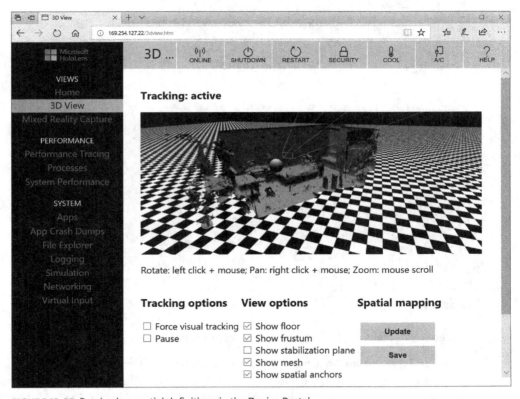

FIGURE 12-25 Previewing spatial definitions in the Device Portal.

Spatial-Mapping Prefab

The spatial-mapping renderer offers the fastest approach to visualize spatial-mapping meshes. If you want to have a more specialized component for that purpose, you can use a spatial-mapping prefab. This prefab comes from the MRTKu package. To use it, simply drag and drop the SpatialMapping. prefab object from the Project window onto the scene. You can then use the Inspector to configure the prefab. (See Figure 12-26.)

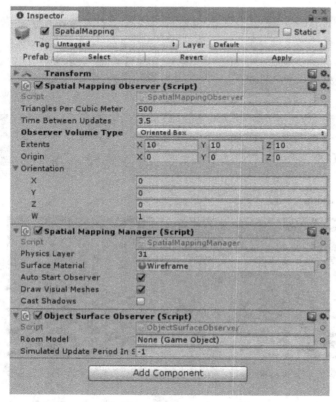

FIGURE 12-26 The SpatialMapping Inspector

Three scripts make up the SpatialMapping.prefab prefab:

- **Spatial Mapping Observer**   This implements the observer that defines the regions in space for which spatial-mapping information will be provided. You can configure this script similarly to the spatial-mapping renderer. For instance, you use the Triangles Per Cubic Meter setting to specify the spatial-mapping quality and the Observer Volume Type drop-down list to choose the volume of the observer.

- **Spatial Mapping Manager**   This implements the class used to control the state of the spatial-mapping observer. You can start and stop the observer using the StartObserver and StopObserver methods. Moreover, you can use the SpatialMappingManager class to load spatial meshes from a file through the Object Surface Observer settings.

- **Object Surface Observer** You can use this script to load mesh data from a file. Specifically, you can import mesh data from modeling software as a game object and then assign it to the Room Model property in the Object Surface Observer group.

At a minimum, to display spatial meshes with the SpatialMapping prefab, add it to the scene (as described previously), and ensure that the **Auto Start Observer** and **Draw Visual Meshes** options in the **Spatial Mapping Manager** group are selected. The actual spatial meshes will be rendered in the same way as with the spatial-mapping renderer but without color coding. To test the SpatialMapping prefab, deselect the Spatial Mapping Renderer checkbox in the HoloLensCamera inspector to disable that component.

Hologram Placement

In this section you will explore how to place holograms within the scene. To achieve this, you will use the TapToPlace script in the MRTKu package. This script uses spatial mapping to place and anchor holograms to a selected surface. The holograms will then stay where you left them even as you move around the scene. You could use this functionality to place virtual content on real surfaces—for example, to place the Ethan model at your desk.

In this section, you will add the Ethan model to the SpatialMapping app and associate it with the TapToPlace script to enable users to anchor the character wherever they like using the tap gesture. Follow these steps:

1. Import the **Ethan** character from the standard Unity package.

2. Add the **Ethan** model to the scene.

3. In the Ethan model's Inspector, change the **X**, **Y**, and **Z Position** settings in the **Transform** group to **0**, **–0.2**, and **2**, respectively.

4. Change the **X**, **Y**, and **Z Rotation** settings to **0**.

5. Change the **X**, **Y**, and **Z Scale** settings to **0.25**, **0.25**, and **0.25**, respectively.

6. In the Project window, type **HumanoidIdle t:Animation** in the search box.

7. Drag the **HumanoidIdle** animation from the search results onto the **Ethan** model.

8. In the Project window, type **TapToPlace** in the search box and drag the **TapToPlace** script onto the **Ethan** model.

The TapToPlace script requires that the collider be added to the hologram being positioned. Because Ethan does not have a default associated collider, you need to add one manually. Here's how:

1. Click the **Add Component** button in the Ethan Inspector and choose **Mesh Collider** from the menu that appears.

2. In the Inspector, click the small icon to the right of the **Mesh** box in the **Mesh Collider** group.

3. The Select Mesh dialog box opens. Select the **EthanBody** object.

4. In the Hierarchy, click the **SpatialMapping** object. Then, in the Inspector, navigate to the **Spatial Mapping Manager** group and deselect the **Auto Start Observer** and **Draw Visual Meshes** checkboxes.

5. In the Hierarchy, select the **HoloLensCamera** object. Then, in the Inspector, select the **Spatial Mapping Renderer** checkbox.

6. Build and deploy the app to the HoloLens emulator.

7. Right-click the **Ethan** model to emulate a tap gesture and gaze around to find a new position for the hologram. (See Figure 12-27.)

8. Tap again. You will see that Ethan is anchored to the selected location.

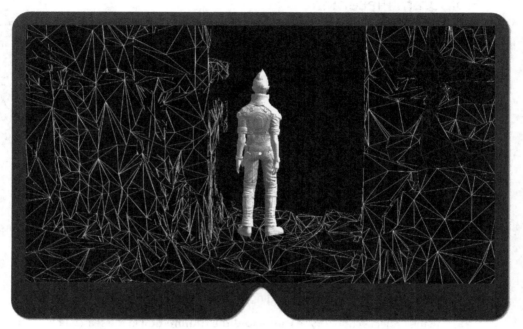

FIGURE 12-27 Positioning the Ethan model on a surface detected by spatial mapping.

Spatial understanding

In some applications, you may want to limit where the hologram can be placed to specific locations. For instance, you may want to place characters only on the floor. To make it easier to identify specific locations in your environment for hologram placement, MRTKu provides a spatial mapping library. This library can detect floors, walls, ceilings, and other objects, as explained in the MRTKu documentation (http://bit.ly/spatial_understanding). This documentation also contains several examples that you can use to extend the SpatialMapping app developed here.

Mixed Reality Toolkit Interfaces

The Mixed Reality Toolkit for Unity provides numerous interfaces to help you significantly reduce the time needed to perform typical tasks related to handling gesture, voice, or gaze input. This section shows you how to quickly handle specific types of gesture and gaze input for a sample app. Specifically, the app will use the following two interfaces:

- **HoloToolkit.Unity.InputModule.IInputClickHandler**   This interface will be used to handle all inputs meant to confirm an action, like an air tap gesture or select voice command. More specifically, you will implement this interface to change the material of the hologram, which was virtually selected.

- **HoloToolkit.Unity.InputModule.IFocusable**   This interface will be used to handle gaze input. You will implement this interface to increase the size of the hologram the user is currently looking at.

To learn how to use these interfaces, proceed as follows:

1. In Unity, create a new 3D app named **HoloToolkitInterfaces**.

2. Open the **Assets** menu, choose **Import Package**, and select **Custom Package**. Then browse for and select the Mixed Reality Toolkit for Unity package to import it. (See the Tools folder from the companion code.)

3. After the package is imported, open the **Mixed Reality Toolkit** menu, select **Configure**, and choose **Apply Mixed Reality Scene Settings**.

4. The Apply Mixed Reality Scene Settings dialog box opens. Leave all the options at their default values and click the **Apply** button.

5. Open the **Mixed Reality Toolkit** menu, select **Configure**, and choose **Apply Mixed Reality Project Settings**.

6. The Apply Mixed Reality Project Settings dialog box opens. Again, leave all options at their default values and click the **Apply** button.

7. In the Hierarchy, click the **Create** drop-down list, choose **3D Object**, and select **Sphere**.

8. Repeat step 7 but choose **Capsule** instead of Sphere.

9. In the Sphere Inspector, set the **X**, **Y**, and **Z Scale** components in the **Transform** group to **0.25**.

10. In the Capsule Inspector, set the **X**, **Y**, and **Z Scale** components in the **Transform** group to **0.25**.

11. In the Sphere Inspector, set the **X**, **Y**, and **Z Position** components in the **Transform** group to **−0.25**, **0**, and **3**, respectively.

12. In the Capsule Inspector, set the **X**, **Y**, and **Z Position** components in the **Transform** group to **0.25**, **0**, and **3**, respectively.

13. To apply materials to Sphere and Capsule objects, open the Project window and type **MRTK_Standard_Red t:Material** in the Search box. Then, drag the **MRTK_Standard_Red** material from the Assets folder onto the Sphere.

14. Repeat step 13 to add the **MRTK_Standard_Cyan** material to the Capsule object. Your scene should resemble the one in Figure 12-28.

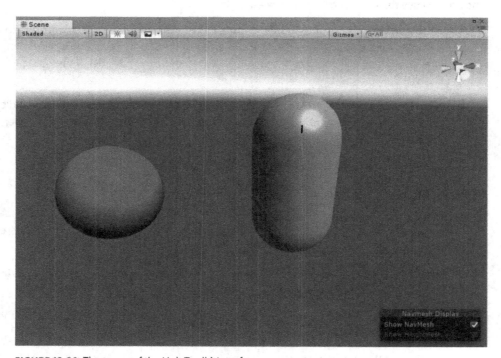

FIGURE 12-28 The scene of the HoloToolkitInterfaces app

You are now ready to create the script that will use the aforementioned interfaces. Follow these steps:

1. In the Project window, create a **Scripts** folder inside the **Assets** folder.

2. Right-click the **Scripts** folder, choose **Create**, and select **C# Script**.

3. Name the new script **SimpleInteraction**.

4. Double-click the script to open it in Visual Studio.

5. To implement the SimpleInteraction script, follow these steps:

6. Import the **HoloToolkit.Unity.InputModule** namespace as follows:

```
using HoloToolkit.Unity.InputModule;
```

7. Change the class declaration to include the IInputClickHandler and IFocusable interfaces like so:

```
public class SimpleInteraction : MonoBehaviour, IInputClickHandler, IFocusable
```

8. Supplement the definition of the `SimpleInteraction` class as shown in Listing 12-33.

   LISTING 12-33 Members of the `SimpleInteraction` class

   ```
   public Material AlternativeMaterial;
   private bool isAlternativeMaterialApplied = false;
   private Vector3 originalScale;
   private Material originalMaterial;
   private Renderer renderer;
   ```

   Listing 12-33 contains one public property: `AlternativeMaterial`. It defines the material that will be applied to the hologram when it is selected. The subsequent four private members store information about whether such an alternative material is currently applied to the hologram (`isAlternativeMaterialApplied`), the original scale of the hologram (`originalScale`), the default hologram material (`originalMaterial`), and a reference to the renderer. The last object is used to dynamically switch hologram materials.

9. Implement the script's `Awake` method to obtain a reference to the renderer, the default hologram scale, and its material, as shown in Listing 12-34.

   LISTING 12-34 Definition of the `Awake` method used to set up the initial script's configuration

   ```
   private void Awake()
   {
       renderer = GetComponent<Renderer>();
       originalScale = transform.localScale;
       originalMaterial = renderer.material;
   }
   ```

10. Implement the `OnInputClicked` method, whose definition is provided by `IInputClick Handler`, as shown in Listing 12-35.

    LISTING 12-35 Handling the input clicked event

    ```
    public void OnInputClicked(InputClickedEventData eventData)
    {
        if (AlternativeMaterial != null)
        {
            if (isAlternativeMaterialApplied)
            {
                renderer.material = originalMaterial;
            }
            else
            {
                renderer.material = AlternativeMaterial;
            }

            isAlternativeMaterialApplied = !isAlternativeMaterialApplied;
        }
    }
    ```

`OnInputClicked` takes one argument, `eventData`, which is an instance of the `HoloToolkit.Unity.InputModule.InputClickedEventData` class. This class provides information about the event, such as the number of taps that triggered the event (TapCount) and a description the input source (`InputSource`). `InputClickedEventData` also has a `Use` method, which can be employed to prevent other parts of the application from handling the click event.

The `OnInputClicked` method first checks whether the `AlternativeMaterial` property is not null. If so, the method checks the value of the `isAlternativeMaterialApplied` field. If this value is true, the hologram's material is reverted to the original one (that is, the material that was applied to the hologram when the application started). Otherwise, the alternative material is attached to the hologram. Finally, the value of `isAlternativeMaterialApplied` is inverted.

11. Implement two methods: `OnFocusEnter` and `OnFocusExit` (see Listing 12-36). Both are declared in the `IFocusable` interface. `OnFocusEnter` is used to slightly increase the size of the hologram the user is currently gazing at. When the hologram is out of the user's focus, `OnFocusExit` restores its size to its original value.

LISTING 12-36 Changing the scale of the focused hologram

```
public void OnFocusEnter()
{
    transform.localScale = (originalScale + Vector3.one * 0.05f);
}

public void OnFocusExit()
{
    transform.localScale = originalScale;
}
```

12. In the Unity Editor, drag the **SimpleInteraction** script onto the **Sphere** and **Capsule** objects.

Finally, set the alternative material for the objects in the SimpleInteraction script as follows:

1. In the Hierarchy, click the **Sphere** object.

2. In the Sphere Inspector, navigate to the **Simple Interaction (Script)** group and click the small circular icon to the right of the **Alternative Material** option.

3. The Select Material windows appears. (See Figure 12-29.) Select the **MRTK_Standard_Magenta** option.

4. Repeat steps 1-3 but select **Capsule** in the hierarchy and choose **MRTK_Standard_Blue** in the Select Material window.

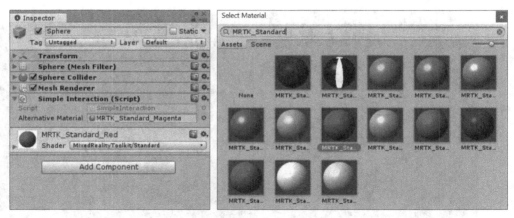

FIGURE 12-29 Configuring the alternative material that will be applied to the hologram.

You can now build the app and deploy it to the HoloLens emulator. After you do, gaze at any hologram. You will see that its scale is changed. (See Figure 12-30.) Then tap on any hologram to invert its material. (See Figure 12-31.)

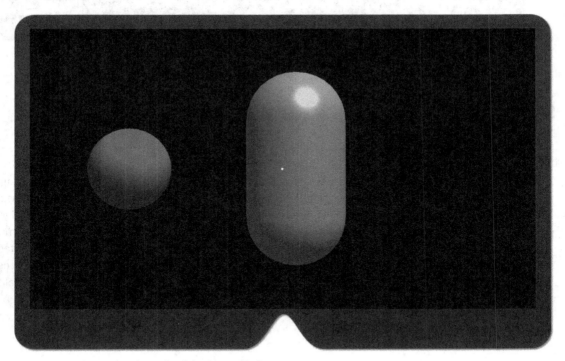

FIGURE 12-30 Increasing the scale of the focused hologram.

FIGURE 12-31 Changing the hologram material. (Compare with Figure 12-30.)

Summary

This chapter investigated HoloLens-specific features of Windows Mixed Reality development. You learned how to implement cursors and position them according to the direction of the user's gaze. You also learned how to use gaze cursors to indicate whether the gaze intersected a hologram. Then, you implemented custom components for handling voice input to control the Ethan model. As a next step, you explored approaches for handling air gestures to resize and manipulate holograms. Finally, you explored spatial-mapping capabilities to detect spatial surfaces, make holograms interact with real objects, and lock holograms within the world coordinate system. Along the way you investigated how to use several components from the Mixed Reality Toolkit for Unity to accelerate the development process. All this information will enable you to quickly parse all samples from the official Mixed Reality academy courses.

CHAPTER 13

An AI-Powered 3D App

Having learned about HoloLens specific functionalities, let's continue to work with the Mixed Reality Toolkit for Unity (MRTKu). In this chapter you will create a new app, VisionAssistant3D. (See Figure 13-1.) In doing so you will learn how to capture photos from the camera on the UWP platform (including the HoloLens world-facing camera) using Unity's PhotoCapture object. You will then learn how to configure the app to display the camera image in a Quad object and utilize artificial intelligence (AI) to describe the camera image. To do so you will send the image to Microsoft Cognitive Services (MCS) for analysis. As in Chapter 6, you will use the Computer Vision API to obtain a text description of the objects in your image. Finally, you will learn how to use billboarding and tag-along hologram behavioral techniques to automatically reposition the Quad object when the user walks or gazes around the scene. So, you will learn how to provide holographic content that is always available to the user. The goal of this project is to implement a 3D version of the vision assistant you created in Chapter 6. The final app will be able to help visually impaired people who are wearing a headset to understand their environment with AI.

FIGURE 13-1 The VisionAssistant3D app.

The VisionAssistant3D app was inspired by the Terminator Vision HUD in a HoloLens project published recently on the Microsoft Blog. (See http://bit.ly/Terminator_Vision.) That project has several shortcomings, however. For instance, the camera image is first saved to a file. Then, the file is read. Finally, it is sent to MCS. In contrast, the VisionAssistant3D app does not create this intermediate file. Instead, it encodes raw binary image data to the PNG format using the Unity `ImageConversion` class. To send requests to MCS, the app uses the Http Client package from the Unity Asset Store.

Configuring Project and Scene Settings

To create the VisionAssistant3D app, start by doing the following:

1. Create a new Unity 3D project named **VisionAssistant3D**.

2. Import the **Mixed Reality Toolkit for Unity** as described in Chapter 12 in the section "Configuring the scene and project settings with Mixed Reality Toolkit."

3. Click the **Mixed Reality Toolkit** menu, choose **Configure**, and select **Apply Mixed Reality Scene Settings**.

4. The Apply Mixed Reality Scene Settings dialog box opens. (Refer to Figure 12-13.) Select the **Add the Mixed Reality Camera Prefab**, **Move Camera to Origin**, **Add the Input Manager Prefab**, and **Add the Default Cursor Prefab** checkboxes and click **Apply**.

5. Click the **Mixed Reality Toolkit** menu, choose **Configure**, and select **Apply Mixed Reality Project Settings**.

6. The Apply Mixed Reality Project Settings dialog box appears. (Refer to Figure 12-14.) Select the **Target Windows Universal UWP** checkbox.

7. Select the **Enable XR, Build for Direct3D, and Enable .NET Scripting Backend** checkboxes and click **Apply**.

Exploring the Mixed Reality Camera Prefab

Before going further, let's quickly explore the Mixed Reality Camera prefab. To start, expand the **MixedRealityCameraParent** object in the Hierarchy and select the **MixedRealityCamera** child object to view its settings in the Inspector. As shown in Figure 13-2, the MixedRealityCamera object has several standard component groups, such as Transform, Camera, and Audio Listener. It also has a Gaze Control group (which is identical to the group of the same name in the HoloLens Camera Inspector) and a Mixed Reality Camera Manager (Script) group.

Mixed Reality Camera Manager is a script that tells you whether your app is running in the opaque or transparent head-mounted device (HMD). You can use this script to adjust your scene much as you did with the Unity XRDevice class in Chapter 10.

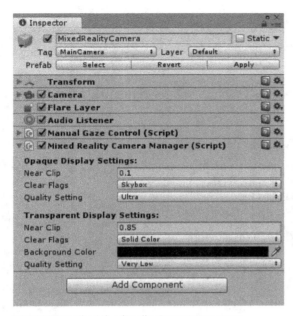

FIGURE 13-2 The MixedRealityCamera Inspector.

Mixed Reality Camera Manager also automatically sets common display parameters, such as Near Clip, Clear Flags, and Quality Setting, for both opaque and transparent HMDs. A shown in Figure 13-2, these settings are adjusted according to Microsoft's recommendation as follows:

- **Opaque Display Settings**

  - **Near Clip: 0.1**

  - **Clear Flags: Skybox**

  - **Quality Setting: Ultra**

- **Transparent Display Settings**

  - **Near Clip: 0.85**

  - **Clear Flags: Solid Color (Black)**

  - **Quality Setting: Very Low**

Mixed Reality Camera Manager detects display settings in the Start method. As shown in Listing 13-1, Mixed Reality Camera Manager obtains the display type (opaque or transparent) from the UnityEngine.XR.WSA.HolographicSettings class. This class has the public, static, read-only property, IsDisplayOpaque, which tells you whether the HMD is opaque. The Start method then stores this display type in the CurrentDisplayType property and adjusts display-specific settings using two helper methods: ApplySettingsForOpaqueDisplay and ApplySettingsForTransparentDisplay.

LISTING 13-1 Mixed Reality Camera Manager Start method

```
public DisplayType CurrentDisplayType { get; private set; }

private void Start()
{
    if (!Application.isEditor)
    {
#if UNITY_WSA
#if UNITY_2017_2_OR_NEWER
        if (!HolographicSettings.IsDisplayOpaque)
#endif
        {
            CurrentDisplayType = DisplayType.Transparent;
            ApplySettingsForTransparentDisplay();
            if (OnDisplayDetected != null)
            {
                OnDisplayDetected(DisplayType.Transparent);
            }
            return;
        }
#endif
    }

    CurrentDisplayType = DisplayType.Opaque;
    ApplySettingsForOpaqueDisplay();

    if (OnDisplayDetected != null)
    {
        OnDisplayDetected(DisplayType.Opaque);
    }
}
```

Listing 13-2 provides definitions of ApplySettingsForOpaqueDisplay and ApplySettingsFor
TransparentDisplay. Both methods adjust three settings—Near Clip, Clear Flags, and Quality—
according to values set through the Inspector.

LISTING 13-2 Applying display settings

```
public void ApplySettingsForOpaqueDisplay()
{
    Debug.Log("Display is Opaque");

    CameraCache.Main.clearFlags = CameraClearFlags_OpaqueDisplay;
    CameraCache.Main.nearClipPlane = NearClipPlane_OpaqueDisplay;
    CameraCache.Main.backgroundColor = BackgroundColor_OpaqueDisplay;

    SetQuality(OpaqueQualityLevel);
}

public void ApplySettingsForTransparentDisplay()
{
    Debug.Log("Display is Transparent");

    CameraCache.Main.clearFlags = CameraClearFlags_TransparentDisplay;
    CameraCache.Main.backgroundColor = BackgroundColor_TransparentDisplay;
```

```
        CameraCache.Main.nearClipPlane = NearClipPlane_TransparentDisplay;

        SetQuality(HoloLensQualityLevel);
}

private static void SetQuality(int level)
{
        QualitySettings.SetQualityLevel(level, false);
}
```

After configuring the display settings, the `MixedRealityCameraManager.Start` method fires the `OnDisplayDetected` event, which can be used to customize display settings depending on the display type.

Creating Quad and 3DTextPrefab Objects

Now that you've configured the scene and project settings, you're ready to add two game objects to the scene:

- **Quad**   This object will depict images captured from the camera.

- **3DTextPrefab**   This object will display a text string containing a description of the image obtained from MCS.

> **Note** You could use the Unity 3D Text object instead of 3DTextPrefab. But as you learned in Chapter 9, the 3D Text object in its default configuration displays strings that appear fuzzy. You can solve this problem by down-scaling the 3D Text object and then increasing the font size, as discussed here: http://bit.ly/Text_in_Unity. However, 3DTextPrefab does all this for you. The bottom line: It's easier to use 3DTextPrefab than to manually configure the 3D Text object.

To create the Quad object, follow these steps:

1.   In the Hierarchy, click **Create**, choose **3D Object**, and select **Quad**.

2.   In the Quad Inspector, type **CameraImage** in the **Name** field.

3.   In the **Transform** group, change the **X**, **Y**, and **Z Position** settings to **0.1**, **0.025**, and **1**, respectively.

4.   Change the **X**, **Y**, and **Z Scale** settings to **0.1**.

Next, you'll add the 3DTextPrefab object from the MRTKu. Here's how:

1.   In the Project window, type **3DTextPrefab** in the search box.

2.   Drag the **3DTextPrefab** entry in the search results onto the scene or the Hierarchy.

3.   In the 3DTextPrefab Inspector, shown in Figure 13-3, type **InfoPanel** in the **Name** box.

4.   In the **Transform** group, change the **X**, **Y**, and **Z Position** settings to **0**, **0.1**, and **1**, respectively.

5. In the **Text Mesh** group, type **Info Panel** in the **Text** box.

6. Type **36** in the **Font Size** box.

7. Click the **Color** box and set the **R**, **G**, **B**, and **A** settings to **255**, **0**, **0**, and **255**, respectively, to select the color red.

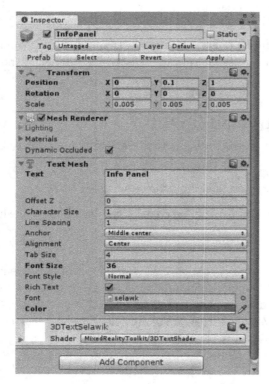

FIGURE 13-3 The 3DTextPrefab Inspector.

Setting Up Photo Capture

To capture images from a camera on UWP (for example, the world-facing camera in HoloLens), you will create a VisionScript script, which will be attached to the MixedRealityCamera. VisionScript will capture photos using the UnityEngine.XR.WSA.WebCam.PhotoCapture class. To create the script, follow these steps:

1. In the Project window, create a **Scripts** folder inside the **Assets** folder.

2. Right-click the **Scripts** folder, choose **Create**, and select **C# Script**.

3. Name the new script **VisionScript**.

4. Double-click the **VisionScript** script to open it in Visual Studio.

Initializing PhotoCapture

Use Listing 13-3 to set up the script to capture photos. But before that, import two namespaces: System.Linq and UnityEngine.XR.WSA.WebCam. Listing 13-3 declares two public properties: ImageRenderer and InfoPanel. You use the Inspector to configure these public properties to choose objects to display an image from the camera (ImageRenderer) and to display their description (InfoPanel). Finally, the script creates three private fields. These private fields store an instance of the PhotoCapture class, camera properties, and a Boolean (isPhotoCaptureReady) indicating whether the capture device was successfully initialized.

LISTING 13-3 Members of VisionScript

```
public Renderer ImageRenderer;
public TextMesh InfoPanel;

private PhotoCapture photoCapture;
private CameraParameters cameraParameters;
private bool isPhotoCaptureReady;
```

Before we move on, let's save the script and associate it with the MixedRealityCamera object. Follow these steps:

1. In the MixedRealityCamera Inspector, click the **Add Component** button and select **VisionScript** to associate the script with that object. Alternatively, drag the **VisionScript** script from the Project window onto the **MixedRealityCamera** object.

2. In the MixedRealityCamera Inspector, click the small circular icon to the right of the **Info Panel** entry.

3. The Select Text Mesh dialog box opens. Select the **InfoPanel** object.

4. Back in the MixedRealityCamera Inspector, click the icon to the right of the **Image Renderer** option.

5. The Select Renderer dialog box opens. Select the **CameraImage** object. Figure 13-4 shows the results.

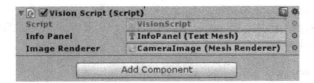

FIGURE 13-4 Configuring the VisionScript script.

Next, implement the Start method in the VisionScript script as shown in Listing 13-4. This listing clears the text displayed in the app's info panel—meaning that when the app starts, there will be no description visible. Then it invokes the CreateAsync static method of the PhotoCapture class. This method takes two arguments:

- **showHolograms** This is a Boolean value that indicates whether the captured image should also contain holograms visible in the scene.

- **onCreatedCallback** This is a callback function that is invoked after the PhotoCapture class is created.

Here, I disabled hologram capture and implemented the OnPhotoCaptureCreated method to handle the creation of the PhotoCapture class.

Note A callback-based approach is necessary here because Unity uses an older .NET API and does not allow you to use a task-based asynchronous pattern.

LISTING 13-4 The Start method for the VisionScript script

```
private void Start()
{
    // Reset the info panel
    InfoPanel.text = string.Empty;

    // Initialize photo capture
    PhotoCapture.CreateAsync(false, OnPhotoCaptureCreated);
}
```

Listing 13-5 presents the implementation of the OnPhotoCaptureCreated callback function. This method has one argument of type PhotoCapture, which is an instance of the created PhotoCapture class. Hence, a reference to that instance is stored in the local photoCapture field. Then, the callback function configures camera parameters such that photos will be taken using the highest possible resolution, in the BGRA format, with 8-bit depth. This format indicates that the image will contain four channels (blue, green, red, and alpha), with each channel represented by an 8-bit integer. Consequently, each pixel is encoded using 32 bits (8 bits per channel). Next, the OnPhotoCaptureCreated callback uses camera parameters to start the capture device. To achieve this, it invokes the StartPhotoModeAsync method. After that the script issues another callback to OnPhotoModeStarted. This checks whether the capture device is ready by reading the success Boolean property of the PhotoCaptureResult struct. The success property is stored in the isPhotoCaptureReady field, which will be used later to determine whether photos can be safely taken. If PhotoCapture initialization fails, the following string will output to the console: Photo capture initialization failed.

LISTING 13-5 The callback invoked after PhotoCapture initialization

```
private void OnPhotoCaptureCreated(PhotoCapture captureObject)
{
    photoCapture = captureObject;

    // Pick the best resolution available
    var resolution = PhotoCapture.SupportedResolutions.OrderByDescending(
        r => r.width * r.height).First();
```

```
    cameraParameters = new CameraParameters(WebCamMode.VideoMode)
    {
        hologramOpacity = 0.0f,
        cameraResolutionHeight = resolution.height,
        cameraResolutionWidth = resolution.width,
        pixelFormat = CapturePixelFormat.BGRA32
    };

    photoCapture.StartPhotoModeAsync(cameraParameters, OnPhotoModeStarted);
}

private void OnPhotoModeStarted(PhotoCapture.PhotoCaptureResult result)
{
    isPhotoCaptureReady = result.success;

    if (!isPhotoCaptureReady)
    {
        Debug.Log("Photo capture initialization failed");
    }
}
```

Taking Photos

After configuring PhotoCapture, you can proceed to take photos from the world-facing camera. To do so, you add the TakePhoto method to the VisionScript script. (See Listing 13-6.) This method checks whether isPhotoCaptureReady is true. If so, the TakePhotoAsync method of the PhotoCapture class instance is invoked. Otherwise, the following string is output to the console: Photo capture is unavailable.

LISTING 13-6 Taking photos with PhotoCapture

```
private void TakePhoto()
{
    if (isPhotoCaptureReady)
    {
        photoCapture.TakePhotoAsync(OnPhotoCaptured);
    }
    else
    {
        Debug.Log("Photo capture is unavailable");
    }
}
```

Again, the TakePhotoAsync method works in the background. After the photo is taken, the custom callback function is invoked. As shown in Listing 13-7 this callback function is provided with two objects:

- **An instance of the PhotoCapture.PhotoCaptureResult struct** Use the success property of this object to determine whether the photo has been successfully acquired.

- **An instance of the PhotoCaptureFrame class** Use this class to obtain image data as well as spatial information about the location where the photo was taken.

This example uses only image data. PhotoCaptureFrame lets you access image data in three ways:

- Use the UploadImageDataToTexture method to read the image as a texture

- Use the CopyRawImageDataIntoBuffer method to read image data as a byte array

- Use the GetUnsafePointerToBuffer method to obtain a pointer to the pixel array

Listing 13-7 uses the first method to obtain the image as a two-dimensional texture. This texture is then displayed in the Quad object using the Renderer.material.SetTexture method.

LISTING 13-7 Displaying a photo as a texture of the Quad renderer

```
private void OnPhotoCaptured(PhotoCapture.PhotoCaptureResult result,
    PhotoCaptureFrame photoCaptureFrame)
{
    if (result.success)
    {
        // Display image
        var texture2D = new Texture2D(
            cameraParameters.cameraResolutionWidth,
            cameraParameters.cameraResolutionHeight);

        photoCaptureFrame.UploadImageDataToTexture(texture2D);

        ImageRenderer.material.SetTexture("_MainTex", texture2D);
    }
    else
    {
        Debug.Log("Photo capture failed");
    }
}
```

Testing the App So Far

Let's test the app in the Unity Editor. First, implement the Update method as shown in Listing 13-8.

LISTING 13-8 Taking photos, when the left mouse button is clicked

```
private void Update()
{
    if (Input.GetMouseButtonDown(0))
    {
        TakePhoto();
    }
}
```

Then, enable holographic emulation as follows and run the app:

1. Open the **Window** menu and choose **Holographic Emulation**.

2. The Holographic window appears. Open the **Emulation Mode** drop-down list and choose **Simulate in Editor**.

3. Click **Play** in the Editor.

4. When the app starts, click the left mouse button. The app captures an image from your webcam and displays it in the Quad object, as shown in Figure 13-5.

 Note The Quad object covers only a very small part of the scene, as it is intended to display information for the user of the HMD without hiding other elements of the scene.

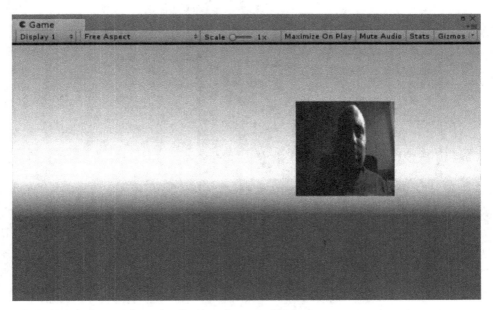

FIGURE 13-5 An image taken using the PhotoCapture object.

Releasing the PhotoCapture Object

To wrap things up, you use the OnDestroy method to release the PhotoCapture object, as shown in Listing 13-9. This script invokes the StopPhotoModeAsync method of the PhotoCapture class instance. This method accepts one argument, the callback function, which is invoked after the capture device is stopped. It uses this callback to explicitly dispose of the PhotoCapture class instance, whose reference is stored in the photoCapture field.

LISTING 13-9 Releasing the PhotoCapture object

```
private void OnDestroy()
{
    photoCapture.StopPhotoModeAsync(
        delegate (PhotoCapture.PhotoCaptureResult result)
        {
            photoCapture.Dispose();
        });
}
```

App Capabilities

Ultimately, you want the VisionAssistant3D app to work on real devices. To achieve this, you need to declare microphone, webcam, and Internet client Server UWP capabilities. Here's how:

1. Open the **Mixed Reality Toolkit** menu and choose **Apply UWP Capability Settings**.

2. The Apply UWP Capability Settings dialog box opens. (See Figure 13-6.) Select the **Microphone**, **Webcam**, and **Internet Client Server** checkboxes.

3. Click the **Apply** button.

FIGURE 13-6 Applying UWP capabilities.

Using the Computer Vision API from MCS

Having configured the app to capture photos, you can now implement the logic responsible for sending these images to the cloud-based Computer Vision API for analysis. To achieve this, you will use the same API as in Chapter 6, so keep your API key and service endpoint ready.

Installing HttpClient

Because Unity does not allow you to install NuGet packages from the Editor, you cannot use the VisionServiceClient class from Chapter 6. You do have two other options, however:

- You can use the UnityEngine.WWW class, as in the Terminator Vision project on the Microsoft Blog.

- You can use the Http Client package from the Asset Store.

This section takes the second approach. To install the Http Client package, follow these steps:

1. Navigate to the Asset Store window.

2. Type **Http Client** in the search box.

3. Select the **Clayton Industries Http Client** entry in the search results.

4. A screen with details about the package opens. (See Figure 13-7.) Click the **Import** button.

5. After a while, the Import Package window will open. Use it to import all objects in the package.

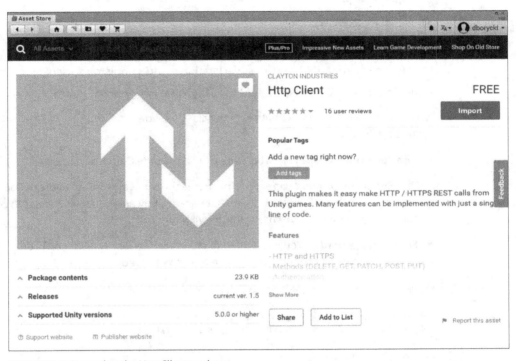

FIGURE 13-7 Importing the HttpClient package.

Building the VisionApiClient Script

After you install the Http Client package, you will create another script, VisionApiClient, which will be used to send requests to MCS. These requests will contain an image to be analyzed. VisionApiClient will also be used to parse the responses it receives, which will consist of an image description. This image description will then be sent to the VisionScript discussed earlier through Unity's messaging system.

Creating the VisionApiClient Script

To create the VisionApiClient script, follow these steps:

1. In the Project window, right-click the **Scripts** folder, choose **Create**, and select **C# Script**.

2. Name the new script **VisionApiClient**.

3. Associate the **VisionApiClient** script with the **MixedRealityCamera** object.

4. Double-click the **VisionApiClient** script to open it in Visual Studio.

5. Add the following namespaces to the header of the **VisionApiClient** script:

   - **using CI.HttpClient;**
   - **using HoloToolkit.Unity;**
   - **using System;**
   - **using System.IO;**
   - **using System.Linq;**

6. Modify the VisionApiClient class declaration to use a singleton pattern as follows:

   - **public class VisionApiClient : Singleton<VisionApiClient>**

7. Add six members to the **VisionApiClient** class, as shown in Listing 13-10. These members include the following:

   - **The Key public property**   This stores the key for the Computer Vision API.

   - **The Endpoint public property**   This stores the service endpoint address. Use the same values as you did in Chapter 6. Note that because Key and Endpoint are both public you can configure these properties from Unity Editor.

   - **Four private fields**   You'll use these to store a reference to the HttpClient class and three constants. These constants will be used to send requests to MCS.

   LISTING 13-10 Members of the VisionApiClient class

   ```
   public string Key = "<TYPE_YOUR_KEY_HERE>";
   public string Endpoint = "<TYPE_YOUR_ENDPOINT_HERE>";

   private HttpClient httpClient;

   private const string subscriptionHeaderKey = "Ocp-Apim-Subscription-Key";
   private const string describeQuery = "/describe?maxCandidates = 1";
   private const string mediaType = "application/octet-stream";
   ```

8. Implement the **Awake** method to instantiate and configure the HttpClient class during initialization of the VisionApiClient class. (See Listing 13-11.)

   LISTING 13-11 The Awake method of the VisionApiClient class

   ```
   protected override void Awake()
   {
       httpClient = new HttpClient();
       httpClient.CustomHeaders.Add(subscriptionHeaderKey, Key);
   }
   ```

9. To instantiate the `HttpClient` class, use a parameter-less constructor.

10. Recall that in Chapter 6, when you implemented the custom Bing search service client, you had to programmatically pass the subscription key. The same thing applies here. To do this, you add one key-value pair to the HTTP request message header. The key should be key `Ocp-Apim-Subscription-Key` and the value equal to the API key you obtained from MCS.

Adding the SendRequest Method

You are now ready to extend the `VisionApiClient` class by adding a `SendRequest` method. (See Listing 13-12.) This method will send requests to MCS.

LISTING 13-12 Sending an image to MCS for analysis

```
public void SendRequest(Texture2D imageTexture)
{
    var imageData = ImageConversion.EncodeToPNG(imageTexture);

    var content = new StreamContent(
        new MemoryStream(imageData), mediaType);

    var uri = new Uri(string.Concat(Endpoint, describeQuery));

    httpClient.Post(uri, content, ParseResponse);
}

private void ParseResponse(HttpResponseMessage<string> response)
{
    Debug.Log(response.StatusCode);
    Debug.Log(response.Data);
}
```

Given an argument of type Texture2D, which represents the previously acquired image, the SendRequest method proceeds as follows:

1. The image is encoded into the PNG format using the EncodeToPNG static method of the `UnityEngine.ImageConversion` class.

2. EncodeToPNG returns a byte array with image data in PNG format.

3. The byte array is wrapped by the `System.IO.MemoryStream` class.

4. The resulting object can be used to create an instance of the `CI.HttpClient.StreamContent` object. HttpClient uses this object to set the request format to satisfy MCS requirements.

5. The SendRequest method creates the request URI by combining an endpoint and the query string stored in the describeQuery field.

6. The URI and image are passed to the Post method of the HttpClient class.

7. The Post method is asynchronous. Like methods in PhotoCapture, this method requires you to provide a callback, which will be invoked when asynchronous operation ends. In this case, the callback is implemented in the ParseResponse method from Listing 13-12.

8. **ParseResponse** is provided with an instance of the generic `HttpResponseMessage` class. This class is an abstract representation of the response received from the web service.

9. Two values that represent the response appear in the console window: a status code and JSON data that contains the result of the image analysis.

To test the app, follow these steps:

1. Modify the **OnPhotoCaptured** callback method in the **VisionScript** class as shown in the bold line in Listing 13-13.

   LISTING 13-13 Modifying the OnPhotoCaptured callback

   ```
   private void OnPhotoCaptured(PhotoCapture.PhotoCaptureResult result,
       PhotoCaptureFrame photoCaptureFrame)
   {
       if (result.success)
       {
           // Display image
           var texture2D = new Texture2D(
               cameraParameters.cameraResolutionWidth,
               cameraParameters.cameraResolutionHeight);

           photoCaptureFrame.UploadImageDataToTexture(texture2D);

           ImageRenderer.material.SetTexture("_MainTex", texture2D);

           // Send image for analysis
           VisionApiClient.Instance.SendRequest(texture2D);
       }
       else
       {
           Debug.Log("Photo capture failed");
       }
   }
   ```

2. Click **Play** and then click anywhere on the Game View screen. The image is acquired and the `VisionApiClient.SendRequest` method is invoked.

3. Observe the debug strings in the console. Notice that instead of displaying the JSON object, the console displays an error. (See Figure 13-8.)

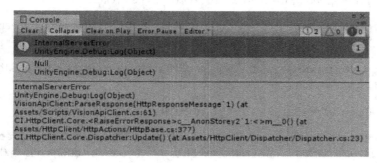

FIGURE 13-8 The console window showing a communication error.

The error shown in the console relates to the use of HTTPS connections by the default MCS endpoint. More specifically, Mono-based platforms—including the C# compiler used by Unity Editor to compile scripts—may encounter certificate exceptions when communicating over the HTTPS protocol. The readme.txt file for the Http Client package contains a solution to this problem: to accept all HTTPS certificates.

4. To accept all HTTPS certificates, extend the **Awake** method of the **VisionApiClient** class as shown in Listing 13-14.

LISTING 13-14 Accepting HTTPS certificates

```
protected override void Awake()
{
    httpClient = new HttpClient();
    httpClient.CustomHeaders.Add(subscriptionHeaderKey, Key);

    System.Net.ServicePointManager.ServerCertificateValidationCallback
        += (o, certificate, chain, errors) =>
    {
        return true;
    };
}
```

5. Rerun the app in Unity Editor to see the image-analysis result in the console window. You should see an image description in a form similar to that presented in Listing 13-15. You will decode this object programmatically in the next section.

LISTING 13-15 An exemplary JSON object received from the Computer Vision API

```
{
  "description": {
    "tags": [
      "person",
      "man",
      "indoor",
      "looking",
      "sitting",
      "front",
      "shirt",
      "camera",
      "holding",
      "glasses",
      "table",
      "wearing",
      "laptop",
      "food",
      "computer",
      "smiling",
      "eating",
      "large",
      "screen",
      "young",
      "mouth",
      "teeth",
```

```
      "pizza",
      "white",
      "phone"
    ],
    "captions": [
      {
        "text": "a man looking at the camera",
        "confidence": 0.9450483492295437
      }
    ]
  },
  "requestId": "9deda88e-c9a5-44ac-bf98-73b8eaf1c987",
  "metadata": {
    "height": 720,
    "width": 1280,
    "format": "Jpeg"
  }
}
```

Parsing Responses

To parse JSON responses, you follow the same approach as in Chapter 6 to decode responses from the Bing Search service. Specifically, you use the JSON Utils website (https://jsonutils.com/). Follow these steps:

1. Copy the JSON string from Listing 13-15 into the **JSON Text or URL** box on the main page of the JSON Utils website.

2. Type **AnalysisResult** in the **Class Name** box.

3. Leave all other settings at their default values and click the **Submit** button.

4. Auto-generated classes should appear in the JSON Utilities panel. Copy these classes and paste them into the **VisionApiClient.cs** file below the curly bracket that closes the definition of the VisionApiClient class.

5. Add a **Serializable** attribute to the **Caption**, **Description**, and **MetaData** classes. (See Listing 13-16.)

    LISTING 13-16 Auto-generated classes mapping JSON responses from the Computer Vision API

    ```
    [Serializable]
    public class Caption
    {
        public string text;
        public double confidence;
    }

    [Serializable]
    public class Description
    {
        public string[] tags;
        public Caption[] captions;
    }
    ```

```
[Serializable]
public class Metadata
{
    public int height;
    public int width;
    public string format;
}

public class AnalysisResult
{
    public Description description;
    public string requestId;
    public Metadata metadata;
}
```

6. Having the auto-generated C# classes comprising the JSON-to-C# mapping, you can now create the final version of the ParseResponse callback as shown in Listing 13-17.

LISTING 13-17 Final definition of the ParseResponse callback

```
private void ParseResponse(HttpResponseMessage<string> response)
{
    Debug.Log(response.StatusCode);
    Debug.Log(response.Data);

    var imageDescription = string.Empty;

    if (!response.IsSuccessStatusCode)
    {
        imageDescription = response.ReasonPhrase;
    }
    else
    {
        var analysisResult = JsonUtility.FromJson<AnalysisResult>(
            response.Data);

        imageDescription = analysisResult.description.
            captions.FirstOrDefault().text;
    }

    BroadcastMessage("OnImageDescriptionGenerated", imageDescription);
}
```

The ParseResponse method now checks whether the response status code is OK (200 HTTP status code). If not, the local variable imageDescription is set to the ReasonPhrase property of the HttpResponseMessage class instance. This property contains a string that represents the error that occurred during the communication with the web service. When the IsSuccessStatusCode property of the HttpResponseMessage class instance is true, the JSON object is deserialized to an instance of the AnalysisResult class. This is done using the FromJson generic method of the UnityEngine.JsonUtility class. An instance of the AnalysisResult class is used to retrieve an image description. This description is then sent to other components via the BroadcastMessage method.

7. To see the image description in the info panel, implement the `OnImageDescriptionGenerated` method in `VisionScript`. (See Listing 13-18.)

LISTING 13-18 Displaying the image description

```
private void OnImageDescriptionGenerated(
    string imageDescription)
{
    InfoPanel.text = imageDescription;
}
```

Let's test the completed app using holographic emulation mode. To do so, simply click **Play** and then click anywhere on the screen to acquire the image and send it to MCS for analysis. The image description will appear in the info panel. (Refer to Figure 13-1.)

Billboarding and Tag-Along

Digital content that should follow the user can make use of two important behavioral concepts that define how objects are oriented and positioned when the user moves or gazes around the scene:

- **Billboarding** With billboarding, objects are always oriented to face the user. However, when the user moves their gaze, the objects can move out of the field of view.

- **Tag-along** With the tag-along behavior, the hologram remains in the user's view even when their gaze shifts. (An example of an object that displays this behavior is the Mixed Reality Start menu, which changes its position as you gaze or move around the scene.)

These behaviors are useful for the VisionAssistant3D app, in which the InfoPanel and Quad objects should always be available for the user. In this section, you will learn how to use billboarding and tag-along to automatically orient and position the InfoPanel and Quad objects so that the latter will remain in the field of view.

You need not independently implement billboarding or tag-along components. They are already available in MRTKu. The MRTKu provides one script for billboarding and the following three tag-along scripts:

- **SimpleTagalong** This script implements a tag-along behavior such that the hologram will always be located in the headset field of view and will be positioned at a fixed distance from the camera.

- **SphereTagalong** This script implements a tag-along behavior in which the object is positioned at a fixed distance from the camera. However, unlike with the SimpleTagalong script, the hologram will stay within the sphere, whose origin is at the camera position.

- **Tagalong** This script extends the `SimpleTagalong` script to enable you to specify the minimum and target percentage of the object to keep in the view.

Let's experiment with these scripts by applying billboarding to the InfoPanel object and tag-along to the Quad object. Follow these steps:

1. In the Project window, type **Billboard** in the search box.

2. Drag the **Billboard** script from the search results onto the **InfoPanel** object.

3. Back in the Project window, type **Tagalong** in the search box.

4. The search results will contain multiple entries: SimpleTagalong, SphereTagalong, and Tagalong. Drag the **Tagalong** entry onto the **Quad** object.

   Open the Quad Inspector. Notice that in addition to a Tagalong (Script) group, the Inspector also contains an Interpolator (Script) group. The Interpolator script will be used internally by the Tagalong component. The Tagalong component also uses the Box Collider component. This will also be added automatically if the game object does not have a box collider.

   At the moment, you cannot test these scripts in the Unity Editor's holographic emulation mode because it requires you to virtually move around the scene. Instead, you will need to build it and deploy it to the HoloLens emulator. This results in two other problems, however.

   The first problem is that the build cannot be completed because the System.Net. ServicePointManager class is not available when building for UWP. To solve this problem, you use preprocessor directives. Depending on the target platform, Unity defines various pre-processor directives, which are listed here: http://bit.ly/platform_dependent_compilation.

5. To detect whether the script is compiled by the Unity Editor, use the **#UNITY_EDITOR** directive and modify the **Awake** method in VisionScript as shown in Listing 13-19. This ensures that the System.Net.ServicePointManager will be accessed only when compiling scripts in the Unity Editor (and not for UWP builds).

   LISTING 13-19 Platform-dependent script compilation

```
protected override void Awake()
{
    httpClient = new HttpClient();
    httpClient.CustomHeaders.Add(subscriptionHeaderKey, Key);

#if UNITY_EDITOR
    System.Net.ServicePointManager.ServerCertificateValidationCallback
        += (o, certificate, chain, errors) =>
    {
        return true;
    };
#endif
}
```

6. Make sure the **Unity C# Projects** setting is enabled. (Open the Build Settings window and select the Unity C# Projects option.) Then build the project for UWP and deploy it to the HoloLens emulator.

After you deploy the app to the HoloLens emulator, you will encounter the second problem: The app cannot start because the world-facing camera is unavailable in the emulator. As such, you will see the following error in the debugger console:

```
Failed to initialize IMediaCapture (hr = 0xC00DABE0)
```

To solve this problem, you must disable two statements in the Start method in VisionScript:

```
    InfoPanel.text = string.Empty;
    PhotoCapture.CreateAsync(false, OnPhotoCaptureCreated);
```

7. To disable these statements, simply comment them out or use the WINDOWS_UWP preprocessor directive as shown in Listing 13-20.

LISTING 13-20 The WINDOWS_UWP preprocessor directive

```
private void Start()
{
#if !WINDOWS_UWP
    // Reset the info panel
    InfoPanel.text = string.Empty;

    // Initialize photo capture
    PhotoCapture.CreateAsync(false, OnPhotoCaptureCreated);
#endif
}
```

8. The WINDOWS_UWP directive also prevents the code from being executed on the real device. To address this, define your own custom symbol using the #define preprocessor directive (for example, #define WINDOWS_UWP_HOLOLENS_EMULATOR), which will be used only when you compile the solution for the HoloLens emulator.

9. Compile and deploy the app from Visual Studio to the HoloLens emulator. You should see a static red string that reads "Info Panel" and a white square that represents the Quad object.

10. Gaze around the scene. (See Figure 13-9.) Notice three things:

FIGURE 13-9 Billboarding and tag-along behaviors in the HoloLens emulator.

- The red text string rotates to always face you.

- When you shift your gaze enough, the Quad object briefly moves out of view. Thanks to the Tagalong component, however, it then quickly moves back into view.

- The Quad object is always at the same distance from you. (You can control this distance using Tagalong parameters, described next.)

You can configure various Tagalong parameters in an object's Inspector. (See Figure 13-10.) I suggest you experiment with these parameters to fine-tune the Quad object's tag-along behavior.

- **Tagalong Distance**   This specifies the distance from the camera (in meters) to the object.

- **Enforce Distance**   This indicates whether the hologram should be at the tag-along distance from the camera even if the hologram does not require repositioning.

- **Position Update Speed**   This is the speed (in meters per second) at which to move the hologram during tag-along.

- **Smooth Motion**   This indicates whether the hologram motion should be smoothed during tag-along.

- **Smoothing Factor**   This controls motion smoothing. The larger the value, the better the smoothing—but at the cost of increased computation, which can slow down the app.

- **Minimum Horizontal Overlap and Minimum Vertical Overlap**   These indicate the minimum horizontal and vertical percentages in the field of view before the object will be tagged along.

- **Target Horizontal Overlap and Target Vertical Overlap**   These indicate the target horizontal and vertical percentages that the tag-along will try to achieve.

- **Horizontal Ray Count and Vertical Ray Count**   These specify the number of rays that will be cast across the object to detect eventual collisions with other objects. Ray casting is used here to position the tagged-along object in front of any other holograms and the spatial mapping mesh.

- **Minimum Tagalong Distance**   This specifies the minimum distance between the user and the hologram being positioned.

- **Maintain Fixed Size**   This indicates whether the angular size of the tag-along object should be kept constant.

- **Depth Update Speed**   This is the speed along the Z axis at which the hologram will tag-along.

- **Debug Draw Lines**   This indicates whether ray casts (used for collision detection) should be displayed in the Scene view.

- **Debug Point Light**   This is used to choose the object that will indicate the depth at which the hologram will be tagged along.

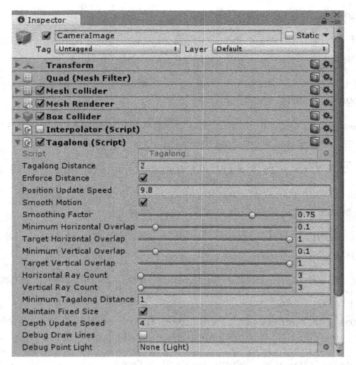

FIGURE 13-10 The Inspector of the CameraImage object showing properties of the Tagalong script.

Summary

In this chapter you learned how to implement an AI-powered 3D app with Unity and MCS, which provide various AI modules. You learned how to display photos captured from the webcam and then send them to the Computer Vision API using the Http Client Unity package. Then you parsed responses from the Computer Vision API using the `JsonUtility` class. Finally, you learned how to use billboarding and tag-along behaviors to enhance the app. You could extend the VisionAssistant3D app by adding voice commands, gestures, and spatial mapping. I will leave this for you as an exercise.

CHAPTER 14

Attaching Holograms to Real Objects with Vuforia

Vuforia is an augmented reality platform that you can use to supplement your HoloLens and mobile apps with robust AR experiences. Vuforia uses computer vision algorithms that recognize and track real objects that you select. Vuforia can track various objects, which Vuforia calls targets, including images, 3D models, and something referred to as VuMarks, which can be understood as colorful two-dimensional barcodes. For UWP apps running on a Surface, Vuforia can also be used to detect ground planes.

When Vuforia recognizes a target, it can automatically attach digital content that you specify to it, essentially augmenting it with virtually generated objects that move with it. Vuforia is great for developing mixed reality (MR) apps in which digital content should be connected with real objects— for example, to provide instructions or to associate a real object with a hologram. Unity version 2017.2 and beyond include Vuforia 7, so you can start using Vuforia capabilities in your HoloLens apps straight away.

> **Note** The Vuforia website features plenty of mobile apps. However, there are not so many examples of HoloLens apps. This leaves you plenty of room to let your imagination run wild!

This chapter shows you how to use Vuforia to attach digital content to a target. When you complete this chapter, you will end up with an app that recognizes a specific image and displays the Ethan character on top of it. The Ethan character will also walk between the two opposite vertices of the recognized image to produce the illusion that the digitally created character is walking on the real surface. (See Figure 14-1.) To create this app, I displayed the X sign on my smartphone. Apart from relatively low image quality, Vuforia correctly recognized the object and attached the Ethan hologram to it. Ethan's position changes when I move my smartphone due to robust tracking provided by Vuforia.

FIGURE 14-1 Ethan is walking on the X recognized by Vuforia.

Creating the Project and Adding the AR Camera Prefab

Your first step is to create the Unity project for the app. Follow these instructions:

1. Create a new 3D Unity project and name it **HoloAugmentedExperience**.

2. Import the Mixed Reality Toolkit for Unity.

3. Apply the default Mixed Reality project and scene settings. (Refer to Chapters 12 and 13 for guidance.)

4. Open the **Mixed Reality Toolkit** menu, choose **Configure**, and select **Apply UWP Capability Settings** to open the Apply UWP Capability Settings window.

5. Select the **Webcam**, **Spatial Perception**, and **Internet Client** checkboxes in the Apply UWP Capability Settings window. Then click the **Apply** button.

The HoloLens project is configured with default MR settings. Your next step is to extend it to support Vuforia capabilities. To that end, you need to add at least two Vuforia prefabs:

- **AR Camera**   Vuforia uses this prefab to recognize and track targets.

- **Image**   This is the image target—a flat two-dimensional object that Vuforia will look for in the real environment.

To add the AR Camera prefab, follow these steps:

1. In the Hierarchy, click **Create**, choose **Vuforia**, and select **AR Camera**. (See Figure 14-2.)

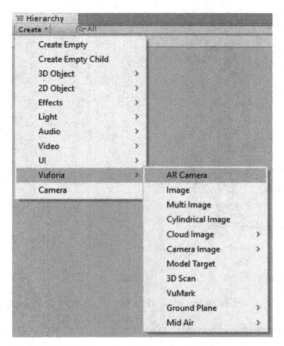

FIGURE 14-2 Adding the AR Camera Vuforia prefab.

2. The Import Vuforia Assets window opens. (See Figure 14-3.) Click **Import** to import the prefab. The import operation may take a short while. When it's finished, you'll see a new object in the Hierarchy: ARCamera.

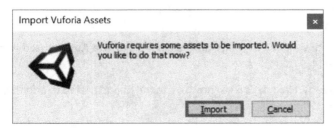

FIGURE 14-3 Importing Vuforia Assets

Click the ARCamera object in the Hierarchy to investigate its properties in the relevant Inspector. As shown in Figure 14-4, the ARCamera prefab has the familiar Transform, Camera, and Audio Listener components. For now, deselect the Audio Listener checkbox. This is to avoid conflicts with the listener from the MixedRealityCamera object. If you have both listeners enabled, Unity will display the following error in the console:

> "There are 2 audio listeners in the scene. Please ensure there is always exactly one audio listener in the scene."

FIGURE 14-4 The AR Camera Inspector.

Notice that ARCamera has two scripts attached:

- **Vuforia Behaviour**   This script implements the base class for all objects delivered by Vuforia.

- **Default Initialization Error Handler**   This script implements a default logic for handling Vuforia initialization errors.

As shown in Figure 14-4, properties of Vuforia behavior are inactive. This is because Vuforia is currently disabled. To enable Vuforia, you must configure PlayerSettings. Follow these steps:

1. Open the **File** menu and choose **Build Settings** or press **Ctrl+Shift+B** to open the Build Settings window.

2. Click **Player Settings**.

3. In the Inspector, scroll down to XR Settings, and select the **Vuforia Augmented Reality** checkbox. (See Figure 14-5.)

The AR Camera prefab is ready. Next, let's learn how to use the Image prefab to add the image target.

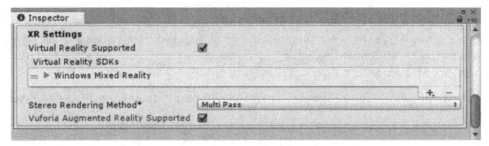

FIGURE 14-5 Enabling Vuforia using Player Settings.

 Note Because you used Mixed Reality Toolkit for Unity to configure the project, the platform is already set to UWP. Similarly, the scripting backend is set to .NET.

Adding the Image Prefab for the Image Target

You add the Image prefab the same way you did the AR Camera prefab: In the Hierarchy, click **Create**, choose **Vuforia**, and select **Image**. (Refer Figure 14-2.) A new object appears in the Hierarchy: ImageTarget. Click this object to investigate its properties using the Inspector. (See Figure 14-6.) For now, leave all options at their default values. By default, image target is a picture of an astronaut.

FIGURE 14-6 The ImageTarget Inspector.

Adding a Hologram to the Target

The Vuforia engine will try to recognize and track the image target you just created. You can go even further and display a hologram whenever the target is recognized. In this section, you will attach the Ethan character to the astronaut image. Follow these steps:

1. In the Unity Editor, open the **Assets** menu, choose **Import Package**, and select **Characters**.

2. The Import Unity Package window appears. Select **All**. Then click **Import**.

3. In the Project window, type **Ethan t:Model** in the search box.

4. Drag the **Ethan** model onto the **ImageTarget** object in the Hierarchy. The Ethan model will become a child of the ImageTarget object.

5. Click Ethan in the Hierarchy. Then, in the **Transform** group of the Ethan Inspector, configure the **X**, **Y**, and **Z Position** settings to **0.0**, **0.1**, and **−0.3**, respectively.

6. Set the **X**, **Y**, and **Z Rotation** settings to **−90**, **0**, and **180**, respectively.

7. Set the **X**, **Y**, and **Z Scale** settings to **0.5**, **0.5**, and **0.5**, respectively. Your scene should look as shown in Figure 14-7.

FIGURE 14-7 The Ethan model lying on top of the astronaut image target.

Testing the App

To test the app, you need some way to place the image target in the real world. There are a couple of ways to do this:

- **Create a printout of the image** Vuforia provides printable versions of its default image targets, including the astronaut image we're using here. You can print out this image and hold it up in front of your web camera. The image is available here: Assets\Editor\Vuforia\ForPrint\ ImageTargets.

- **Display the image on your smartphone** Vuforia provides textures, which are stored as JPEG files, for each image target. You can import the texture for the astronaut image target to your smartphone and then hold the smartphone in front of your web camera. The texture is available here: Assets\Editor\Vuforia\ImageTargetTextures\VuforiaMars_Images.

Once you have the image target ready, follow these steps:

1. Click the **Play** button to enable the editor Play mode. Unity will run the app in the Mixed Reality simulator and in the Game view. (I used the Game view.)

2. Hold up the image (either the printout or your smartphone) in front of the camera. Vuforia will recognize the target and display the Ethan character on top of it. (See Figure 14-8.)

FIGURE 14-8 Attaching a hologram to the image target.

3. Move the image around in front of the webcam. The Ethan character follows the target as long as the target can be seen by the camera. Notice that Vuforia recognizes and tracks the image target even if you rotate the image or move it closer or further away.

Adding a Text Description

In practical applications, you will most likely supplement the real object with digital content that provides textual instructions or some description of the detected object. To add text, you can use the 3DTextPrefab from the MRTKu package. Let's see how this works:

1. In the Project window, type **3DTextPrefab** in the search box.

2. Drag the **3DTextPrefab** entry in the search results below the **ImageTarget** object.

3. Open the 3DTextPrefab Inspector and type **Description** in the **Name** field to rename it.

4. In the **Transform** group of the Inspector, configure the **X**, **Y**, and **Z Position** settings to **0.5**, **0**, and **0**, respectively.

5. Set the **X**, **Y**, and **Z Rotation** settings to **90**, **0**, and **0**, respectively.

6. In the **Text Mesh** group, change the Text setting to **Target Detected**, the Font Size setting to **90**, and the Color to **Red**.

7. Run the app and hold the image target in front of the webcam. Text that reads "Target detected" will appear when the app recognizes the image target.

Implementing Extended Tracking

Vuforia automatically displays the selected hologram when the target is recognized. However, the digital content disappears when the image target moves out of the camera field of vision (FOV). Such behavior is not desirable when you want to display larger holograms. You don't want the hologram to disappear as the user gazes around the scene. Instead, you would like to let the user see the whole hologram. This is where extended tracking comes in. With extended tracking, Vuforia extrapolates the target position based on its past trajectory as shown here: http://bit.ly/extended_tracking.

The best way to visualize this effect is to use an example. Follow these steps:

1. Open the Ethan Inspector and, in the **Transform** group, change the **X**, **Y**, and **Z Scale** settings to **2**.

2. Open the ImageTarget Inspector, expand the **Advanced** option in the **Image Target Behaviour** group (refer to Figure 14-6), and select the **Extended Tracking** checkbox to enable this feature.

3. Click **Play** button in Unity Editor.

4. Hold the image target in the camera's FOV. The Ethan hologram should be displayed over the image target.

5. Move the image target out of the camera's FOV. Although the image target is no longer visible, Vuforia uses extended tracking to determine Ethan's location.

Implementing Augmented Navigation

This section shows you how to extend the HoloAugmentedExperience app so that Ethan will walk on the target recognized by Vuforia. (See Figure 14-9.) In Chapter 11, you learned how to implement natural character movement using a navigation mesh. Here, you will use the EthanAnimatorController you developed in that chapter to configure Ethan to switch between idle and walking states.

FIGURE 14-9 Ethan is walking on the recognized image target.

Using the DefaultTrackableEventHandler Script

In the app, Ethan will walk on the target whenever the target it is actively tracked. To achieve this, you need to know when Vuforia recognizes the target. You can obtain this information from the DefaultTrackableEventHandler script. This script is automatically attached to every image target, which you can quickly verify in the ImageTarget Inspector.

As shown in Listing 14-1, the DefaultTrackableEventHandler class, like any other C# script, derives from the UnityEngine.MonoBehaviour class. The script implements the Vuforia. ITrackableEventHandler interface, which declares the OnTrackableStateChanged method. This method is invoked when the tracking state changes. The object being tracked (here, the image target) is represented by an instance of the Vuforia.ImageTargetBehaviour class. This class derives from Vuforia.DataSetTrackableBehaviour and then from Vuforia.TrackableBehaviour. DefaultTrackableEventHandler stores a reference to the image target in an mTrackableBehaviour field of type TrackableBehaviour. An instance of this type is achieved using the GetComponent generic method. (See the Start method in Listing 14-1.) After that, the current instance of DefaultTrackableEventHandler is registered as a handler that tracks state changes of the image target. (See the last statement of the Start method in Listing 14-1.) In practice, this means that whenever the tracking state changes, OnTrackableStateChanged will be invoked.

LISTING 14-1 Default definition of DefaultTrackableEventHandler

```
public class DefaultTrackableEventHandler : MonoBehaviour, ITrackableEventHandler
{
    protected TrackableBehaviour mTrackableBehaviour;

    protected virtual void Start()
    {
        mTrackableBehaviour = GetComponent<TrackableBehaviour>();
        if (mTrackableBehaviour)
            mTrackableBehaviour.RegisterTrackableEventHandler(this);
    }

    // Definition of the OnTrackableStateChanged

    // Definitions of the OnTrackingFound and OnTrackingLost methods
}
```

Listing 14-2 shows the default definition of the OnTrackableStateChanged method.

LISTING 14-2 Handling tracking state changes

```
public void OnTrackableStateChanged(
    TrackableBehaviour.Status previousStatus,
    TrackableBehaviour.Status newStatus)
{
    if (newStatus == TrackableBehaviour.Status.DETECTED ||
        newStatus == TrackableBehaviour.Status.TRACKED ||
        newStatus == TrackableBehaviour.Status.EXTENDED_TRACKED)
    {
        Debug.Log("Trackable " + mTrackableBehaviour.TrackableName + " found");
        OnTrackingFound();
    }
    else if (previousStatus == TrackableBehaviour.Status.TRACKED &&
            newStatus == TrackableBehaviour.Status.NOT_FOUND)
    {
        Debug.Log("Trackable " + mTrackableBehaviour.TrackableName + " lost");
        OnTrackingLost();
    }
    else
    {
        OnTrackingLost();
    }
}
```

As shown in Listing 14-2, this method supports two arguments, `previousStatus` and `newStatus`. Both arguments are of type `Vuforia.TrackableBehaviour.Status`, which is an enumeration that defines the following values:

- **NOT_FOUND**   This indicates that the target has not been found.

- **UNKNOWN**   This specifies that the tracking state is unknown.

- **UNDEFINED**   This indicates that the tracking state is undefined.

- **DETECTED**   This informs you that the target has been detected.

- **TRACKED**   This indicates that the target is being tracked.

- **EXTENDED_TRACKED**   This specifies that the target is under an extended tracking.

- **DEGRADED**   This indicates that the tracking quality has degraded.

The `OnTrackableStateChanged` method uses an `if` clause to check whether `newStatus` equals DETECTED, TRACKED, or EXTENDED_TRACKED. If so, the method executes two statements. The first statement uses the `Debug.Log` method to display a string in the console with information about the detected target. (It uses the `TrackableName` property of the `TrackableBehaviour` class instance to obtain the name of the target.) The second statement invokes the `OnTrackingFound` method (discussed later). If `newStatus` does not equal DETECTED, TRACKED, or EXTENDED_TRACKED, the `OnTrackableStateChanged` method uses another `if` clause to determine whether the `previousStatus` was TRACKED and the `newStatus` is NOT_FOUND. When this condition is `true`, the `OnTrackableStateChanged` method outputs a debug string that indicates which target tracking has been lost. Again, the target's name is obtained from the `TrackableName` property. If none of the aforementioned conditions is `true`, the `OnTrackingLost` method will be called. (See the statement under the `else` clause in Listing 14-2.)

Listing 14-3 presents definitions of the `OnTrackingFound` and `OnTrackingLost` methods. These methods work in a similar manner. First, they obtain lists of child renderers, colliders, and canvases with respect to the target. Then, the `OnTrackingFound` method sets the `enabled` property of each element to `true`, while the `OnTrackingLost` method sets the `enabled` property to `false`. As a result, `OnTrackingFound` will show all child holograms of the target, while `OnTrackingLost` will hide them. Vuforia is no longer able to track the target.

LISTING 14-3 Showing and hiding holograms when the tracking state changes

```
protected virtual void OnTrackingFound()
{
    var rendererComponents = GetComponentsInChildren<Renderer>(true);
    var colliderComponents = GetComponentsInChildren<Collider>(true);
    var canvasComponents = GetComponentsInChildren<Canvas>(true);

    foreach (var component in rendererComponents)
        component.enabled = true;
```

```
        foreach (var component in colliderComponents)
            component.enabled = true;

        foreach (var component in canvasComponents)
            component.enabled = true;
    }

    protected virtual void OnTrackingLost()
    {
        var rendererComponents = GetComponentsInChildren<Renderer>(true);
        var colliderComponents = GetComponentsInChildren<Collider>(true);
        var canvasComponents = GetComponentsInChildren<Canvas>(true);

        foreach (var component in rendererComponents)
            component.enabled = false;

        foreach (var component in colliderComponents)
            component.enabled = false;

        foreach (var component in canvasComponents)
            component.enabled = false;
    }
```

These definitions are the defaults. You can freely adjust them to your needs. Later in this chapter you will use `OnTrackingFound` and `OnTrackingLost` to invoke statements that will send a message to another script that will make Ethan walk. Before doing that, however, let's prepare the scene.

Preparing the Scene

To prepare the scene, start by modifying Ethan's properties. Follow these steps:

1. In the Ethan Inspector, in the **Transform** group, change the **X**, **Y**, and **Z Position** settings to **0**.

2. Change the **X**, **Y**, and **Z Rotation** settings to **0**.

3. Change the **X**, **Y**, and **Z Scale** settings to **0.2**, **0.2**, and **0.2**, respectively.

4. In the Project window, create a new folder called **Animations** inside the **Assets** folder.

5. Right-click the **Animations** folder and choose **Import New Asset** from the menu that appears.

6. In the Import New Asset window, import the **EthanAnimatorController.controller** file you created in Chapter 11. (You can find this file with the companion code in the following folder: Chapter_11\AnimatedHumanoid\Assets\Animations.)

7. Drag the **EthanAnimatorController** object that appears in the Hierarchy onto the **Ethan** model in the scene.

8. In the Ethan Inspector, click **Add Component**, choose **Navigation**, and select **Nav Mesh Agent**.

9. In the Project window, create a new folder called **Scripts** in the **Assets** folder.

10. Right-click the **Scripts** folder, choose **Create**, and select **C# Script**. Name the new script **Patrolling**.

11. Drag the **Patrolling** script onto the **Ethan** model in the scene.

Now that you've configured Ethan, you're ready to create two new objects: the plane used to define the navigation mesh and an empty object with a LineRenderer component. The LineRenderer component will draw a line connecting Ethan's current position with the position he is moving toward.

To create the navigation mesh, proceed as follows:

1. In the Hierarchy, right-click the **ImageTarget** object, choose **3D Object**, and select **Plane** to add a Plane object to the scene.

2. In the Plane Inspector, change the name of the Plane object to **ReferencePlane**.

3. Open the **Window** menu and choose **Navigation** to open the Navigation window.

4. Select the **ReferencePlane** object in the Hierarchy. Then, in the Navigation window, click the **Object** tab.

5. Select the **Navigation Static** checkbox in the Object tab.

6. Open the **Navigation Area** drop-down list and choose **Walkable**.

7. Click the **Bake** tab in the Navigation window. Then click the **Bake** button to construct the navigation mesh. (This could take a moment.)

> **Tip** If you do not see the navigation mesh, enlarge the ReferencePlane object—for example, change the **X** and **Z Scale** settings in the **Transform** group in the ReferencePlane Inspector to **10**. Then re-bake the navigation mesh.

8. In the ReferencePlane Inspector, change the **X**, **Y**, and **Z Scale** settings in the **Transform** group to **0.055**, **1**, and **0.1**, respectively.

The walkable area is already defined. However, there is no need to render this plane when the target is displayed. The plane is used only to define the walkable area, and to easily find points that will be used to set destinations for patrolling. To easily hide the ReferencePlane object, you can use the transparent_background material from the MRTKu. Follow these steps:

9. In the Project window, type **transparent t:Material** in the search box.

10. Drag the **transparent_background.mat** entry in the search results onto the **ReferencePlane** object in the scene.

11. In the ReferencePlane Inspector, in the **transparent_background** group, open the **Cull Mode** drop-down list and choose **Front**. (See Figure 14-10.) The ReferencePlane will now be enabled when the image target is recognized but will remain invisible.

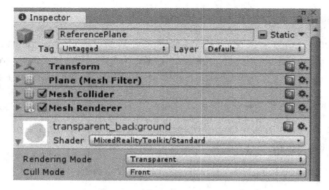

FIGURE 14-10 Configuring the transparent background shader.

Next, you will create the object that will indicate the path Ethan will follow when walking, which I will call the TargetIndicator. You will design this object using an empty GameObject object with a LineRenderer component. This component draws a straight line between two or more points. To create the TargetIndicator, follow these steps:

1. In the Hierarchy, right-click the **ImageTarget** object and choose **Create Empty**.

2. Name the new object **TargetIndicator**.

3. Open the Inspector for the TargetIndicator object.

4. Click the **Add Component** button and choose **LineRenderer** to add a LineRenderer component.

5. Expand the **Position** settings in the **LineRenderer** group in the Inspector.

6. Type **2** in the **Size** box; type **0** in the **Element 0 X**, **Y**, and **Z** boxes; and type **0** in the **Element 1 X**, **Y**, and **Z** boxes.

7. Select the **Use World Space** checkbox and type **0.001** in the **Width** box. (See Figure 14-11.)

FIGURE 14-11 Configuring the LineRenderer component.

Now you need to set the color used by the LineRenderer component by creating a material. Follow these steps:

1. In the Project window, create a new folder named **Materials** in the **Assets** folder.

2. Right-click the **Materials** folder, choose **Create**, and select **Material**.

3. Click the material and, in the Inspector, change its name to **TargetIndicatorMaterial**.

4. Click the **Emissive Color** box. (See Figure 14-12.)

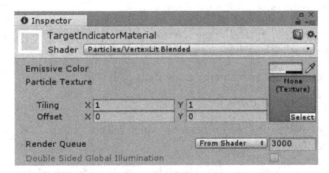

FIGURE 14-12 Configuring the TargetIndicatorMaterial.

5. In the color window that opens, set the **R**, **G**, **B**, **A** properties to **0**, **255**, **0**, and **127**, respectively. Then close the color window.

6. Drag the **TargetIndicatorMaterial** object from the Project window onto the **TargetIndicator** object in the Hierarchy.

Implementing the Patrolling Script

You are now ready to implement the logic that will cause the Ethan model to continuously walk between two edges of the ReferencePlane object. (Vuforia will automatically position this plane.) This type of continuous movement between given positions is called patrolling. Basically, whenever the tracking state of the image target changes, either the OnTrackingFound or OnTrackingLost method of the DefaultTrackableEventHandler script will send a message to the Patrolling script, which will be responsible for controlling Ethan's state.

To implement this logic, follow these steps:

1. In the Project window, right-click the **Scripts** folder, choose **Create**, and select **New C# Script**. Name the new script **Patrolling**.

2. Drag the **Patrolling** script from the Project window onto the **Ethan** object in the scene.

3. Double-click the **Patrolling** script in the Project window to open it in Visual Studio.

4. Replace the default using statements in the header of the Patrolling.cs file with the following two statements:

```
using UnityEngine;
using UnityEngine.AI;
```

5. Extend the class declaration with two instances of the UnityEngine. RequireComponentAttribute:

```
[RequireComponent(typeof(NavMeshAgent))]
[RequireComponent(typeof(Animator))]
```

These attributes will ensure that the NavMeshAgent and Animator components will always be available for your script. If you do not add these components through the Editor, Unity will automatically add them to the object using the script.

6. In the Patrolling class, implement the helper method from Listing 14-4. This method obtains references to all components that will be used later, including the following:

    - **NavMeshAgent**   This will be used to set the character's path.

    - **Animator**   This will be used to animate the character.

    - **MeshRenderer**   This renders the reference plane, which will be used to determine the points between which Ethan will walk.

    - **LineRenderer**   This is a reference to the line renderer, which indicates where Ethan is going.

    LISTING 14-4 Obtaining references to required components

```
private NavMeshAgent navMeshAgent;
private Animator animator;
```

```
private MeshRenderer referencePlaneRenderer;
private LineRenderer targetIndicator;

private void ObtainReferencesToRequiredComponents()
{
    navMeshAgent = GetComponent<NavMeshAgent>();
    animator = GetComponent<Animator>();

    referencePlaneRenderer = GameObject.
        Find("ReferencePlane").GetComponent<MeshRenderer>();
    targetIndicator = GameObject.
        Find("TargetIndicator").GetComponent<LineRenderer>();
}
```

7. Implement the ConfigureAgent helper method. (See Listing 14-5.) This method sets public properties of the NavMeshAgent instance to configure Ethan's linear and angular speeds, stopping distance, and braking mode. (The braking mode is set to false, so the Ethan model will not slow down as it approaches its destination.)

LISTING 14-5 Configuring the agent's properties

```
private void ConfigureAgent()
{
    navMeshAgent.speed = 0.05f;
    navMeshAgent.angularSpeed = 300.0f;
    navMeshAgent.stoppingDistance = 0.01f;
    navMeshAgent.autoBraking = false;
}
```

8. Use the preceding helper methods to implement the Start method of the Patrolling script. (See Listing 14-6.)

LISTING 14-6 Initializing the Patrolling script

```
private void Start()
{
    ObtainReferencesToRequiredComponents();

    ConfigureAgent();
}
```

9. Implement the UpdatePatrollingStatus method. (See Listing 14-7.) This method handles messages sent from DefaultTrackableEventHandler. UpdatePatrollingStatus accepts one Boolean argument: isPatrolling. The value of this argument indicates whether or not Ethan should walk. Therefore, UpdatePatrollingStatus uses the input argument to set the local member isPatrolling, update the IsWalking animation parameter (refer to Chapter 11), and configure Ethan's target position using another method, UdpateAgentDestination. Additionally, UpdatePatrollingStatus sets the isStopped property of the NavMeshAgent instance to !isPatrolling. This ensures that Ethan will not be moved by Unity's navigation engine when the image target is not recognized.

LISTING 14-7 Updating the patrolling status

```
private bool isPatrolling;

private void UpdatePatrollingStatus(bool isPatrolling)
{
    this.isPatrolling = isPatrolling;

    animator.SetBool("IsWalking", isPatrolling);

    navMeshAgent.isStopped = !isPatrolling;

    UpdateAgentDestination();
}
```

As shown in Listing 14-7, the UpdateAgentDestination method uses the bounds property of the MeshRenderer associated with the ReferencePlane object. This property is represented as an instance of the UnityEngine.Bounds struct and represents the bounding box of the plane. This property has min and max properties. They are both of type Vector3 and represent minimum and maximum points of the box plane. Practically, these points are calculated as follows, where *center* denotes the middle point of the bounding box:

$$min = center - \frac{perimeter}{2}, max = center + \frac{perimeter}{2}$$

10. The min and max points are used to initialize a two-dimensional array of name destinations. This collection stores objects of type Vector3. They define the locations between which Ethan will walk. To determine which of those points should be set as the next Ethan destination, implement a private currentDestinationIndex member, which stores an array index. As shown in Listing 14-8, the value of currentDestinationIndex is incremented right after setting the new destination. However, the array index cannot be larger than the length of the array. Accordingly, an incremented value is then divided by the array length and the currentDestinationIndex is set to the remainder of that division (modulo operator).

LISTING 14-8 Updating the agent destination

```
private int currentDestinationIndex = 0;

private void UpdateAgentDestination()
{
    if (referencePlaneRenderer != null)
    {
        var destinations = new Vector3[]
        {
            referencePlaneRenderer.bounds.min,
            referencePlaneRenderer.bounds.max
        };

        navMeshAgent.destination = destinations[currentDestinationIndex];

        currentDestinationIndex = (currentDestinationIndex + 1) % destinations.Length;
    }
}
```

11. Implement the `IndicateDestination` helper method from Listing 14-9. This method dynamically sets the `positions` property of the `LineRenderer` component to draw the line (refer to Figure 14-11). One end of this line is set to Ethan's current position, while the other is set to Ethan's destination. So, `IndicateDestination` dynamically shows Ethan's current path.

LISTING 14-9 Indicating the destination position

```
private void IndicateDestination()
{
    if (targetIndicator != null)
    {
        targetIndicator.SetPositions(new Vector3[]
        {
            navMeshAgent.transform.position,
            navMeshAgent.destination
        });
    }
}
```

12. Use the helpers to implement the `Update` method of the `Patrolling` script as shown in Listing 14-10. This implementation checks whether the `isPatrolling` member is `true` (see the first `if` clause). If so, the second `if` clause is used to determine whether the agent's path is not currently being calculated (see the `pathPending` property) and whether the remaining distance is not smaller or equal to the agent's stopping distance. If these logical conditions evaluate to `true`, the agent's destination is modified using the `UpdateAgentDestination` method. (Refer to Listing 14-9.) Whenever the agent is patrolling the image target area, the `IndicatePosition` method is invoked to update the `LineRenderer` to reflect the agent's path.

LISTING 14-10 Ethan's destination is updated at every frame, provided the `isPatrolling` member is `true`

```
private void Update()
{
    if (isPatrolling)
    {
        if (!navMeshAgent.pathPending
            && navMeshAgent.remainingDistance <= navMeshAgent.stoppingDistance)
        {
            UpdateAgentDestination();
        }

        IndicateDestination();
    }
}
```

13. Extend the `OnTrackingFound` and `OnTrackingLost` methods of `DefaultTrackableEventHandler` as shown in Listing 14-11. When tracking is found or lost, this broadcasts the `UpdatePatrollingStatus` message to all child components (including Ethan). A Boolean parameter supplements the message to indicate whether Ethan should walk (`true` in the `OnTrackingFound` method) or not walk (`false` in the `OnTrackingLost` method).

LISTING 14-11 Broadcasting a message to the child components

```
protected virtual void OnTrackingFound()
{
    var rendererComponents = GetComponentsInChildren<Renderer>(true);
    var colliderComponents = GetComponentsInChildren<Collider>(true);
    var canvasComponents = GetComponentsInChildren<Canvas>(true);

    // Enable rendering:
    foreach (var component in rendererComponents)
        component.enabled = true;

    // Enable colliders:
    foreach (var component in colliderComponents)
        component.enabled = true;

    // Enable canvas':
    foreach (var component in canvasComponents)
        component.enabled = true;

    BroadcastMessage("UpdatePatrollingStatus", true);
}

protected virtual void OnTrackingLost()
{
    var rendererComponents = GetComponentsInChildren<Renderer>(true);
    var colliderComponents = GetComponentsInChildren<Collider>(true);
    var canvasComponents = GetComponentsInChildren<Canvas>(true);

    // Disable rendering:
    foreach (var component in rendererComponents)
        component.enabled = false;

    // Disable colliders:
    foreach (var component in colliderComponents)
        component.enabled = false;

    // Disable canvas':
    foreach (var component in canvasComponents)
        component.enabled = false;

    BroadcastMessage("UpdatePatrollingStatus", false);
}
```

Testing the App

Let's test the app to see how it works so far. Follow these steps:

1. Click **Play** to start the Editor play mode.

2. Place the image target in the camera's FOV. As shown in Figure 14-13, both Ethan and the target indicator are properly displayed, and Ethan is walking. However, there is an extra gray plane below them, which blocks the image target.

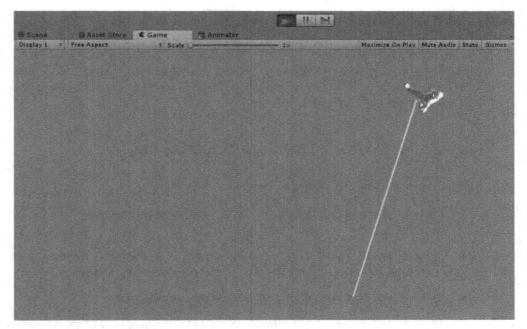

FIGURE 14-13 Unwanted boundary rendering.

The gray plane is a product of the MixedRealityCameraParent object, which has a Boundary child object. The Boundary object renders the floor and boundaries of the headset's user. Specifically, the ReferencePlane is interpreted as the floor, so the Boundary object renders a gray plane.

3. To disable this unwanted effect, expand the **MixedRealityCameraParent** object in the Hierarchy and click the **Boundary** object.

4. In the Boundary Inspector, deselect the **Render Floor** checkbox. (See Figure 14-14.)

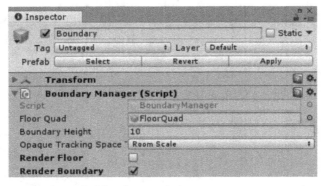

FIGURE 14-14 Disabling floor rendering.

5. Click **Play** to restart the Editor play mode. You should finally see the result shown in Figure 14-9.

Adding a Custom Image Database

You just learned how to use Vuforia to detect one of its own built-in image targets. For practical applications, however, you will likely want the app to recognize custom images rather than one of Vuforia's predefined ones. To achieve this, you will need to create a custom image database. To find out how, read on.

Obtaining a Vuforia Developer License Key

Before you can create a custom image database, you must register as a Vuforia developer and obtain a Development License Key. Follow these steps:

1. Enter the requested information on the following page to register as a Vuforia developer: http://bit.ly/Vuforia_registration.

2. Once registered, log in to the Vuforia Development Portal (https://developer.vuforia.com/), accept the license terms, click **Develop**, and choose **License Manager**.

3. In the License Manager, click the **Get Development Key** button.

4. In the Add a Free Development License Key page (see Figure 14-15), type the name of the app in the **App Name** box (in this case, **HoloAugmentedExperience**), select the checkbox at the bottom of the page to agree to the terms and conditions, and click **Confirm**. A hyperlink for your new app will appear in the License Manager.

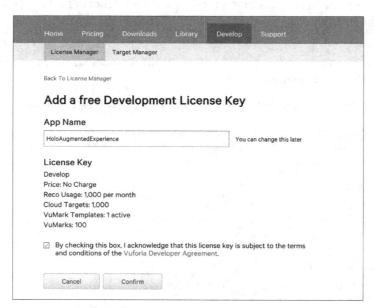

FIGURE 14-15 Obtaining a Vuforia Development License Key.

5. Click the hyperlink to obtain your Development License Key.

6. Copy the Development License Key to the clipboard.

7. In the Unity Editor Hierarchy, click the **ARCamera** object.

8. In the ARCamera Inspector, scroll down to the **Vuforia Behaviour (Script)** group, and click the **Open VuforiaConfiguration** button.

9. A VuforiaConfiguration group appears in the Inspector. Paste the Development License Key into the **App License Key** box. (See Figure 14-16.)

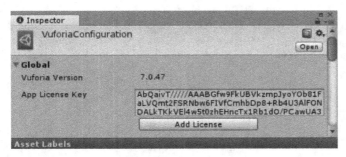

FIGURE 14-16 Configuring the Vuforia Development License Key.

Creating a Database

To create your custom image database, follow these steps:

1. In the Vuforia Developer Portal, click **Develop**, and then click **Target Manager**. (See Figure 14-17.)

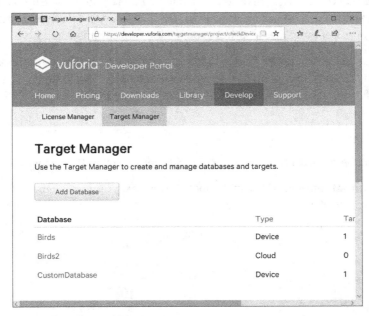

FIGURE 14-17 Target Manager.

2. Click the **Add Database** button. A Create Database dialog box opens. (See Figure 14-18.)

3. Type **CustomDatabase** in the name box, select the **Device** option button under **Type**, and click the **Create** button. Vuforia creates a new database, which is displayed as a hyperlink in the Target Manager.

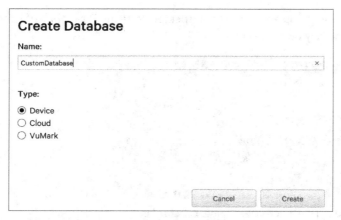

FIGURE 14-18 Creating a device-based database.

Notice in the Create Database dialog box that you can create three types of databases:

- **Device**   Device-based databases are added to your app and used locally. They are recommended for AR apps that need to recognize fewer than 1,000 targets.

- **Cloud**   Cloud-based databases are hosted within the Vuforia cloud. They're used for apps that must recognize large numbers of targets—even more than 1 million. However, if you use this approach, the app user must have a network connection to access the database.

- **VuMark**   These are databases for storing VuMarks. Each VuMark is represented as an SVG file. VuMarks let you design custom targets that represent a company logo or some other custom symbol. For a full description of VuMarks, see http://bit.ly/VuMarks.

Adding a Target

Initially, the custom database will contain no targets. To add a target, follow these steps:

1. Click the **CustomDatabase** hyperlink in the Target Manager. A CustomDatabase window opens. (See Figure 14-19.)

FIGURE 14-19 The CustomDatabase window.

2. Click the **Add Target** button.

An Add Target dialog box opens, which enables you to upload an image target. (See Figure 14-20.) You can choose between four types:

- **Single Image**   Choose this to select an image file as the image target.

- **Cuboid**   Choose this to select a cuboid as the image target. You can specify the cuboid's width, height, and length.

- **Cylinder**   Choose this to select a cylinder as the image target. You can specify the cylinder's height as well as the diameter of its base and top.

- **3D Object**   Choose this to use Vuforia Object Scanner data. (Available for Android only.)

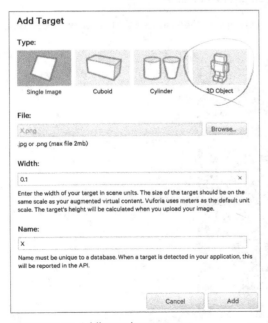

FIGURE 14-20 Adding an image target.

3. Click the **Single Image** option under **Type**.

4. Click the **Browse** button and locate and select the image file you want to use. (For this example, I selected a simple 380 x 500-pixel bitmap of a black X on a white background.)

5. In the **Width** box, type a value to specify the width of the image target. Vuforia will use this value to calculate the image target's height automatically; Unity Editor will apply these dimensions to scale the target. (I entered **0.1** to produce an image target roughly as wide as the astronaut used earlier.)

6. Type a name for the image target in the **Name** box to identify it in the database. (I named my image target **X**.)

7. Click the **Add** button to upload the image to the database.

Downloading the Database and Importing It into Unity

Your next step is to download the database containing the image target and import it into Unity. Follow these steps:

1. Click the **Download Database** button on the Target Manager page. (Refer to Figure 14-19.)

2. In the window that appears, select **Unity Editor** as the database format. Then click the **Download** button. The database is saved as a custom Unity package.

3. In Unity **Editor**, open the **Assets** menu, choose **Import Package**, and select **Custom Package**.

4. Locate and select the database you just downloaded.

5. The Import Unity Package dialog box opens. (See Figure 14-21.) Ensure that all objects are selected, and click **Import**.

FIGURE 14-21 Importing a custom database.

Selecting the Custom Image Target

Now that you've imported the database, you can select the custom image target for use in your app. Follow these steps:

1. Select the **ImageTarget** object in the Hierarchy.

2. In the ImageTarget Inspector, in the **Image Target Behaviour (Script)** group, open the **Database** drop-down list and choose **CustomDatabase**.

3. The Image Target drop-down list is updated to contain any image targets within the selected database. In this case, the database contains only one image target: X. (See Figure 14-22.) Select **X** from the **Image Target** drop-down list. The X image will replace the astronaut image in the Scene view.

FIGURE 14-22 Setting the image target to the custom image.

4. To ensure that the custom database is loaded and activated, open the ARCamera Inspector and, in the **Vuforia Behaviour (Script)** group, click the **Open VuforiaConfiguration** button.

5. Expand the **Databases** setting and select both the **Load CustomDatabase Data** checkbox and the **Activate** checkbox underneath it. (See Figure 14-23.)

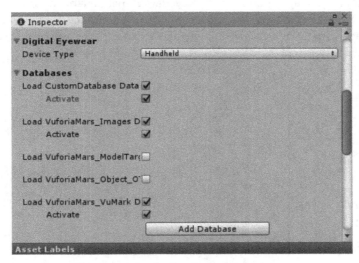

FIGURE 14-23 Loading and activating the target database.

6. To test the app, you need to print out the image or send it to your phone. Then, click the **Play** button to start Unity Editor Play mode and place the image target within the camera's FOV. You should see Ethan walking on this new image target.

 Tip If the size of the custom image target differs significantly from that of the astronaut image, you will need to adjust the scale of the ReferencePlane as well as the width of the LineRenderer accordingly.

Configuring for HoloLens

You've created a custom image target. Now all you need to do is enable the integration of Vuforia with HoloLens. Here's how:

1. Open the ARCamera Inspector and, in the **Vuforia Behaviour (Script)** group, click the **Open VuforiaConfiguration** button.

2. Expand the **Digital Eyewear** setting, open the **Device Type** drop-down list, and choose **Digital Eyewear**.

3. Open the **Device Config** drop-down list that appears and choose **HoloLens**.

4. Deploy the app to the HoloLens device and test it. (Note that you cannot test Vuforia in the HoloLens emulator.)

Summary

In this chapter you learned how to create augmented reality experiences with Vuforia. Specifically, you created an app that recognizes image targets and then overlays virtual content on top of them. In this example the virtual content was a character that moved intelligently between two corners of a bounding box around the image target. The presented content applies to HoloLens only because immersive headsets do not provide AR experiences.

CHAPTER 15

UrhoSharp

U rhoSharp is the cross-platform .NET binding to the C++ Urho3D game engine. It provides a power-ful 3D rendering engine that is useful for Mixed Reality development, including physics simula-tions, scene handling, navigation, networking, and more. Importantly, you can access all this directly through the C# code. Unlike with Unity, which you used in Chapters 9 through 14, you will now build your app directly from the code. This allows you to implement the whole scene and related logic in a separate .NET library, which you can later reuse on other projects. These projects can target not only the Windows Mixed Reality platform but also iOS, Android, and Mac.

You can add UrhoSharp to your project as a NuGet package. There is one main package, UrhoSharp, and a number of platform-specific extensions. In this chapter you will learn how to use the UrhoSharp. SharpReality extension, which targets HoloLens. After you set up a project and create a hologram, you'll explore several features of this package in this chapter, including physics simulations and spatial mapping. You'll also explore HoloLens-specific features (called SharpReality).

 Note Everything in this chapter will be built using Visual Studio 2017 without Unity.

Setting Up the Project

You can build your Mixed Reality app that uses UrhoSharp on top of the Universal Windows Platform Visual C# project. You have already used this kind of project template in this book. By default, the Blank App UWP project comes with elements that handle app activation (App.xaml) and implement the default view (MainPage.xaml). Additionally, when you build the app, the entry point (the static Main method of the Program class) is automatically generated. (You can check this by inspecting the App.g.i.cs file located in the Obj subfolder of the Output directory.) For MR applications, the UrhoSharp engine can run in its own view source, which does not require any of the default elements included in the Blank UWP project template (App.xaml and MainPage.xaml). Also, UrhoSharp should be instanti-ated within the entry point.

To create the UrhoSharp MR app, start by creating the UWP project template you used previously to create 2D apps. Proceed as follows:

1. In Visual Studio, open the **File** menu and choose **New Project** to open the Add New Project dialog box.

2. In the Add New Project dialog box, type **Blank App Visual C#** in the search box.

3. Select the **Blank App (Universal Windows) Visual C#** template in the search results.

4. Type **ExploringUrhoSharp** in the Name field and click **OK**. (See Figure 15-1.)

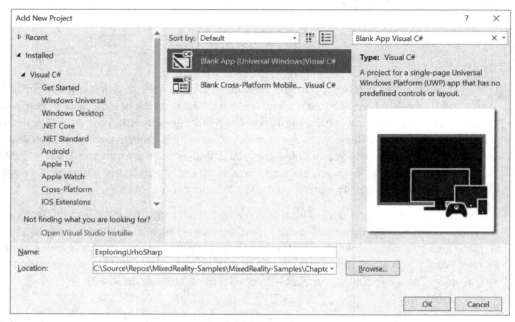

FIGURE 15-1 Creating the blank UWP app.

5. In the New Universal Windows Platform Project dialog box (see Figure 15-2), open the **Target Version** drop-down list and choose **Windows 10 Creators Update (10.0; Build 15063)**. Then open the **Minimum Version** drop-down list and choose **Windows 10 November Update (10.0; Build 10586)**, and click **OK**.

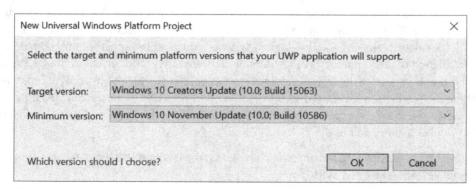

FIGURE 15-2 Configuring target and minimum versions.

6. In Solution Explorer, right-click **App.xaml** and choose **Delete** from the menu that appears. Then click **OK** in any dialog box that appears.

7. Repeat step 6 for **MainPage.xaml**.

8. To install and set up UrhoSharp, open the **Tools** menu, choose **NuGet Packet Manager**, and select **Package Manager Console** to open the NuGet Package Manager Console. Then type the following command:

```
Install-Package UrhoSharp.SharpReality -ProjectName ExploringUrhoSharp
```

The last argument of this command (ProjectName) is optional. It specifies the project in which UrhoSharp should be installed. This is especially useful when you install NuGet packages in solutions composed of many projects.

After the package is installed, the Package Manager Console should display the following confirmation:

```
Successfully installed 'UrhoSharp.SharpReality 1.8.93' to ExploringUrhoSharp
Executing nuget actions took 1.24 sec
Time Elapsed: 00:00:03.3766804
```

Subsequently, you can proceed to the actual implementation, which proceeds as follows:

9. In Solution Explorer, right-click the **ExploringUrhoSharp** project, select **Add**, and choose **Class**. The Add New Item – ExploringUrhoSharp dialog box opens.

10. Ensure the **Class Visual C#** item is selected. Then type **Program.cs** in the **Name** box and click **OK** to add the Program.cs file to the project.

11. Modify the contents of the Program.cs file as shown in Listing 15-1.

LISTING 15-1 A custom app entry point that launches the UrhoSharp view source

```csharp
using System;using Urho;
using Windows.ApplicationModel.Core;

namespace ExploringUrhoSharp
{
    public static class Program
    {
        [MTAThread]
        static void Main() => CoreApplication.Run(
        new UrhoAppViewSource<MixedRealityApplication>());
    }
}
```

12. Visual Studio displays a message indicating that it cannot resolve the MixedRealityApplication class. To create the class in a separate file, click the yellow light bulb icon next to the

message, select **Generate Type 'MixedRealityApplication'**, and choose **Generate Class 'MixedRealityApplication' in New File**. (See Figure 15-3.) The ExploringUrhoSharp project will now include a new MixedRealityApplication.cs file.

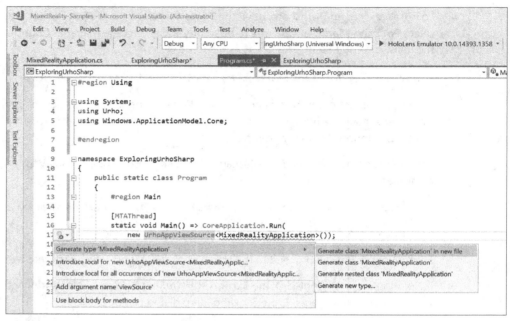

FIGURE 15-3 Creating a definition of the missing class.

Before we proceed, let's discuss the code from Listing 15-1. This code implements the app entry point—the static `Program.Main` method from which the app will start its execution. The `Main` method invokes a single statement, which runs the application. Thus, the `Main` method is defined using an expression body in which the method definition starts after the `=>` operator. As shown in Listing 15-1, to start the 3D engine from UrhoSharp you use the `Run` method of the `CoreApplication` class. This method, defined under the `Windows.ApplicationModel.Core` namespace, provides the basic functionality for each UWP app for handling state changes and managing windows. An instance of the `CoreApplication` class is created by the operating system when it runs the app. There is only one instance of `CoreApplication` per application. Moreover, the `CoreApplication` requires threads created from it to be decorated with the `MTAThread` attribute. Hence, the declaration of the `Main` method is supplemented by this attribute.

The Run method of the `CoreApplication` class accepts one argument, which implements the `IFrameworkViewSource` interface. This interface represents the provider for the app view. UrhoSharp implements this provider within the `UrhoAppViewSource` class. This is a generic class whose concrete type defines the entry point of the UrhoSharp application. For Windows Mixed Reality applications, the entry point should derive from `UrhoSharp.SharpReality.StereoApplication`. This base class initializes the underlying Urho3D engine, creates a basic scene, provides an interface to handle gesture and voice input, and provides access to speech-synthesis and spatial-mapping features.

Implementing the Entry Point

After you create and configure the project, it's time to implement the `MixedRealityApplication` class that will serve as the entry point for UrhoSharp. You will now implement `MixedRealityApplication` so that it derives from `StereoApplication`. To do so, open the MixedRealityApplication.cs file and modify its contents as shown in Listing 15-2.

LISTING 15-2 A minimum entry point for the UrhoSharp app

```
using Urho;
using Urho.Gui;
using Urho.SharpReality;

namespace ExploringUrhoSharp
{
    public class MixedRealityApplication : StereoApplication
    {
        public MixedRealityApplication(ApplicationOptions options) : base(options) { }
    }
}
```

The code from Listing 15-2 implements the minimal entry point for the UrhoSharp app. The class presented there derives from `StereoApplication` and implements an empty constructor. The constructor is the only required element to be implemented manually. The app, however, does not do anything. To rectify that, let's create the `Text` class in UrhoSharp to display static text that reads "Hello, UrhoSharp!" (See Figure 15-4.) To implement this functionality, add the field and method in Listing 15-3 to the `MixedRealityApplication` class.

Hello, UrhoSharp!

FIGURE 15-4 A simple Hello, World–like app created with UrhoSharp.

LISTING 15-3 Creating static text

```
private Text text;

private void CreateText(string caption, Color color, float fontSize = 48.0f)
{
    text = new Text()
    {
        Value = caption,
        HorizontalAlignment = HorizontalAlignment.Center,
        Position = new IntVector2(0, 50)
    };

    text.SetColor(color);
    text.SetFont(CoreAssets.Fonts.AnonymousPro, fontSize);

    UI.Root.AddChild(text);
}
```

The CreateText method from Listing 15-3 accepts two arguments:

- **caption**   This argument specifies the text to be displayed.

- **fontSize**   This argument specifies the font size. It is optional and has a default value of 48.

Given these arguments, CreateText proceeds as follows:

1. It instantiates the Urho.Gui.Text class and stores the resulting object in the private text field.

2. During initialization, the following public members of the Text object are configured:

    - **Value**   This indicates the text to be displayed. Here, this value is set according to the caption argument passed to the CreateText method.

    - **HorizontalAlignment**   This specifies the horizontal text alignment. Here, the text is centered.

    - **Position**   This allows you to indicate the absolute text position, represented as a two-dimensional vector of integers. These vectors are represented in UrhoSharp as instances of the Urho.IntVector2 struct. Here, this struct is used to add a vertical shift by 50 pixels with respect to the top edge of the view.

3. The SetColor instance method is used to change the foreground color of the text.

4. The font and font size are set for rendering using the SetFont method. This method has two versions. Both accept two arguments:

- **font** or **fontName** This specifies the font to be used. In the first case, the argument is an instance of the Urho.Gui.Font class, being an abstract representation of the font. In the second case, you need to provide the string representing the font.

- **fontSize** This indicates the font size.

   You can access all fonts available by default through the Fonts property of the Urho. CoreAssets static class. By default, there is only one font, AnonymousPro. This font is used in Listing 15-3.

5. The text is added to UI of the UrhoSharp application using the following statement:

```
UI.Root.AddChild(text);
```

Let's use the CreateText method. To do so, you override the Start method, as shown in Listing 15-4. You can now run the app in the HoloLens emulator to see results from Figure 15-4.

LISTING 15-4 Creating the text object

```
protected override void Start()
{
    base.Start();

    CreateText("Hello, UrhoSharp!", Color.Magenta);
}
```

To wrap up this section, let's discuss the Start method. This method is similar to the Unity script Start method. In UrhoSharp, the Start method is invoked to start the application. So, you typically use Start method to set up your scene. Hence, the CreateTest method is invoked there. As with Unity, the Start method is supplemented by the OnUpdate method, which is invoked whenever the application is updated during runtime, including scene rendering.

Let's implement the OnUpdate method in the ExploringUrhoSharp app, as shown in Listing 15-5. The app will now display the time elapsed since it was started instead of a static string. (See Figure 15-5.)

LISTING 15-5 Updating text

```
protected override void OnUpdate(float timeStep)
{
    base.OnUpdate(timeStep);

    // Update text
    text.Value = $"Elapsed time: {Time.ElapsedTime:F1} s";
}
```

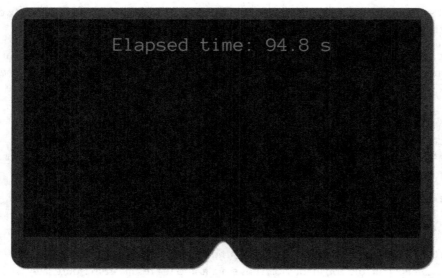

Elapsed time: 94.8 s

FIGURE 15-5 Displaying the elapsed time using the OnUpdate method.

The OnUpdate method takes one argument, timeStep. This is a floating number that represents the time since the last application update. In principle, this argument can be used to manually calculate the time since the app was started. However, this time is already determined by UrhoSharp, and as Listing 15-6 shows, can be obtained by reading the ElapsedTime property of the Urho. Application class.

Adding Primitive Components and Materials

Like Unity, the Urho3D engine arranges all scene objects into a hierarchy of nodes, with the scene node on top. These nodes are represented as instances of the Urho.Node class. As with Unity, you can create new nodes as descendants of the scene node. These descendants can become ascendants for other nodes. Multiple descendants can have the same parent. So, objects in the scene can be easily grouped to manipulate them quickly.

Nodes are like Unity's game objects. They have a specified scale, rotation, and position in the scene, but are not very useful until you supplement them with components. These components define a node's appearance and behavior. To define a node's appearance, you can use external models or start with primitive 3D components. In UrhoSharp, primitive 3D shapes are represented as classes, declared under the Urho. Shapes namespace:

- Box
- Cone

- Cylinder
- Plane
- Pyramid

- Sphere
- Torus

All these classes derive from a base Shape class. This class provides basic functionality used by the Urho engine to render the component. In particular, the Shape class has a Model property that returns the path used to render an object. The Shape class also has a Color property, which you can use to quickly change the shape material.

When the UrhoSharp app starts, the root node is created automatically. You can access this node by reading the Scene property of the StereoApplication class. Then, to create a new node, you can use either the constructor of the Node class or the Scene.CreateChild method. After the node is created, you add it to the scene using the Scene.AddChild method.

To see how this approach works in practice, implement the CreateNode method in the MixedRealityApplication class. (See Listing 15-6.) This method takes two arguments: position and scale. Then, the method creates a new instance of the Node class and sets the node position and scale according to input arguments. Finally, the node is added to the scene using the Scene.AddChild method.

LISTING 15-6 Creating the scene node

```
private Node CreateNode(Vector3 position, float scale)
{
    var node = new Node()
    {
        Position = position,
        Scale = scale * Vector3.One
    };

    Scene.AddChild(node);

    return node;
}
```

Listing 15-6 uses the Node class constructor. An alternative approach would be to use the Scene.CreateChild method as shown in Listing 15-7. The difference is that with the Scene.CreateChild method, you need not invoke the Scene.AddChild method (because the node is automatically added as the scene's descendant), but you cannot use the C# object initializer syntax to set the node's property.

LISTING 15-7 Creating the child node

```
private Node CreateSceneChildNode(Vector3 position, float scale)
{
    var node = Scene.CreateChild();

    node.Position = position;
    node.Scale = scale * Vector3.One;

    return node;
}
```

You will now use the `CreateNode` method to add three primitive objects to the scene: a sphere, pyramid, and box. Each of these will be created using a dedicated helper method. Start by implementing the `CreateSphere` method from Listing 15-8.

LISTING 15-8 Creating the sphere node

```
private Node sphereNode;

private void CreateSphere(Color color)
{
    sphereNode = CreateNode(new Vector3(0.15f, 0, 1f), 0.1f);

    // Add sphere component
    sphereNode.CreateComponent<Sphere>().Color = color;
}
```

Listing 15-8 shows how to add a sphere component to the node. To add a component, you use the `Node.CreateComponent` generic method, whose parameter defines the component type. This type must derive from the `Urho.Component` class that serves as the base for all components in UrhoSharp. The `Component` class is also used to define the `Shape` class through the following level of inheritance:

```
Shape -> StaticModel -> Drawable -> Component
```

Accordingly, you can use any of the previously listed classes representing a shape as a parameter of the `Node.CreateComponent` method. Listing 15-8 uses this functionality to add a sphere. Once this is done, the sphere color is adjusted according to the input argument of the `CreateSphere` method. (See the method declaration in Listing 15-8.)

After implementing the `CreateSphere` method, you place it in the `Start` method, as shown in Listing 15-9. You can then run the app in the HoloLens emulator to see the results depicted in Figure 15-6. Note that the sphere is located in the right part of the view. This is controlled by the node position (refer to Listing 15-7 and Listing 15-8). It is instructive to experiment with this position to see how it affects the appearance of the sphere in the scene.

LISTING 15-9 Displaying the sphere

```
protected override void Start()
{
    base.Start();

    CreateText("Hello, UrhoSharp!", Color.Magenta);

    CreateSphere(Color.Red);
}
```

FIGURE 15-6 A scene with the sphere added in.

Let's continue this example and implement another helper method: `CreatePyramid`. (See Listing 15-10.) `CreatePyramid` works a lot like `CreateSphere`. However, `CreatePyramid` uses a `Material` property to change the primitive's color. To programmatically create the material, you use static methods of the `Urho.Material` class. For example, to make a uniform material of a specified color, you use the `Material.FromColor` method. (See Listing 15-10.) You can also create a material from an image using `Material.FromImage`. In this latter case you will need to specify the image path.

LISTING 15-10 Creating a pyramid

```
private Node pyramidNode;

private void CreatePyramid(Color color)
{
    pyramidNode = CreateNode(new Vector3(-0.2f, 0, 1.25f), 0.1f);

    // Add pyramid component
    pyramidNode.CreateComponent<Pyramid>().Material = Material.FromColor(color);
}
```

Implement a third helper method, `CreateBox`. Listing 15-11 shows how to do so, and how to rotate the box component 30 degrees along the x-axis. The rotation occurs in the last statement in Listing 15-11, which uses the `Rotate` method of the `Node` class instance. This method accepts two arguments:

- **delta** This is an instance of the `Quaternion` class that represents the rotation. In Listing 15-11 an instance of the `Quaternion` class is created with the `FromAxisAngle` static method. This method requires you to provide information about the axis along which the rotation will occur and an angle of rotation expressed in degrees. (The axis is represented as a `Vector3` class instance because you can rotate an object along three axes at once.)

- **space** This represents the space in which the rotation should be performed. It can be a local, parent, or world space. These spaces are represented by corresponding values from the `Urho.TransformSpace` enumeration.

LISTING 15-11 Creating a box

```
private Node boxNode;

private void CreateBox(Color color)
{
    boxNode = CreateNode(new Vector3(0, -0.025f, 1f), 0.1f);

    // Add box component
    boxNode.CreateComponent<Box>().Color = color;

    // Rotate the node
    boxNode.Rotate(Quaternion.FromAxisAngle(Vector3.Right, 30));
}
```

Finally, use the `CreatePyramid` and `CreateBox` methods to display the pyramid and the box within the scene. (See Listing 15-12.)

LISTING 15-12 A modified `Start` method of the `MixedRealityApplication` class

```
protected override void Start()
{
    base.Start();

    CreateText("Hello, UrhoSharp!", Color.Magenta);

    CreateSphere(Color.Red);
    CreatePyramid(Color.Green);
    CreateBox(Color.Blue);
}
```

Run the modified app. You should get the result depicted in Figure 15-7.

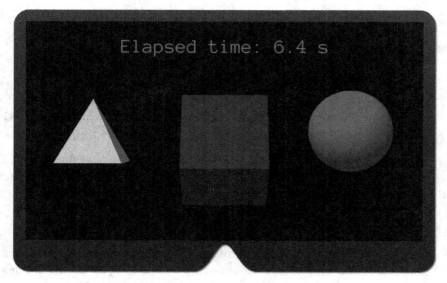

FIGURE 15-7 A final scene that we created in this chapter.

Handling the Gaze

You will now extend the ExploringUrhoSharp app by another node, which will serve as the gaze indicator. The SharpReality extension to UrhoSharp provides a dedicated component for just this purpose: `Urho.SharpReality.SpatialCursor`. This component acts as a virtual pointer, showing which direction the user is looking. `SpatialCursor` also implements raycasting logic, which can be used to interact with holograms.

By default, `SpatialCursor` displays a cyan torus. (See Figure 15-8.) Whenever the user gazes at the hologram, `SpatialCursor` plays an animation that enlarges the cursor by a factor of six. (See Figure 15-9.) In this section, you will learn how to use this cursor in the ExploringUrhoSharp app to indicate gaze direction. Then you will alter the cursor color and use raycasting to store a reference to the node (representing a hologram) the user is gazing at. You will use this reference later in this chapter to manipulate the holograms with gestures.

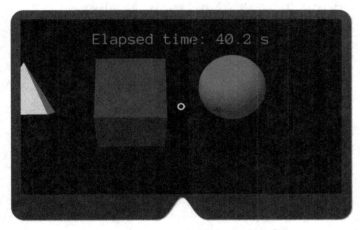

FIGURE 15-8 A gaze indicator created with the `SpatialCursor` component.

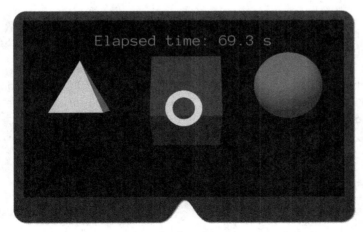

FIGURE 15-9 THE cursor changes when the user gazes at the hologram.

Indicating Gaze Direction

To indicate the gaze direction, extend the MixedRealityApplication class by adding the CreateSpatialCursor helper method from Listing 15-13. This method adds a new child node to the scene, and then supplements that node with the SpatialCursor component and the Node.CreateComponent generic method.

LISTING 15-13 Creating a spatial cursor

```
private Node spatialCursorNode;

private void CreateSpatialCursor()
{
    // Create cursor node
    spatialCursorNode = Scene.CreateChild();

    // Add SpatialCursor component
    var spatialCursorComponent = spatialCursorNode.CreateComponent<SpatialCursor>();
}
```

Next, invoke the CreateSpatialCursor in the Start method, as shown in Listing 15-14.

LISTING 15-14 Adding the gaze indicator to the scene when the app is started

```
protected override void Start()
{
    base.Start();

    // Text
    CreateText("Hello, UrhoSharp!", Color.Magenta);

    // 3D primitives
    CreateSphere(Color.Red);
    CreatePyramid(Color.Green);
    CreateBox(Color.Blue);

    // Spatial cursor (gaze indicator)
    CreateSpatialCursor();
}
```

Run the app to see the results shown in Figures 15-8 and 15-9. While gazing around the scene, you will see that the cyan torus is not very visible on the green pyramid. To fix this, change the cursor color to yellow to increase the contrast between the cursor and all holograms in the scene. To do so, you must modify the cursor's shader by setting the MatDiffColor parameter by extending the CreateSpatialCursor method as shown in Listing 15-15.

LISTING 15-15 Modifying the cursor color

```
private void CreateSpatialCursor()
{
    // Create cursor node
    spatialCursorNode = Scene.CreateChild();

    // Add SpatialCursor component
    var spatialCursorComponent = spatialCursorNode.CreateComponent<SpatialCursor>();

    // Get the static model of the cursor
    var staticModel = spatialCursorComponent.CursorModelNode.GetComponent<StaticModel>();

    // ... and change its color from cyan to yellow
    staticModel.Material.SetShaderParameter("MatDiffColor", Color.Yellow);
}
```

The CreateSpatialCursor method in Listing 15-15 obtains a reference to the StaticModel component associated with SpatialCursor. StaticModel represents the torus. After the reference to this model is obtained, you can use its Material property to set the shader parameter using the SetShaderParameter method. As shown in the last statement in Listing 15-15, SetShaderParameter accepts two arguments:

- **name** This is the name (represented as a string) of the shader parameter. You can obtain a list of available shader parameter names by reading static properties of the CoreAssets. ShaderParameters class. For instance, to obtain MatDiffColor (a parameter name used in Listing 15-14), you could use CoreAssets.ShaderParameters.MatDiffColor.

- **value** This is the value for the parameter. This value can be one of 14 types, including simple types like bool, int, and float, or complex types like Vector3, Color, or Quaternion.

Run the app. You will see that the cursor color has changed from cyan to yellow. (See Figure 15-10.)

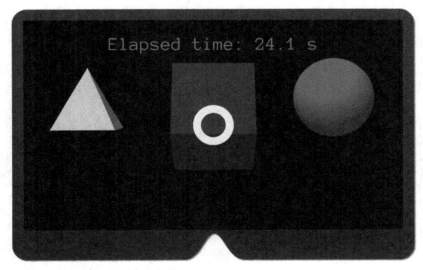

FIGURE 15-10 A modified gaze indicator.

Raycasting

To detect whether the gaze indicator intersects a hologram, the SpatialCursor component uses raycasting. Raycasting in UrhoSharp works like it does in Unity. A 3D engine sends a ray toward the scene and checks whether it has intersected an object. To create a ray, you use the Urho.Ray structure with a default constructor that accepts two arguments: origin and direction. Alternatively, you can use one of the following from the Camera component:

- **GetScreenRay** This accepts two arguments, x and y (representing normalized coordinates), to create an instance of the Ray struct that originates from the camera position and moves toward a given point.

- **GetScreenRayForMouse** This works like GetScreenRay, but the ray origin is set according to the pointer position within the scene view.

After the ray is created, you send it toward the scene using the Raycast or RaycastSingle method of the Octree class. Octree is the component that implements spatial partitioning. An instance of this component is automatically added to StereoApplication. Raycast and RaycastSingle return either a collection (Raycast) or a single instance (RaycastSingle) of the RayQueryResult struct. This struct contains information about the node hit by the ray (Node) and the point of the intersection (Position).

Listing 15-16 shows code that casts a ray toward the middle of the screen and then prints an identifier of the detected scene's node in the debugger console. If the ray does not intersect any node, the code outputs a Nothing detected string instead. To create a ray, I used the GetScreenRay method of the LeftCamera property. This is the Camera component that corresponds to the left eye of the user and was automatically created by the StereoApplication class.

LISTING 15-16 A sample usage of raycasting

```
private void RaycastTest()
{
    // Create ray
    var ray = LeftCamera.GetScreenRay(0.5f, 0.5f);

    // Send the ray toward the scene
    var raycastResult = Octree.RaycastSingle(ray);

    // Debug information about the detected nodes
    var debugInfo = "Nothing detected";
    if (raycastResult.HasValue)
    {
        debugInfo = $"ID from the RaycastTest: {raycastResult.Value.Node.ID}";
    }

    System.Diagnostics.Debug.WriteLine(debugInfo);
}
```

We will test this method in the next section, when learning about gestures. The reason I'm showing it here is that a similar approach is used internally by the SpatialCursor component. Moreover, SpatialCursor fires a Raycasted event whenever the ray is cast, which is provided with an instance of the RayQueryResult struct. So, you can use this event to quickly detect whether the user is gazing at the hologram without the need to write the raycasting logic yourself. You only need to analyze RayQueryResult.

Listing 15-17 shows how to use the Raycasted event to obtain a reference to the scene's node, representing a hologram. First, you wire the method with a Raycasted event (see the last statement of the CreateSpatialCursor method in Listing 15-17). Then, you declare a private member, focusedNode, of type Node. Finally, you define the event handler (SpatialCursorComponent_Raycasted) that rewrites the reference of the intersecting node to focusedNode (when the hologram is detected) or sets it to null (when the user is not looking at the hologram). In this way you achieve a logic similar to that discussed in the "Configuring Gaze Input" section of Chapter 12. Note that here we implemented the gaze-related logic more easily than with Unity.

LISTING 15-17 Using the Raycasted event of the SpatialCursor component

```
private void CreateSpatialCursor()
{
    // Create cursor node
    spatialCursorNode = Scene.CreateChild();

    // Add SpatialCursor component
    var spatialCursorComponent = spatialCursorNode.CreateComponent<SpatialCursor>();

    // Get the static model of the cursor
    var staticModel = spatialCursorComponent.CursorModelNode.GetComponent<StaticModel>();

    // ... and change its color from Cyan to Yellow
    staticModel.Material.SetShaderParameter("MatDiffColor", Color.Yellow);

    // Handle raycasted event
    spatialCursorComponent.Raycasted += SpatialCursorComponent_Raycasted;
}

private Node focusedNode;

private void SpatialCursorComponent_Raycasted(RayQueryResult? obj)
{
    if (obj.HasValue)
    {
        focusedNode = obj.Value.Node;
    }
    else
    {
        focusedNode = null;
    }
}
```

Adding Gestures and Actions

In this section you will extend the ExploringUrhoSharp app by adding support for gestures. Specifically, you will implement methods to handle tap, double-tap, and manipulation gestures. The tap gesture will be used to verify the RaycastTest method from the previous section. The double-tap gesture will be used to animate focused holograms with actions. Finally, the manipulation gesture will be used to translate a hologram that was selected through the user's gaze. You will also implement a hold gesture.

To detect gestures, the SharpReality extension of the UrhoSharp uses a SpatialGestureRecognizer class, which comes from the Windows 10 API, declared under the Windows.UI.Input.Spatial namespace. SharpReality implements a thin layer on top of the SpatialGestureRecognizer to further simplify the code that you need to handle gestures.

The general approach is to first enable the recognizer for the particular gesture. To enable or disable a gesture recognizer, you use the following properties of the object, deriving from StereoApplication:

- **EnableGestureTapped**   Use this to enable or disable the tap and double-tap gesture recognizer. (These are detected through the same recognizer.)

- **EnableGestureManipulation**   Use this to enable or disable the manipulation gesture.

- **EnableGestureHold**   Use this to enable or disable the hold gesture. To perform the hold gesture you start with a tap and then keep your fingers together.

You enable gesture recognizers in the Start method. You then override the event handler that is fired whenever a particular gesture is detected. These events handlers must be overridden within the class that derives from StereoApplication. Here is the list of gestures along with their associated event handlers:

- **Tap**   OnGestureTapped

- **Double-tap**   OnGestureDoubleTapped

- **Manipulation**   OnGestureManipulationStarted, OnGestureManipulationUpdated, OnGestureManipulationCompleted, and OnGestureManipulationCanceled

- **Hold**   OnGestureHoldStarted, OnGestureHoldCompleted, and OnGestureHoldCanceled

This is similar to what you can do with Unity, except that UrhoSharp.SharpReality does not provide a recognizer for the navigation gesture.

Let's see how to use this approach in practice. Along the way, you will use actions to modify the hologram's properties. Actions are reusable objects that let you smoothly modify scene node properties over a specified time frame. In this respect, actions are like animations, since both change object's properties temporarily. There are numerous built-in actions. All of them are defined under the Urho.Actions namespace. Moreover, you can create your own actions by subclassing the Urho.Actions.BaseAction class. Later in this chapter you will learn how to use the ScaleTo and TintBy actions.

Tap

To implement the logic for the tap gesture, begin by adding two statements to the Start method of the MixedRealityApplication class as shown in Listing 15-18.

LISTING 15-18 Enabling recognizers for tap gestures

```
protected override void Start()
{
    base.Start();

    // Text
    CreateText("Hello, UrhoSharp!", Color.Magenta);

    // 3D primitives
    CreateSphere(Color.Red);
    CreatePyramid(Color.Green);
    CreateBox(Color.Blue);

    // Spatial cursor (gaze indicator)
    CreateSpatialCursor();

    // Gestures
    EnableGestureTapped = true;
    EnableGestureManipulation = true;
}
```

Then, you implement the event handler for the tap gesture as shown in Listing 15-19.

LISTING 15-19 Handling tap gesture

```
public override void OnGestureTapped()
{
    base.OnGestureTapped();

    RaycastTest();
}
```

To test this example, run the app in the emulator. Then gaze at the hologram and right-click the pointer. An identifier of the scene's node associated with the hologram will be displayed in the debugger console, as shown in Figure 15-11.

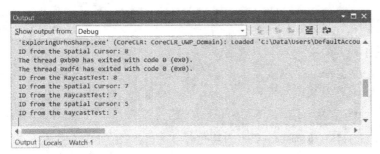

FIGURE 15-11 Previewing the ID of the hologram's node obtained with custom raycasting and from the SpatialCursor component.

You can confirm that this ID agrees with the raycasting used internally by the SpatialCursor component. To do so, modify the SpatialCursorComponent_Raycasted event handler (refer to Listing 15-17) as shown in Listing 15-20.

LISTING 15-20 Obtaining the ID of the hologram at which the user is gazing

```
private void SpatialCursorComponent_Raycasted(RayQueryResult? obj)
{
    if (obj.HasValue)
    {
        if (focusedNode != obj.Value.Node)
        {
            System.Diagnostics.Debug.WriteLine(
                $"ID from the Spatial Cursor: {obj.Value.Node.ID}");
        }

        focusedNode = obj.Value.Node;
    }
    else
    {
        focusedNode = null;
    }
}
```

Double-tap

You will now write the logic for the double-tap gesture. To do so, you modify the OnGestureDouble Tapped event handler such that the focused hologram will be rescaled by 50% before reverting to the original value after a short while. To make this scaling smooth, you will use ScaleTo action. To proceed, add the following statement to the MixedRealityApplication.cs file:

```
using Urho.Actions
```

Then implement the OnGestureDoubleTapped event as shown in Listing 15-21.

LISTING 15-21 Rescaling the focused hologram with the double-tap gesture

```
public override void OnGestureDoubleTapped()
{
    base.OnGestureDoubleTapped();

    if (focusedNode != null)
    {
        var duration = 0.5f;

        var originalScale = focusedNode.Scale.X;
        var intermediateScale = originalScale * 1.5f;

        focusedNode.RunActions(
            new ScaleTo(duration, intermediateScale),
            new ScaleTo(duration, originalScale));
    }
}
```

The method from Listing 15-21 works as follows:

1. It invokes the base `OnGestureDoubleTapped` functionality.

2. It uses an `if` statement to check whether the user is gazing at a hologram. The `if` statement ensures that a value stored in the `focusedNode` private member is not `null`.

3. If the `focusedNode` private member is not null, three local variables are declared:

   - **duration** This variable specifies how long the rescaling action will apply. Here, this value will be half a second for each action. In this time, the hologram will change from the original scale (obtained by reading the `Scale.X` property of the `focusedNode` field; uniform scaling is assumed) to its intermediate scale and back to its original scale.

   - **originalScale** This stores the value for the original scale.

   - **intermediateScale** This stores the value for the intermediate scale. In this example the `intermediateScale` value is 1.5 times larger than the `originalScale` value.

4. The `duration`, `originalScale`, and `intermediateScale` variables are used to instantiate two instances of the `ScaleTo` class. This class changes the scale of the selected node from the current value to the specified one. In the preceding code, the first instance of the `ScaleTo` class rescales the hologram to the scale stored in the `intermediateScale` variable, while the second instance changes the scale back to the scale stored in the `originalScale` variable. As the last statement in Listing 15-21 shows, these actions are invoked by a `RunActions` method of the Node class. `RunActions` accepts a list of actions to be invoked. You can add as many actions as you wish.

To test the preceding code, run the app in the HoloLens emulator, gaze at any hologram, and then right-click the pointer twice. The hologram will be rescaled. (See Figure 15-12.)

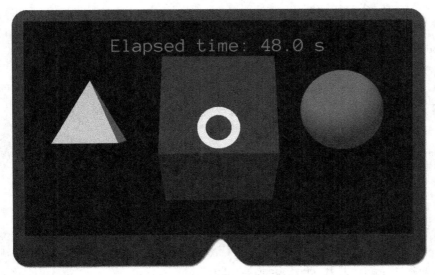

FIGURE 15-12 Resizing a focused hologram with the double-tap gesture.

Manipulation

Typically, the manipulation gesture is used to manipulate the hologram to change its location or size. Here, you will implement logic that translates a scene's node associated with the hologram that was previously selected by a user's gaze.

Start by implementing the OnGestureManipulatonStarted event handler, as shown in Listing 15-22. This event, along with supporting private members, is used to configure logic to translate the hologram. The supporting private members are as follows:

- **manipulatedHologram**   This is used to store the reference to the hologram at which the user is gazing when the manipulation gesture begins. (The reference is stored because focusedNode, which is a reference to the gazed hologram, can change to null when the hologram is translated out of the SpatialCursor component.)

- **previousHandPosition**   This is used to implement the OnGestureManipulationUpdated event handler. (See Listing 15-23.) Specifically, previousHandPosition calculates the relative difference of user's hand position when he or she performs the manipulation gesture. Hand positions are provided to OnGestureManipulationUpdated as an instance of the Vector3 vector.

LISTING 15-22 Handling of the manipulation gesture

```
private Node manipulatedHologram;
private Vector3 previousHandPosition;

public override void OnGestureManipulationStarted()
{
    base.OnGestureManipulationStarted();

    manipulatedHologram = focusedNode;
    previousHandPosition = Vector3.Zero;
}
```

LISTING 15-23 Updating a hologram position during a manipulation gesture

```
public override void OnGestureManipulationUpdated(Vector3 relativeHandPosition)
{
    base.OnGestureManipulationUpdated(relativeHandPosition);

    if (manipulatedHologram != null)
    {
        manipulatedHologram.Position += (relativeHandPosition - previousHandPosition);
        previousHandPosition = relativeHandPosition;
    }
}
```

As shown in Listing 15-23, OnGestureManipulationUpdated proceeds as follows:

1.   It invokes the functionality of the base class (base.OnGestureManipulation).

2.   It checks whether manipulatedHologram is not null.

3. If it is not `null`, the object's `Position` property is changed according to the tracked user's hand position. This difference is calculated by subtracting the `previousHandPosition` value from the `relativeHandPosition` value. (The `relativeHandPosition` value is provided to the `OnGestureManipulationUpdated` handler by UrhoSharp.SharpReality.)

4. The value from `relativeHandPosition` is rewritten to the `previousHandPosition` field.

To complete the implementation, you need to add the `OnGestureManipulationCompleted` and `OnGestureManipulationCanceled` event handlers. As shown in Listing 15-24, you use these to reset the `manipulatedHologram` member to its default `null` value. This is used to prevent the manipulation of holograms not selected by the user when the manipulation gesture starts.

LISTING 15-24 Restoring the value of the `manipulatedHologram` field to its default value when the manipulation gesture ends or is canceled

```
public override void OnGestureManipulationCompleted(Vector3 relativeHandPosition)
{
    base.OnGestureManipulationCompleted(relativeHandPosition);

    manipulatedHologram = null;
}

public override void OnGestureManipulationCanceled()
{
    base.OnGestureManipulationCanceled();

    manipulatedHologram = null;
}
```

To test this code, run the app in the HoloLens emulator. Then, gaze at any hologram, press Alt on the keyboard, right-click the pointer, and start moving it to emulate a manipulation gesture. A focused object will be translated according to your input. (See Figure 15-13.)

FIGURE 15-13 Translating a hologram with gesture manipulation.

Applying Physics

As discussed in previous chapters, one key element of many mixed reality apps is a physics simulation that makes holograms in the app behave like real objects. With UrhoSharp, you can quickly add components to nodes for these types of simulations. You control these simulations using the `Urho.PhysicsWorld` component, which interfaces with the Bullet library. An instance of the `PhysicsWorld` component is added to the root scene node. (This is performed automatically in `StereoApplication`, however.) You generally do not modify the default configuration of `PhysicsWorld` unless you need to optimize it. Instead, you add three other components to the child nodes associated with your holograms:

- **RigidBody** This represents a rigid body (similar to the `Rigidbody` component in Unity).

- **CollisionShape** This defines the shape of an object that is used to detect collisions.

- **Constraint** This is used to define joints used to constrain two rigid bodies such that the movement of one body depends on the other one. (For instance, the distance between objects can be kept constant.) Joints can also define a constraint between a rigid body and an anchor point. Such a function is typically used to create a rope.

In this section, you will learn how to use `RigidBody` components so that holograms will be affected by gravity. When the user taps a focused hologram, it will fall down, as a real object would when released. Then, you will add a plane to the scene. After that, you will use `CollisionShape` to make this plane a virtual ground for holograms. Holograms will fall down on the plane. Next, you will use collision detection and actions to change the hologram's color while it is bouncing off the plane. Finally, you will create a projectile that can be thrown toward other objects in the scene.

RigidBody

Start by adding the following statement to the MixedRealityApplication.cs file:

```
using Urho.Physics;
```

Then, extend the `MixedRealityApplication` class by adding the `AddRigidBody` helper method. (See Listing 15-25.)

LISTING 15-25 Adding a RigidBody component to the node

```
private RigidBody AddRigidBody(
    Node node,
    float mass = 1,
    bool useGravity = true,
    bool isKinematic = false,
    float bounciness = 0.75f)
{
    // Check whether RigidBody was already created
    var rigidBody = node.GetComponent<RigidBody>();

    if (rigidBody == null)
    {
        // If not, create the new one
```

```
        rigidBody = node.CreateComponent<RigidBody>();

        // Set the mass, gravity, and restitution (bounciness)
        rigidBody.Mass = mass;
        rigidBody.UseGravity = useGravity;
        rigidBody.Kinematic = isKinematic;
        rigidBody.Restitution = bounciness;
    }

    return rigidBody;
}
```

The method from Listing 15-25 accepts five arguments:

- **node**   This is an instance of the Node class, representing the hologram to which the RigidBody component should be added.

- **mass**   This is a mass of the rigid body. (The default value is **1**.)

- **useGravity**   This is a Boolean value indicating whether the rigid body should be affected by gravity. (The default value is **true**.)

- **isKinematic**   This a Boolean value indicating whether the rigid body is kinematic. Kinematic rigid bodies do not change their position during physics simulations. This is useful for creating walls or blocking planes (as in this section).

- **bounciness**   This value indicates how much the rigid body will bounce off the colliders. The higher the value, the lower the energy loss on collision. A value of 0 indicates total loss, while a value of 1 indicates no loss. The default value is 0.75.

These arguments (except node) are used to add a RigidBody component to the given node and configure it. In principle, the node can have the RigidBody component already attached. Hence, the method from Listing 15-24 uses a generic GetComponent method to check whether the node has this component. If the RigidBody component is not available, the AddRigidBody method will create a new instance of the component. Then, AddRigidBody sets the four properties of the RigidBody: Mass, UseGravity, Kinematic, and Restitution. The last of these defines the bounciness of the body as described. (I use the term bounciness to conform to the discussion in Chapter 10.)

You can now extend the OnGestureTapped event handler such that the focused hologram will be supplemented by the RigidBody component. (See Listing 15-26.)

LISTING 15-26 A modified version of the OnGestureTapped method

```
public override void OnGestureTapped()
{
    base.OnGestureTapped();

    RaycastTest();

    if (focusedNode != null)
    {
        AddRigidBody(focusedNode);
    }
}
```

To ensure everything is working as expected, run the app in the HoloLens emulator. Then, gaze at any hologram and right-click the pointer. The hologram should fall down. (See Figure 15-14.) Currently, it falls continuously, because there is nothing to stop it. In the next section, you will create the plane and use CollisionShape components so the hologram will fall on the plane.

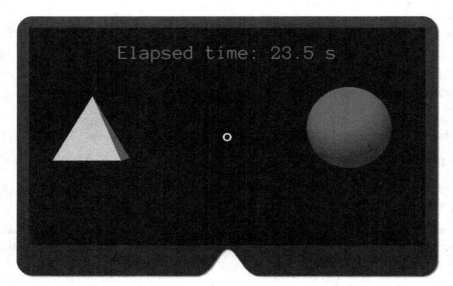

FIGURE 15-14 The blue box is missing because it fell down due to gravity.

CollisionShape

To configure the app so the scene nodes can collide with each other, you add a CollisionShape component. Afterward, you need to define the collider shape. This shape is used by the physics engine to calculate collisions between nodes. In general, the displayed shape can differ from the collider shape. This happens for complex objects that would require a lot of calculations to satisfy physical bounds. To optimize performance, it is reasonable to use an approximate geometry for collision detection.

To add colliders to the ExploringUrhoSharp app, start by adding a plane to the scene. This plane will be positioned below other 3D primitives to stop the primitives when they are falling down. To start, implement the CreatePlane method from Listing 15-27.

LISTING 15-27 Creating a plane

```
private Node planeNode;

private void CreatePlane(Color color)
{
    planeNode = CreateNode(new Vector3(0, -0.25f, 1f), 0.75f);
    planeNode.CreateComponent<Urho.Shapes.Plane>().Color = color;

    AddRigidBody(planeNode, 10, false, true, 1);
    AddCollisionShape(planeNode);
}
```

The method from Listing 15-27 proceeds similarly to the methods used to create a sphere (refer to Listing 15-8), pyramid (refer to Listing 15-10), and box (refer to Listing 15-11). First, it creates the new node (stored in the planeNode member), creates a Plane component, and sets its color. (Note that in this case, the fully qualified type name is used as a parameter of the CreateComponent method to avoid name conflicts.) After the Plane component is added to the node, the CreatePlane method invokes the AddRigidBody method to add the RigidBody component to planeNode. In this case, the mass of the planeNode's rigid body is set to 10 (in the second argument of the AddRigidBody method), meaning the plane will be 10 times heavier than the other 3D primitives (the pyramid, box, and sphere). This mass difference will ensure that the plane will stop the primitives. Moreover, the plane will not use gravity (see the third argument of AddRigidBody), will be kinematic (see the fourth argument), and will have maximum bounciness (see the last argument). Finally, the CreatePlane method invokes the method to create and configure the collider for a plane. (See Listing 15-28.)

LISTING 15-28 Adding the collision shape

```
private CollisionShape AddCollisionShape(Node node)
{
    var shape = node.GetComponent<Shape>();

    if (shape == null)
    {
        return null;
    }
    else
    {
        return SetCollisionShape(node, shape);
    }
}
```

The method from Listing 15-29 accepts one argument of type Node. This is an instance of the scene's node, which should be supplemented by the CollisionShape component. Then, the method checks whether the provided node has an assigned Shape component. If not, the method returns null. Otherwise, the helper SetCollisionShape method is invoked. (See Listing 15-29.)

LISTING 15-29 Setting a shape for the collider

```
private CollisionShape SetCollisionShape(Node node, Shape shape)
{
    var collisionShape = node.CreateComponent<CollisionShape>();

    var one = Vector3.One;
    var position = Vector3.Zero;
    var rotation = Quaternion.Identity;

    if (shape.GetType() == typeof(Sphere))
    {
        collisionShape.SetSphere(1, position, rotation);
    }
    else if (shape.GetType() == typeof(Box))
    {
        collisionShape.SetBox(one, position, rotation);
    }
```

```
        else if (shape.GetType() == typeof(Urho.Shapes.Plane))
        {
            var size = new Vector3(planeNode.Scale.X,
                0.01f, planeNode.Scale.Z);

            collisionShape.SetBox(size, position, rotation);
        }
        else if (shape.GetType() == typeof(Pyramid))
        {
            collisionShape.SetConvexHull(CoreAssets.Models.Cone,
                0, one, position, rotation);
        }

        return collisionShape;
}
```

The SetCollisionShape method creates and adds the CollisionShape component to the given node. Then it declares three local variables: one, position, and rotation. These are reusable components used to configure the CollisionShape component. To that end, you use one of the methods that set the actual collider shape (or form). In Listing 15-29, the form of the collider is set depending on the Shape component previously associated with the node. Note that the Shape component defines what the node will look like, while CollisionShape determines how the node will act under collisions with other nodes.

To set the actual form of the collider, the SetCollisionShape uses four if statements. Each of these compares the node's shape (obtained through the GetType method of the shape argument) to one of four types: Sphere, Box, Plane, and Pyramid. Then, the SetCollisionShape method invokes the corresponding method of the CollisionShape class instance:

- **SetSphere**   This sets the form of the collider to a sphere. This method accepts three arguments, which define the collider diameter, position, and rotation,

- **SetBox**   This sets the form of the collider to a box. Again, this method accepts three arguments, which define the collider size, position, and rotation. This method is used for the box and for the plane. In the second case, the size of the collider along the y-axis is set to 0.01.

- **SetConvexHull**   This sets the form of the collider to a convex hull depending on the model. In the preceding example, the Cone model is used to approximate the pyramid shape. (See the first argument of the SetConvexHull method.) The model is obtained from the Cone property of the CoreAssets.Model object. The second argument of the SetConvexHull method lets you specify the level of detail, and the next three arguments define the scale, position, and rotation, respectively.

You use the CreatePlane and AddCollisionShape methods in the Start method of the MixedRealityApplication class as shown in Listing 15-30.

LISTING 15-30 A modified `Start` method of the `MixedRealityApplication` class

```
protected override void Start()
{
    base.Start();

    // Text
    CreateText("Hello, UrhoSharp!", Color.Magenta);

    // 3D primitives
    CreateSphere(Color.Red);
    CreatePyramid(Color.Green);
    CreateBox(Color.Blue);

    // Spatial cursor (gaze indicator)
    CreateSpatialCursor();

    // Gestures
    EnableGestureTapped = true;
    EnableGestureManipulation = true;

    // Physics
    CreatePlane(Color.Gray);

    AddCollisionShape(sphereNode);
    AddCollisionShape(pyramidNode);
    AddCollisionShape(boxNode);
}
```

Test the solution by deploying the app to the HoloLens emulator. Then, press and hold the S key on the keyboard to virtually move backward within the scene. Keep the key pressed until you see the plane. Next, tap either the pyramid, box, or sphere. It will fall down and bounce off the plane. (See Figure 15-15.)

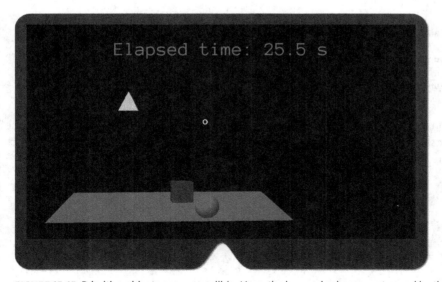

FIGURE 15-15 Primitive objects can now collide. Here, the box and sphere are stopped by the plane.

Detecting and Handling Collisions

The physics engine uses the following three events of the Node class to notify you when a collision happens and what the collision's status is:

- **NodeCollisionStart** This event is fired when the collision starts.

- **NodeCollision** This event is raised when two colliders come in contact.

- **NodeCollisionEnd** This event is fired when the collision ends.

These events are accompanied by corresponding structs that describes them: NodeCollision StartEventArgs, NodeCollisionEventArgs, and NodeCollisionEndEventArgs. Each of these structs has an OtherNode property, which identifies the node with which your node collided.

Listing 15-31 shows how to use the NodeCollision event of planeNode to change the tint of the node that hits the plane. First, you subscribe to the NodeCollision event. (See the first bolded statement in Listing 15-31.) Then, in the event handler (PlaneNode_NodeCollision), you obtain a reference to the node that collided with the plane (OtherNode). Finally, you run the TintBy action against OtherNode.

LISTING 15-31 Handling the plane's NodeCollision event

```
private void CreatePlane(Color color)
{
    planeNode = CreateNode(new Vector3(0, -0.5f, 1f), 1f);
    planeNode.CreateComponent<Urho.Shapes.Plane>().Color = color;

    AddRigidBody(planeNode, 10, false, true, 1);
    AddCollisionShape(planeNode);

    planeNode.NodeCollision += PlaneNode_NodeCollision;
}

private void PlaneNode_NodeCollision(NodeCollisionEventArgs obj)
{
    var otherNode = obj.OtherNode;

    otherNode.RunActions(new TintBy(0.5f, Color.White));
}
```

Run the app in the HoloLens emulator and move backward to see the whole scene. Then, tap the pyramid, box, or sphere. As it falls down and collides with the plane, the color gradually changes to white. (See Figure 15-16.)

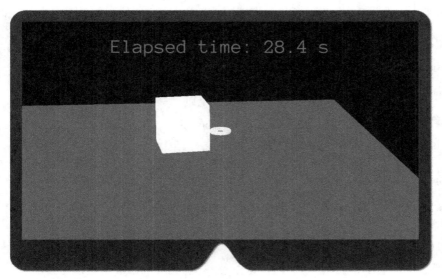

FIGURE 15-16 Using collision detection to alter the color of the node.

Projectiles

In this section you will create a projectile similar to the yellow ball you created in Chapter 10. This ball will be thrown toward the scene on the double-tap gesture.

To begin, add a ThrowTheBall method to the MixedRealityApplication class. (See Listing 15-32.) Then, invoke it in OnGestureDoubleTapped, as shown in Listing 15-33.

LISTING 15-32 Creating and firing a projectile

```
private void ThrowTheBall(float speed)
{
    // Create the new node
    var ballNode = CreateNode(HeadPosition, 0.1f);

    // Create the sphere component
    ballNode.CreateComponent<Sphere>().Color = Color.Yellow;

    // Configure physics
    var ballRigidBody = AddRigidBody(ballNode, 0.5f);
    AddCollisionShape(ballNode);

    // Throw the ball toward the gaze direction
    var ray = LeftCamera.GetScreenRay(0.5f, 0.5f);
    ballRigidBody.SetLinearVelocity(ray.Direction * speed);
}
```

LISTING 15-33 Throwing the ball

```
public override void OnGestureDoubleTapped()
{
    base.OnGestureDoubleTapped();

    if (focusedNode != null)
    {
        var duration = 0.5f;

        var originalScale = focusedNode.Scale.X;
        var intermediateScale = originalScale * 1.5f;

        focusedNode.RunActions(
            new ScaleTo(duration, intermediateScale),
            new ScaleTo(duration, originalScale));
    }

    ThrowTheBall(10);
}
```

The ThrowTheBall method (refer to Listing 15-32) creates a new node that will host the ball. The initial position of this node is the same as the user's head position, which you obtain by reading the HeadPosition property of the StereoApplication class. The scale of the ball node is set to 0.1f. (See the second argument of the CreateNode method in Listing 15-32.) After the node is created, the ThrowTheBall method adds a Sphere component to the node whose color is Color. Yellow. Then, the ThrowTheBall method adds RigidBody and CollisionShape components to the sphere. The mass of the sphere is half the unit. This is controlled through the second argument of the AddRigidBody method. All other arguments of that method are left at their default values. So, RigidBody will use gravity, will not be kinematic, and will have a bounciness of 0.75. Afterward, ThrowTheBall defines the ball's velocity vector using SetLinearVelocity of the RigidBody class instance. The velocity vector defines where and how fast the ball will go. Here, the ball will move toward the gaze direction. To determine this direction, ThrowTheBall creates a ray originating from the screen toward the middle of the view. Lastly, the velocity vector is multiplied by a speed scaling factor (obtained as a method argument). The larger the value, the faster the ball will move.

Run the app and perform a double-tap gesture. The yellow ball will be thrown toward the scene. The yellow ball will also change color after colliding with the plane due to the collision handler from Listing 15-31. (See Figure 15-17.)

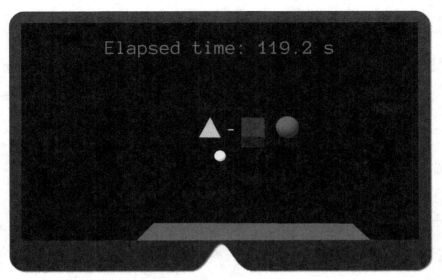

FIGURE 15-17 Throwing the ball toward the scene.

Spatial Mapping

In this section you will learn how to use the spatial mapping by extending ExploringUrhoSharp to display surfaces detected by the HoloLens spatial-perception system. UrhoSharp.SharpReality provides a straightforward API to obtain spatial information. To begin, use the StartSpatialMapping method to start the observer. This method accepts an instance of the Vector3 class that defines the bounding box, which tells the spatial perception system which area should be observed to generate spatial mesh info. You can stop spatial perception by invoking the StopSpatialMapping method. When spatial perception is running, any updates to the recognized spatial mesh will be reported using the OnSurfaceAddedOrUpdated method. This method has two arguments:

- **surface** This an instance of the SpatialMeshInfo struct, which contains details about the detected spatial mesh. This includes the unique identifier (SurfaceId), the timestamp (Date), a collection of spatial vertices that define the surface (VertexData), a collection of indices (IndexData), the location of the surface (BoundsCenter), its rotation (Rotation), and its size (Extents).

- **generatedModel** This an instance of the Model class that represents the shape of the surface.

In the following example, I will show you how to use the spatial mapping API from UrhoSharp. SharpReality to draw detected surfaces and then configure them as colliders. As a result, the yellow ball will bounce off the spatial meshes (similar to Chapter 12). Follow these steps:

1. To declare the Spatial Perception capability, double-click the **Package.appxmanifest** file in the Solution Explorer.

2. In the window that opens, click the **Capabilities** tab, and select the **Spatial Perception** checkbox. (See Figure 15-18.)

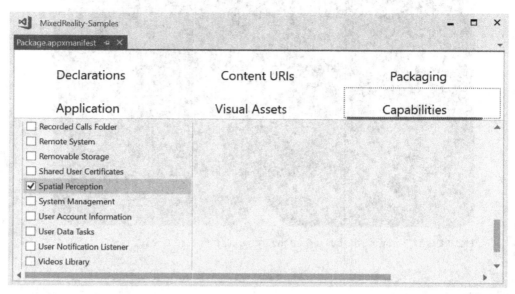

FIGURE 15-18 Declaring the Spatial Perception capability.

3. To enable spatial perception, modify the `Start` method of `MixedRealityApplication` as shown in Listing 15-34. In this listing, the spatial observer is configured to monitor the spatial area within the volume of dimensions 5x5x5 m³.

Note `StartSpatialMapping` is an asynchronous method. Hence, you need to add an async keyword to the `Start` method declaration.

LISTING 15-34 Starting the spatial mapping

```
protected override async void Start()
{
    base.Start();

    // Text
    CreateText("Hello, UrhoSharp!", Color.Magenta);

    // 3D primitives
    CreateSphere(Color.Red);
    CreatePyramid(Color.Green);
    CreateBox(Color.Blue);

    // Spatial cursor (gaze indicator)
    CreateSpatialCursor();

    // Gestures
```

```
        EnableGestureTapped = true;
        EnableGestureManipulation = true;

        // Physics
        CreatePlane(Color.Gray);

        AddCollisionShape(sphereNode);
        AddCollisionShape(pyramidNode);
        AddCollisionShape(boxNode);

        // Spatial mapping
        await StartSpatialMapping(new Vector3(5, 5, 5));
    }
```

4. Implement OnSurfaceAddedOrUpdated as shown in Listing 15-35. This method is invoked whenever the spatial info changes. To ensure this, you change the room definition as in Chapter 12. You will see that the spatial meshes are redrawn.

LISTING 15-35 Displaying the spatial mesh that will act as colliders

```
public override void OnSurfaceAddedOrUpdated(
    SpatialMeshInfo surface, Model generatedModel)
{
    base.OnSurfaceAddedOrUpdated(surface, generatedModel);

    // Create the node for the spatial surface
    var surfaceNode = CreateNode(surface.BoundsCenter, 1.0f);
    surfaceNode.Rotation = surface.BoundsRotation;

    // Create and configure the static model component
    var staticModelComponent = surfaceNode.CreateComponent<StaticModel>();
    staticModelComponent.Model = generatedModel;
    staticModelComponent.ViewMask = 0x80000000;

    // Set the wireframe material for the model
    var material = Material.FromColor(Color.Gray);
    material.FillMode = FillMode.Wireframe;
    staticModelComponent.SetMaterial(material);

    // Add the rigid body
    AddRigidBody(surfaceNode, 10, false, true, 1);

    // Create and configure the collider
    var collisionShape = surfaceNode.CreateComponent<CollisionShape>();
    collisionShape.SetTriangleMesh(generatedModel, 0, Vector3.One,
        Vector3.Zero, Quaternion.Identity);
}
```

To display spatial meshes and configure them as colliders, the method from Listing 15-35 proceeds as follows:

1. After invoking the base functionality (base.OnSurfaceAddedOrUpdated), the method creates a new node for the spatial surface, stored in the surfaceNode local variable.

2. The position and rotation of the node are set according to the `BoundsCenter` and `Rotation` properties obtained from the instance of the `SpatialMeshInfo` struct.

3. You create the `StaticModel` component, which defines the visual appearance of the node.

4. The rendering model shape is set to an instance of the `Model` class obtained from the second argument of the `OnSurfaceAddedOrUdpated` method. This ensures that the surface will resemble the shape of the recognized real object.

5. The `ViewMask` property of `StaticModel` is configured to prevent raycasting of spatial meshes. As a consequence, `SpatialCursor` will not be upscaled when the user gazes at the spatial mesh.

6. The default material of the `StaticModel` is changed to the gray wireframe. To set the wireframe rendering, you use the `FillMode` property of the `Material` class instance.

7. `RigidBody` is added to `surfaceNode`.

8. `CollisionShape` is created and configured. In this example, the collider shape is configured using the `SetTriangleMesh` of the `CollisionShape` class. This lets you precisely match the collider to the model.

Deploy the app in the HoloLens emulator. You will see various lines representing the detected spatial meshes. To see that they indeed act as colliders, throw the ball toward them. The ball will bounce off them and can eventually stay put on flat surfaces. (See Figure 15-19.)

FIGURE 15-19 Rendering the spatial mesh.

Summary

This chapter explored the most important features of UrhoSharp in terms of HoloLens development. You learned how to set up a project, implement the entry point, and create holograms with primitive components and materials. Then, you used `SpatialCursor` to indicate the gaze direction and employed raycasting to interact with holograms. After that you learned how to handle spatial gestures and use actions to quickly manipulate objects in the scene. In the last two sections you learned about components used for physics simulations and used spatial mapping to render spatial meshes.

Although all examples were shown in the HoloLens emulator, you can also execute ExploringUrhoSharp in the immersive headset without making any code changes. Just change the debug target from HoloLens emulator (see the top-right corner of Figure 15-3) to Local Machine. The app will be executed in the Mixed Reality Portal as shown in Figure 15-20. You can then test all the features except spatial mapping, which is unavailable with immersive headsets. Note that everything works the same as in HoloLens. The only difference is the larger field-of-view.

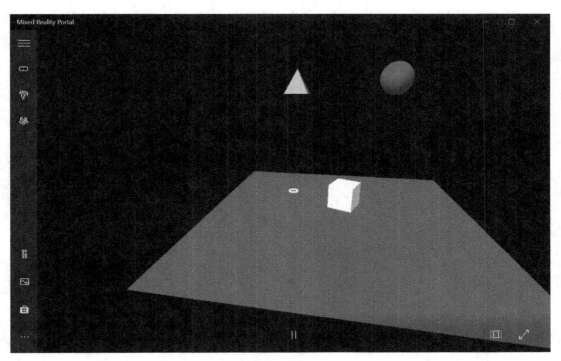

FIGURE 15-20 The ExploringUrhoSharp app executed in the immersive headset simulator.

Index

Numbers

A

X